MW01699035

Unexpected Fire

A Powerful New Study on the Book of Revelation

by Dr. Peter Wyns

Great Reward Publishing

Copyright © 2007 by Peter D. Wyns

Great Reward Publishing
PO Box 36324
Rock Hill, SC 29732
www.peterwyns.org
e-mail: wynsusa@comporium.net

All scriptures used are taken from the New International Version unless otherwise noted Scriptures taken from the Holy Bible, New International Version® NIV®. Copyright© 1973, 1978, 1984 by International Bible Society. Used by permission.
All rights reserved worldwide.

All rights reserved. No part of this publication may be reproduced without prior permission of Great Reward Publishing

First Great Reward Publishing edition published 2007

Manufactured in the United States of America
By BooksJust Books

Contents

DEDICATIONS

"TO MY WONDERFUL FATHER, Irvine George Wyns," who demonstrated more faith than anyone I know. He was born and raised in the deserts of Northern China. He never saw his father, but his mother championed the cause of Mongolia for Messiah Missions. Years of famine, poverty and marauding thieves ravaged their tiny village of Gashatay. Dad learned the importance of faith as he watched his mother and other mission workers stand firm in the middle of great tribulation.

As a young boy, his family moved to England where he grew up under the teachings of Smith Wigglesworth and George Jefferies.

Dad's faith grew, but he faced great trials. As a young man he lost his first wife and their seventh child at the time of the baby's birth. It was devastating for him, but somehow his faith grew stronger.

Dad was a powerful preacher and miracles followed his ministry. As a young man, I was called to preach the gospel, and dad was my mentor. He amazed me for nothing seemed impossible to him. He had a faith that was always reaching far beyond the ground on which he stood. He was as bold as a lion, bursting with Holy Spirit fire.

A year ago he graduated and went to receive his reward in the courts of heaven. I know he is watching me from the throne room. As I write about the book of Revelation and the tribulation period, I picture a new church emerging, a church filled with people just like my dad.

"And to my cousin, Stephen Hedges." Like my Mother, Stephen's mother was a forsaken Jewess who was adopted by Lydia and Derek Prince when she was a child living in Palestine.

As young men, Stephen and I became Derek Prince disciples. More than thirty-five years ago, we traveled with Grandpa Derek. We cast out demons, prayed for the sick, and taught what he taught.

Stephen has always challenged me to wrestle with the scriptures in order to discover what they are really saying. That continues to be my life's journey. More than that, Stephen has helped me connect with my Jewish roots. He, more than any other person, has helped me find my Jewish identity. Stephen, I am eternally grateful.

ACKNOWLEDGMENTS

THE FOLLOWING IS A list of people whom I acknowledge as being special partners with me in the writing and publishing of this book. I am very grateful for the different contributions that each one has given.

THANK YOU:

Jesse David Enns, for the months of hard work that you gave to help me with the first edits of *Unexpected Fire*. You properly challenged my theology as well as my grammar.

Joy Wyns, Rachel Joy Enns, Joshua Enns, Andrew Peter Wyns, Strachelle Wyns, Elizabeth Joy Enns, Jesse Enns, and Matthew Peter Wyns are my family. You have encouraged me over many years. You never wavered in your belief that what I was teaching from the book of Revelation was inspired by God. When I became tired or discouraged, you added your faith to mine and helped me continue on my journey.

Steve and Laurie Martin, David and Vickie Bogar, Gary and Jeri Updegraft, Jim and Ruth Bruce, Jorge and Anna Parrott, Matthew and Darlene Woodhouse, Diana and Ian Ramsey, Jerry and Peggy Boggus, Raul and Karen Molina, Ronnie and Clarice Holden, Richard and Susan

Tompkins, Bobby and Jane Causey, John and Anna Rambeau, Stephen and Maureen Wyns, Gary and Charlot Steele, Jesse and Elizabeth Enns, Bob and Marion Varden, Joe and Sharon Clunk, Miriam Longland, Marvin and Candi Rollins, Robert and Mary Henderson, Mary (Penny) Morrison, Freda Fincher, Faith and Bruce Wilson, Katherine Wells-Farley, Denise and Eric Young, Lynn and Susan Purdy, Russ and Danielle Elliott, Ivonne Arce, Juan Carlos and Maria Haydar, Ruth-Ann Phelps, David and Vickie Foster, Jake and Sharon Jacobsen, Judy Bondurant, Bobby and Kim Rutherford, Stan and Barbara Felix, Chris and Jennifer Updegraft, John and Helene Morrison, David and Anne-Renee Heinrich, Robert and Rochelle Gager, Maria Cuebas, and Larry and Linda Wentz.

You are among the many people across the country who have encouraged the writing of this book and the call of God on my life in recent years. You have each been exceptional, and Joy and I are grateful for you. Some of you have helped us financially; others have prayed for us and encouraged us to press on. Many of you have begged me to hurry up and finish the book. We thank God for all of you.

Introduction

Welcome to the Unexpected

NOT SO DIFFICULT

THE BOOK OF REVELATION is difficult for many to understand, and some lay it aside for the more studious to interpret. That is about to change. The Holy Spirit is giving insight as we approach the tribulation period (the trauma of the end times as described in the book of Revelation), and increased revelation must come to fulfill God's plan for Israel and the church. What I have written will be a great surprise for most people because it will reveal the unexpected. From the very start of this book, I call on you to expect the unexpected.

Revelation is a perfect book designed by God for us, and it cannot be improved upon. It is a gift for God's sons and daughters. In it, the Almighty shows the victory of Jesus over Satan.

The first verse says, "The Revelation .... which God gave ... to show his servants" (Rev. 1:1).

God did not give us the book of Revelation to confuse us. As you read this interpretation of Revelation, I hope you will become enlightened and excited about the future.

Revelation is not complicated once a person understands its language. It is by far the most detailed prophecy in the Bible, and, with some guidance, it becomes an easy read. God gave Revelation to the church not to puzzle her but to prepare her, not to frighten her but to encourage her. It brings a blessing: "Blessed is he who reads, hears the words and keeps the things which are written in it" (Rev. 1:3).

We will take God at his word, and, as we read the book, we will look to find the blessings, and we will not give way to worry or fear.

THE CLOCK IS TICKING

The book of Revelation is like a time bomb with its internal clock ticking. Unexpected fire is about to fall from heaven, and the events recorded in the pages of Revelation will soon light up. Two thousand years ago, God released the vision to travel along a descending chain of authority. It was given to Jesus, who gave it to an angel, and he in turn gave it to John. John gave it to the seven churches of Asia, and now it has come to us. The window of Revelation provides the best view of the future that we have received to date. There is no book more relevant for us, no book more up-to-date. As I write, the nations are lining up to fulfill the plans and purposes of God. We are moving at breakneck speed toward the unfolding of the great tribulation.

TWO MAIN THEMES

Revelation has two main themes:

1. The complete exposure and destruction of Satan
2. The complete release of God's promises and blessings to the Church and Israel

In a sentence, it brings completion to all that has been promised in the Bible.

The book contains graphic details of the most cataclysmic events. We are given a description of unprecedented tribulation and a preview of God's unbridled judgments. We also catch a glimpse of the angels. They are overflowing with extravagant worship and excitement as they witness the end-time plans of God unfolding. Nothing seems more thrilling for the host of heaven than these end-time events, and when we understand what is happening, nothing will be more exciting for us either.

IMPORTANT GUIDELINES

Here are some basic but important guidelines to help us study the book of Revelation. Revelation is apocalyptic, which means, "an unveiling of the end times." It is different than other books in the Bible because much of it is written in signs and symbols, which must be decoded.

I will go through every chapter and do my best to describe what is happening. Some of the book is obvious; some symbols are clearly explained, and many explanations are given in other parts of the Bible. We can depend on the word of God for answers. Regardless of people's opinion, the Bible is always its own best commentary.

FOUR MAIN INTERPRETATIONS

Put simply, there are four main schools of thought concerning the interpretation of the book of Revelation:

1. Preterists suppose that most of Revelation was completed during the lifetime of the first disciples.
2. Historicists say that Revelation can be divided into parts that each represent a period in church history. They claim that the problems and victories described in each letter to the seven churches (in chapters 2 and 3) each line up with a different season of church history and that we are presently in the Laodicean Church age.
3. Idealists say that Revelation is not a factual book. They say it is a symbolic explanation of spiritual warfare written for God's people in any era and is only given to teach the church how to understand the attacks of Satan and the victorious ways of God.
4. Futurists believe that the book is primarily about the end times.

Although each of these views has a valid application, I believe in the futuristic view. Revelation has been instructive and inspirational for every age, but its events are still before us.

REVELATION IS CHRONOLOGICAL

After part one, where we find the initial introductions of Revelation, I will attempt to explain the events of each chapter in the order they appear. I believe the events of Revelation flow one after the other in real time. In other words, the events of chapter 12 follow the events of chapter 11, and the events of chapter 16 follow those in chapter 15.

Many scholars shift the chapters chronologically. Some who believe that most of Revelation is still ahead of us position chapter 12, for example, as though it happened thousands of years ago. I respect their viewpoints; many who follow this line of thought are godly scholars. From my study, however, I find that the book has a chronological timeline.

CHAPTERS OF REVIEW AND PREVIEW

There are chapters in Revelation in which the events are momentarily put on hold. There is a pause in the action while an angel gives a deeper explanation of what has happened or a brief preview of what is to come. These chapters serve to help us summarize and gather our thoughts and posture us for the next unveiling.

UNEXPECTED FIRE

I have titled the book *Unexpected Fire* because Revelation is about the holy fire of God. Jesus is revealed as a burning fire, bright as the sun. His angels are flaming torches and ministers of fire. The prayers of the saints are flames of fire burning on the altar. The wrath of God is a consuming fire hurled down upon the planet. Revival fires will cover the earth as God's people are on fire with the anointing of the Holy Spirit. And the final judgment for the devil and his allies is hell fire.

The fire is unexpected because the church, as a whole, is unaware of the extent of the Holy Spirit fire that will empower her. Unexpected fire of a different kind will fall on those without Christ. The world is unaware of the reality and scope of the judgment fires that are coming.

Revelation fire is the passion, purity, and power of God. It refines and protects the saints, and it is also an instrument of divine justice. Fire from heaven will soon fall on the good and the bad. It is so close that the prophets today could appropriately warn us with a shout, "Fire in the Hole!" It is time to make ready and pray. Let the fire of God come, for its coming will be the fulfillment of God's perfect and unchangeable plan. It is his refining fire.

WE CANNOT BE DOGMATIC

Finally, I cannot and will not be dogmatic with my interpretation of Revelation. None of us should be immovable or unteachable. Many believers have different views on Revelation. I will share what I believe the Lord has revealed to me and teach my beliefs with conviction, as every preacher should. I do, however, humbly bow to the lordship of Jesus and the ongoing revelation of the scriptures that will come from the Holy Spirit. The Lord is continually speaking, and more understanding will emerge. He speaks in many ways, through many different people. One day we will understand fully and be united in truth under the banner of Christ. Until then, we reason together and look to God for greater revelation.

To better understand this teaching, I recommend that you pray and carefully read the suggested portion of scripture at the start of each chapter.

The fire that is coming is unexpected. May the Holy Spirit give you eyes to see, grace to understand, and faith to embrace God's plan. May you find your place of partnership with the Holy One of Israel.

Part One
Royal Introductions

Chapter One

REVELATION IS ABOUT JESUS

The revelation of Jesus Christ, which God gave him to show his servants what must soon take place ... Blessed is the one who reads the words of this prophecy, and blessed are those who hear it and take to heart what is written in it, because the time is near. (Rev. 1:1–3)

SUGGESTED READING: REVELATION 1

CHAPTER TOPICS

1. Jesus;
2. The revelation being given to John;
3. John being spared from martyrdom;
4. The Island of Patmos;
5. A new Jesus;
6. Jesus on fire;
7. Jesus the revelator.

THE JESUS REVELATION

REVELATION IS ABOUT JESUS. The opening words of the first chapter put us in the right frame of mind. The book opens, "The revelation of Jesus Christ, which God gave him to show his servants" (Rev. 1:1).

The book is not called *Revelations* although there are many revelations in it. It is titled *the* Revelation of Jesus Christ. All other information in the book is part of this revelation. If we fail to grasp this, we miss the main directive and purpose of the book. Revelation is about Jesus' identity, his church, his angels, his blood, his salvation, his Father, his love, his testimony, his battle, his kingdom, his millennial rule, his glory, and his victory over the devil.

THE REVELATION WAS GIVEN TO JOHN

One of Jesus' closest friends was John, the son of Zebedee. He was a disciple and was chosen to receive the book of Revelation. He was called John the Beloved. He was a tender man, totally devoted to Jesus. At the Last Supper, he leaned on Jesus' breast and was know as the Apostle of Love.

Inspired by the Holy Spirit, John recorded the words of Jesus: "A new commandment I give to you, that you love one another: as I have loved you" (John 13:34 NKJV).

John was not always full of love, however. When he first met Jesus, he was known for his anger. He was a rugged fisherman, impulsive and harsh. He was sectarian, proud, and ready to stop any who did not conform to his understanding of the faith. He was ready to call fire from heaven upon any who would not accept Jesus (Luke 9:54). Jesus corrected John, teaching him to be gracious, patient, and caring to others. John was a responsive student, and the Holy Spirit changed his character. He became a man of gentle grace and genuine love. Perhaps that is why he was chosen to receive the book of Revelation. He was humble and could be trusted to properly handle the testimony of Jesus.

It says in Rev. 1:2 that John testified "to everything he saw." He would not embellish the book of Revelation to sensationalize it, nor delete the troubling spots of judgment and suffering to avoid criticism. He did not need to be politically correct. John was the chosen disciple; he was the perfect man for the task.

JOHN WAS NOT MARTYRED

The disciples loved the Lord Jesus and were prepared to die serving him. Ten of the twelve were martyred for their faith. Some were crucified; Peter was crucified upside down. Others were stoned. James was beheaded, Nathanael was flogged to death, and Thomas was killed by a sortie of arrows on the beaches of Madras, India. The Roman Empire persecuted the early church with incarcerations, barbaric tortures, and brutal killings. Christians were fed to lions and bears before great crowds in public arenas. Some were put in sacks with venomous snakes and thrown into rivers. Others were tied with loose ropes to the horns of wild bulls where they were pummeled and gored to death. Many were crucified, ripped in two by catapults, or covered with pitch and hung on poles. They were lit on fire to give light to the cities at night. For three hundred years, the Christians of the Middle East, Europe, and Asia were tortured for sport by wicked Roman Emperors. Through all of this, the Church continued to grow rapidly until Roman temples were forsaken and entire towns were converted to Christ.

John was an exception to the other disciples; he lived a long life and died of natural causes. His life, however, was not without pain. He was banished by Emperor Domitian to hard labor in a rock quarry on the Island of Patmos. While John was suffering abuse under harsh and inhumane treatment, God revealed to him what would become the book of Revelation.

John said, "I John ... was on the Island of Patmos because of the word of God and the testimony of Jesus" (Rev. 1:9).

NOT THE JESUS HE KNEW

The first revelation John received was, in fact, a vision of Jesus. John was quietly worshipping the Lord; he was in the Spirit on the Lord's Day when suddenly he heard a voice as loud as a trumpet. It was Jesus. He identified himself and said, "Write on a scroll what you see and send it to the seven churches" (Rev. 1:11).

John spun around and saw the Lord standing in the middle of seven golden lampstands. This was not the Jesus John had known, and John had to be reeducated. Until that point, John had only known Jesus from their friendship on earth, and his earthly perspective of Jesus was insufficient.

He knew Jesus as the master teacher, healer, and lover of mankind. He knew the man who had comforted the weary, saved the sinner, calmed the storm, lifted the oppressed, and shielded the defenseless. He knew the compassionate Lamb of God who had died for the sins of the world. Yet before him stood a heavenly person, blazing with unexpected fire. John needed a vision of the warrior king who was about to unleash the great tribulation.

This is the clearest picture that scripture gives of how Jesus looks today. He is not the babe in the manger or the sandaled journeyman of dusty towns. Nor is he the weary teacher sleeping in the bow of a boat on the Sea of Galilee. He is much more than that.

Jesus is the Lord of heaven and the King of Glory. He is, undeniably, the Alpha and the Omega, the Beginning and the End. Jesus is the light that destroys every dark and evil thing. He has no enemy that can rival him, no equal beyond the Trinity. He is the all-powerful commander of heaven's armies, and he will speak the word, wield the sword, and make all things right. He is not only the Lamb; he is the Lion, the warrior, the King of kings, and the Lord of Battles. Before John could even hope to understand the revelation he was about to receive, he had to see the awesome magnitude and unrivaled authority of the living Christ.

JESUS ON FIRE

John saw Jesus shining in all of his brilliance up close and personal. Jesus' eyes were blazing fires, flaring with holy passion. His feet were glowing with brazen fire like metal in a blast furnace, and his face radiated with the full force of the sun when it shines with all of its brightness.

Like any of us who have foolishly looked into the sun, John's eyes were stinging, and he turned away to shield them. His heart pounded hard as fear and death closed in around him. He knew from the holy writings that any man who came this close to the holiness of God was going to die. He stared at the imprint of Jesus that was burned on his retinas.

His momentary glance remembered snow white hair and a brilliant white gown with a golden sash that hung over the shoulder and crossed the chest. Jesus' face was of fire, and his mouth was not normal—out of it came a gleaming, double-edged sword that was honed deadly sharp. It was a fearsome weapon, and nothing could deny its intent. One would think that the sword would be in his hand, but instead his hand held glittering stars.

FEAR OF DEATH

The fear was not isolated to John's heart; it spread like a raging flood through his entire body, as if it were the poison of a scorpion's sting. He became weak, his mind lost all avenues of escape, and his body went limp. Fully drained of energy, John must have thought, 'he is Jesus for sure, but this is not the tender rabbi I used to know.' He collapsed to the ground, helpless, motionless, and bereft of strength. He was as good as dead and had no ability to resist.

Immediately, to his shock and surprise, John felt the hand of Jesus on his back. He heard Jesus speak: "Do not be afraid. I am the First and the Last. I am the Living One; I was dead, and behold I am alive for ever and ever! And I hold the keys of death and Hades. Write, therefore, what you have seen, what is now and what will take place later" (Rev. 1:17–19).

Fear left John's body as quickly as it had come. He knew now, that this was indeed his friend, his rabbi, the Lord Jesus Messiah. At that moment, he knew he was about to receive an eternal message.

John's frightful introduction to the new Jesus was exhausting, but it was inescapable. Jesus did not want to frighten John, but to enlighten him. Heaven's power must first be seen in heaven's awesome king.

Now that John had seen the real Jesus, every detail of the end of the age would fall into place. John's heart was still racing, but he was prepared to receive the message. He would handle the message in the fear of the Lord and send it without hesitation or adjustment to the seven churches of Asia. There the message would be kept safe until it was canonized, and finally released for the end-time church. John saw the unexpected fire in heaven's king, and that opened the door for him to see all the different kinds of fire that are destined to fall upon the earth.

Chapter Two

Revelation Is About the Church

To the angel of the church of Ephesus write: These are the words of him who holds the seven stars in his right hand and walks among the seven golden lampstands. I know your deeds, your hard work and your perseverance. (Rev. 2:1–2)

SUGGESTED READING: REVELATION 2–3

CHAPTER TOPICS

1. Jesus loving his church
2. Jesus communicating his love to his church
3. Jesus as the best coach
4. The devil's lies
5. The failure of the church
6. The power to overcome
7. The preparation of the church

JESUS LOVES HIS CHURCH

IN THE FIRST FEW chapters of Revelation we receive the royal introductions. I have designated eight chapters in the book to focus on these introductions. Following the introductions, the great tribulation is revealed.

After being introduced to the new Jesus, John was introduced to the church. When John heard the voice of Jesus and turned to see him, Jesus was standing in the middle of seven golden lampstands (Rev. 1:12–13). Jesus said, "The seven lampstands are the seven churches" (Rev. 1:20).

Jesus stood in the middle of the church and identified himself as being one with his people. He is the head, and the church is his body. He is the husband, and the church is his bride. And he will not be separated from his bride.

At the very beginning of John's report to the churches, he communicated Jesus' love for them. He wrote, "To him *who loves us* and freed us from our sins ... be glory ... for ever" (Rev. 1:5–6).

John described to us what he felt and saw. He was moved by Christ's love for his church. If we miss this emphasis we will distance ourselves from the Lord and hide from his wrath. We will become far removed from the book of Revelation, as if it is some strange, foreign writing. We will envision heaven's king releasing his sovereign will without our involvement. That is not Jesus' intention. He stood with his church around him to indicate that he will not unfold the book of Revelation without us. He wants us at his side, for that is an essential and mandatory part of his victory. He died and rose to life to bring forth a glorious church in this life and in the next.

LOVING THE SEVEN CHURCHES

The book of Revelation was sent to the seven churches of Asia because John had a relationship with those churches. He extended personal apostolic care to them. They looked to him as a spiritual father and would take his writings seriously. They would treasure the apocalyptic writing and keep it safe until it could be canonized and made part of the Holy Scriptures.

Seven times, John wrote, "He who has an ear, let him hear what the Spirit says to the churches" (Rev. 2:7, 11, 17, 29; 3:6, 13, 22). John was emphatic about this, because the book of Revelation is not just for the seven churches, but for all who have ears to hear. It is for all who will listen to what the Spirit of God is saying.

The seven churches found wisdom and comfort from the letters, but more importantly, the churches were the keepers of the letters, tasked with preserving them for future generations. Where else could these writings have gone for safekeeping until the appointed time of action?

Jesus dictated the seven letters to John. He started with a reminder that he is the one who walks with his church in the middle of the lampstands (Rev. 2:1). He was not scolding the churches; he was giving them wisdom from above.

"The wisdom that comes from heaven is first of all pure; then peace-loving, considerate, submissive, full of mercy and good fruit, impartial and sincere. Peacemakers who sow in peace raise a harvest of righteousness" (James 3:17–18). This is a description of the Lord's method of counsel to his children. Jesus gives strong corrections, but he gives them with love, mercy, and peace.

He said, "Those *whom I love* I rebuke and discipline. So be earnest, and repent. Here I am! I stand at the door and knock. If anyone hears my voice and opens the door, *I will come in and eat with him, and he with me*" (Rev. 3:19–20).

Jesus tenderly corrects and looks for our response. He stands at the door of our hearts and knocks, and we must open the door to hear and receive his words. When we open up and obey, he shares his life with us, and we have fellowship with him.

THE NATIONAL FOOTBALL LEAGUE

The way the seven letters are written reminds me of a National Football League (NFL) coach who is meeting with his team at half-time. Both are private encounters, behind closed doors. Jesus loves his church and tells each one what they have done right and what they have done wrong. He tells them how to make their churches better and encourages them to overcome. He is not beating them, but preparing them for the end-time battle—the second half of the game.

Jesus is like a football coach who shares his heart in the locker room. The coach says to his team, "You did well. You got two touchdowns, and your passing game was outstanding. Still you made some big mistakes. You let the other team get a touchdown when you fumbled the ball, and your running game was terrible. This is how you can fix it. The blockers will need to rise up and stay the course. You must hold your positions. Then watch out for the unnecessary penalties that drive you back and cause you to lose ground. Team, you can win this game; you can overcome. Do the things that you have been taught, and you will succeed and go all the way to the Super Bowl."

The tenor of the coach's words is authoritative but positive. This was Jesus' tone in the letters. Only one who does not grasp the love of Jesus for his church would think that he was angry, unsympathetic, or hardhearted.

LETTERS FOR US ALL

These letters were written for the churches of Asia, but they also address God's concerns for us today. Every Christian can find a personal message in chapters 2 and 3 of Revelation. We are all different, but Jesus exposed everyone in these letters. As you read them, I trust you will hear the Holy Spirit correcting you. I trust you will discover the passionate love of Jesus as he coaches you to be the best you can be.

Jesus tells each church their strengths and where they missed the mark. He warns them what will happen if they do not change and tells them of the blessings they will receive if they overcome. Except for the church at Philadelphia, the churches were in need of major adjustments. Each was caught in some kind of sin because they believed a lie from the deceiver, the devil.

LIES ALL LIES

The lies for which Jesus rebuked the churches are the same lies that Christians entertain today. See if you can identify them. Ask yourself if any of these lies have found a place in your life.

The List of Lies include:

1. The lie at Ephesus: *You do not need to be a passionate disciple. It is okay for Christians to leave their first love and just be casual toward Christ.* Jesus said, "You have forsaken your first love. Remember the height from which you have fallen! Repent and do the things you did at first" (Rev. 2:4–5).
2. The lie at Smyrna: *Christianity is not worth the persecution it may bring.* Jesus said, "Do not be afraid of what you are about to suffer. I tell you, the devil will put some of you in prison … and you will suffer persecution … Be faithful, even to the point of death, and I will give you the crown of life" (Rev. 2:10).
3. The lie at Pergamum: *You can be sexually immoral and get away with it.* Jesus said, "I have a few things against you: You have people there who … entice the Israelites to sin by eating food sacrificed to idols and by committing sexual immorality. Repent therefore!" (Rev. 2:14, 16).
4. The lie at Thyatira: *You must tolerate the spirit of Jezebel (witchcraft). Society says she is to be given equal rights, and it is politically incorrect to resist her.* Jesus said, "I have this against you: You tolerate that woman Jezebel, who calls herself a prophetess. By her teaching she misleads my servants … To the rest of you in Thyatira, to you who do not hold to her teaching and have not learned Satan's so-called deep secrets (I will not impose any other burden on you): Only hold on" (Rev. 2:20, 25).
5. The lie at Sardis: *The church can sleep and ignore sin in society. It is okay to be apathetic about the moral decay in society.* Jesus said, "Wake up! Strengthen what remains … for I have not found your deeds complete … Remember, therefore, what you have received and heard; obey it, and repent" (Rev. 3:2–3).

6. The lie at Laodicea: *Earthly riches will bring security; materialism will satisfy our deepest needs*. Jesus said, "You say, 'I am rich; I have acquired wealth and do not need a thing.' But ... you are wretched, pitiful, poor, blind and naked. I counsel you to buy from me gold refined in the fire, so you can become rich; and white clothes to wear, so you can cover your shameful nakedness; and salve to put on your eyes, so you can see. Those whom I love I rebuke and discipline. So be earnest and repent" (Rev. 3:17–19).

THOSE WHO OVERCOME

These same lies are popular today. Many in the church are lukewarm, fearful, immoral, compromising, idolatrous, and materialistic. These failures will become even more prevalent as we approach the tribulation.

Jesus gives grace for all to overcome these lies. He is the author and finisher of our faith (Heb. 12:2). In other words, he invented our faith and knows how to make it work for us. It is his place to prepare the end-time church for the days ahead. He will have an overcoming church to partner with in the hour of tribulation.

Jesus ends each letter with an exhortation to overcome. He says in effect, "Listen to what I have said, overcome the sin and the obstacles in your way, and I will reward you." The Lord would not ask us to do these things if they were not possible. As end-time pressures mount, persecution and judgment will humble and purify the church. The saints will rise up and overcome.

When gross darkness covers the earth, God's glory will rise upon his people.

"Arise, shine for your light has come, and the glory of the Lord rises upon you. See, darkness covers the earth and thick darkness is over the peoples, but the Lord rises upon you and his glory appears over you" (Isa. 60:1–2).

This scripture was first given to Israel (the Jewish people), but it applies to the gentile church as well. Jesus loves his church. He will cause her to overcome the devil. He will release his glory upon her as we enter the tribulation period. Then all will see God's love.

Think for a moment, about one of the most popular scriptures: "For God so loved the world [people] that he gave his one and only Son." (John 3:16).

The awesome love of God for people will be demonstrated when the book of Revelation becomes reality. Expect the unexpected.

Chapter Three

Revelation is About Almighty God

After this I looked, and there before me was a door standing open in heaven. And the voice I had first heard speaking to me like a trumpet said, "Come up here, and I will show you what must take place after this." At once I was in the Spirit, and there before me was a throne in heaven with someone sitting on it. And the one who sat there had the appearance of jasper and carnelian. A rainbow, resembling an emerald, encircled the throne. (Rev. 4:1–3)

Then I saw in the right hand of him who sat on the throne a scroll with writing on both sides and sealed with seven seals. And I saw a mighty angel proclaiming in a loud voice, "Who is worthy to break the seals and open the scroll?" (Rev. 5:1–2)

CHAPTER TOPICS

1. John's experience
2. An open door in heaven
3. No mention of a rapture
4. God's throne room
5. He who sits on the throne
6. Worshipping the Almighty

7. The scroll in God's hand
8. A call to the saints

JOHN IS STRETCHED

JOHN SAW JESUS. HE heard the words of the Great Shepherd for his church. Revelation began, and John was about to receive a vision so big that he would have difficulty recording it. The vision would be much like a three-dimensional movie being shown on screens all around him, and he would have to turn completely around, three hundred sixty degrees, to catch a glimpse of all that was happening. Besides this, the vision would come quickly. It would appear like a movie in fast-forward speed, and there would be so much information to take in that it would be difficult to describe every detail and give a complete commentary. John was forced to be concise.

These were early introductions for John, but they were essential. John would see the grandeur of heaven before he would see the frailty of the earth. Without a revelation of the throne room, he would not be able to fit the coming tribulation in proper context. If he did not see the glory of God Almighty, he would be overtaken with fear when he was shown Satan's violent assaults and heaven's judgments. If he did not grasp the love of God, he would panic when wrath came. Who could bear such a vision unless God prepared him? John would understand that God is love, and that he has all wisdom and absolute authority.

The book of Revelation is the disclosure of God's sovereign plan. At the very heart of his plan is his love for people.

THE THRONE ROOM REVEALED

It was time for John to see the power-grid of heaven. There were two cosmic armies who were about to fight a seven-year war—the war that would end all wars. John was about to be introduced to the troops. When he saw them, he would be glad that he was on the Lord's side. He was on his way to the throne room, the headquarters of heaven.

Several individuals mentioned in scripture had already visited the throne room. Ezekiel (Ezek. 1 and 10), Isaiah (Isa. 6), Daniel (Dan. 7), Micaiah (1 Kings 22:19), and Stephen (Acts 7:55–56) were all given a revelation of heaven.

Even the apostle Paul received a vision of heaven. He told us of someone, probably himself, who was caught up into heaven. He said, "I know a man ... who was caught up to the third heaven ... to paradise. He heard inexpressible things, things that a man is not permitted to tell" (2 Cor. 12:2, 4).

Although Paul was not permitted to tell what he saw, others were. Their descriptions of the throne room differ slightly. Each recorded what he saw from his vantage point. Just as when several witnesses report an event, their stories fit together but differ in minor details, so do the Gospels differ slightly. Matthew, Mark, Luke, and John each recorded the ministry and life of Jesus, but some details differ according to the writer's vantage point or research. While some might say that these differences invalidate the Gospels, the opposite is true. The fact that minor details vary further validates that different disciples saw these events with their own eyes or, as in Luke's case, recorded other people's eyewitness accounts. They did not copy the writings of others; rather, they had slightly different perspectives of the same events.

Likewise, the writers of the Bible who received a vision of God's throne room described it with minor differences. This helps to substantiate the fact that the throne room is real and was actually seen by different people at different times. One writer did not copy the writings of another.

"COME UP HERE" IS NOT THE RAPTURE

The first thing John saw was an open door. An open door in heaven is an open invitation to come into the presence of God. (See Hebrews 4:16 and 10:19–22.) It is a call, a beckoning, and a personal opportunity for people to come to God.

The door will not always be open. It makes sense that the door will one day be closed; if not, why would there be a door when a hallway would suffice? Suddenly, Jesus spoke to John as he had earlier, with a voice as loud as a trumpet.

John wrote: "After this I looked, and there before me was a door standing open in heaven. And the voice I had first heard speaking to me like a trumpet said, *'Come up here, and I will show you* what must take place after this.' At once I was in the Spirit, and there before me was a throne in heaven" (Rev. 4:1).

Some godly teachers, whom I regard highly, believe that the statement, "Come up here and I will show you," is the rapture. The rapture is a doctrine that suggests that Jesus will come in the clouds and take his followers with him back into heaven. I respectfully disagree, this is not the rapture. That idea does not fit the context of the chapter. The words, "Come up here," are directed to John, not to the people of the earth. Immediately following, John responded and was taken up into the throne room. He would soon discover God's purpose. He saw into the future.

John sees the open door and goes inside the throne room. The angel introduces him to the host of heaven. I searched for the rapture in this text, but I could not find it. I do not believe there is any connection to a worldwide rapture in this verse.

GOD'S THRONE

At once, John saw a throne in heaven with someone sitting on it. He saw the Lord God Almighty, he who is above all others. John was struck with reverence and awe. He felt the powerful presence of God for the room was charged with God's majesty. He could not see clear details of God's face or his form, but he knew who was sitting before him, and he was humbled by God's unapproachable light.

The Bible says that God dwells "in unapproachable light, whom no one has seen or can see" (1 Tim. 6:16).

Moses came close when he said to God, "Show me your glory." And the Lord said, "I will cause all my goodness to pass in front of you ... But ... you cannot see my face, for no one may see me and live" (Exod. 33:18–20).

John tried to describe the Almighty from the partial revelation he was given.

He said, "The one who sat there had the appearance of jasper and carnelian. A rainbow, resembling an emerald, encircled the throne" (Rev. 4:3). Jasper and carnelian are two semiprecious stones, which are blood red, bright yellow, or honey brown in color. They are striated and translucent, and when light glitters through them, they give the appearance of dancing embers in a fire. When I lived in Canada I saw the aurora borealis. Known as the northern lights, the glow in the sky is brilliant and beautiful, glimmering and shifting like a luminous curtain full of dazzling color and light. I imagine that John saw light like that shooting out in every direction from the throne.

Ezekiel told us that the throne itself is the color of sapphire, which is a dark royal blue (Ezek. 1:26; 10:1). From John's description, we know that the air in the throne room is brushed with an emerald green light in the shape of a rainbow. Green is the easiest and most comfortable color to the human eye. Even though God's presence is awesome, he designed this room for people. God's throne room, his place of power—wonder of wonders—has been fashioned with people in mind.

Yet God is omnipotent, and he will not be contained. In this description of the throne room, John noted that "From the throne came flashes of lightning, rumblings and peals of thunder" (Rev. 4:5). Energy bursts from the throne. Shards of electrical power slice through the air. Lightning crackles, and peals of thunder boom through the atmosphere.

ALL WHO APPROACH WILL WORSHIP

John was in the presence of the Almighty, the sustainer of life, and the judge of all and he could not help but worship him.

John noted that everyone in heaven worshipped God; four seraphim stood around the throne, and night and day they continued worshipping him. They constantly repeated the words, "Holy, holy, holy is the Lord God Almighty, who was, and is, and is to come" (Rev. 4:8).

In addition the twenty-four people, known as elders, surrounded the throne worshipped the Almighty as well. They had crowns that they had earned because of their good deeds, and they cast their crowns before the throne, saying "You are worthy, our Lord and God, to receive glory and honor and power, for you created all things, and by your will they were created and have their being" (Rev. 4:11).

THE SCROLL

As John watched and worshipped, one part of God's body became visible. John saw God's hand, and he could not take his eyes off the object that God was holding: "Then I saw in the right hand of him who sat on the throne a scroll with writing on both sides and sealed with seven seals" (Rev. 5:1).

God revealed the contents of his right hand. In it was the scroll of Revelation. It contained the plans, the blueprints, and the edicts of the Almighty for the end of the age. It was sealed, and had two inscriptions written on it.

The Bible does not say what those inscriptions were, but I believe the writing on the outside of the scroll was the title of its contents. The scroll had two parts. I think that the words read something like, "The Judgment of the devil" on one side of the scroll and something like, "Blessings for Israel and the Church" on the other side.

The scroll has yet to be opened, but one day it must be opened.

HEAVEN AND EARTH ARE WAITING

John saw God Almighty sitting on the throne, shining with unapproachable light. Angels and men were gathered around worshipping him. In his hand, he carried what was foremost on his mind and heaven and earth were waiting to see its contents.

When the scroll is taken from the hand of the Almighty, it will be time for heaven and earth to agree with his design. God's will is nonnegotiable—it cannot be stopped or delayed. God's plan will fall in place according to his divine schedule. The book of Revelation is his mandate. The saints on earth are being called to come into agreement with the edicts of the scroll. The full account of the apocalypse is prerecorded in that scroll, and the book of Revelation is a glimpse of its contents. We are being commissioned for partnership with God.

In Amos 3: 7– 8, we are told, "Surely the Sovereign Lord does nothing without revealing his plan to his servants the prophets. The lion has roared—who will not fear? The Sovereign Lord has spoken—who can but prophesy?"

It is hard to comprehend, but the Almighty includes us as coworkers and partners.

The psalmist said, "What is man that you are mindful of him, the son of man that you care for him? You made him a little lower than the heavenly beings and crowned him with glory and honor. You made him ruler over the works of your hands; you put everything under his feet: all flocks and herds and the beasts of the field, birds of the air and the fish of the sea. ... O Lord, our Lord, how majestic is your name in all the earth!" (Ps. 8:4–9).

God loves the human race and is determined to bring us into his glory. There is no God like our God.

Chapter Four

Revelation is About the Seraphim

In the center, around the throne, were four living creatures, and they were covered with eyes, in front and in back. The first living creature was like a lion, the second was like an ox, the third had a face like a man, the forth was like a flying eagle. Each of the four living creatures had six wings and was covered with eyes all around, even under his wings. Day and night they never stop saying: "Holy, holy, holy is the Lord God Almighty, who was, and is, and is to come."
Whenever the living creatures give glory, honor and thanks to him who sits on the throne and who lives for ever and ever, the twenty-four elders fall down before him who sits on the throne, and worship him who lives for ever and ever. (Rev. 4:6–10)

CHAPTER TOPICS

1. The servants of heaven
2. The visitation of angels
3. The mighty seraphim
4. The prophetic power of the seraphim
5. The four living creatures
6. Angelic fire
7. Wheels within wheels

8. The worship of the seraphs
9. The Amen arrow

SERVANTS OF HEAVEN

ALL ANGELS ARE WORSHIPPING warriors. They are servants of heaven who visit the earth as wind and flames of fire to serve Christians.

In Heb. 1:7 and 14, we read, "In speaking of angels he [God] says, 'He makes his angels winds, his servants flames of fire.' Are not all angels ministering spirits sent to serve those who will inherit salvation?"

ANGELS COME OFTEN

Angels fight demons and help people, yet most of the time we do not detect their presence. They extend supernatural protection to children and to all servants of God. They orchestrate circumstances to assist the Holy Spirit in fulfilling the redemptive plans of heaven. On a regular and frequent basis, majestic and powerful angels are sent to answer our prayers.

A VISITATION

Many people can tell a story of a providential situation where they were protected, shielded, had a door of opportunity opened, or received a needed provision.

I remember playing alone in the back yard of my home when I was six years old. Our family was in transition, and we had lived at that home for only a few months. Behind a row of thick bushes at the very back of the garden was a cliff that was hidden from view. The bushes were meant to serve as a barrier.

I was a carefree child, full of adventure and eager to explore. One day I pushed my way through the bushes and, to my surprise, I came upon the cliff. I was standing on the very edge of it when suddenly the ground beneath me gave way, and I fell. Twisting around, I grasped hold of the roots of the bushes that dangled over the cliff. There I hung, high up in the air with table rock seventy-five feet below. I looked at the roots in my hands as one by one they snapped and broke away.

Suddenly, a hand reached down and grabbed my wrist. I was lifted up onto the grass. I think it was the neighbor boy who, I guess, was about fifteen years of age. I had only seen him once before, and that glimpse had been from a distance. I never saw him again. After lifting me up, he looked at me and simply said, "Be more careful." Then he turned and walked away.

I never told Mom or Dad or anyone else what had happened until many years later, but I never forgot that day. Now, I look back and wonder if the person I thought was my "neighbor" was actually an angel. If the young man who helped me was not an angel, I have no doubt that angels were involved in the rescue.

FOUR LIVING CREATURES

In God's throne room, John discovered different types of angels, but the seraphim and cherubim stood out in a class of their own. John saw four of them around the throne. Seraphim and cherubim differ, but for the purposes of this book I will refer to them both as seraphim.

Seraphim are huge, and—perhaps to distinguish them from the muscular but lifeless Greek and Roman stone statues of his day—John described them as "four living creatures."

Seraphim are actively engaged as warriors and worshippers. Besides the Father, Son, and Holy Spirit, these angels are the most powerful creatures in the universe. Consider Isaiah's reference to these angels. He wrote, "In the year that King Uzziah died, I saw the Lord seated on a throne, high and exalted, and the train of his robe filled the temple. Above him were seraphs, each with six wings: with two they covered their faces, with two they covered their feet, and with two they were flying. And they were calling to one another: 'Holy, holy, holy is the

Lord Almighty; the whole earth is full of his glory.' At the sound of their voices the doorposts and thresholds shook and the temple was filled with smoke" (Isa. 6:1–4).

Each has six wings. With two they cover their faces for worship; with two they cover their feet for humble service; and with two they fly as aggressive prophets.

Isaiah, upon seeing the Lord Almighty and the incredible seraphim, was so awestruck that he thought he would die. Instead of killing him, the seraphim ministered holy fire to him. (See Isaiah 6:6-8)

He was instantly cleansed and sanctified as the angel took a live coal from heaven's altar and touched his lips with it. Isaiah was then commissioned for prophetic service. It is possible that the seraphim will minister to many in a similar fashion at the end of the age.

HOLY CHARACTER

The four living creatures are not just soldiers of brawn, lacking depth of character or intelligence; the grace of God upon them is seen on every side. John informed us that one had a face like a lion's, and another's face was like an ox's; one had the face of a man, and one had the face of an eagle.

Ezekiel had a closer look at them, from a different angle. He said, "Each of the four had the face of a man, and on the right side each had the face of a lion, and on the left the face of an ox; each also had the face of an eagle" (Ezek. 1:10).

Four different faces are on each of the seraphim to describe their character and purpose. The seraphim are holy, and they demonstrate the highest standards of godly character. They move with dignity and power at the same time. They are focused as if there is nothing in the universe more important than their assignments.

The lion speaks of authority and power. The ox speaks of submission and service. The man speaks of humility and dependence on God. The eagle speaks of wisdom and prophecy.

EAGLE EYES

The eagle nature of the seraphim sees far, and they go after what they see with great speed. Each seraph is full of eyes. Eyes cover their entire bodies, front and back and even under their wings. Eyes and wings typify the gifts of the prophet. Prophets are seers and fliers. Nothing escapes the vision of the seraph. Nothing takes them by surprise, and they are ready to do the Lord's bidding at an instant.

GENERALS OF FIRE

The four living creatures are the Almighty's personal generals. They will launch the first campaign, the first sortie of judgments in the great tribulation. They are military commanders, and their armies are unequaled in power.

They are the windstorm coming from the north. Ezekiel noted, "Behold a whirlwind was coming out of the north, a great cloud of raging fire engulfing itself; and brightness was all around it and radiating out of its midst like the color of amber, out of the midst of the fire. Also from within it came the likeness of four living creatures" (Ezek. 1:4–5 NKJV).

"They sparkled like the color of burnished bronze" (Ezek. 1:7 NKJV).

"As for the likeness of the living creatures, their appearance was like burning coals of fire, like the appearances of torches going back and forth … And the living creatures ran back and forth, in appearance like a flash of lightning" (Ezek. 1:13–14 NKJV).

They come with the awesome power of lightning and thunder. Fire moves among them, and they speed back and forth as flashes of fire.

REFINERS FIRE

Seraphim can overpower every demonic creature, but they will also attack evil people. When the time comes, seraph fire will purge the church of hypocrites and remove the ungodly from the earth. On that day, no one will want to have these angels as enemies. The fear of God will purify the lives of many, but there will be hypocrites in the church—religious people involved in the church who are not disciples of Christ. The seraphim will remove the weeds, those who are really wolves living among the sheep.

We read, "As the weeds are pulled up and burned in the fire, so it will be at the end of the age. The Son of Man will send out his angels, and they will weed out of his kingdom everything that causes sin and all who do evil" (Matt. 13:40–41).

Seraphim are the whirlwind, the harvesters, and the death angels. They will be on the front lines of battle at the end of the age.

WHEELS WITHIN WHEELS

Each seraph is a commander. He has wheels within wheels accompanying him. The wheels are covered in fire and eyes just like the seraph who leads them (see Ezek. 1:4–5, 12–21; 10:2–19).

In Ezek. 10:16–17, we read, "When the cherubim [seraphim] moved, the wheels beside them moved; and when the cherubim spread their wings to rise from the ground, the wheels did not leave their side. When the cherubim stood still, they also stood still; and when the cherubim rose, they rose with them, because the spirit of the living creatures was in them."

Also, in Ezek. 1:20, we read, "Wherever the spirit would go, they would go, and the wheels would rise along with them, because the spirit of the living creatures was in the wheels."

The spirit of the seraphim is in the wheels, which glow like brilliant gems At first glance, the wheels seem to be described as some sort of spacecraft. However, I do not believe this to be the case. They are ministering spirits, able to fly and fight without the aid of any craft. I believe the wheels full of eyes and fire are battalions of angelic armies under the seraphim's command, which move as one with their commanders.

Another verse in Ezekiel says: "The creatures sped back and forth like flashes of lightning" (Ezek. 1:14).

If a seraph darts one way, the wheels move with him in synchronized harmony and absolute unity. Like a flock of birds or a school of fish, the entire group instinctively moves as one.

Thousands of migrating birds swarm together, diving and shifting this way and that in unison, as if they were one. Likewise, fish school together and shift and dive in synchronized fashion. From a distance, such flocks and schools appear as a single organism. If this can happen in the natural world, be sure that it is not beyond the realm of angels.

The seraphim are led by the Spirit of God, and the wheels are led by the seraphim.

What a magnificent army—a troop of fighting angels so powerful and moving in such unity that no enemy can penetrate their defenses. None can outflank them or stand before them with any strength.

WORSHIP LEADERS

The seraphim warriors are also the worship leaders of heaven. Night and day they cry, "Holy, holy, holy is the Lord." When they worship, a chain reaction of extravagant worship explodes throughout the heavens. The elders join in, other angels join in, and ultimately every creature in heaven and earth joins the irresistible worship they initiate.

"Whenever the living creatures give glory, honor and thanks to him who sits on the throne … the twenty-four elders fall down before him … and worship him" (Rev. 4:9–10).

"Then I looked and heard the voice of many angels … ten thousand times ten thousand. They encircled the throne … In a loud voice they sang: 'Worthy is the Lamb'… Then I heard every creature in heaven and on earth and under the earth and in the sea, and all that is in them, singing: 'To him who sits on the throne and to the Lamb be praise and honor and glory and power, for ever and ever!'" (Rev. 5:11–13).

THE AMEN ARROW

After recording this amazing expression of worship, John recorded a further detail of importance. He wrote, "The four living creatures said, 'Amen,' and the elders fell down and worshiped" (Rev. 5:14).

When the prophetic seraphim said, "Amen," it was not a simple acknowledgement or a mere agreement of the proclamation that had been made. Amen is a powerful word. It literally means "so be it." Alternately, it could be translated, "Now let it happen!" So when the seraphim said amen, it released God's word into existence. Here, amen is the release that sends the arrow flying from the bow of prophecy and prayer.

After worship and the prophetic word, the living creatures said "amen," and the arrow was sent. Just as when you push the "send" key on your computer after your message has been composed, the message is gone instantly, when the seraphim said "amen,"' the word was sent forth, and it could not be retrieved. In the case of heaven's prophetic words, they suddenly became reality.

THANK GOD FOR SERAPHIM

Personally, I am thrilled that the seraphim will lead the way. I am grateful for their powerful army. I am thrilled that I will be fighting alongside them. I am so glad that they are friends and not enemies. I am eager to learn how to better prophesy and worship by observing their lead. I say, "Thank you, Heavenly Father, for creating the seraphim. You do all things well."

Chapter Five

REVELATION IS ABOUT HUMAN ELDERS IN HEAVEN

Surrounding the throne were twenty-four other thrones, and seated on them were twenty-four elders. They were dressed in white and had crowns of gold on their heads. The twenty-four elders fall down before him who sits on the throne, and worship him who lives for ever and ever. They lay their crowns before the throne and say: "You are worthy …"
The twenty-four elders fell down before the Lamb. Each one had a harp and they were holding golden bowls full of incense, which are the prayers of the saints. And they sang a new song … The elders fell down and worshiped. (Rev. 4:4, 10; 5:8–9, 14)

SUGGESTED READING: REVELATION 4–5

CHAPTER TOPICS

1. The elders in heaven
2. Identifying the elders
3. The elder's golden crowns
4. The elder's harps
5. The elder's bowls
6. Prophets, priests and kings

7. The temple worship
8. Elders who teach

THE ELDERS ARE PEOPLE

WE ARE STILL STUDYING the royal introductions, and I am glad to report that people are included. We have human representatives before the throne of God in heaven. Twenty-four elders sit on thrones around the Almighty's throne. The four living creatures John described were angelic seraphim, but the elders were people.

I once heard about a pastor, who was experiencing conflict with his church elders. He said to his wife, in jest, "I don't want to go to heaven. There are twenty-four elders there."

All joking aside, the elders are amazing. They have become part of heaven's elite worship and military team. They are part of the special-forces tactical unit in the throne room. They are coworkers with God, engaged in the vital initiatives of Revelation's mandate. We are not told who they are, but I imagine they are famous. I think we have read about them, and one day when we hear their names, we will recognize them.

IDENTIFYING THE ELDERS

John was looking into the future when he saw the elders. I wonder if he recognized anyone. Some of the Old Testament patriarchs were raised from the dead when Jesus died and was resurrected. They walked through the streets of Jerusalem before ascending to heaven

We read in Matthew, "And when Jesus had cried out again in a loud voice, he gave up his spirit. At that moment the curtain of the temple was torn in two from the top to the bottom. The earth shook and the rocks split. The tombs broke open and the bodies of many holy people who had died were raised to life. They came out of the tombs, and after the resurrection, they went into the holy city and appeared to many people" (Matt. 27:50–53).

John may have recognized some of the twenty-four elders. Perhaps he saw Abraham, Moses, David, or Daniel sitting before God's throne. It would have been such a shock if he saw his fellow disciples or even himself, sitting on one of the twenty-four thrones. It is possible for John was looking into the future. I am sure that John remembered the words of Jesus: "You who have followed me will also sit on twelve thrones" (Matt. 19:28).

THEY HAVE GOLDEN CROWNS

The twenty-four elders, like the angels, were dressed in white, but they had golden crowns on their heads. They were already kings and priests unto God.

At the end of the great tribulation, Jesus will reward the rest of the saints according to their service records. The judgment seat of Christ, known in the Greek language as the *bema* is not the judgment that determines one's destination to heaven or hell. Rather, it is for recognizing excellence and for handing out awards. It is different from the great white throne, which is the judgment seat of God Almighty.

Speaking to the church, Paul wrote, "For we must all appear before the judgment seat of Christ, that each may receive what is due him for the things done while in the body" (2 Cor. 5:10).

Golden crowns will be awarded to those who have served the Lord in some outstanding way. The placing of a crown on one's head is a validation of authority and rulership. Those who serve well will rule and reign with Christ (see Rev. 20:4–6).

Scripture records several different crowns that will be awarded at the *bema*. The crowns include:

The martyr's crown (James 1:12, Rev. 2:10)
The shepherd's crown (1 Pet. 5:2–4)
The soul winner's crown (1 Thess. 2:19–20)
The crown for righteous living (2 Tim. 4:8)
The crown for walking in the Spirit (1 Cor. 9:25–27)

As the elders worshipped, they took the crowns that had been awarded to them and cast them before the Lord, signifying that their own accomplishments and rewards were as nothing compared to what God had done for them. All of the honor they received, they gave back to him in holy adoration.

ELDERS ARE ACTIVE IN HEAVEN

The elders have many responsibilities in heaven. They worship, prophesy, sing, administrate prayer power, and prophesy on their instruments. They teach by example and by giving wise counsel as they rule from thrones of power.

John wrote, "The twenty-four elders fell down before the Lamb. Each one had a harp and they were holding golden bowls full of incense, which are the prayers of the saints. And they sang a new song" (Rev. 5:8–9).

Each has tools to accomplish their tasks. In their hands are two powerful instruments: musical harps and golden bowls. The harps are the elder's prophetic instruments; the bowls are their priestly instruments.

Among other things, the elders are vital players in the cycle of prayer and agreement between heaven and earth. Prayer agreement is essential to God's plans. He will not complete his plans unless people agree with him in prayer. The elder's role will be extremely important during the great tribulation. With their harps, they communicate God's plans to the intercessors. Intercessors are people who have been called by God to partner with him in prayer. With God, they have the ability to change the world.

The elders also have bowls. With their bowls, they collect the prayers of the intercessors and faithfully hold them before the throne.

HARPS

When the elders play their harps, the sound is like the roar of rushing waters and loud peals of thunder (see Rev. 14:2). There is no biblical record of any angels playing harps. The fictitious Valentine's cupids dressed as chubby babies and holding harps must be insulting images to real angels.

As far as we know, only humans play harps in heaven. Besides the elders, the entire multitude of saints in heaven play on harps as they participate in throne room prayer, prophesy, and worship (see Rev. 15:2–3).

John wrote, "The sound I heard was like that of harpists playing their harps. And they sang a new song before the throne … No one could learn the song except … the redeemed from the earth" (Rev. 14:2–3).

The elders are powerful warriors assigned as part of heaven's military. They play their harps, and earth-shattering songs resonate like thunderous war cries through the universe. Besides invigorating the redeemed in heaven, the elders' songs find their way to the ears of the faithful on earth. This is their prophetic ministry. They send God's word to the saints. Their music is the sound of revelry for the troops. It causes demons to tremble and saints to rise up in faith and purpose. The saints on earth sing the song of the intercessor. It is a secret song of prayer that no one else can learn. They pray the hidden plans of heaven—the prayer of agreement that God requires before he will release his will for humanity.

BOWLS

Besides harps, the elders carry bowls. When Christians pray, their prayers are collected in heaven. The throne room is filled with the aroma of prayer, which is the incense of heaven. Prayers burn on a huge altar, and some smolder and flare up in bowls, or censers, that the elders hold (Rev. 5:8).

Prayer requests are not ignored. They are kept before the Lord until the time is right for their answer, and the elders play an important role in this process. Elders are honored with the priestly call; as priests of the sanctuary, they carry earth's prayers and present them to the Lord.

The elders (priests) fulfill their duties under the direction of the high priest of heaven, the Lord Jesus. He is the high priest of our confession (Heb. 3:1). "He daily lives to make intercession for us" (Heb. 7:25).

Prayer agreement is essential for the fulfillment of Revelation. The Lord has his prayer team in heaven, and he will have agreement from his prayer team on earth. Elders and angels hold the prayers of people before Almighty God. He will summon those prayers at the appropriate time and, with them, he will light the fires of his purpose.

"The eyes of the Lord are on the righteous and his ears are attentive to their prayer" (1 Pet. 3:12).

PRIESTS, PROPHETS, AND KINGS

The elders are priests, prophets, and kings. A priest sacrifices unto the Lord and represents the people before Almighty God. As priests, the elders worship, lay down their lives in sacrifice, and hold our prayers before the throne of heaven.

As prophets, the elders see and proclaim the plans of God, both verbally and on their harps. The prophecies fill the air with the will of the Lord, instructing the saints by giving them direction and faith for the work ahead.

As kings, the elders sit on twenty-four thrones. They are rulers, and they give oversight to the multitudes of saints in the heavens. Along with others, they will rule the world in the ages to come.

The elders will help fulfill the pattern that God has established for the tabernacle. The tabernacle and temple that the children of Israel built on earth are but shadows of that which is in heaven. To the Jews (not the gentiles), belongs the temple worship. (see Romans 9:4–5.)

These elders lead heaven's human population in temple worship. The twenty-four elders are likely patriarchs and disciples, and, most likely, they are all Jews.

ELDERS ARE TEACHERS

The elders will help us find and understand our places in the pattern of the tabernacle and teach us how to come into agreement with the Lord. They lead by example and teach by giving instruction. The elders counseled John as he received and recorded the book of Revelation. At poignant moments they stepped forward to give John much needed help, and they will do the same for us.

The elders know the way humans think so they will be great teachers for us in the days ahead. They will help us embrace the end times and help us shift to kingdom-of-God thinking. We will discover this as we see them bringing many details to light in the book of Revelation. For starters, (see Rev. 5:5 and 7:13–14).

The elders are active participants in God's end-time plans, but they are not the only people in heaven. In the next chapter, we will discover what has happened to all of the righteous people who have died since the creation of mankind.

Chapter Six

Revelation is About People in Heaven

Also before the throne there was what looked like a sea of glass, clear as crystal. (Rev. 4:6)

CHAPTER TOPICS

1. People getting ready for heaven
2. Jesus' explanation of Hades
3. Jesus preaching in Hades
4. Jesus leading the saints into heaven
5. The church triumphant in session
6. The sea of glass

PEOPLE IN HEAVEN

BEFORE STUDYING ABOUT THE sea of glass, it will be helpful to gain a biblical perspective about dead people. Heaven was not always inhabited with people. In ancient times, even good people did not go there after they died. Before Christ died, only angels gathered around God's throne. Jesus had to change that.

It used to be that when Old Testament believers died, they went to a place in the lower parts of the earth called "Hades," "Abraham's bosom" or "paradise." Only after Jesus died could godly people enter

God's throne room. Jesus had some work to do in Hades before the change could take place.

Jesus said to the thief on the cross, "I tell you the truth, today you will be with me in paradise" (Luke 23:43).

After dying Jesus and the thief went immediately to Abraham's bosom, or paradise. Souls were waiting there for a special visit from Jesus.

Peter wrote, "Christ died for sins ... but made alive by the Spirit ... he went and preached to the spirits in prison who disobeyed long ago" (1 Pet. 3:18–19).

Hades has two parts: paradise for believers and hell or the place of torment [prison] for those who reject God and his ways. Peter's words infer that Jesus preached to those on both sides of Hades—even to those who had disobeyed God's commandments long ago who were in the side of Hades called hell. Hades was neither the final hell nor the final paradise. People in the hell part of Hades are still waiting for the final day of judgment, those in paradise experienced a transition into heaven after Jesus visited them. Jesus told a story about Hades.

JESUS TAUGHT ABOUT HADES

Jesus told a story of two men who died. He said: "The beggar died and the angels carried him to Abraham's side. The rich man also died and was buried. In hell ... he saw Abraham far away, with Lazarus (the beggar) by his side. So he called to him, "Father Abraham, have pity on me ..." Abraham replied ... "in your life time you received your good things, while Lazarus received bad things, but now he is comforted here and you are in agony. And besides all this, between us and you a great chasm has been fixed, so that those who want to go from here to you cannot." (Luke 16:22–26)

Jesus taught that the rich man's body had been buried, but his spirit had gone to Hades. The beggar's spirit went to Hades also, but to a different part. The rich man's spirit was tormented while the beggar was experiencing comfort. They could see each other and even speak to each other, but neither could cross over the gulf that was between them.

JESUS PREACHES IN HELL

When Jesus died, he descended into Hades and spent three days there. His body was in the tomb, but his Spirit was visiting a multitude of dead souls. Every person who had died since Adam was there in Hades, on one side or the other. Those with Abraham were captives of time, waiting for the blood of Jesus to pay for their sins so they could be escorted to heaven.

Jesus preached the gospel in Hades. He most likely told of his death on the cross and of his imminent resurrection. His message was a seal of judgment for the wicked and resurrection to life for the righteous.

JESUS LEADS THE SAINTS TO HEAVEN

Following his preaching in Hades, three days after his death, Jesus rose. Accompanying him were millions of souls. All who had died as followers of God had been in paradise with Father Abraham. When Jesus died and paid for their sins, the souls were able to leave Hades. "When he ascended on high, he led captives in his train ... (What does "he ascended" mean except that he also descended to the lower, earthly regions? He who descended is the very one who ascended higher than the heavens, in order to fill the whole universe.)" (Eph. 4:8–10).

With great excitement they left their place of waiting. They were translated through the atmosphere, into the presence of Almighty God. That day, Jesus took the keys of death and of Hades, and he unlocked the door. He released the captives of paradise and took them into God's presence.

A monumental shift took place because the blood of Jesus, at long last, had paid for the sins of humanity. Jesus died to bring us to God.

The righteous in Hades followed in his train. Their bill had been paid, and they left the debtor's prison. Abraham's bosom (paradise) was once full of souls, and heaven was empty of them. Now Abraham's bosom is totally vacant, and heaven is full of souls.

NOW WE GO TO HEAVEN

The apostle Paul made it clear that, after Christ's resurrection, the righteous would no longer go to Hades. He said that when we die, we are, "away from the body and at home with the Lord" (2 Cor. 5:8).

At death, the soul of a Christian is immediately transported into God's presence. Today heaven is the dwelling place for all dead believers. They are the spirits of righteous men made perfect, which we read about in Hebrews: "But you have come to the heavenly Jerusalem ... to the spirits of righteous men, made perfect" (Heb. 12:22–23).

RESURRECTION DAY

Each day the massive multitude of Christians in heaven grows larger. The saints are not there in body, but in spirit, and their spirits wait for resurrection day. The exact moment when that will take place has been predetermined, but only God knows the hour. Resurrection day is set for the redemption of our bodies. The spirits in heaven are already perfect, but they need new bodies to be complete.

"But we ourselves who have the first fruits of the Spirit [Holy Spirit], groan inwardly as we wait eagerly for our adoption as sons, the redemption of our bodies" (Rom. 8:23).

On resurrection day, the spirits of the righteous will descend with the Lord to be reunited with their new and perfected bodies.

"See, the Lord is coming with thousands upon thousands of his holy ones" (Jude 1:14).

"Listen, I tell you a mystery: We will not all sleep, but we will all be changed—in a flash, in the twinkling of an eye, at the last trumpet. For the trumpet will sound, the dead will be raised imperishable and we shall be changed" (1 Cor. 15:51–52).

It is no wonder that heaven bursts into glorious praise as Revelation unfolds.

HEAVEN'S CHURCH IN SESSION

My mother passed away recently. She was only sixty-seven years old, and, although my family and I thought that her time of departure was premature, the Lord took her. She was God's friend, and she is more his friend now than ever before. We read in the scriptures, "Therefore, since we are surrounded by such a great cloud of witnesses, let us throw off everything that hinders … and let us run with perseverance the race marked out for us" (Heb. 12:1).

I am aware that my mother sees me even though I cannot see her. She is part of the church triumphant, assembled with the courts of heaven. Heaven's church is in session, and I know she is playing an active part in it. She is praying and worshipping and, as a part of the great cloud of witnesses that see our daily events and surround us as we walk with the Lord, she is prophesying the plans of God over her family and others.

Those who have gone ahead, watch us, expecting to see heaven reflected in us. My mom is just one of millions who are cheering us on from the throne room. We are linked with angels, with God, and with the church triumphant. We read of this in Hebrews: "You have come to Mount Zion, to the heavenly Jerusalem, the city of the living God. You have come to thousands upon thousands of angels in joyful assembly, *to the church of the firstborn, whose names are written in heaven.* You have come to God, the judge of all men, to the spirits of righteous men made perfect, to Jesus the mediator of a new covenant" (Heb. 12:22–24; italics added).

As John was being introduced to the dignitaries of heaven, he was overwhelmed with what he saw. At a glance, John saw the church in heaven and the hosts of people who were there in spirit, not in body.

THE SEA OF GLASS

John described the souls in heaven later in the book; but for now, as we look at Revelation chapter 4, we find that he could only mention them in passing, as a 'sea of glass' before the throne. He wrote, "From the throne came flashes of lightning, rumblings and peals of thunder. Before the throne, seven lamps were blazing. These are the seven spirits of God. *Also before the throne there was what looked like a sea of glass, clear as crystal,"* (Rev. 4:5–6; italics added).

The sea of glass, clear as crystal, is an enormous entity that stretches out before the throne of God. Ezekiel described the sea of glass differently: "Spread out above the heads of the living creatures was what looked like a great expanse, sparkling like ice, and awesome" (Ezek. 1:22, see also Ezek. 1:23–25; 10:1).

Three times, Ezekiel described the sea as a great expanse. It must have extended far out toward the horizon. He said that it was awesome and that it sparkled and glittered like ice.

"Clear as crystal," is the same phrase that John used to describe God's people, the bride of Christ, later in the book of Revelation. He said, "One of the angels said to me, 'Come, I will show you the bride, the wife of the Lamb'… And he showed me the Holy City, Jerusalem, coming down out of heaven from God. It shone with the glory of God, and its brilliance was like a jasper, *clear as crystal."* (Rev. 21:9–11; italics added).

The heavenly city—which is full of people, not buildings—is the church, and the people in heaven are awesome. They are brilliant and clear as crystal, and they shine like ice and look like jasper. A gem used in fine jewelry, jasper is a type of quartz that comes in a variety of colors, and, when jasper is polished, it glitters like ice. The church triumphant is awesome; it stretches far and shines brilliantly, before God's throne.

MANY WATERS

A great multitude of justified spirits is in heaven. These spirits are the sea of glass. To further tie this in with the symbolism of Revelation, we look at another multitude that is compared to a sea: those who follow the devil. Satan's disciples are also a large company of people, and they are described as a large body of water, an ocean; however, there is no mention of brilliance over them.

The angel said to John, "Come, I will show you the great prostitute who sits on many waters." ... "Then the angel said to me, 'The waters that you saw, where the prostitute sits, are people, multitudes, nations, and languages'" (Rev. 17:1, 15).

Revelation has its own language. A sea, or large body of water, most often represents people. This is where the phrase, 'a sea of people,' comes from.

RESURRECTION

One day, the glorious sea of souls in heaven will follow Jesus to the earth, and their dead bodies will rise. Graves will open; decomposed bodies will be remade, will receive life again, and will become incorruptible. The bodies will reunite with their spirits. That is the resurrection. All of God's creation, in the natural world, wait for that great day of resurrection. Even the animals and the environment will be made new.

We read, "For the creation was subjected to frustration, not by its own choice, but by the will of the one who subjected it, in hope that the *creation itself will be liberated from its bondage to decay* and brought into the glorious freedom of the children of God" (Rom. 8:20–21; italics added).

All of nature groans for man's resurrection day. Multitudes of people in heaven are looking at us, full of faith. There is a buzz in heaven; people are excited. They are anticipating the unfolding of the book of Revelation. They are active participants in the kingdom of God and are cheering us on to be the same.

Chapter Seven

Revelation is About the Lion of Judah

Who is worthy to break the seals and open the scroll? But no one in heaven or on earth or under the earth could open the scroll or even look inside it. I wept and wept because no one was found who was worthy to open the scroll or look inside.
Then one of the elders said to me, "Do not weep! See, the Lion of the tribe of Judah, the Root of David, has triumphed. He is able to open the scroll and its seven seals." Then I saw a Lamb, looking as if it had been slain, standing in the center of the throne, encircled by the four living creatures and the elders. He had seven horns and seven eyes which are the seven spirits of God sent out into all the earth. He came and took the scroll from the right hand of him who sat on the throne.
And when he had taken it, the four living creatures and the twenty-four elders fell down before the Lamb … They sang a new song: "You are worthy to take the scroll and to open its seals, because you were slain, and with your blood you purchased men for God from every tribe and language and people and nation" …
Then I looked and heard the voice of many angels, numbering thousands upon thousands and ten thousand times ten thousand … In a loud voice they sang: "Worthy is the Lamb who was slain, to receive power and wealth and wisdom and

strength and honor and glory and praise." Then I heard every creature in heaven and on earth and under the earth and on the sea and all that is in them singing, "To him who sits on the throne and to the Lamb be praise and honor and glory and power forever and ever!" (Rev. 5:3–13)

SUGGESTED READING: REVELATION 5

CHAPTER TOPICS

1. Jesus being more than what we see
2. Focusing on the scroll
3. Patience and expectation
4. The one who is worthy
5. The Jewish Lion
6. The Lion who is a Lamb
7. Jesus taking the scroll

MORE ABOUT JESUS

THERE ARE MANY NAMES for God the Father. Each name describes an aspect of his glory and character and helps us grasp the magnitude of his greatness. It is the same with Jesus, his Son. John previously knew Jesus as the Jewish Messiah, the rabbi of Galilee. Now he knew him as the Alpha and Omega, the warrior king who has the keys of death and hell. He had not however, seen all that he must in order to understand the book of Revelation. The book of Revelation is the revelation of Jesus Christ. John had seen the Lord in a new light, but there was much more to know about Jesus. At this point in our study, John was still being introduced to him.

ATTENTION ON THE SCROLL

As the prophecy unfolds our attention is drawn to the scroll in the hand of the Almighty who sits on the throne. It is sealed with seven seals. The scroll is rolled up and the seven seals are running down the length of it. All of them must be broken before anyone will be able to see inside. We know by inference that in the scroll are the plans of God for the defeat of Satan and the victory of the saints. When all that has been written in the scroll is complete, the earth will be filled with the glory of God. In answer to the prayer of Jesus, God's kingdom will be on earth as it is in heaven (Matt. 6:10).

PATIENCE AND EXPECTATION

Most Christians do not feel the pent-up excitement that is in the host of heaven. Most of us see only the world around us, and we do not understand what heaven understands. We do not know what we are missing. The corruption in the world has brought depravity, and many of us have become desensitized to it. We do not know how good it will be once God's kingdom comes, but those in heaven know what is coming.

As John received the Revelation, the shortsightedness he once had was removed. As he joined the ranks of heaven, his soul must have cried, "Lord, let your kingdom come; let your will be done on earth as it is in heaven." He looked at the scroll, which was in the Father's hand, knowing that the full release of God's kingdom was locked up in it. John understood that the time for action had come. He was breathless with anticipation as he watched for the next move.

NO ONE WORTHY

Suddenly, a mighty angel proclaimed with a loud voice, "Who is worthy to break the seals and open the scroll? But no one in heaven or earth or under the earth could open the scroll or even look inside it" (Rev. 5:2–3).

John began to cry because heaven gave no answer—no one responded to the angel's question. John had come this far, seen the glories of heaven, but in one cold and frightful moment, all hope had suddenly gone. (see Rev. 5:4)

For certain he had wondered, as many Christians do, why the promises of God were delayed. Now heaven was on the very brink of action, but there was a roadblock. No one was found worthy to open the scroll and release that which had been promised.

The sin of mankind had sealed God's blessings in the scroll, and no one could open it. John wept because no one was worthy, and, unless the scroll could be opened, nothing on earth would change. Humankind would live with corruption and forever suffer under a tyrannical devil. It must change.

THE JEWISH LION

Then one of the twenty-four elders spoke up: "Do not weep! See, the Lion of the tribe of Judah, the Root of David, has triumphed. He is able to open the scroll and its seven seals" (Rev. 4:5).

An angel had asked, who was "worthy," and a human had come back with the answer. An elder comforted John, telling him to cry no longer—someone was able to open the scroll. It was Jesus, the Lion from the tribe of Judah. It is amazing: the Alpha and the Omega, the Beginning and the End, is God, but he is also a Jew. There in heaven, he retained his Jewish identity—he was called the Lion from the tribe of Judah and was further named, the Root of David, both of which refer to him as the Jewish king.

One might think that at this crossroads in history, when the scroll is about to be opened, the Jewishness of Jesus would be a moot point, but not so. The Jewishness of Jesus is emphasized because the Lord refuses to forget Israel. This opening of the scroll is about heaven coming down to earth, and as it does, the Jews will receive their inheritance.

One day, millions of Jews will embrace their Lion. He is part of their family. Because of him, Israel will receive every God-given promise, and Jesus, King of the Jews, will lead his family to a special place of glory and honor. He is proud to identify with his brethren, and he is determined to rule humanity from a Jewish throne. The book of Romans says it like this: "Theirs [the Jews] are the patriarchs, and from them is traced the human ancestry of Christ" (Rom. 9:5).

Jesus is called "the Lion" of the tribe of Judah because he is ferocious and unstoppable in his conquest. When the lion roars, his enemies become weak in the knees and lose all strength. Jesus is about to step forward and prove it.

THE LION IS A LAMB

John was looking at the Lion of Judah, but suddenly he saw a Lamb: "Then I saw a Lamb, looking as if it had been slain, standing in the center of the throne" (Rev. 5:6).

I cannot grasp the full picture of what John saw when he looked at the Lamb of God. The Lamb was standing, but looked as if he had been slain. It must have been a sight of blood and trauma, one of complete weakness and humiliation. It is a confirmation that Jesus gave all he had to save the world. This view of Jesus is important for us to see as we prepare to look at the great tribulation, because he is still saving people. Jesus was slaughtered; his blood was emptied from him. When a lamb was sacrificed in biblical times, its blood was drained before it was placed on the altar. A lamb slain was an awful sight. Jesus died as a lamb. He became God's lamb, and he was sacrificed to pay for sin because he and the Father really love people. He is consumed with saving souls from hell, and he is determined that many more will be saved as the tribulation unfolds.

No single picture can fully describe all that Jesus is. He is both the powerful lion and the sacrificial lamb. To his enemies he is the lion of wrath, but to his friends and to lost humanity, he is the lamb who lays down his life. John the Baptist called Jesus the Lamb of God. He wrote, "Behold, the Lamb of God, who takes away the sin of the world!" (John 1:29).

The Lamb is the only one in the universe worthy to open the scroll because he is the only one who paid the price to remove man's sin. He died to break the scroll's seals and release God's blessings on his people. If someone else tried to take the scroll or attempt to open it, they would not get past God Almighty. Humanity does not deserve the blessings that come at the end of the Revelation, but Jesus will make sure that those blessings come.

There is another reason why the Lamb is the only one worthy to open the scroll. When the scroll is opened, the events foretold in the book of Revelation will begin and God's clock for the end of the age will start ticking. This has monumental ramifications for the unsaved because, when the prophesies of Revelation are completed, no more souls can be saved.

Jesus is the only one worthy to bring an end to the season of saving grace, which is what will happen when the plans inside the scroll are completed. Jesus gave his life to save people; only he can say when there are enough people saved. Once the scroll is opened, the end of salvation is fixed.

Suddenly the elders and the four living creatures sang to Jesus; "You are worthy to take the scroll and to open its seals, because you were slain, and with your blood you purchased men for God from every tribe and language and people and nation. You have made them to be a kingdom and priests to serve our God, and they shall reign on the earth" (Rev. 5:9–10).

The open scroll will announce the final chapter of salvation. Although it is essential, it is sad to think a time will come when no one else can be saved. Such is the kindness and the severity of the Lion and the Lamb. He alone is worthy.

JESUS TAKES THE SCROLL

When John saw Jesus take the scroll from the hand of God Almighty, all of heaven exploded in unparalleled, extravagant praise. The four living creatures and the twenty-four elders fell to the ground and began worshipping the Lamb. They sang a new song of praise that has never been sung before. Then one hundred million angels filled the throne room, swirling around the throne of God and flooding the air with energy as they sang, "Worthy is the Lamb." Then every creature in heaven and on earth and under the earth joined the worship and sang, "To him who sits on the throne and to the Lamb be praise and honor and glory and power, forever and ever" (Rev. 5:13).

When Jesus takes the scroll, praise and prophetic worship will resound from one end of the universe to the other. The praise will ignite the universe with unexpected fire, and the purpose and release of God's holy plans will be set in motion. Worthy is the Lord and worthy is the Lamb.

Open our eyes, Lord, that we might see what the host of heaven sees in the scroll and in the power of the Lamb who takes it. Teach us to embrace the excitement of heaven. Teach us to embrace the book of Revelation.

Chapter Eight

Revelation Is About Seven Angels

Before the throne seven lamps were blazing. These are the seven spirits of God. (Rev. 4:5)
He [Jesus the Lamb] had seven horns and seven eyes, which are the seven spirits of God sent out into all the earth. (Rev. 5:6)

CHAPTER TOPICS

1. The government of heaven
2. God's amazing angels
3. The angels in Jesus' hand
4. The archangels
5. The names of the seven angels
6. The activity of the seven angels
7. The seven spirits of God

GOVERNMENT IN HEAVEN

GOD CREATED GOVERNMENT: "FOR by him all things were created: things in heaven and on earth, visible and invisible, whether thrones or powers or rulers or authorities" (Col. 1:16).

God has a highly organized chain of command, both in heaven and on earth. In the first few chapters of Revelation, John was introduced to the senior officials of heaven. He experienced a meeting with the Trinity. He saw God's throne and the Lion and the Lamb. He also discovered the seraphim, the twenty-four elders, and the awesome sea of glass. John saw one hundred million angels flying above the throne, and his entire perspective of God's throne room was elevated to a new level.

By reading John's description we become aware of the immensity of God's throne room. It is not like any room we have ever known; it is vast. The Lord said, "Heaven is my throne and the earth is my footstool" (Isa. 66:1, Matt. 5:35).

All of heaven is his house of worship, his war room, and the dwelling place of his friends.

SEVEN GENERALS

Heaven is united in purpose, and everyone there has a specific function. There is still one celestial group that we must speak of. Seven heavenly beings are gathered around the Lamb. God Almighty has four living creatures who serve as his personal generals, and Jesus has seven angels who serve as his. The seven are called horns, eyes, spirits, winds, stars, torches, angels, thunders, and lamps.

John wrote, "He [Jesus] had seven horns and seven eyes, which are the seven spirits of God sent out into all the earth" (Rev. 5:6).

These angels are commanders of angelic armies, and they are sent into the world with strategic assignments. They are ambassadors of heaven, archangels involved with the needs of humanity. In Jude 1:8, we read of Michael, and Luke 1 talks of Gabriel, but they are only two of the seven. At lease five other archangels are presently ministering on the earth. One day we will meet them and know their names.

I believe that guardian angels, messenger angels, and many political angels follow the commands of the seven. Sometimes the seven must get involved directly when fallen angels and demons come against the purposes of God with great force. Such an occurrence is recounted in Daniel 10, when Daniel's end-time vision was given to him, and another is recorded in Luke 1 and 2, which recounts the birth of Jesus.

ANGELS IN HIS HAND

The seven angels and their armies are central to the plans of Revelation. In the first chapter of Revelation, Jesus is seen standing with his church, and these angels are in his right hand. He will not direct the events described in Revelation without the help of angels and humans.

Take note of the following verses. Notice that the seven spirits of God are the seven stars, and the seven stars are the seven angels. Jesus said, "The mystery of the seven stars that you saw in my right hand … is this: The seven stars are the angels …" (Rev. 1:20).

We have seen that the seven stars are angels. We also discover that the seven stars are the seven spirits of God. "These are the words of him who holds the seven spirits of God and the seven stars" (Rev. 3:1).

The seven angels, stars and spirits are one and the same. Further reading confirms that they are also called lamps. "Before the throne, seven lamps were blazing, these are the seven spirits of God" (Rev. 1:6).

The book of Hebrews gives us additional information about the angels. It says, "In speaking of angels he says, 'He makes his angels winds, his servants flames of fire'" "Are not all angels ministering spirits sent to serve those who will inherit salvation?" (Heb. 1:7, 14).

Angels are spirits. In this case, they are the seven spirits of God that go out into all the earth. Just as God and Jesus each have many names, these seven angels have many names as well. Each of their names describes a characteristic or role that they play in the work of the Lord:

1. They are called seven horns to emphasize their power.
2. They are called seven eyes to emphasize their prophetic vision.

3. They are called seven lamps to emphasize their understanding and wisdom.
4. They are called seven stars to emphasize their majesty and government.
5. They are called seven thunders to emphasize their passion as they serve as heralds.
6. They are called winds when they function as celestial ambassadors.
7. They are called seven spirits to emphasize their supernatural capabilities.

THE ACTIVITY OF THE SEVEN

Here are some key functions that the angels are involved in during the great tribulation.

1. The seven angels will *blow seven trumpets* and release the judgments of God on the earth during the second and third campaigns: "And I saw the seven angels who stand before God, and to them were given seven trumpets ... Then the seven angels who had the seven trumpets prepared to sound them" (Rev. 8:2, 6).

2. The seven angels *will pour the wrath of God upon the earth* from the seven bowls: "Out of the temple came the seven angels with the seven plagues." ... "Then I heard a loud voice from the temple saying to the seven angels, 'Go and pour out the seven bowls of God's wrath on the earth'" (Rev. 15:6, 16:1).

3. As heralds, *the seven angels will proclaim* the edicts and judgments of the Lord with prophetic voices that sound like thunder, the entire universe will one day hear the powerful decrees that come from their mouths. John wrote, "When he shouted, the voices of the seven thunders spoke. And when the seven thunders spoke, I was about to write, but I heard a voice from heaven say, 'Seal up what the seven thunders have said and do not write it down'" (Rev. 10:3–4).

One day we will hear what the seven thunders have proclaimed. The time for that piece of revelation and much more is still hidden in the scroll.

4. The seven angels are *instructors* who helped John see the glories of heaven. They were able to carry him away in the Spirit and show him the bride of Christ: "One of the seven angels … said to me, 'Come, I will show you the bride, the wife of the Lamb.' And he carried me away in the Spirit" (Rev. 21:10).

The seven angels not only showed John good things, but they also revealed evil things: "One of the seven angels who had the seven bowls came and said to me, 'Come, I will show you the punishment of the great prostitute, who sits on many waters.' Then the angel carried me away in the Spirit into a desert" (Rev. 17:1, 3).

5. The seven angels are *ambassadors of heaven*. They are messengers sent out into all the earth: "Then I saw a Lamb … He had seven horns and seven eyes which are the seven spirits of God sent out into all the earth" (Rev. 5:6).

SEVEN PRINCES

The seven angels are called horns. Horns are a symbol of power and authority. These are archangels—angelic princes who stand with the Lamb in the presence of God Almighty. A prince rules a principality, or in this case, a dominion of angels. In Rev. 12 we read that Michael, the archangel, will lead a massive army of angels who fight and defeat the devil and his angels: "And there was war in heaven. Michael and his angels fought against the dragon … The dragon was hurled down … to the earth, and his angels with him" (Rev. 12:7).

The seven angles stand before God, but they are sent into the world.

Gabriel who visited Mary said, "I am Gabriel. I stand in the presence of God, and I have been sent to speak to you and to tell you this good news" (Luke 1:19).

The angel Michael is called the great prince who protects and watches over the Jewish people. He has watched over the Jewish people as far back as Daniel's time (Dan. 10:21). It is prophesied that the archangel Michael will help the Jewish people and deliver them during the tribulation period.

We read in Daniel, "At that time *Michael, the great prince who protects your people,* will arise. There will be a time of distress such as has not happened from the beginning of nations until then. But at that time your people—everyone whose name is found written in the book—will be delivered. Multitudes who sleep in the dust of the earth will awake: some to everlasting life, others to shame and everlasting contempt" (Dan. 12:1–3; italics added).

ANGELS ON FIRE

In the book of Daniel, we read that Gabriel appeared. Daniel described Gabriel as awesome. Gabriel shone with a brilliance that was similar to the description John gave of Jesus in Revelation chapter 1.

Daniel wrote, "I looked up and there before me was a man dressed in linen, with a belt of the finest gold around his waist. His body was like chrysolite, his face like lightning, his eyes like flaming torches, his arms and legs like the gleam of burnished bronze, and his voice like the sound of a multitude" (Dan. 10:6).

As with John who saw Jesus, Daniel became like a dead man when he saw Gabriel. He said, "I had no strength left, my face turned deathly pale and I was helpless ... my face to the ground" (Dan. 10: 8–9).

Gabriel spoke, "Daniel ... I have been sent to you ... your words were heard and I have come in response to them. But the Prince of Persia resisted me twenty-one days. Then *Michael, one of the chief princes,* came to help me ... soon I will return to fight ... No one supports me against them except Michael, your prince" (Dan. 10:10–21).

Gabriel was awesome, but he needed Michael's help. Michael came to help his coworker in a time of trouble.

We do not know for sure if either Gabriel or Michael is a member of the seven, but they both fit the description. I believe they are two of the seven. They provide a clear picture of senior angels who are sent from the throne room to minister to God's people on earth.

UNDER THE COMMAND OF JESUS

It is clear that the seven angels are with the Lord Jesus: "Then I saw a Lamb ... He had seven horns and seven eyes which are the seven spirits of God" (Rev. 5:6).

The seven take their orders directly from Jesus. As his horns, they are instruments of government and power. As his eyes, the seven see much of what is happening on the earth and direct the armies of God accordingly.

The blueprints of Revelation, which are in the scroll, come from God Almighty. He drew up the plans, but Jesus will put them into action. He champions the forces of heaven and the seven stand ready. They stand at his side.

KINGDOM ANGELS

Revelation is about the kingdom of God's dear Son. It is about his church and angels working with him. It is about his seven special angels.

One day, Jesus will give the kingdom back to his Father, but for now, he is in charge. The seven are at his side receiving and distributing his authority. The stars are in his right hand. Jesus reigns through his church and his angels. With their help, he will overcome and destroy every wicked government.

We read, "Then the end will come, when he [Jesus] hands over the kingdom to God the Father after he has destroyed all dominion, authority and power. For he must reign until he has put all his enemies under his feet" (1 Cor. 15:24–25).

SEVEN SPIRITS OF GOD

The book of Isaiah speaks of several wonderful dynamics of the Holy Spirit. The Spirit of Jesus is the Holy Spirit and that means he has all of the qualities referred to in Isaiah's list. He has the Spirit of the Lord, the Spirit of wisdom, the Spirit of understanding, the Spirit of counsel, the Spirit of power, the Spirit of knowledge, and the Spirit of the fear of the Lord (see Isa. 11:2).

Many fine Bible teachers believe that these qualities of the Holy Spirit are the seven Spirits of God sent out into the world. They believe that the seven Spirits mentioned in the book of Revelation are these attributes of the Holy Spirit. I respect many of these teachers and hold them in high esteem. From my personal study, however, I must conclude that the scriptures are referring to angels. I do not believe that these seven attributes of the Holy Spirit are the seven spirits of God mentioned in the book of Revelation. I do not think that the seven attributes of the Holy Spirit fit the depictions of the seven spirits such as horns, eyes, thunders, and stars, but these angels do. It is important to identify the seven angels of the Lamb. They will play an important role in the unfolding of Revelation.

THE ROYAL INTRODUCTIONS ARE OVER

By the end of Revelation chapter five, most of the royal introductions are complete. The great tribulation may now be revealed. In our reading thus far, we have seen the mighty power-grid of heaven. This is not a time for us, the church on earth, to be fearful or anxious. The kingdom and glory of the Lord is coming to earth, and we are being called to play an important role in the drama. The stage is set. Unexpected fire is about to fall.

Part Two
The First Campaign

Chapter Nine

REVELATION IS ABOUT THE GREAT TRIBULATION

I watched as the Lamb opened the first of the seven seals… The great day of their wrath has come, and who can stand? (Rev. 6:1, 17)

SUGGESTED READING: REVELATION 6

CHAPTER TOPICS

1. An introduction to the great tribulation
2. Righteousness prevailing
3. The Lamb breaking the seals
4. The purpose of the cross continuing
5. The tribulation as a series of three military campaigns
6. The tribulation humbling people

INTRODUCTION

IN THIS CHAPTER I will give an introduction to the great tribulation. Before I explain the events in other chapters, I will give a brief overview. This will help us grasp the big picture and provide us with some parameters.

RIGHTEOUSNESS WILL PREVAIL

We have studied the royal introductions in which John was made aware of heaven's military might. But he had not yet been shown the forces of darkness. By the end of the fifth chapter of Revelation John was convinced that God would fulfill all he had promised.

During his lifetime, John had seen the evils of Roman decadence and the trauma of human failure and corruption. These horrors were real, but they were now irrelevant in the light of what he had seen in God's throne room. He was convinced that righteousness would prevail.

THE LAMB BREAKS THE SEALS

John saw the scroll of Revelation move from the hand of the Almighty to the hand of the Lamb, and he saw the Lamb begin to break the seals that had bound it. Although Jesus commands multitudes of angels and men, he will not delegate this task. Just as Jesus did not assign an angel to die on the cross, no one will break the seven seals except him.

When all that is written in the scroll is fulfilled, the events of the book of Revelation will be complete, and opportunity for salvation will be gone. Jesus alone is worthy to end the day of salvation, and, thus, he alone could break the seals. Even during the tribulation period, Jesus will extend his saving grace to humanity. The Lamb will continue to take away the sins of the world right up to the very end.

PLEASE GET READY

The great tribulation will simultaneously release God's judgments and reveal the greatest revivals of all time. A Christian revival is a move of God that results in a massive number of people being converted to Christ.

Revelation tells us that the tribulation will include three series of judgments which I call campaigns. The tribulation stretches from the first campaign, (the first series of judgments) which is recorded in chapter 6, to the judgments in chapter 19. This devastating period of time will last for seven years, and a major paradigm shift will occur at the halfway point.

Christians will be present throughout the entire tribulation and many will die. In our study of the tribulation period, we will see the activity of angels, saints, demons, and evil men. Most of all, we will see the eternal plans of Almighty God as they unfold. It is time to make sure that each of us is on the Lord's side.

COMPLETING THE EXCHANGE

The great tribulation will change the world forever. It will conclude the work of the cross. The crucifixion of Christ was the pivotal point that released the divine exchange. Derek Prince, the famous Bible teacher, explained the divine exchange in his book, *Atonement*. He wrote, "All the evil due, by justice, to come to us came on Jesus, so that all the good due to Jesus, earned by his sinless obedience, might be made available to us.

1. Jesus was punished that we might be forgiven.
2. Jesus was wounded that we might be healed.
3. Jesus was made sin for our sinfulness that we might be made righteous with his righteousness.
4. Jesus died our death that we might share his life.
5. Jesus was made a curse that we might receive the blessing.
6. Jesus endured our poverty that we might share his abundance.
7. Jesus bore our shame that we might share his glory.
8. Jesus endured our rejection that we might enjoy his acceptance.
9. The old man died in Jesus that the new man might live in us."[a]

The great exchange was initiated at the cross. When all of the events written about in the book of Revelation have come to pass, all of those blessings will have been delivered in full. The details of the book of Revelation complete the extreme transaction. The church (all true believers in Christ) and Israel have been waiting to receive the full package of their blessings for a long time, and they will receive it. God, who gave up his own Son to die on the cross, will be faithful to his promise to give us all things. We will be joint heirs with Christ.

PIVOTAL IMPORTANCE

No future event prophesied in scripture has been described in more detail than the tribulation period. Many events have been prophesied in the Bible, including Israel's return to her land, the day of Pentecost, and of highest importance, the birth and life of Jesus the Messiah. None of these events, however, were prophesied in as much detail as the end times.

There can be no doubt that the Lord wants us to understand the book of Revelation. It was given to bless us. Blessed is he who reads and understands this book.

CHRISTIANS ARE THERE

Many preachers teach that the church will be raptured before the great tribulation begins. I respectfully disagree. I will explain my findings when we look at the second coming of Christ. If you would like to see that study before reading further, please read chapter 51.

I know that the thought of no pre-tribulation rapture will be difficult for many to embrace, but a new understanding is coming to God's people. The church around the world will undergo a major teaching shift on this theme as the time of Revelation draws near. The Lord will prepare us for the tribulation period. By the time it arrives, many Christians will consider themselves privileged to be part of it. They will feel honored to participate in the victory of the king. They will witness God's judgments, but they will also see the glory of his saving grace, the awesome power of miracles, and the kingdom of Christ coming upon the earth.

They will not be mere spectators, but coworkers with the Lamb. The church's brightest hour will come during earth's darkest hour. Like lighthouses in the storm, the saints (God's people) will lead multitudes of sinners to the eternal harbor of Christ. Christians will be a flame of fire in the hands of their God.

The book of Revelation is a prayer manual. Saints are already praying in agreement with God. They are walking with him as they read it. They are asking for more revelation on Revelation, and as they receive it, they begin to pray passionately.

THREE CAMPAIGNS

The great tribulation is a war. Heaven's strategy, as described in Revelation, can be seen as three military campaigns and a final sortie to cancel Satan's rule forever. I will discuss these campaigns in the next few chapters. The tribulation will end with the second coming of Christ. I can find no place in the entire book of Revelation that suggests that Christ will return to earth before the end. And no verse in the entire Bible says that he will come and remove his church prior to the great tribulation.

Each of the military campaigns, contain three noticeable dynamics:

1. Devastating judgments that become increasingly more intense
2. Massive revivals that cause vast multitudes to come to Christ
3. The saints arising with holy passion, godly character, and supernatural power

The first campaign will take place when Jesus breaks the seals and the four living creatures make war.

During the second campaign, the seven angels will make war. They will blow the seven trumpets, and judgments worse than the previous ones will hit the earth.

The third campaign will begin during the days of the seventh trumpet. All the armies of heaven will be involved. The seven angels will pour out bowls of wrath that the four living creatures give them.

God's judgments will be completed with the destruction of Satan's armies.

JESUS COMES AT THE LAST TRUMP

Jesus will return at the end of the third campaign. He will come during the days of "the last trumpet."

Scripture says, "Listen, I tell you a mystery: we will all be changed—in a flash, in a twinkling of an eye, *at the last trumpet.* For the trumpet will sound and the dead will be raised" (1 Cor. 15:51–52; italics added).

Believers will receive resurrected bodies when Jesus returns. He will come at the sounding of the *last trump,* not the first trump or sometime before. He does not tell us of a third coming. We will study these points in detail later.

THE LOVE OF GOD

A few important questions loom before us:

1. Why does God have three military campaigns or series of judgments during the tribulation period?
2. Why must the tribulation period last for seven full years?
3. Why not wipe out the devil and take us into the new millennium at the beginning of the great tribulation?

The answers are extremely important. It is God's mercy and love that will stay his hand and extend the great tribulation period. He will extend it to allow many more people to be saved. He wants everyone to come to repentance.

The Bible says, "The Lord is not slow in keeping his promise, as some understand slowness. He is patient with you, not wanting anyone to perish, but everyone to come to repentance" (2 Pet. 3:9).

THE JUDGMENTS WILL HUMBLE PEOPLE

As the tribulation begins, the hearts of many people will be hardened against God. Their minds will have been twisted by doctrines of devils.

"The Spirit clearly says that in latter times some will abandon the faith and follow deceiving spirits and things taught by demons. Such teachings come through hypocritical liars, whose consciences have been seared as with a hot iron" (1 Tim. 4:1–2).

Hardness of heart comes:

1. When people are abused
2. When people continuously sin
3. When people rise up with arrogant pride
4. When people are defiant toward God

Worldwide judgments, however, will bring many to their knees. Most people are humbled when trauma and suffering come. When severe trauma comes, people lose confidence in themselves, and they reach out to God. They do this when:

1. They lose control of their future
2. They cannot fix the devastation around them
3. They find themselves and their families in great pain

In times of trouble, people become aware of their weaknesses, and they begin to call on God for help. During the tribulation, many will be humbled because of fear, closed hearts will be opened, and multitudes will come to Christ.

Between each campaign (series of judgments), time will be given for salvation, and billions of people will be saved. The shed blood of the Lamb that saves man from sin and eternal damnation will stretch to the very end of the tribulation. More souls will be saved during the time of Revelation than in all of man's previous history.

THE SEALS ARE THE SIGNAL

John wrote, "I watched as the Lamb opened the first of the seven seals. Then I heard one of the four living creatures say in a voice like thunder, 'Come'!" (Rev. 6:1).

As Jesus breaks the seals from the scroll, a seraph will cry, "Come!" in a voice as loud as thunder. He will be the first of four to summon the four horsemen who will release the initial wave of judgments upon the earth.

So it will begin. The breaking of the seals will release the great tribulation. Jesus will unleash the judgments of God, and no man, angel, or demon will be able to stop them. He is in complete control, and he will soon call upon his angels and his church to help, as he wages war on all that is evil and rescues many who have suffered because of it.

Chapter Ten

Revelation is About Riders on Horses

I watched as the Lamb opened the first of the seven seals. Then I heard one of the four living creatures say in a voice like thunder, "Come!" I looked, and there before me was a white horse! Its rider held a bow and he was given a crown, and he rode out as a conqueror bent on conquest. (Rev. 6:1–2)

SUGGESTED READING: REVELATION 6

CHAPTER TOPICS

1. The four horses from heaven
2. The white horse (a call to arms)
3. Two kinds of judgment
4. The red horse (war)
5. The Muslim threat
6. The black horse (famine)
7. The pale horse (plague)
8. The first apocalyptic revival

THE WHITE HORSE

JOHN WATCHED AS JESUS broke the first seal. Immediately, one of the seraphim launched the first campaign. With a voice like thunder, his primal battle cry shook the universe. The residents of heaven had been waiting for eons to hear this upward call of God.

The creature will cry, "Come!" and all of heaven will respond. The host of heaven have long anticipated this moment, and they will immediately come to attention. Stillness will fill the air, and all eyes will look toward the throne.

Suddenly, John saw a white horse mounted by an angel who was holding a bow. Jesus placed a crown on the rider's head.

Once he is commissioned, the angel will ride to conquer, determined to achieve his mission. He will be going to war, and heaven will be going with him.

PURITY, PASSION, AND POWER

The warhorse is white, representing purity, passion, and power. John felt the power and the passion with which the angel rode, and he stared at the horse's brilliant coat, which points to the righteousness and purity of the one he represents. This was God's war, and it was holy.

This rider will not release judgment like those that follow. Rather, he will give the call to arms. With his bow, he will fire the flare to initiate heaven's charge, and all of heaven will snap to attention. As all armies should, heaven will declare war before attacking, and so the white charger will release the declaration of war to the enemies of God.

He will come as a prophetic sign. Like a banner flapping in the wind, he will ride out before the armies of God. His presence will announce God's victory and Satan's defeat. He will be bent on conquest because heaven cannot fail and he is a conqueror.

THE HORSES OF HEAVEN

There are four different colored horses that come from heaven and the book of Revelation is not the only book in the Bible that makes mention of them. Heaven's horses are also found in 2 Kings (2:11; 6:17) and Zechariah (1:8–11; 6:1–7).

We are introduced to the same colored horses by Zechariah. He said, "During the night I had a vision—and there before me was a man riding a red horse! Behind him were red, brown and white horses. The angel … answered, 'They are the ones the Lord has sent to go throughout the earth'" (Zech. 1:8–10).

Again, Zechariah was shown the horses of heaven. "I looked again—and there before me were four chariots. The first chariot had red horses, the second black, the third white, and the fourth dappled—all of them powerful. I asked the angel …'What are these?' The angel answered me, 'These are the four spirits of heaven, going out from standing in the presence of the Lord'… So they went throughout the earth" (Zech. 6:1–7).

The horses come from the throne room of God. They are holy ambassadors; messengers of the Lord. They are called the four spirits of heaven who stand in the presence of the Lord.

The white horse and his rider are servants of the Most High God. Some suggest that the white horse is the Antichrist, but that does not fit the Bible as I understand it. These horses are not from Satan.

HORSES OF JUDGMENT

After we are introduced to the white horse, three others follow. They will bring devastating judgments that will affect every person on the planet. Global catastrophes will strike the good and the bad. Judgments have come throughout history, even in our lifetimes. The ones that will come when the events in Revelation unfold, however, will be much more intense.

"They [the colored horses and their riders] were given power over a fourth of the earth to kill by sword, famine and plague, and by the wild beasts of the earth" (Rev. 6:8).

War, famine, and plague will destroy a quarter of the earth's population. It will likely happen within a one-year period.

Today, more than six billion people inhabit the earth. A fourth of the earth is more than one and a half billion people. That is how many will die at the beginning of the first campaign. Although there are other signs that tell us that the end of the age is near, when one and a half billion people die within a year, we will know that the great tribulation has begun.

We see from the limited perspective of earth. God sees from eternity. Whether we live on earth for a week or for eighty-five years, our time here is only a blip on the computer screen of eternity. The trials of this life are but a vapor, but the joys of eternity will last forever. Without this perspective, we can never understand the plans of God.

The people of God will have a special grace during the great tribulation. It will be said of them: "They overcame him [the devil] by the blood of the Lamb and by the word of their testimony; they did not love their lives so much as to shrink from death" (Rev. 12:11).

The saints who are present during the tribulation will not shrink back, as do many today. Rather they will stand as great warriors who will overcome the devil and are not afraid to die.

The righteous who die will wake up in the presence of the Lord, as have billions before them. The unsaved will open their eyes in Hades. Many judgments will fall on both the good and the bad. Both will die, and we cannot determine who will go to heaven and who will go to Hades. All must come through Christ, but where sin abounds, God's grace abounds more. I believe that many more people will go to heaven than we think.

JUDGMENTS ON EARTH

There is a difference between judgments that take place in heaven and those we receive while still on earth. In heaven every individual will be judged by what he or she did in life. It will not matter what others from a persons' family did; each will stand alone before God.

That is not the case with the judgments that fall on the earth. Here, judgment comes upon families, communities, and nations. Many families and nations are under a curse because of sin. Leaders who rule with evil intent bring judgment upon themselves, their families, and their nations. That is called a curse. When judgment falls on those nations, all within them are affected.

THE RED HORSE

John saw Jesus remove the second seal and heard the second seraph cry "Come!"

He wrote, "Then another horse came out, a fiery red one. Its rider was given power to take peace from the earth and to make men slay each other. To him was given a large sword" (Rev. 6:4).

John saw a fiery red horse step forward. The rider, who carried a sword, opened the floodgates of war on the earth.

Nations will attack nations, and civil war will erupt in many countries. Hundreds of city gangs will launch assaults on their neighbors, and violence will rule the streets of major cities. Racial arrogance will lead to ethnic cleansings and genocide. Entire peoples will be decimated. Some nations will be completely obliterated, for not every nation will survive and make it to the new millennium. God will lift his hand, and human restraint will be cast aside. Greed, oppression, and pride that will have simmered for centuries will be allowed free course. The cup of pent-up malice and chaos will be unleashed.

The apostle Peter explained the root cause of corruption in the world. He said, "Corruption in the world [is] caused by evil desires" (2 Pet. 1:4).

People's evil desires for selfish gain, their hatred of those different from themselves, and their pride will undermine tolerance and kindness. A global bloodbath will erupt as peace is taken from the world.

THE MUSLIM THREAT

War will erupt around the world, and vast multitudes will die. As I write, influential voices in the United States are saying that World War III has already begun, but most in the west do not recognize it.

Presently, the number one enemy of the free world is Muslim fanaticism. A new documentary called "Obsession" was aired during the month of January, 2007 on national television in the United States. I saw it on the Fox News station. It showed dozens of Mullahs (Islamic Muslim Priests) giving public speeches in different nations, including European nations such as England.

They were declaring war on the world. One Mullah after the other repeated the message that Islam once ruled the world and will rule the world again. They unashamedly announced that it is Allah's will to kill all people who do not convert to Islam. They say they will overtake America and Europe and will completely annihilate Israel.

More than one billion Muslims are on earth. If only 1 percent of them were fanatical suicide killers, they would number more than ten million committed warriors. Since September 11, 2001, when Muslim terrorists flew two airliners into the World Trade Center, the world went on alert. Many terrorist attacks have now taken place in dozens of other nations. The trauma and fear of the Islamic threat is growing daily, and fanatical Muslims are emerging on the global stage with unprecedented frequency.

If not for the promise of the scriptures, my heart would sink. Although fanatical Muslims will not be the only enemy of Israel and the free world during the first part of the great tribulation, they will be a major force. They will be the flash-point group that will draw the world to war.

As Muslim terrorists step up their agenda, it will reach a level of combustion that will eventually bring massive retaliation from the west and from other non-terrorist nations. Within a year or two, at the very start of the great tribulation, the power of the fanatics within Islam, will be broken. Major Arab cities will be totally destroyed, and although Islam will continue, the terrorists who exercise global manipulation and a worldwide campaign of fear will lose their power.

Once this happens, all nations will be forced to embrace democracy. This catastrophic shift in politics will prepare the way for the political events of the last days. We will study this in detail later.

Here are some scriptures that announce the destruction of major Islamic cities at the end of time.

"An Oracle concerning Damascus: 'See, Damascus will no longer be a city but will become a heap of ruins" (Isa. 17:1).

"The word of the Lord is against ... Tyre and Sidon, though they are very skillful. Tyre has built herself a stronghold; she has heaped up silver like dust, and gold like the dirt of the streets. But the Lord will take away her possessions and destroy her power on the sea, and she will be consumed by fire" (Zech. 9:1–4).

Damascus is the capital of Syria, and Tyre and Sidon are two of the main cities of Lebanon. They suffered heavy bombings from Israel in the summer of 2006. This attack from Israel was done in retaliation, because the Lebanese Hezbollah provoked them with an act of war.

The very next verse in Zechariah prophesied the reaction of the Palestinians in Gaza who are hoping that the Muslim nations involved in this conflict will defeat Israel and enable them to possess all of the Holy Land. The Bible says that will not happen; rather, the Palestinians will be in fear and writhe in agony when they see Lebanon consumed by fire.

"Tyre ... will be consumed by fire. Ashkelon will see it and fear; Gaza will writhe in agony, and Ekron too, for her hope will wither. Gaza will lose her king and Ashkelon will be deserted. Foreigners will occupy Ashdod, and I will cut off the pride of the Philistines" (Zech. 9:5–6).

As the Muslim world is being reduced, Israel will receive all of her promised land. Israel will defend herself from the attacks of the surrounding nations, and in so doing, her land will be increased to the dimensions that God promised Abraham. Israel will extend from the Nile to the Euphrates in the early days of the great tribulation. This will happen because God will release supernatural military power to Israel and will defend her. All who attack Israel in those days will injure themselves.

The Bible says, "On that day the Lord made a covenant with Abram and said, 'To your descendants I give this land, from the river of Egypt to the great river, the Euphrates'" (Gen. 15:18–19).

"I will make Jerusalem an immovable rock for all the nations. All who try to move it will injure themselves ... I will keep a watchful eye over Judah ... They will consume right and left all the surrounding peoples, but Jerusalem will remain intact in her place ... On that day I will set out to destroy all the nations that attack Jerusalem" (Zech. 12:3, 4, 6, 9).

The wars of the first campaign will take a heavy toll on the nations, but they will prepare the world for the events predicted in later chapters of Revelation. Israel will finally possess her land and she will defend it until the Lord returns.

THE BLACK HORSE

John saw Jesus remove the third seal and heard the third seraph say, "Come!"

"I looked and there before me was a black horse! Its rider was holding a pair of scales in his hand." (Rev. 6:5).

John saw a black horse charge from heaven whose rider held a pair of weight scales in his hand, and famine covered the earth.

An angel called out, "Then I heard what sounded like a voice among the four living creatures, saying, 'A quart of wheat for a days wages, and three quarts of barley for a days wages, and do not damage the oil and the wine'" (Rev. 6:6).

Strange weather patterns, drought, agricultural disease, and natural disasters will cause crop failures around the world. Famine will not only affect third world countries, but the developed nations as well. Epidemics like hoof-and-mouth disease, mad cow disease and Asian bird flu will devastate livestock while new strains of plant diseases and mutant insects will destroy the fruit and vegetables of entire regions.

Millions of people will die from starvation, and the price of food will skyrocket out of control.

GROSS INFLATION

In 2005 a hurricane named Katrina slammed into the gulf coast of the United States. Momentarily, the oil refineries were shut down, and the price of gasoline rose. Before the hurricane, the average U.S. gasoline price was $2.30 per gallon, but within a day it rose to more than $6 per gallon in some places.

When global famine hits, a loaf of bread will rise from $2 to $100. A quart of wheat will produce only one or two loaves of bread, but, as the angel says, it will cost a day's wages. Estimating that the average wage is $100 per day, $100 will be the new price of bread. Food prices will rise beyond the reach of average people.

COMPASSION AND MERCY

When catastrophe takes hold of the world, the church will rise up and partner with God. Miracles and supernatural provisions will come to multitudes, and newly commissioned Christians and redeemed Jews will give generously to those in need. The angel prophesied it. He said, "A quart of wheat for a days wages … and do not damage the oil and the wine" (Rev. 6:6).

Famine and lack will be everywhere, but the oil and wine will not be damaged. These are the classic symbols of Christian care and compassion. This is the mercy ministry of the church. Mission efforts will supply food, water, clothing, shelter, and medical supplies to the poor and needy. Christian relief programs will be everywhere. Help will come from organized church groups as well as individual Christian families. They will have supplies because God will provide supernaturally. Testimonies of food coming from the hand of God and provisions being multiplied are common Bible stories. Many modern day disciples have also seen these kinds of miracles. It is not strange to expect them during the tribulation. The angel prophesied it when he said, "Do not damage the oil and the wine."

THE GOOD SAMARITAN

A Jewish politician asked Jesus, "What must I do to inherit eternal life?" he answered, 'Love the Lord your God with all your heart ... and love your neighbor as yourself.' But he asked, 'Who is my neighbor'?" (Luke 10:25–29).

In response, Jesus told the story of the Good Samaritan, who found a wounded traveler lying half dead on the side of the road. The man was a Jew, and normally the Samaritan would have no contact with him. Jesus taught us to express care beyond cultural and ethnic lines. Our neighbor is anyone in need. Jesus said that we are to love others as much as we love ourselves. In the story, the Samaritan cared for the wounded man.

Jesus said, "He went to him and bandaged his wounds, pouring on oil and wine" (Luke 10:34).

The oil and wine symbolize Christian compassion and mercy ministries. We must extend it to those in need. During the great tribulation, heaven's compassion will open the door for heaven's anointing. Believers will experience great joy as they serve others. Unbelievers will realize that society can offer no solutions, and multitudes will turn to Christ as they witness his miraculous power and see his love coming from his people. This will produce the first of many revivals in the great tribulation.

Jesus will unfold the end times with the help of his servants. He will enlist both angels and humans as he reaches out to a dying world. The angel told John of this three-way partnership.

John wrote, "Then the angel said to me, "I am a fellow servant with you and with your brothers who hold to the testimony of Jesus" (Rev. 19:9–10).

THE PALE HORSE

When Jesus broke the fourth seal, the fourth living creature cried, "Come!"

"I looked and there before me was a pale horse! Its rider was named Death, and Hades was following close behind him. They were given power over a fourth of the earth to kill by sword, famine and plague, and by the wild beasts of the earth" (Rev. 6:8).

John saw a gray or dappled horse come forward. This horse brought the judgment of plagues and disease to earth. Its rider was named Death, and Hades followed close behind him.

Diseases like the Asian bird flue, the bubonic plague, the Ebola virus, and AIDS will kill whole communities. The medical experts of the world will not be able to stop the outbreaks, and viruses will mutate at such a speed that yesterday's cures will be ineffective today. Huge numbers of people will die due to the plagues, so the rider on the horse is called Death.

I believe, although it is not stated, that these plagues will not affect believers—Hades follows close behind, and believers do not go to Hades. When believers die, they go to be with the Lord.

The combination of war, famine, disease, and wild beasts will kill a quarter of the people on the planet. The mourning and loss among the nations will be unrelenting. Everyone will know a friend or family member who has died, and pain will cover the earth. Without Christ, it will be unbearable.

BIRTH PAINS

Jesus spoke of these days. He said, "You will hear of wars and rumors of wars, but see to it that you are not alarmed. Such things must happen, but the end is still to come. Nation will rise against nation, and kingdom against kingdom. There will be famines and earthquakes in various places. All these are the beginning of birth pains" (Matt. 24:6–8; see also Mark 13; Luke 21).

It is only natural to be alarmed when we read these things, but Jesus tells us not to be alarmed for these things must happen. He says that they are just the beginning. He tells us that they are birth pains. What is about to be born?

We discover the answer to that question further on in the book of Revelation. It is the powerful end-time church that will be born. The prophetic church of the last days will emerge. The world will step back and notice the glory of the Lord upon his people. Jesus will make his stand among the golden lampstands. His promise of miraculous power has not yet been fulfilled, yet he spoke of greater miracles working through his disciples.

He said, "Anyone who has faith in me will do what I have been doing. He will do greater things than these, because I am going to my Father. You may ask for anything in my name, and I will do it" (John 14:12–14).

Scripture says that God's glory will come on his people the Jews and also on the gentile church. It will come when gross darkness covers the earth. We have not yet seen God's glory come to his people as described in Isaiah.

It reads, "Arise, shine, for your light has come, and the glory of the Lord rises upon you. See darkness covers the earth and thick darkness is over the peoples, but the Lord rises upon you and his glory appears over you. Nations will come to your light and kings to the brightness of your dawn" (Isa. 60:1–3).

This scripture will apply to both, the gentile church and to Israelites who receive Jesus as Messiah. It will happen when gross darkness comes. God will bring revival to the earth as he shines through his people.

FOR YOU

If you are a Christian who has prayed and not yet seen God's power as much as you believe it should come, look with faith to the days that lie ahead. God's miraculous power will come to the church and to redeemed Israel during the first half of the tribulation period. We will discover this more as we proceed in our study. That anointing will remain on God's people for all eternity.

"He who did not spare his own Son, but freely gave him up for us all—how will he not … graciously give us all things" (Rom. 8:32).

Chapter Eleven

Revelation is About Martyrs

When he opened the fifth seal, I saw under the altar the souls of those who had been slain because of the word of God and the testimony they had maintained. They called out in a loud voice, "How long, Sovereign Lord, holy and true, until you judge the inhabitants of the earth and avenge our blood?
Then each of them was given a white robe, and they were told to wait a little longer, until the number of their fellow servants and brothers who were to be killed as they had been was completed. (Rev. 6:9–11)

CHAPTER TOPICS

1. The altar of prayer
2. The angels of fire
3. The martyrs of the faith
4. Heaven honors the martyrs
5. Martyrs are a part of God's plan

DIFFERENT VANTAGE POINTS

THE BREAKING OF THE first four seals will release the first wave of apocalyptic judgments upon the earth. The breaking of the fifth seal will take us back to the throne room to see the altar and the martyrs. This back and forth pattern happens often throughout the book of Revelation. At one point we see what is happening on earth; then suddenly we are taken into the spirit realm to catch a glimpse of heaven. This pattern shows us the battlefield from different vantage points. The Lord continues to give us detailed intelligence.

THE FIFTH SEAL

As Jesus breaks the fifth seal, he will show us the martyrs. The Lord will honor those who have died defending the faith. Seeing the martyrs will help us stay on course as others are killed. We must have an accurate picture of the coming battle. This is so important that one of the seven seals is dedicated in honor of the martyrs.

ALTAR OF PRAYER

The fiery altar contains the prayers of God's people, and the souls of the martyrs are beneath it. It is positioned in front of God's throne. This tells us that God cares about the prayers people pray. Prayer is cooperation with God, and he will do nothing on earth without it. He will involve us in every part of his plan, and Revelation is his end-time prayer manual for the planet.

Grandma's prayers, our children's prayers, desperate prayers, and casual prayers become the prayers of agreement that fuel the fire on God's altar. They become flaring flames of fire before the throne. They continue burning without burning out, until finally they are answered and fulfilled. Prayer emits an aroma of incense that floods the throne room. It produces a continual link between mortal man and immortal God.

We are called to partner with God through the Spirit. God communicates his will to his saints, and they in turn speak his will back to him in prayer. The plan originates in heaven, comes to earth, and is echoed back. This circle of agreement must be completed.

Prayer is vital. God-initiated prayer becomes the fragrance of his will that lingers in the throne room. Each prayer is a time capsule that must be answered. Some prayers are answered immediately, while others are answered over long periods of time. Some prayers are held back for a season, and then suddenly they are answered in an instant. Without exception, all God-initiated prayer will be answered in time. Prayer is the most potent perfume in the universe—more powerful than the most exotic fragrances—for it holds its authority with God.

HOLY ACTION

When people hear from God and obey, their actions become holy. Moses heard God speak from a burning bush, and suddenly the desert became holy ground.

The Lord said, "Take off your sandals for the place where you are standing is holy ground" (Exod. 3:5).

What made the ground holy? It was not because God was there; God is everywhere, and all ground is not holy. The ground became holy because holy instructions were given, and man was about to obey them. Whenever we receive instructions from God and obey them, we stand on holy ground. When God's plans were transferred to Moses, Moses became holy. Whenever you follow the Lord, you walk in holiness.

The altar in the throne room releases holiness. Plans are revealed, stirred with fire, spoken, and answered on the altar. They are waiting to spring into action. The potential energy of prayer becomes kinetic. God's holy plans become God's holy acts. Even now, the book of Revelation is burning on the altar.

ANGELS OF THE HOLY FIRE

Angels work with human prayers to both - bless and judge humanity. The angels follow God's timing. Even though angels are more powerful then men, they must serve them. One day however, humans will be more powerful than angels.

Hebrews says, "It is not to angels that he has subjected the world to come. 'What is man that you are mindful of him? You made him a little lower than the angels; you crowned him with glory and honor and put everything under his feet.' In putting everything under him, God left nothing that is not subject to him. Yet at present we do not see everything subject to him" (Heb. 2:5–10).

Validation of man's higher call can be seen in the following verse: "Now we are the children of God, and what we will be has not yet been made known. But we know that when he appears, we shall be like him [Jesus], for we shall see him as he is" (1 John 3:2).

At this time, the awesome angels are commissioned to serve the lesser saints: "Are not all angels ministering spirits sent to serve those who will inherit salvation?" (Heb. 1:14).

CLEANSING FIRE

The altar fire is also used to cleanse and commission us for service. This is how saints are prepared for ministry. In every generation, God looks for people to partner with him. Years ago he found Isaiah. The prophet was given a vision of God's throne, and immediately he became aware of his frailty and his own sinfulness.

Isaiah said, "Then one of the Seraphs flew to me with a live coal in his hand, which he had taken with tongs from the altar. With it he touched my mouth and said, 'See, this has touched your lips; your guilt is taken away and your sin atoned for'" (Isa. 6:5–7).

Isaiah was cleansed with fire from the altar of prayer. The encounter prepared him for service. Perhaps faithful saints had prayed for him to fulfill his destiny, and those prayers had burned before the Lord until

Isaiah was ready. Then the angel administered the fire from the altar, and the prophet came into his own.

MARTYRS

Beneath this amazing altar live the souls of the martyrs—the millions who have died for the word of God and his testimony (Rev. 6:9).

History tells a story of a passionate man named Nicander. He was just an average soldier in the Roman army who had been away from home for ten years. He was fighting on a foreign field. He lived during the first century, and, while in the emperor's service, he heard the message of Christ. He became a disciple and an outspoken advocate of the Christian faith. After many years he was able to return to his family in Rome. Upon his arrival, Nicander was apprehended and thrown in prison. When anyone refused to worship the emperor, it was considered a crime against Rome, and those people paid with their lives.

Nicander was led to the arena where he was tied to a pole and left for the lions to eat. A great crowd assembled in the arena and, as was custom, the emperor delayed the proceedings to give Christians opportunity to recant. Family members were invited to walk down onto the arena floor to help persuade their relatives to renounce Christ. If the prisoners would recant, they would be released unharmed. The crowds would cheer and watch with fascination as family members pleaded with loved ones, hoping they would compromise.

It is said that Nicander's wife was brought into the arena. She stepped down onto the dusty field and crossed over to the place where her husband was tied. She looked into his eyes and said, "Be of good cheer; be a hero. Ten years I spent at home without you and I prayed that I might see you. Now I see you, and I rejoice that you are set for life." (see website – Saints O' the Day – Nicander and Marcian MM (RM) – June 17)

That day Nicander's blood was spilt on Roman soil, but his soul was lifted to the throne room of heaven.

Fox's Book of Martyrs: A History of the Lives, Suffering, and Deaths of the Early Christian and Protestant Martyrs[b] and hundreds of other writings tell the stories of thousands who have died for their faith. Untold millions, nevertheless, have been forgotten. Their deaths have not been recorded in our history books. Even the Bible does not name most of the persecuted who were martyred during the time it was written.

Scripture says, "Others were tortured and refused to be released, so that they might gain a better resurrection. Some faced jeers and flogging, while still others were chained and put in prison. They were stoned; they were sawn in two; they were put to death by the sword ... the world was not worthy of them" (Heb. 11:35–38).

HEAVEN REMEMBERS

Many martyrs of Christ are unsung heroes of the faith. Humankind does not remember all of these outstanding people, but heaven does. The souls of martyrs live with the Lord, and, of all the souls in heaven, they are closest to him. They cry out, and God does not turn away from their cries. He does not allocate them to a back room; nor does he patronize them. God listens to them intently and responds in four specific ways:

1. Giving them white robes of dignity and righteousness (Rev. 6:11, 19:8)
2. Telling them to wait a little longer and justice will come (Rev. 6:11, 16:7)
3. Telling them that more Christians will be martyred (Rev. 6:11)
4. Telling them that martyrdom is necessary for the completion of his plan (Rev. 6:11)

Our partnership with Christ may involve pain and even death, but it will result in eternal glory. Christians will be present in every part of the tribulation, and many will die for their faith. God will reach out with patience to his enemies. He will extend compassion and love through the very saints who are being martyred.

Paul reminded us, "I consider that our present sufferings are not worth comparing with the glory that will be revealed in us" (Ro. 8:18).

Suffering is referred to in Philippians as "the fellowship of his sufferings" (Phil. 3:10).

Peter told us that suffering completes our calling as followers of Christ: "If you suffer for doing good and you endure it, this is commendable before God. To this you were called, because Christ suffered for you, leaving you an example, that you should follow in his steps. He committed no sin, and no deceit was found in his mouth. He did not retaliate; when he suffered. Instead he entrusted himself to him who judges justly" (1 Pet. 2:20–23).

Suffering may come for a moment, but Revelation shows us that suffering for Christ leads to glory.

A MARTYR'S FAITH

It is important for us to hear God's conversation with the martyrs. The dialogue has been canonized. Perhaps, it is more important for us than for the martyrs themselves. They have faith, and we are in need of it. Sometime well-intentioned people can refuse the plan of God because of fear. When Jesus told his disciples he was going to the cross, they did not like what they heard.

Peter said, "Never Lord! This shall never happen to you.' Jesus turned and said to Peter, 'Get behind me, Satan! You are a stumbling block to me; you do not have in mind the things of God but the things of men'" (Matt. 16:22).

The book of Revelation reveals that great numbers of people will become martyrs. It says, "This calls for the patient endurance and faithfulness of the saints" (Rev. 13:10; see also Rev. 14:12).

The Bible reveals that many saints will carry a cross during the great tribulation. These will not be crosses that will pay for man's sin—that was done once and for all—but crosses of love and evangelism. Many will be willing to die for the cause of Christ.

Some even today speak as Peter did, telling the Lord that he would surely not allow his people to suffer. The Bible does not teach the absence of suffering, in fact, it teaches the opposite. There is a good fight to be fought and sometimes it involves pain. Peter lacked foresight regarding Christ's death—looking back we see that the greatest blessings came because of Christ's death on the cross.

Suffering and love will release magnificent revivals during the great tribulation. God will extend grace, and many will be protected from martyrdom. Signs and wonders will flourish at the hands of the saints, and the glory of the Lord will shine through his people. Whether we are taken beforehand or we live or die during the great tribulation, we need the martyr's faith. All of us are called to shine as bright lights before a needy world.

"They overcame him [the devil] by the blood of the Lamb and by the word of their testimony; they did not love their lives so much as to shrink from death" (Rev. 12:11).

GOD IS IN CONTROL

Revelation teaches us that God is in control. That is why we are told about the martyrs. People are not dying because Satan has the upper hand, but because God is allowing their deaths to turn hardened hearts to him. After seeing the patient mercies of God in the midst of judgment, multitudes will repent. Longsuffering saints will give hardcore sinners no excuses, and many will be saved in the final hours. God's plan reveals his amazing love for sinners. He calls us to partner with him for those who are perishing.

Recall that in Revelation 13:10 we read, "This calls for the patient endurance and faithfulness on the part of the saints"

NOT SUICIDE BOMBERS

Today, some fanatical Muslims and other zealots outside of Christianity commit suicide as a religious duty. Suicide bombing is an act of terror. The aim of suicide bombers is to kill people who differ from them and to kill themselves in the process. This is the opposite of Christian martyrdom.

True Christians aim to save lives. Christianity does not teach us to murder ourselves or anyone else. A fanatical Muslim will kill people; a fanatical Christian will turn the other cheek. Christians will love their attackers and pray that God will forgive them and rescue them from their sins.

Martyrs who die for the cause of Christ will receive a special crown. We read, "Do not be afraid of what you are about to suffer. I tell you, the devil will put some of you in prison to test you, and you will suffer persecution ... Be faithful, even to the point of death, and I will give you a crown of life" (Rev. 2:10).

The martyrs will pass from this life to the next, but their blood will not be wasted. It has been said that revival is fueled by the blood of the saints. Their momentary pain opens hearts so that many others can come to Christ.

Chapter Twelve

Revelation is About Hell on Earth

I watched as he opened the sixth seal. There was a great earthquake. The sun turned black like sackcloth made of goat hair, the whole moon turned blood red, and the stars in the sky fell to earth, as late figs drop from a fig tree when shaken by a strong wind. The sky receded like a scroll, rolling up, and every mountain and island was removed from its place.
The kings of the earth, the princes, the generals, the rich, the mighty, and every slave and every free man hid in caves and among the rocks of the mountains. They called to the mountains and the rocks, "Fall on us and hide us from the face of him who sits on the throne and from the wrath of the Lamb! For the great day of their wrath has come, and who can stand?" (Rev. 6:12–17)

CHAPTER TOPICS

1. The judgments getting worse
2. Everything being shaken
3. People experiencing hell on earth
4. The persecution of the saints
5. Great numbers of angels descend from heaven
6. The financial securities of the rich are removed

EARTHQUAKES AND WORSE

THE GREAT TRIBULATION IS from God, not the devil. It will begin with judgment, but it will end with the kingdom of righteousness. This chapter reveals a judgment that is like a momentary hell on earth. Several things will happen to make the planet a living hell.

John wrote, "I watched as he opened the sixth seal. There was a great earthquake. The sun turned black like sackcloth" (Rev. 6:12).

John watched as Jesus opened the sixth seal, and the earth experienced hell. It began with a great earthquake that ripped the world in pieces. Earthquakes were prophesied by Jesus when he spoke of wars, famines, and plagues. Matthew 24, Mark 13, and Luke 21 foretell these calamities. Three campaigns will be launched from heaven, and during the first one, wars, famines, and plagues will strike the planet. It will seem that things cannot get worse, but they will. Over a period of seven years, things will become much worse. Great revivals will also come. As horrible as the judgments will be, the revivals will be wonderful.

The earthquake described in Rev. 6 will be the worst in human history. The major fault lines of earth will shift simultaneously and damage the entire globe. It will devastate cities and villages around the world. The dead and injured will number in the millions, and the damage to property will rise to trillions of dollars.

Wars, plagues, famines, and earthquakes are unbearable, but they are not as dreadful as the trauma that accompanies them. The physical earthquake reflects a spiritual earthquake that is far more devastating. Panic and fear will rise on a scale unknown since the beginning of man. Darkness, like hell itself, will roll over the earth and shake the heart of humanity.

Hebrews forewarned of this malaise: "See to it that you do not refuse him who speaks. If they did not escape when they refused him who warned them on earth, how much less will we if we turn away from him who warns us from heaven. At that time his voice shook the earth, but now he has promised, "Once more I will shake not only the earth but also the heavens." The words "once more" indicate the removing of what can be shaken—that is, created things—so that that which cannot be shaken may remain. Therefore since we are receiving a kingdom that cannot be shaken let us be thankful, and so worship God acceptably with reverence and awe, for our God is a consuming fire." (Heb. 12:25–29)

The spiritual shaking in Hebrews is a description of the shaking foretold in the book of Revelation. Hebrews compares this shaking with the trauma the children of Israel faced when they refused Moses. He came down from the mountain carrying the Ten Commandments. The people were in sin, and God judged them. The earth shook and severe warnings were given.

On another occasion, Korah and his followers rebelled against Moses and the Lord. Suddenly, an earthquake erupted and swallowed them (Exod. 19:20; see also Num. 16:28–35). That was a preview of the earthquakes that will come during the great tribulation.

The book of Hebrews not only warns of this, but gives reasons for it. It is necessary to shake everything that can be shaken so that only God's kingdom will remain. The entire book of Revelation is about this spiritual shaking, and the first campaign will start the process. The natural world will be shaken: it will crumble and fall. The spiritual world will also be shaken and all that is not of God will fall. It will be so devastating that, when it is over, we will need a new heaven and a new earth.

A MOMENT OF HELL

The earthquake will signal the beginning of a momentary hell. It is momentary because, like all earthquakes, it will run its course and then it will be over. It is like hell because the Lord will turn his face away from the earth.

One definition of hell is, "An horrible place totally void of God's presence and blessings." This is indicated in 2 Thessalonians. Referring to those who will be sent to hell, it says, "They will be punished with everlasting destruction and *shut out from the presence of the Lord* and from the majesty of his power" (2 Thess. 1:9; italics added).

COMMON GRACE

Hell is the absence of grace. Common grace is God's natural blessing upon humanity. It is the kindness of God that enables people to enjoy life with necessary provisions and protections. It is different from saving grace, which enables people to find salvation and eternal life.

Common grace is given to everyone, but if it were to be removed, the world would become a place of torment. It would be hell on earth. When the sixth seal is broken, God will remove common grace for a moment of time, and those without saving grace will be terrified. This will be a call for people to turn to God, who alone can save and provide peace in the hour of tribulation.

GOD TURNS HIS FACE

John wrote, "The sun turned black like sackcloth made of goat hair" (Rev. 6:12).

One cannot be dogmatic with this scripture, but I believe "the sun turned black" refers to God turning his face away from the world. Revelation 1:16 says that the Lord's face is like the sun shining in all its brilliance. In Mal. 4:2 the Lord is called "The Sun of Righteousness."

In the book of Psalms, we read, "For the Lord God is a sun and shield; the Lord bestows favor and honor" (Ps. 84:11).

John said, "In him was life, and that life was the light of men" (John 1:4).

In Rev. 6, everything becomes black because the light of God is removed, as if his face is covered by thick "sackcloth made of goat's hair."

This happened when Jesus hung on the cross. Jesus took on himself the sin of the world and, for a moment, God turned his face from his Son. Here, is Matthew's account: "From the sixth hour until the ninth hour darkness came over all the land. About the ninth hour Jesus cried out in a loud voice ... 'My God, my God, why have you forsaken me?' The curtain in the temple was torn in two from top to bottom. The earth shook and the rocks split. The tombs broke open" (Matt. 27:45, 46, 51).

When the events of Rev. 6 come to pass, only the light of God in his people will shine. He has promised never to leave nor forsake them, but this will be a horrible time for those without Christ. When God turns his face from the earth, the world will be plunged into darkness, depression, and absolute depravity. Evil will raise its ugly head. Demons will torment and ravage the minds of people, and wicked men will take advantage of the darkness. Crime will escalate, violence will soar, and occult activity will become rampant. Depraved men will be free to revel in the lusts of the flesh. Strife and anger will erupt, and witchcraft will rise to that of the worst horror movie. People groping in the darkness will be overtaken with fear. They will run and hide and call upon the mountains and the rocks to cover them.

It is no wonder that the prayer of Aaron is so powerful and that for thousands of years after it was penned, men have continued to pronounce its blessings.

It says, "The Lord bless you and keep you; the Lord make his face shine upon you and be gracious to you; the Lord turn his face toward you and give you peace" (Num. 6:24–26).

Without God's face shining on us, all grace, goodness, and peace are gone.

HORRIFIC PERSECUTION

Revelation says, "The whole moon turned blood red" (Rev. 6:12).

Typically, the moon represents the church. It reflects the light of the sun, which is the Lord. Genesis 37:9–10 records the first mention of the word moon in the Bible. Here the moon is compared to Rachel, Israel's bride. Israel, the husband, is compared to the sun.

The wife is to reflect the glory of her husband as scripture says, "The man is the image and glory of God; but the woman is the glory of man" (1 Cor. 11:7).

A bride has light in herself, but she is also called to reflect the light of her husband. This goes a step further with the church. The church has no light in itself. The church is the bride of Christ and must reflect his light. Like the moon, the church has no light, but it is brilliant because it reflects the light of the sun (Christ). The express calling of the moon is to reflect the glory of the sun.

In a much later chapter of Revelation than the one we are studying now, John will see the church, the bride of Christ, coming out of heaven. This is the city of God, and it reflects God's glory.

We read, "It shone with the glory of God, and its brilliance was like that of a very precious jewel, clear as crystal" (Rev. 21:9–11).

Returning to the study at hand, at this point of the tribulation, the moon turns blood red. Joel 2:31 says the moon will turn to blood before the dreadful day of the Lord. Likewise, in Acts 2:20, we read that the moon will be turned into blood before the coming of the Lord. The next verse in Acts says that everyone who calls on the name of the Lord will be saved. It is instructive to notice that this happens before the second coming of the Lord.

These verses describe the event with stronger language than what we find in Rev. 6. The moon not only turns blood red in color, it actually turns to blood. This is a picture of persecution. The persecution of God's people is common in the book of Revelation. At some points, the blood of the saints will run freely in the streets.

Later, in Revelation, we read concerning the beast, "He was given power to make war against the saints and to conquer them" (Rev. 13:7).

We also read about the great Harlot: "I saw that the woman was drunk with the blood of the saints, the blood of those who bore testimony to Jesus. In her was found the blood of prophets and of the saints" (Rev. 17:6; see also 18:24).

Many Christians will be martyred during the tribulation. Near the end of the first campaign, violence will erupt against Christ and his people. When hell breaks loose, the church will come under demonic fire, and many will die and go to be with the Lord. Figuratively speaking, the moon will turn to blood. It has been said that the blood of the martyrs fuels the fires of revival, and that will happen again. As sinners see the persecution of God's people, multitudes will come to Christ. As the church turns to blood, grace will come, and God will strengthen the hands and hearts of his people.

A DROP ZONE FOR ANGELS

The drama continues, "The stars in the sky fell to earth, as late figs drop from a fig tree when shaken by a strong wind" (Rev. 6:13).

Stars in the book of Revelation are symbolic of angels. As terror floods over the world, angels will engage in spiritual warfare. Both good and evil angels will fall from the sky.

On a recent visit to Ephesus and Pergamum in Turkey, I picked a ripe fig from a tree. The fig was yellow and luscious, and it tasted absolutely delicious. As I touched it, the heavy fig literally dropped from the tree into my hand. If a strong wind blew through the tree that I took the fig from, all the fruit would immediately drop like rocks.

The angels will drop to earth like that. They will arrive in large numbers and come with amazing speed, like heavy figs falling to the ground when the tree is shaken by a strong wind. The wind of God will blow upon the angels, and there will be an instantaneous migration to earth. Evil ones will come from the second heaven to join the festival of evil. Godly ones will come to defend the cause of Christ and minister to the saints.

THE COVERING REMOVED

Revelation continues, "The sky receded like a scroll, rolling up" (Rev. 6:14).

The blue sky that covers the world represents God's protection and provision that covers humanity. All of us live under God's blue sky.

Isaiah wrote, "He stretches out the heavens like a canopy and spreads them out like a tent to live in" (Isa. 40:22).

Scripture describes the sky as a tent that God draws over us. It provides shelter, a breathable atmosphere, and a planet we call home.

Suddenly his covering will be drawn back like a scroll. God's spiritual provision will be momentarily removed. Prior to the apocalypse, man will have enjoyed God's spiritual protection. That is why, in this present age, demons are not able to torment any person at will—not even the unsaved. Demons must gain access through legal doors to trouble people. Certain sins and sometimes the sins of past generations bring curses and demonic interference to people's lives (Deut. 27), but even then the demonic license is limited. Jesus tells us that Satan has come to kill, steal, and destroy. That is what demons do (see John 10:10).

God's grace over the earth restrains that evil. It will be a terrible day when the sky is rolled back like a scroll, and demons are free to trouble humanity. This will be a moment of hell. It will be a further wake-up call for all who have decided not to take God seriously. God's people will have a special care. Throughout the book of Revelation, the saints are protected from demonic torment.

As God steps back from the world, the nations will go into shock. Many people will repent, but multitudes will still harden their hearts toward him.

FINANCIAL SECURITIES SMASHED

Revelation continues, "Every mountain and island was removed from its place" (Rev. 6:14).

Mountains are high places. In the Bible, they represent places of power, strength and security. While in Israel, I have often visited the military stronghold of Masada. It is a mountaintop fortress that rises out of the wilderness overlooking the Dead Sea. The kings of Israel used it as a hideaway, and Herod stored enough food there to last him for ten years, just in case he needed a permanent place of escape. In its day, its cisterns could hold enough water to supply five thousand people for one full year. When Jerusalem was destroyed in 70 AD, the Essenes (religious zealots) held their ground on the mountain of Masada, against a much stronger enemy. Eventually the Romans built a ramp using Jewish slaves as workers. When they captured the mountain, they discovered that the Jews had committed suicide rather than be made slaves.

Bank accounts are the mountains of security for modern people. Financial security is a stronghold of independence for people in every nation. The American dollar bill has written on it, "In God We Trust," but for many, the greenback is known as the almighty dollar. Even when famine, war, and poverty hit the world, the rich will have their securities.

People of wealth have learned to protect themselves with layers of financial holdings. They know not to put all their eggs in one basket, so that if one basket comes up empty, they can go to another. They have diversified because deep down they fear that one day their security may come crashing down.

On September 11, 2001, The World Trade Center was struck by terrorists. It was a catastrophe that shocked the world, devastated families, and put the nations on alert. We realized how vulnerable we are.

It was a relatively small attack compared to what could happen. Even so, the global economy slid into trauma and momentary failure. If hundreds of natural disasters or terrorist attacks occur simultaneously it would devastate the world's financial community.

Revelation's reference to every mountain being removed points to our personal and national securities being stripped away. Terrorist activities and natural disasters will wipe out most computers making financial transactions impossible. Even the very rich will lose access to their resources.

When the catastrophes are compounded, the collective cost of repair will bankrupt us. Insurance agencies will immediately go broke, business will grind to a halt, and banks will shut their doors. The National Guard will be called into populated areas to stem the tides of chaos and riot. Food supplies and utility services will shut down, and people will focus on personal survival. Mass hysteria will erupt everywhere.

ISLANDS COLLAPSE

The book of Revelation reveals amazing details. If the super-rich think they will elude the problem, they should read on. Revelation highlights the failure of all contingency plans. Many think they have enough protection devices in place, but one by one, all will fail.

People with money know that a nation's economy may fail, so they have back-up plans. They have offshore bank accounts and holdings—nest eggs that are hidden from government scrutiny—which provide them with a false sense of security. Revelation announces that *every island,* as well as every mountain, will be removed from its place. The remote, hidden islands of financial strength will be removed. The problem will be global, and the kingdom of God will be our only place of security.

God's judgments will fall on the earth, and no one outside of Christ will endure them. The super wealthy, the elite, the kings, and the presidents will have no strength if they resist the God of heaven.

Isaiah said: "Surely the nations are like a drop in the bucket; they are regarded as dust on the scales; he weighs the islands as though they are fine dust. He brings princes to naught and reduces the rulers of this world to nothing … No sooner are they planted, no sooner are they sown, no sooner do they take root in the ground, than he blows on them and they wither, and a whirlwind sweeps them away like chaff ... Have you not heard? The Lord is the everlasting God, the creator of the ends of the earth. He will not grow tired or weary, and his understanding no one can fathom. He gives strength to the weary and increases the power of the weak." (Isa. 40:15, 22–24, 28, 29)

EXPLOSION OF FEAR

People of every financial bracket and social status—whether they are rich or poor, humble or elite, slave or free, mighty or weak—will be filled with fear. They will run and hide, and many will commit suicide. Others will wish they could die, because every pleasure and security they had built their lives on will have disintegrated before their eyes. Many will understand that what is happening is divine judgment and that it is the wrath of the Lord. Nevertheless, some will still refuse to call on him. They will run to hide because they are guilty of rebellion against their creator, but it will not help. Some will cry for death to swallow them, yet they will resist salvation. Their pride will imprison them, and their anger will blind them. In that day Christ will be mankind's only hope.

WINDFALL REVIVAL

While terror and judgment are falling, and many are refusing to heed the call of God, multitudes will bend their knees and come to Christ.

There will be another side to the drama, and God wants to share it with us. The next chapter of Revelation describes the greatest revival in history, to date. The number of people who will find salvation is staggering. The Lord of the harvest will rescue vast multitudes of souls.

It is amazing that God can take enemies and turn them into disciples. Once they are in the fold, they will receive revelation from the Holy Spirit. Then they will realize how foolish they were and how blessed they are going to be. The blood of Jesus will reach into the tribulation period to rise above the judgments and extend the mercies of God. The weary and the destitute will turn to God and he will receive them.

Chapter Thirteen

Revelation is About God's Protection

After this I saw four angels standing at the four corners of the earth, holding back the four winds of the earth to prevent any wind from blowing on the land or on the sea or on any tree. Then I saw another angel coming up from the east, having the seal of the living God. He called out in a loud voice to the four angels who had been given power to harm the land and the sea: "Do not harm the land or the sea or the trees until we put a seal on the foreheads of the servants of our God."
Then I heard the number of those who were sealed: 144,000 from all the tribes of Israel. (Rev. 7:1–4)

CHAPTER TOPICS

1. Angels that minister protection
2. Revival fires that touch the earth
3. The mark of God on the foreheads of the saints
4. Salvation coming to the Jews

DIFFERENT VIEW POINTS

AS I WRITE, I am aware that many Christian groups espouse interpretations of Revelation. It is not my intention to offend the many wonderful Christians who teach different perspectives. I honor many of them. Nevertheless, I am writing what I believe the scriptures teach, regardless of popular interpretations. It is my desire to teach God's word accurately, no matter how different it may be from other teachings. May God help all who teach to rightly divide the word of truth. May each of us teach Revelation with humility and personal conviction. It is possible for Christians to differ on some points of doctrine and still walk in harmony with other members of Christ's church. That is my goal.

ANGELS MINISTER PROTECTION

At the beginning of Rev. 7, we read of four angels who will be given power to harm the land and sea. The environment of earth will suffer greatly before the tribulation is over. The devastation will make the planet a hostile and, eventually, an all but uninhabitable place.

The four winds (angels) of judgment will be restrained for a brief season until God's people have received protection. Then these angels will release tormenting demons who will haunt those who refuse Christ. This will not happen until a seal of protection—a barrier that the demon spirits cannot cross—has been applied to the foreheads of the saints. During the tribulation period, God will not allow demons to torment the minds of his children.

REVIVAL FIRES

God will do more than extend protection; he will also bring revival. Three things will happen: the church will receive God's blessings, Satan will be judged, and the great end-time harvest will come. That is the reason why the tribulation must last for seven years. It cannot be over in one massive judgment because the Lord desires to rescue many more souls from damnation. There will be both Jewish and gentile revivals.

THE SEAL OF GOD

God will cover his people with a seal. It will be like a security seal that is designed to protect a precious package or guard confidentiality over documents or products so they will not be opened at the wrong time or by the wrong people. In this case, we are God's precious packages.

An NIV Study Bible note explains, "Ancient documents were folded and tied, and a lump of clay was pressed over the knot. The sender would then stamp the hardening clay with a signet ring or roll it with a cylinder seal, which authenticated and protected the contents. The sealing in chapter 7 … is to protect the people of God in the coming judgments." [c]

In reviewing Rev. 5, we discovered how powerful God's seal is. No one in heaven or on earth could remove the seals on the scroll except Jesus himself. Now in chapter 6, we learn that a similar seal will be placed on the foreheads of the servants of God. No creature can break the seal of God, which is the most effective protection for one's mind. When the seal covers our thinking, no deception, lie, or trick of Satan will have any effect on us.

THE HELMET OF SALVATION

Unfortunately, all Christians do not guard their minds with the helmet of salvation (see Eph. 6:17). Presently, we live in an age of information overload. Mixed with the good, we are fed enormous amounts of information and knowledge that is not good. We have too much information. Filtering the valuable from the worthless is a consuming task. Deceptive or demonic information will undermine one's faith. Wrong information will produce doubt, double-minded thinking, and spiritual confusion.

It is easy to understand how demonic mind games would be devastating, even for Christians, during the tribulation period. That is why God will not allow demons to play mind games with his followers. He will protect the thoughts of the saints with a seal.

Spiritual warfare will often come as an attack on one's minds. We read of this in 2 Corinthians: "The weapons we fight with are not weapons of the world. On the contrary they have divine power to demolish strongholds. We demolish *arguments* and every *pretension* that sets itself up against the *knowledge* of God, and we take captive every *thought* to make it obedient to Christ" (2 Cor. 10:4, 5; italics added).

Strongholds are spiritual, emotional, and psychological attacks aimed at the mind. The words, "arguments," "pretension," "knowledge," and "thought" tell us that the battle is often in the mind. Satan is the father of lies. He is the deceiver and the creator of disloyalty and confusion. No matter how skilful his demons are, during the tribulation, they will not be able to penetrate the seal of God.

MARKED BY GOD

The seal of God is not an external, visible mark like a tattoo or an ink stamp. It is invisible to the natural eye, but is extremely powerful. It has a twofold application. It will provide a shift in our thinking and a firewall that evil cannot penetrate. It is the mind of Christ, full of wisdom and discernment. It is also a protective guard like the angel that stood before the Garden of Eden with a flaming sword. No one could pass while the guard was present (Gen. 3:24).

THE MIND OF CHRIST

Our minds need transformation. Romans, instructs us, "Be transformed by the renewing of your mind. Then you will be able to test and approve what God's will is" (Rom. 12:2).

Paul says, "Let this mind be in you that was also in Christ" (Phil. 2:5).

The mind of Christ is available to all Christians. When we have the mind of Christ, we have wisdom, love, and a clear conscience. During the tribulation this impartation will be essential. The mind of every believer will be renewed as well as protected.

This renewed mind will release in us a powerful new anointing. We will minister with great skill to those without Christ. The saints will lead many suffering people to the knowledge and love of Jesus.

THE JEW FIRST

The seal mentioned in Rev. 7 will specifically be placed on the foreheads of the Jews who believe in Jesus. We read, "Then I heard the number of those who were sealed: 144,000 from all the tribes of Israel" (Rev. 7:4).

The 144,000 are clearly identified as Jews. We will look at this in the next chapter. I believe that all saints will receive this provision of protection, but the scripture does not say that in these verses. At the end of Revelation, however, all God's people, Jews and gentiles alike, will have his name written on their foreheads. We read, "They will see his face, and his name will be on their foreheads" (Rev. 22:4).

In Rev. 9 we read of demons attacking the nations. There we discover that they are unable to hurt God's people. It says, "They were told not to harm the grass of the earth or any plant or tree, but only those people who did not have the seal of God on their foreheads. They were not given power to kill them, but only to torture them for five months" (Rev. 9:4, 5).

The 144,000 redeemed Jews are further mentioned in Rev. 14. Again we are told of the mark of God on their foreheads. Here we discover that they have both Christ's and the Almighty's name on their foreheads: "Then I looked, and there before me was the Lamb, standing on Mount Zion, and with him 144,000 who had his name and his Father's name written on their foreheads" (Rev. 14:1).

INVISIBLE SEAL

This is an invisible stamp. I do not believe that an angel will place a tattoo on the saints. If this mark is invisible, then the counterfeit mark on the enemies of God may also be invisible. The mark of the beast may be the thinking of the beast. Perhaps the mark of the beast is more an evil way of thinking—an individual's mindset or worldview—than it is a tattoo.

A defiled conscience or an evil conscience is a demonic stronghold. Instead of the mind of Christ, some will posses the mind of Satan. I will discuss the power of a demonic worldview in another chapter.

The seal on the saints speaks of God's approval and protection. It is the Father's identifying mark that is given to his children—whoever has this mark is part of his family. Like the blood on the doorposts of the Jewish homes in Egypt, Christians will have the blood of Christ on the doorposts of their hearts.

OTHER PROTECTION MARKS

Most of Revelation is a repeat of events that have already happened at some other time in history. The difference between those events that have already occurred and those that will come is the magnitude and intensity of the events. Judgments and revivals have come before, but the scope of those foretold in Revelation is greatly increased.

Like other dynamics of the book of Revelation, marks of God's protection were given on previous occasions in history. They are mentioned in other parts of the Bible. As mentioned earlier, the children of Israel were instructed to smear the blood of a lamb on the doorposts of their homes. This happened when God's judgments were falling upon Egypt just prior to the Exodus. The death angel passed over the homes of Egypt, killing the firstborn of each family that did not have the mark on their homes. The people of God who had the mark were protected.

Likewise, Ezekiel recorded a vision of God's protection and judgment at a time when the Israelites were involved in idolatry. We read,

"Go through the city of Jerusalem and put a mark on the forehead of those who grieve and lament over the detestable things that are done in it. Follow him through the city and kill, but do not touch anyone who has the mark" (Ezek. 9:4, 6).

This mark was not an external imprint that the neighbors could see, but an invisible, spiritual one that only the angels could detect.

YOUR PERSONAL SEAL

"Then I saw another angel coming up from the east, having the seal of the living God. He called out in a loud voice to the four angels who had been given power. Do not harm the land or the sea or the trees until we put a seal on the foreheads of the servants of our God" (Rev. 6:2–3).

We should not fear the tribulation period. God will cover and care for his people. The Christians and redeemed Jews who are there will not live in fear. They will know God's power and love, and they will posses a sound mind.

A person's theology (understanding of God) determines their philosophy (values), and one's philosophy or values determines one's actions. A Christian in the tribulation will not act like others in the neighborhood; they will have the mind of Christ. They will not live in fear nor will the vices of the flesh rule over him. While others are in panic, Christians will walk in peace. This will be very attractive to a world in pain. People will want what the Christians have. The seal of God will serve as a powerful testimony of inner strength, and multitudes will come to Christ for salvation.

STRONG MINDS FOR MARTYRS

Throughout the ages, the Christian church has produced amazing men and women. Many have walked in the power of the Holy Spirit. They have stood against injustice and spread the gospel in the face of aggression and wickedness. Some have died for their faith, but maintained love and power and a sound mind. The world does not understand the power of Christ that enables a person to go through the fires of persecutions with victory.

Many modern-day Christians lack this understanding as well, but the Lord will prepare them. Demons will not torment the people of God, but many will give up their lives for the faith. Through it all, they will possess the peace that passes understanding.

Chapter Fourteen

Revelation is About a Jewish Revival

Do not harm the land or the sea or the trees until we put a seal on the foreheads of the servants of our God.
Then I heard the number of those who were sealed: 144,000 from all the tribes of Israel. From the tribe of Judah 12,000 were sealed, from the tribe of Reuben 12,000, from the tribe of Gad 12,000, from the tribe of Asher 12,000, from the tribe of Naphtali 12,000, from the tribe of Manasseh 12,000, from the tribe of Simeon 12,000, from the tribe of Levi 12,000, from the tribe of Issachar 12,000, from the tribe of Zebulun 12,000, from the tribe of Joseph 12,000, from the tribe of Benjamin 12,000. (Rev. 7:3–8)

CHAPTER TOPICS

1. A revival coming to Israel at the start of the tribulation
2. Salvation for Jews who were cut off
3. The temporary cutting off of the Jews
4. The Church fathers who preached about a Jewish revival
5. The Jewish revival that comes after Jerusalem is an immovable rock
6. The majority of Israel, but not every Jew, receiving Jesus as Messiah

ıtion of more Jews at the end of the tribulation

THE JOY OF REVIVAL

CHRISTIANS FAIL TO observe the joys and hope elation. The angels in heaven rejoice during the great ıuse they see something that many Christians do not ..ıey see the blessings of God coming to the church and to Israel, and they see the defeat of Satan. This will be the Churches' finest hour prior to the new millennium. The momentary, chilling trials of the tribulation will turn into extravagant expressions of evangelism and joy.

Revelation 7 reveals two great revivals. First we see the 144,000 Jews who recognize Jesus as Messiah and stand as redeemed Israel. Immediately following that vision, we see a multitude of gentile converts that cannot be numbered. Different from the first revival, these are not Jews, but Christians. They will come from every nation, tribe, language, and people. Here are some interesting facts from Rev. 7:

1. There will be a great Jewish revival in the tribulation period (symbolically, 144,000 Jews will be saved).
2. During the tribulation, there will be a massive revival of gentiles who represent every nation on earth.
3. The number of gentile Christians saved during the first part of the tribulation period will be so large that no human will be able to count them.
4. Jews and Gentile saints are one in Christ, but the Jewish identity will be preserved.

In this chapter we will discuss the Jewish revival.

ONE HUNDRED AND FORTY-FOUR THOUSAND

Numerology is the study of numbers, and the Bible has a definite numerology woven into it. God's mark of protection will be put on the foreheads of 144,000, and that is a number of great importance in the book of Revelation because it symbolizes the family of God. The number *12* stands for family or nation, and 12 times 12 equals 144. Jesus chose twelve disciples to be with him as his earthly family. God chose the twelve tribes of Israel to be his chosen nation.

The city of God in Rev. 21 is a picture of the bride of Christ—the family of God. Its dimensions are twelve thousand stadia in each direction. It has twelve foundation stones and twelve gates. The leaves of its tree will bear twelve fruit, which are for the healing of the nations. The number twelve seems to be everywhere. That is because it represents God's family, city, or nation.

Twelve times twelve equals 144. Multiply that times 1,000, and it gives us 144,000. That is the expanded number of a great family. The family of God is also a city, and 144 cubits is the thickness of the walls of the city. The city of God is a nation and a family.

THE JEWISH FAMILY

The first mention of 144,000 refers specifically to the Jewish family who are part of God's larger family of Jews and gentiles. The entire family incorporates redeemed Jews and saved gentiles, which are the two branches of the olive tree mentioned in Rom. 11. The Jews are the natural branches, and the gentiles are the wild olive branches.

"If some of the branches have been cut off, and you, though a wild olive shoot, have been grafted in among the others and now share in the nourishing sap from the olive root … If you were cut out of an olive tree that is wild by nature, and contrary to nature were grafted into a cultivated olive tree, how much more readily will these, the natural branches, be grafted into their own olive tree" (Rom. 11:17, 24).

Just in case we are predisposed to think that Israel, mentioned here in Rev. 7 is only symbolic, God clarified the matter. Some believe that the 144,000 refers to a spiritual Israel made up of gentile believers, but the Lord identifies each of the twelve tribes by name. It would be a gross mistreatment of scripture to try to spiritualize these names and eradicate natural Israel from the pages of the book. It has been done throughout history, but I would not want to be guilty of mishandling these scriptures. The fact that these are real Israelites is very important to God. He records their names emphatically. These are Israelites indeed who will become followers of Jesus during the great tribulation.

Twelve thousand Jews will be saved from each tribe, and each tribe is mentioned by name. It is reasonable to conclude that the number *twelve* is a symbolic number; it represents family. The fact remains that all the tribes are included except for the tribe of Dan.

As Judas was eliminated from the twelve disciples and replaced by another, perhaps Dan has been disqualified from the twelve tribes of Israel and replaced by another. Some believe this happened because his tribe chose to remain in idolatry. We read of this in the book of Judges:

"The Danites rebuilt the city and settled there. They named it Dan after their forefather Dan, who was born to Israel. There the Danites set up for themselves idols. They continued to use the idols Micah had made all the time the house of the Lord was in Shiloh" (Judg. 18:30).

Some contend that all twelve tribes do not exist anymore. Only God knows, and no person can make that assumption. For centuries, thousands of Jews have changed their names to escape persecution. Their lineage is no longer traceable by humans. It is likely that many people in the world are partly Jewish, but are unaware of it. God knows who they are. Like lost orphans who find their true parents later in life, many Jews will discover their identity in the end.

ISRAEL'S FOLLY IS NOT PERMANENT

Although we will not devote much time to this theme, it is necessary to clarify this next point for some Christians. The Jews fell from God's grace, but they will be restored. After coming to Christ, they will play a significant role in the tribulation period.

Israel wandered from the ways of the Lord through unbelief and hardness of heart (see Rom. 11:20). She further departed from following the Lord when she rejected her Jewish Messiah, Jesus. The Jews, as a whole, lost the kingdom of God for a season of time. We read of this in the book of Matthew. Jesus said to the Jews, "The kingdom of God will be taken away from you and given to a people who will produce its fruit" (Matt. 21:43).

The kingdom of God was taken from the Jews and given to the gentile church, but that is not the end of the story.

The book of Romans highlights the painful judgment that fell upon Israel. It says, "Some of their branches have been broken off … They were broken off because of unbelief" (Rom. 11:17, 20).

Praise God that that was not the end of the story; Israel will be reunited with her God.

Isaiah said, concerning Israel, "Can a mother forget the baby at her breast and have no compassion on the child she has borne? Though she may forget I will not forget you! 'See I have engraved you on the palms of my hands; your walls are ever before me'" (Isa. 49:15).

Romans says, "Again I ask: Did they stumble so as to fall beyond recovery? Not at all!" (Rom. 11:11).

In the early days of the tribulation period, during the first campaign, revival will come to the nation of Israel. A symbolic 144,000 will stand as evidence of a huge ingathering of Jewish believers.

JEWISH REVIVAL

A massive Jewish revival is prophesied throughout scripture and has been preached by saints throughout history. It will happen in the end times, just prior to the return of Christ. This is indicated in the book of Luke. Here, Israel is pictured as a fig tree: "Look at the fig tree and all the trees. When they sprout leaves, you can see for yourselves and know that summer is near. Even so, when you see these things happening, you know that the kingdom of God is near ... At that time they will see the Son of man coming in a cloud with power and great glory" (Luke 21:27, 29).

Romans, speaks of the Jewish revival: "I do not want you to be ignorant of this mystery, brothers, so that you may not be conceited: Israel has experienced a hardening in part until the full number of the Gentiles has come in. And so all Israel will be saved, as it is written: 'The deliverer will come from Zion; he will turn godliness away from Jacob. And this is my covenant with them when I take away their sins.' For God's gifts and his call are irrevocable" (Rom. 11:25–29).

Scripture tells us that there is a specific number of gentiles that will be saved, and after that a great multitude of Jews will be converted. God has not forgotten his people. He will fulfill all of his promises to them. His gifts and call toward the Jewish people remain irrevocable.

We read in Zechariah, "And I will pour out on the house of David and the inhabitants of Jerusalem a spirit of grace and of supplication. They will look on me, the one they have pierced, and they will mourn for him as one mourns for an only son" (Zech. 12:10).

"On that day a fountain will be opened to the house of David and the inhabitants of Jerusalem, to cleanse them from sin and impurity" (Zech. 13:1).

It will be a sovereign act of grace that will lead the Jews to sorrow, supplication, and salvation. They will weep when they finally realize that Jesus is their Messiah. They will pray the prayers of supplication. It is likely that millions of Jews will be saved during the tribulation period. The number 144,000 is a symbolic numeral that speaks of this great family.

CHURCH FATHERS SPEAK UP

Many of the church fathers have preached about a Jewish revival at the end of the age. The historical quotes in this section are taken from the book, *The Puritan Hope: Revival and Interpretation of Prophecy*, by Iain H. Murray.

In the eighteenth century, Jonathan Edwards, a revivalist of a movement called the "Great Awakening in American Christianity," wrote, "Nothing is more clearly foretold than this national conversion of the Jews in Romans eleven." [d]

Can you imagine what will happen to the Church around the world when multitudes of Israelites receive Jesus as their Messiah?

Romans 11:15 says, "If the casting away of them be the reconciling of the world, what shall the receiving of them be but life from the dead."

When revival comes to Israel, the Church will also be invigorated to new life.

The early Puritans believed this. In 1652 William Gouge, Edmund Calamy and Simeon Ashe wrote, "The Scripture speaks of a double conversion of the Gentiles, the first before the conversion of the Jews, the second after the conversion of the Jews."[e]

Thomas Boston of The Church of Scotland also preached this message. A sermon recorded from 1716 declares, "Are you longing for a revival to the churches, then pray for the Jews. 'For if the casting away of them be the reconciling of the world; what shall the receiving of them be but life from the dead.' That will be a lively time, a time of great outpouring of the Spirit, that will carry reformation to a greater height than yet has been." [f]

In 1855, Charles Spurgeon preached the following: "I think we do not attach sufficient importance to the restoration of the Jews. We do not think enough of it. But certainly, if there is anything promised in the Bible it is this. The day shall yet come when the Jews, who were the first apostles to the Gentiles, the first missionaries to us who were afar off, shall be gathered in again. Until that shall be, the fullness of the restoration of Israel; their gathering in shall be as life from the dead."[g]

JEWISH REVIVAL COMES DURING WAR

Revival will come to Israel when the nations are gathered around her in a time of war.

Read Zech. 12 and 13:1, and discover the following truths:

1. Israel's revival takes place after Israel has been brought back to her homeland.
2. When the nations gather against her, Jerusalem becomes an immoveable rock. That began in May 1948 and continues today. It will escalate in the future.
3. The nations will conspire against her, but her leaders will rise up with new strength.
4. God will protect Israel supernaturally, and all nations who attack her injure themselves.
5. During the tribulation war, when tanks are in motion and missiles are exploding, God will lift the spiritual veil from Israel's eyes.
6. The people of Israel will begin to weep, repent, and pray as the grace of God floods over them.
7. The Holy Spirit will pour salvation over them, and all the families with their wives will mourn with repentance as they receive a revelation of Jesus as Messiah.

We will discover later in our study that not all of Israel will be saved during this first revival, but God will be persistent with his chosen people. God will continue to bring the Jewish people to salvation.

Chapter Fifteen

Revelation is About Worldwide Revival

After this I looked and there before me was a great multitude that no one could count, from every nation, tribe, people and language, standing before the throne and in front of the Lamb. They were wearing white robes and were holding palm branches in their hands. And they cried out in a loud voice: "Salvation belongs to our God, who sits on the throne, and to the Lamb."
Then one of the elders asked me, "These in white robes—who are they, and where did they come from?" I answered, "Sir, you know." And he said, "These are they who have come out of the great tribulation: they have washed their robes and made them white in the blood of the Lamb." (Rev. 7:9, 13–14)

SUGGESTED READING: REVELATION 7:9–17

CHAPTER TOPICS

1. Revivals that are prophesied
2. Two great revivals that are coming
3. A massive worldwide revival, which will reach all nations
4. Multitudes of new converts, who will stand before God's

throne
5. The persecution that follows the revival
6. A glory explosion in heaven

SOME ARE SLEEPING

AS I'VE TRAVELED THROUGHOUT the United States, I've discovered that an incredible number of Christians do not attend church regularly. There are multitudes of people who love the Lord but do not enjoy the blessings of church life. I do not agree with this practice of not attending church, but I am aware that there are reasons for it.

Many have fallen because of sin, and, as a result, they have become distracted from their devotion to Christ. Others have been wounded by church leaders who are often more legalistic than merciful. Multitudes of people who are spiritually gifted have been overlooked by church leaders. They have been given no opportunity for development and functionality. It is painful and exhausting to sit and listen to leaders whose ministry is not anointed. Many of those leaders function as a cork in a bottle. They make no room for others to mature. Some Christians try for a long time to fit in a church like that, but eventually they feel as though they are drying up. Unfortunately, some decide to put organized church on the shelf.

Others with better attitudes do not have a spiritual church in their community and cannot find a genuine church home. The truth is, it may be wrong, but there are many reasons why multitudes of believers do not attend church. Thousands of genuine Christians are part of a sleeping army that will rise again in the hour of God's power.

REVIVAL IS PROPHESIED

The great tribulation will activate the end-time church. When discouraged and distracted believers see the hand of God at work, they will leave the prodigal pigpen, be washed clean, and rise to stand at his side. Many will repent of lukewarm lifestyles, and God will forgive them and put a new fire in their souls. The tribulation church will rise with unity as well as power, because leaders will function at a different level of spiritual anointing, and God's people will follow. This will happen in every nation on earth.

"There before me was a great multitude that no one could count, from every nation, tribe people and language, standing before the throne and in front of the Lamb. They were wearing white robes" (Rev. 7:9).

An excited elder in heaven asked John who these people were and answered his own question: "These are they who have come out of the great tribulation; they have washed their robes and made them white in the blood of the Lamb" (Rev. 7:14).

TWO REVIVALS

Revelation 7 reveals two great revivals. First will come the revival of the 144,000 redeemed Jews. Immediately following that revival, the gentiles will experience a revival so large that it will be impossible for the people on earth to count the number of souls that are saved. In contrast to those who will have participated in the first revival, these will not be Jews, but gentile Christians from every nation, tribe, and people.

The salvation of thousands of Jews will have a spin-off effect upon the rest of the world. Breaking news of revival in Israel will warm the hearts of the members of Christ's church around the world. Holy Spirit flames will become roaring fires as Christians witness the nation of Israel receiving Jesus as Messiah. Great faith will fall upon the earth, and passion for Jesus and his kingdom will launch the church into a new level of action.

Millions of supernatural testimonies will become the focus of the day. Every possible vehicle of travel will be busy as gentile and Jewish pilgrims connect for the purposes of God. Jewish evangelists will join gentile evangelists to preach the gospel of the kingdom in every nation. This new excitement will feel like resurrection from the dead. It is foretold in the book of Romans: "If their [The Jewish People's] rejection is the reconciliation of the world, what will their acceptance be but life from the dead?" (Rom. 11:15).

WORLDWIDE REVIVAL

Revival will erupt around the world as God's two historical witnesses, the Jews and the church, partner as one new man. The natural and the wild olive branches will function together as the people of God. The first campaign will have left the world in pain. Billions will be ready to give their lives to God. There will be an open heaven over the earth, and the greatest anointing for salvation will be released.

Many voices of sin, perversion, idolatry, greed, and ungodly entertainment will be silenced because of God's judgments. Many TV networks and media facilitators will no longer function. People who are hurting will be hungry for God. It is not the judgments alone that will catch the attention of the masses; the love and compassion of the saints will soften the hearts of multitudes. The world will witness a great expression of love from Israel and the newly empowered church as well as demonstrations of supernatural signs and wonders. Miracles will follow the preaching of God's word, and multitudes will fall on their knees before the God of heaven.

This revival will be greater than any in previous history. Church buildings will be far too small, and there will not be enough of them. Homes and stadiums will become the most common sites for spiritual gatherings. Every day will bring new purpose and adventure for the spiritual soldiers of the cross. Finally they will see the power of God at the level their hearts have expected. The judgments of the tribulation are dreadful, but they will bring man's greatest blessings. Evangelism will become more important than human survival because saints will understand the book of Revelation. They will know that the window for salvation, like the door on Noah's ark, will soon be shut. For those who enlist in God's army, the joy of the Lord and the call of God to partner with him in the harvest will overpower every pain that they or the human race will suffer.

CHINA EXPERIENCE

Recently, I enjoyed a visit to China. Another pastor and I traveled there to see some Christians and to witness for Christ. In Xian we met a friend who traveled with us and translated for us. Each day we prayed for souls and met with many Chinese people. With only one exception, every person we witnessed to opened their hearts to Christ. We led each in a prayer of salvation. We saw genetic scientists, businessmen, doctors, engineers, university students, and even a communist soldier surrender their lives to Christ. Each day we saw God save people in China. I have traveled to more than thirty-five nations, but I have never experienced such an open heaven over a nation like I did in China. There are many more Christians in China than in any other nation in the world including the United States.

After my encounter there, I can understand how ripe the harvest of the world will be during the tribulation period. We will witness worldwide revival. The evangelism explosion will fulfill Bible prophecy. The number of new Christians will be so large that no one will be able to count them. I can see billions coming to Christ.

REVIVAL BRINGS PERSECUTION

Multitudes will be converted and many will die because of persecution. The book of Revelation is a book of martyrs. We know that many of the new Christians will die because we see them standing before the throne of God in heaven.

In Rev. 7, an elder asks John, "Who are these people who make up this multitude and where have they come from" (Rev. 7:13). The elder answers, "These are they who have come out of the great tribulation; they have washed their robes and made them white in the blood of the Lamb?" (Rev. 7:14).

These are not those who were saved throughout history. This verse establishes a last days revival comprised of souls who have been saved during the great tribulation. The fact that these souls are standing before the throne tells us that they died soon after coming to Christ.

Natural judgments and persecution will claim the lives of many newborn Christians. These people will literally be plucked from the fires of hell, and their momentary trials will be quickly turned into joy.

Many Christians think of Revelation as a frightful time, but they fail to observe the growing crowd in heaven. The Lord is reaping his reward. It is the latter rain, the massive end-time harvest.

STANDING BEFORE THE THRONE

We are not sure if the saints who John saw standing before God's throne will have resurrected bodies at this time. The fact that John saw them standing before the throne clothed in white robes does not mean they had bodies. The souls of the deceased can be seen, and they can function as if they have bodies.

In Luke 16:19–31 Jesus tells the story of two deceased men. Both Lazarus and Abraham are recognized in that scripture passage. The bodies of the men were buried, but their souls were still very functional. They felt pain, recognized each other, talked with each other, and had spiritual body parts such as eyes and tongues. They could drink water, experience comfort, and feel the burning heat of fire. We are given a picture of souls in a fully functional state even though they are without earthly bodies.

EXPERIENCING GLORY

The Lord will pour his blessings on the saints as he gathers them together in the throne room. He will eliminate their pain. We read about the saints in Rev. 7: "They are before the throne of God and serve him night and day in his temple; and he who sits on the throne will spread his tent over them. Never again will they hunger; never again will they thirst. The sun will not beat on them, nor any scorching heat. For the Lamb at the center of the throne will be their shepherd; he will lead them to springs of living water. And God will wipe away every tear from their eyes" (Rev. 7:15–17).

The tribulation will have brought suffering, and everyone will have known hunger, thirst, and scorching heat. The saints will cry out to the Lord, and they will be heard. Once in heaven they will stand before Jesus, their shepherd and king. They will be under the tent of the Lord. No longer will they hunger or thirst, and the sun will not scorch then anymore. They will be comforted from the pains of life. They will have arrived at the land of the living water, and they will be eternally grateful.

ANGELS AND ELDERS REJOICE

The angels and the elders in heaven will rejoice. John wrote, "All the angels were standing around the throne and around the elders and the four living creatures. They fell down on their faces before the throne and worshipped God, saying: 'Amen! Praise and glory and wisdom and thanks and honor and power and strength be to our God for ever and ever. Amen'!" (Rev. 7:11–12).

The entire host of heaven have been, and are now, waiting patiently alongside the Almighty. Elders, angels, and the four living creatures are in unity with the Lord. When they see this harvest of souls standing with them in the throne room, the excitement will be absolutely electric. This is why Jesus died. This great crowd of sons and daughters will justify the longsuffering that heaven and earth have endured throughout the ages. God will have received part of his inheritance—the reward for which the Lamb shed his blood. God loves people; and as they stand before him in robes of brilliant white, all of heaven will fall prostrate to worship the Lamb and the Lord God Almighty.

A BRIEF SUMMARY

Here is a brief summary of the revivals of Rev. 7:

1. There will be a huge revival among the Jews (symbolically 144,000 are saved.)
2. There will be a massive revival of gentiles, who will be saved

from every nation.

3. The number of new Christians will be so large that no human can count them.
4. Multitudes of Jews and gentiles will actually be saved during the tribulation.
5. Jews and gentiles are one in Christ, but the Jewish identity the Jews will be preserved.
6. Together Jews and gentiles will evangelize the world.
7. Most of the new converts will die during the tribulation.
8. Those who die will stand before God and receive their eternal reward.
9. The heavenly host will fall down and worship the Lord when they see this amazing harvest of souls in heaven.

Chapter Sixteen

Revelation is About Explosive Prayer

When he opened the seventh seal, there was silence in heaven for about half an hour. And I saw the seven angels who stand before God, and to them were given seven trumpets.
Another angel, who had a golden censer, came and stood at the altar. He was given much incense to offer, with the prayers of all the saints, on the golden altar before the throne. The smoke of the incense, together with the prayers of the saints, went up before God from the angel's hand.
Then the angel took the censer, filled it with fire from the altar, and hurled it on the earth; and there came peals of thunder, rumblings, flashes of lightning and an earthquake. (Rev. 8:1–5)

Chapter Topics

1. The breaking of the final seal
2. Silence that captivates the heavens
3. The keeper of the altar fire
4. Prayers being answered
5. The shaking of the earth as prayer is answered

THE FINAL SEAL

WHEN JESUS BREAKS THE seventh and final seal on the scroll the details of God's end-time plans will be fully revealed. Until the seventh seal is open, the final acts of God cannot be known. Even though the book of Revelation tells a great deal about the end times, many details remain hidden. That is one of the reasons for such a wide interpretation of doctrine and opinions on the book. Only the Almighty knows the details of the future, and the scroll is still sealed as I write. We only know what has been revealed.

It is will be an awesome moment when the last seal is broken. The last seal is dedicated to God's friends. The opening of each seal will release a powerful statement from heaven. We know that the first four seals will release the four horses of judgment, and the fifth seal will give honor to the martyrs. The breaking of the sixth seal will release more judgments and a trauma that will be like hell on earth. When the seventh seal is removed, the focus of heaven's attention will shift to the prayers of the saints.

God highlights two themes through the breaking of the seven seals: judgments for sinners and endearment for saints. These are incorporated in the prayers of his people.

SILENCE IN HEAVEN

The opening of the scroll will move heaven to a new level. John described a sober hush that filled the throne room as angels, elders, and saints became silent. This was the point of no return.

John's heart was pumping with adrenaline as he tried to understand the dynamics behind the ominous silence. It was amazing; it felt like someone had pushed a button, and the entire universe had stopped.

To our knowledge, this is the only moment in eternity, when heaven will be totally quiet. By order of the Almighty, everything will stand still for half an hour. Even the Seraphim who cry "holy, holy, holy" before the throne day and night will have to restrain themselves. It is a matter of honor. The loudness of the silence will be profound. God appreciates the prayers of the faithful and focuses on the patient suffering and the faith of his children.

Down through the centuries, mothers, fathers, kids, and grandparents have prayed in the face of adversity. Many God-inspired prayers have remained unanswered, but none have fallen to the ground. Prayers have come from nations, leaders, churches, and forsaken ethnic groups. They have come in times of war, famine, and disease. Whenever the human race has groveled in the mire of hopeless suffering and desperate failure, somebody has prayed.

Many prayers have not been answered, but God does not forget. He will have the last word, and when the seventh seal is broken, these prayers will be brought from the files of the fire to be reclaimed for the glory of God. These prayers are crucial and they have earned reverence. As far as the heavens extend, all the way to the horizons of eternity, all will become quiet.

For half an hour, God will look intently at the altar, focused on the prayers that are burning upon it. His thoughts will be on the multitudes who have laid down their lives for him.

God will have waited patiently for the harvest to be ripe, and his people will have waited with him. Many will have suffered because he has been longsuffering. Now, those who have suffered will be honored. The flames will jump higher and sparks will fly, as ancient prayers come to resolve. It is not only fire, but indignation that churns on the altar. Living prayers do not lose passion. Every creature in heaven will look toward the fire. They will hear the inner voice of the Holy Spirit as he speaks worth and value over the prayers. All will stand in awe of the potency of the moment.

These prayers have made it to the throne room because God requested them. Jesus paid the price for their admission, and they have become God's treasures. They are the essence of agreement between man and God, and they are so necessary that without them the great tribulation will not come. Every one of them will now be answered. The zeal of the Lord will finish what has been echoed in prayer. No negotiations can change the outcome.

TRUMPETS GET READY

John watched as the silence ended, movement stirred, and the seven angels prepared themselves. They stood before God, and each received a trumpet, which they would soon blow to release the second wave of judgments. The first campaign was over—severe judgments had fallen, multitudes had been saved, and God's grace toward the rebellious was growing thin. The second campaign was on its way.

Power and anointing rests on the trumpets. They are the holy shofars, the rams' horns of heaven. The seven, knowing their assignment, will hold rank and wait for the Lamb's command.

THE ALTAR OF FIRE

Besides God's throne, the altar of fire is the most notable piece of furniture in the throne room. The furniture in heaven has counterparts in the Jewish temple on earth. Moses was given strict instructions to build the tabernacle according to God's heavenly pattern.

Exodus 37 tells us that the furniture in the Jewish temple was made of acacia wood overlaid with pure gold. The wood represents our humanity, and the gold overlay symbolizes God's divinity. The wood is combustible, but the gold is only made more brilliant by fire. The wood represents man's weakness—it would be consumed by judgment fires. But God covers his people with righteousness, and the saints shine as pure gold. The mystery of the God-man factor can be seen in the wood-gold combination. God's divinity covers man's humanity.

The furniture in heaven's throne room however, is made of solid gold with no wood at all. The frail human element is totally gone there. The prayer altar is made of gold. Only God-inspired prayers find their way to this altar.

THE ANGEL OF THE ALTAR

Revelation 14:18, reads, "Still another angel, who had charge of the fire, came from the altar."

This verse tells us that there is an angel who is in charge of the altar fire. As God draws on specific prayers at set times, the altar angel releases them into action. Sometimes, the answers to prayers are personally delivered by angels, who may bring us a subtle sign or cause a massive shift in the elements of nature. The angels may bring judgment or blessings. They may minister comfort to a single Christian or bring about events that will change an entire nation. Prayer is our agreement with God, and angels turn them into action.

The altar angel is the keeper of the sacred fire.

Recall that we read about him earlier when Isaiah encountered him. "Then one of the seraphs flew to me with a live coal in his hand, which he had taken with tongs from the altar. With it he touched my mouth and said, 'See this has touched your lips; your guilt is taken away and your sin atoned for'" (Isa. 6:6).

This altar angel is one of the four living creatures who worship God around the throne. This is indicated in the same passage of scripture: "Above him were seraphs, each with six wings: With two they covered their faces, with two they covered their feet, and with two they were flying. And they were calling to one another: 'Holy, holy, holy is the Lord Almighty; the whole earth is full of his glory.'" (Isa. 6:2–3).

The seraph is the angel we read about in Rev. 8: "Another angel … stood at the altar … given much incense to offer with the prayers … The prayers went up before God from the angel's hand … the angel took the censer and filled it with fire from the altar, and hurled it on the earth" (Rev. 8:3–5).

Human prayers fuel the fires of heaven, and angels are commissioned to serve the saints. In eternity we will enjoy a working relationship with angels. We have already been working together with them, although for the most part, the angels have been incognito. Our partnership efforts will greatly increase when the great tribulation comes.

TRIBULATION PRAYERS

The church is being prepared for tribulation warfare. Christians will not be mere bystanders who hope to survive the horrors of judgment. They will play a dynamic role in the saving of souls. They will walk in harmony with the Holy Spirit, and he will give understanding. Then the church will rise with prayers of agreement and acts of mercy.

The demise of Satan will unfold as weak humanity prophesies and prays God's will into existence. Evil men will be brought to nothing, and demonic armies will be torn apart. The intercessors cannot fail in their mission, for the Lord is their strength. The end will come, not by any human strength, but by the Spirit of the Lord. There has never been a time of such prophetic cooperation like the Revelation time that looms on the horizon. The altar of fire will be constantly refueled. The altar angel will be working overtime.

A century ago, members of the Moravian church held a prayer meeting that lasted for one hundred years. Their efforts energized one of the greatest mission movements in history.[h]

That intensity will burn again, but this time, the flames will leap much higher.

ACTION FROM THE ALTAR

John watched and, as the half hour of silence ended: "Then the angel took the censer, filled it with fire from the altar, and hurled it on the earth; and there came peals of thunder, rumblings, flashes of lightning and an earthquake" (Rev. 8:5).

As the angel throws prayer fire upon the planet, there will be peals of thunder, rumblings, flashes of lightning, and an earthquake. Angels will fly with lightning speed into position, and the natural elements will find themselves being realigned to play their part in the great judgment. The earth will be traumatized, and will shift on its tectonic plates. Continents will slide as earthquakes shake the earth. Men will look to the skies with fear. Justice will find its way to earth. Out of the holy silence will come an all-consuming fire.

Part Three
The Second campaign

Chapter Seventeen

Revelation is About Trumpets

Then the seven angels who had the seven trumpets prepared to sound them. The first angel sounded his trumpet, and there came hail and fire mixed with blood, and it was hurled down upon the earth. A third of the earth was burned up, a third of the trees were burned up, and all the green grass was burned up.

The second angel sounded his trumpet, and something like a huge mountain, all ablaze, was thrown into the sea. A third of the sea turned into blood, a third of the living creatures in the sea died, and a third of the ships were destroyed.

The third angel sounded his trumpet, and a great star, blazing like a torch, fell from the sky on a third of the rivers and on the springs of water—the name of the star is Wormwood. A third of the waters turned bitter, and many people died from the waters that had become bitter.

The fourth angel sounded his trumpet, and a third of the sun was struck, a third of the moon, and a third of the stars, so that a third of them turned dark. A third of the day was without light, and also a third of the night. (Rev. 8:6–12)

CHAPTER TOPICS

1. The second military campaign from heaven
2. The seven trumpets (with a preview of the last trump)
3. Asteroids and meteors falling from the sky
4. The environment being decimated
5. The drinking water turning poisonous
6. The earth falling into gross darkness

A TWOFOLD MANDATE

WE HAVE LEARNED THAT the first campaign will be led by the four living creatures, who will go on the offensive as the seven seals are broken from the scroll. Two other military campaigns will follow. The three campaigns are marked by seals, trumpets, and bowls. The twofold mandate of the tribulation will begin; the Lord will begin to destroy his enemies and he will rescue those who accept his grace.

In 2 Corinthians we read, "For we are … the aroma of Christ among those who are being saved and those who are perishing. To the one we are the smell of death; to the other, the fragrance of life" (2 Cor. 2:15).

The tribulation will bring life and death, and both will come like speeding trains that stop at a station for only a moment to collect passengers.

THE SECOND CAMPAIGN

Once the first campaign is completed, the scroll will be fully opened, and the blueprints of the book of Revelation will be revealed in detail.

At the start of the second campaign, the seven angels will step forward to lead the battle. As officers directly under Jesus, they will lead the "Battalions of the Lamb." They are archangels, like Michael and Gabriel—princes who rule principalities—and each will command a vast army of angels. The battle they initiate will be more intense than that of the first campaign. Their mission will not be defensive, as it has been for most of man's history. It will be aggressive. They are warriors, and they will be commissioned to avenge the Lamb and secure the interests of heaven. Each is ready to sound his trumpet.

As the edicts of heaven are spoken, the seven angels will expose the demonic powerbase. Then the wicked armies will be drawn out into the open to fight, and they will be no match for the generals of heaven.

THREE THINGS WILL HAPPEN

During the second campaign three things will occur.

1. The church will become more powerful than ever before.
2. Demons will be unrestrained and will manifest their full expression of evil.
3. Ungodly men will do all they can to undermine the Lord and his people.

When every army rises to the height of its power, Jesus will demonstrate that he is King of kings and Lord of lords.

TRUMPETS BLOW

The war cry of the seven trumpets will begin to sound, and fire from heaven will follow. The trumpets will signal the release of a measured, but powerful, attack upon the earth. Heaven's vengeance will come in systematic stages, but eventually full retribution will fall.

The seventh and last trumpet is very unique. When it sounds, the final days of the tribulation battle and the last campaign will be set in motion. In the days of the sounding of that trumpet, the Lord himself will come to earth.

THE LAST TRUMP: CHRIST'S RETURN

The seventh trumpet is the last trumpet. In the days of the seventh trumpet, the bowls of God's wrath will be poured upon the earth. Then the Lord Jesus will return to earth. He will not come at the beginning of the tribulation, nor will he come at the blowing of the first trumpet. He will come at the blowing of the last trump.

Revelation says, "In the days when the seventh angel is about to sound his trumpet, the mystery of God will be accomplished, just as he announced to his servants the prophets" (Rev. 10: 7).

That mystery is the return of the Lord and the resurrection of those who are in Christ.

We read in the book of Corinthians, "Listen, I tell you a mystery: We will not all sleep, but we will all be changed—in a flash, in the twinkling of an eye, *at the last trumpet*. For the trumpet will sound, the dead will be raised and we will be changed ... Therefore, my dear brothers, stand firm. Let nothing move you. Always give yourselves fully to the work of the Lord, because you know that your labor in the Lord is not in vain" (1 Cor. 15:51–58; italics added).

We read about the second coming in Thessalonians: "For the Lord himself will come down from heaven, with a loud command, with the voice of the archangel and with the trumpet call of God, and the dead in Christ will rise first. After that, we who are still alive and are left will be caught up together with them in the clouds to meet the Lord in the air. And so we will be with the Lord forever" (2 Thess. 4:16–17).

Again, we discover that the trumpet is blown.

RAGE OF THE NATIONS

The seven trumpets (the second campaign) will bring judgments on the earth that will be more intense than the judgments brought on by the seven seals (the first campaign), but the seven bowls (the third campaign) will bring judgments that will be even more devastating. The nations will be in the valley of decision. They will have to choose to bow before King Jesus or be destroyed.

An ominous warning was prophesied in the book of the Psalms. It reveals the disposition of the nations and what their options will be when the seven trumpets sound. It says:

"The nations conspire and the peoples plot in vain? The kings of the earth take their stand and the rulers gather together against the Lord and against his anointed one. "Let us break their chains," they say, "and throw off their fetters." The One enthroned in heaven laughs; the Lord scoffs at them. Then he rebukes them in his anger and terrifies them in his wrath saying, "I have installed my king on Zion, my holy hill." I will proclaim the decree of the Lord: He said to me, "You are my Son; today I have become your Father. Ask of me and I will make the nations your inheritance, the ends of the earth your possession. You will rule them with an iron sceptre; you will dash them to pieces like pottery." Therefore you kings be wise; be warned, you rulers of the earth. Serve the Lord with fear and rejoice with trembling. Kiss the Son, lest he be angry and you be destroyed in your way, for his wrath can flare up in a moment. Blessed are all who take refuge in him" (Ps. 2:1–12).

The warning goes out to the nations. The day of choice was prophesied long ago. Now the peoples of the earth are in the valley of decision, and eternity hangs in the balance.

DEMOLITION

The first three judgments of the second campaign will bring asteroids and meteors from the sky. The environment will be devastated. Instead of creation, the natural world will experience de-creation. The natural world will be pummeled, torn apart, and ruined.

John wrote that when the first angel sounded his trumpet, "there came hail and fire mixed with blood, and it was hurled down upon the earth" (Rev, 8:6).

Suddenly, flaming meteors will break through the atmosphere. An asteroid cloud will pass too close to the planet, and billions of rocks will burst into flames, gathering speed as gravity sucks them toward earth. It will be a hailstorm, not of wind and ice, but of rocks, fire, and brimstone.

Years ago my family and I experienced a dangerous hailstorm in Niagara Falls, Canada. Chunks of ice about the size of golf balls hurled down for about five minutes. The toll was far-reaching. The damage soon reached many millions of dollars. Niagara Falls is an agricultural region with many fruit orchards. Within moments, entire crops were ruined. Hundreds of cars required extensive bodywork, and homes needed re-roofing. The shingles on our roofs were destroyed in minutes. Property damage of all kinds resulted in huge insurance claims. Companies doled out the money without hesitation because the damage was so intense. Relatively speaking, it was a small catastrophe, but the cost was nevertheless, significant. The cost of global judgments during the second campaign will be more than anyone can estimate.

BRIMSTONE

John wrote, "A third of the earth was burned up, a third of the trees were burned up, and all the green grass was burned up." (Rev. 8:7)

Our Niagara experience involved ice, not rock and fire. The Revelation hail will crush everything in its path and set the world on fire. It will be so widespread that it will hit every region of the planet, destroying a third of the earth's environment. While only a third of the trees will be destroyed, all of the green grass will be burned. The hail will be hit-and-miss, but the fires will go everywhere. The brimstone will drive toward the earth from space, and it will come from one specific direction. So it stands to reason that the world will have to rotate before the other side will be hit. Since the catastrophe will strike the entire world, the storm must last for hours with spurts of lesser and greater intensity. In the end, one third of the planet's vegetation will be flattened and a third of the earth will be burnt to a crisp.

The scripture is even more descriptive. It says that the hail and fire will be mixed with blood (see Rev. 8:7). This indicates that multitudes will die as flaming shrapnel strikes them. No wartime bombing raid compares with the intensity of this preemptive strike.

During the Second World War, Europeans were terrified when the bombing campaigns begun. My father remembered the awful droning noise of Nazi buzz bombs circling high above the city of London. When the noise stopped, the people knew that the internal engines in the bombs had shut off, and the shell would fall.

One of my aunts was killed during such a bombing raid. She went into shock as bombs whistled around her in a hospital bed. By the time the nurses reached her, she was gone.

Many who survive the initial downpour of flaming meteors will die from fear, and others will die from toxic poison or starvation.

THE ASTEROID

"The second angel sounded his trumpet, and something like a huge mountain, all ablaze, was thrown into the sea." (Rev. 8:8).

When the second archangel blows his trumpet, a huge asteroid, the size of a mountain, will plummet into the ocean. Many meteors, will hit the planet. One of them will be several miles wide and will burst into flames as it drives through the earth's atmosphere. It will slam into the ocean, and its effects will be beyond most people's wildest imagination.

I have seen blockbuster movies with this theme. In *Armageddon,* a huge asteroid is set on a collision course with the planet, but Harry Stamper (played by Bruce Willis) and his team land on it while it is still out in space. They blow it apart with nuclear bombs. It explodes into pieces, and the larger segments are diverted enough to veer past the earth.

When the asteroid mentioned in Revelation is heading toward the earth, Harry Stamper will not be able to save us. I think there will be too many asteroids to deal with. All of man's efforts will not be able to stop or divert this judgment.

Another movie I saw was called *Deep Impact*. In that movie, a huge asteroid splashes into the Atlantic Ocean. Although the sudden impact occurs hundreds of miles out to sea, it has the power of a thousand nuclear explosions. It produces a tsunami wave that quickly reaches the eastern seaboard of the United States. The entire city of New York is instantly leveled as a mountain of water smashes into it. The oncoming wave is taller than the Empire State building, and its destruction stretches hundreds of miles inland. An asteroid the size of a mountain would devastate every coastal city that borders the Atlantic.

Although the movie portrayed the catastrophe well, it will be much worst in real life. The depth of human pain will be far more intense than what the film portrayed. The movie also failed to expose the resultant trauma in the sea and in the atmosphere. Besides the devastation that hits coastal cities, the ocean will suffer immensely.

"A third of the sea turned into blood, a third of the living creatures in the sea died, and a third of the ships were destroyed" (Rev. 8:-9) A third of all ocean-going vessels will immediately be crushed, capsized, and destroyed. Nuclear fallout will be produced, sending radioactive poison through the water. Intense shockwaves will rifle through the depths, killing everything within hundreds of miles.

One-third of all living things in the ocean will die. The sea will turn to blood as death permeates its realm and bodies of all sorts float to the surface. Soon the shorelines will be piled high with rotting carcasses. The fallout will bring disease and gross biological pollution.

WORMWOOD

"The third angel sounded his trumpet, and a great star, blazing like a torch, fell from the sky on a third of the rivers and on the springs of water—the name of the star is Wormwood"(Rev. 8:10).

When the third angel sounds his trumpet, another massive asteroid will break into the atmosphere. This one will burn so profusely that John described it as a great star and a blazing torch. Due to a lack of structural integrity, the asteroid will suddenly explode in midair, shattering into billions of pieces. The sky will be impregnated with spewing sulfur, heavy metals, and poisonous chemicals, which will result in lethal acid rain. Deadly ash and poisonous grit will fall to the earth covering forests, plains, mountains, and valleys. Worst of all, it will clog streams and poison the surface water.

A third of the waters turned bitter, and many people died from the waters that had become bitter" (Rev. 8:11). Dark rain clouds will fill the sky as flaming rocks heat the lakes and oceans. Steam and excessive evaporation will billow into the air. The steam will mix with ash and smoke and record rainfalls will wash even more pollutants into the rivers and lakes. The ground water will be totally fouled, and even freshwater springs will begin to percolate with deadly toxins.

The exploding star is called "wormwood." The name comes from the Greek word meaning undrinkable. Wherever wormwood's ash and soot touch down, the drinking water will be ruined. The ecosystems will be decimated beyond all natural means of recovery. This will be far worse than any oil spill or industrial dumping catastrophe.

Chaos and panic will grip the globe as people everywhere die from thirst or from drinking toxic water. Water purification plants and distillation systems cannot keep up with the demand, and much of what is available will be sold on the black market. Only those with vast amounts of money or those who find special privilege will secure a reliable source of water.

GROSS DARKNESS

The fourth angel sounded his trumpet, and a third of the sun was struck, a third of the moon, and a third of the stars, so that a third of them turned dark. A third of the day was without light, and also a third of the night. (Rev. 8:6–12)

The fourth angel will blow his trumpet, and a black shadow—a darkness that is a consequence of steam, smoke, and ash left behind by the asteroids—will cover the earth. Adding to the devastation, active volcanoes will begin to erupt because of the earthquakes. More ash and smoke will travel around the globe.

When Mount St. Helens in Washington exploded, a dark cloud could be seen in Japan within a few days. Scientists tell us that it takes seven years for the air to be completely rid of the pollution from one volcanic eruption.

The ancient city of Pompeii sat in the foothills of Mount Vesuvius. When it exploded, the entire city was buried. *Encyclopedia Britannica* describes the destruction as follows:

> The whole city was overwhelmed by the great eruption of Vesuvius, A.D. 79. Pompeii was merely covered with a bed of substances, cinders, small stones and ashes, which fell in a dry state. The whole of the super incumbent mass, attaining to an average thickness from 18 to 20 ft., was the product of one eruption. The materials may be divided generally into two distinct strata, the one consisting principally of cinders and small volcanic stones, and the other and uppermost layer of fine white ash. From the number of skeletons discovered, about 2,000 persons may have perished in the city itself.[i]

When Vesuvius erupted, the people in Pompeii died instantly so the excavations reveal amazing details. When the city was destroyed, the people were caught off-guard. The place was frozen in time. Food and table settings were left in mealtime positions. People who had died in there sleep were found lying in their beds. The eruption happened so quickly that they had no opportunity to wake and run, and even if they had been awake, they would not have been able to outrun the spewing dust clouds from the volcano that traveled toward them at speeds of two hundred miles per hour.

The asteroid shower described in Revelation will be far more devastating than a dozen volcanoes. It will cause a third of the earth's atmosphere to be smothered with a blanket of smoke. During the day, the light of the sun will be blocked from a third of the earth, and at night the moon and stars will be hidden from a third of the planet.

A depression far darker than the sky will grip the hearts of people. Spiritual "cabin fever" will invade humanity. In Canada people often stay indoors during the cold winter months. For some, the snow and frigid weather are best viewed through the window of a warm home. But after a few months of staying indoors, folks are negatively affected. The lack of fresh air and outdoor activity causes them to become irritable and depressed, which creates anger, panic, and domestic violence. The darkness of the tribulation will be far more traumatic than any Canadian winter. The world will suffer intense cabin fever, and despair will cover the human race.

The physical darkness will be a reflection of humanity's spiritual condition. God will be showing mankind a mirror image of himself, and it will be far more terrible for those who do not know the Lord. Severe trials will uncover our frailty as well as the source of our security. Some will cry out to God in humble repentance, and they will find him. Others will curse and scream in anger. Both groups will stand or fall before the living God. Those who refuse to kiss his Son will find no path of escape.

It would appear that things could not get worse, but this is not even the end of the second campaign. Things will become much worse. It is easy to understand that another great revival will be on its way. More people will begin to cry out to God for mercy.

Chapter Eighteen

Revelation is About Three Woes

As I watched, I heard an eagle that was flying in midair call out in a loud voice: "Woe! Woe! Woe to the inhabitants of the earth, because of the trumpet blasts about to be sounded by the other three angels!" (Rev. 8:13)
The fifth angel sounded his trumpet, and I saw a star that had fallen from the sky to the earth. The star was given the key for the shaft of the Abyss. When he opened the Abyss, smoke rose from it like the smoke from a gigantic furnace. The sun and sky were darkened by the smoke from the Abyss. (Rev. 9:1–2)

CHAPTER TOPICS

1. The eagle prophet
2. Middle heaven
3. The warning of the three woes
4. The four kinds of hell
5. The bottomless pit called the Abyss
6. The one with the keys

AN UNEXPECTED PROPHET

JOHN WAS IN SHOCK because of the destruction he had seen and because he knew that these events were not preventable. He must have been wondering if people would believe him when he shared the vision or if they would think that he was just a doomsday prophet whose emotional passions had run away with him. Suddenly, a prophetic messenger declared that the situation would get much worse.

He wrote, "I heard an eagle that was flying in midair call out in a loud voice: 'Woe! Woe! Woe to the inhabitants of the earth, because of the trumpet blasts about to be sounded by the other three angels" (Rev. 8:13).

John had already seen great disasters ravage the earth during the first part of the tribulation, and now he witnessed an eagle warning of three "woes" That would be much worse.

THE EAGLE

The eagle John saw was probably one of the four living creatures, as they are anointed with several mantels of service. This time the seraph will come as an eagle prophet, not a humble man, a servant ox, or a lion ruler, and he will bring a dramatic warning. He has eyes to see what is coming and wings to travel through the realm of the spirit. He will scream with the voice of the eagle, and a fear will rip the skies.

The Lord will inform the good and the bad that extreme horror is coming. The word is a sword that pierces the darkness. Hebrews 4:12 tells us that "the Word of God divides soul and spirit, joints and marrow." It cuts to the depth of one's being. Our response to it will bring blessings or judgment. It will reveal our loyalties and determine our destiny.

MIDAIR

The eagle flies in midair. Middle-air, or mid-heaven, is also called the second heaven.

Paul told us, "I know a man in Christ who fourteen years ago was caught up to the third heaven" (2 Cor. 12:2).

If there is a third heaven, then logic dictates that there is also a second and a first heaven. Theologians generally concur that the first heaven is earth's atmosphere and the third heaven is where God's throne room is. The second heaven is a realm between the throne room and earth's atmosphere. When angels leave the presence of God with a mission to serve mankind, they must first pass through middle-heaven. This is where Satan and his fallen angels dwell.

Derek Prince, the late international Bible teacher wrote, "It seems clear to me that even fallen angels still maintain their dwelling place somewhere in 'the heavenly places' (Ephesians 6:12)—although not in 'the third heaven' where God dwells (2 Corinthians 12:2-4)."[j]

We get a glimpse of angels fighting in middle heaven when we read the book of Daniel: "Daniel ... your words were heard and I have come to respond to them. But the prince of the Persian kingdom resisted me twenty-one days. Then Michael, one of the chief princes came to help me, because I was detained there with the king of Persia" (Dan. 10:12–14).

It is likely that the angel talking with Daniel was Gabriel. He was sent from heaven with an answer to prayer on the first day that Daniel prayed. For twenty-one days, he was resisted somewhere in the second heaven by an evil spirit identified as the Prince of Persia. Finally, Michael the archangel came to his defense, and he was able to break through enemy lines and reach Daniel.

John watched the eagle of Revelation fly through the second heaven and announce the warning of the three woes, and he knew that demons, angels, and spiritual people would hear the eagle's prophecy.

THE FIRST WOE

As John watched, as a new kind of terror was about to come to earth in three distinct waves. These are the trilogy of woes, which heaven prophesies that all should heed. In a sense, the eagle–angel will warn us to brace yourselves and prepare for three judgments that are far worse than anything you have seen so far.

The three woes will be attacks from demonic beings who will be given license to terrorize humanity. The first woe is a demon hoard that will rise from the Abyss. (Rev. 9:3-12)

HELL, PRESENT AND ETERNAL

Hell has at least four applications:

1. The first hell is extensive trauma on earth that feels like a living hell.
2. The second hell is a temporary restraining place for demons. It is called the Abyss or the bottomless pit.
3. Third hell is in Hades. It is the waiting place of torment for unrighteous people. They dwell on the other side of a great gulf from a place called Abraham's bosom. See Luke 16:19–31.
4. The fourth hell is the eternal lake of fire that was made for the devil and his angels. Humans who side with Satan will also go there. We will say more about this hell later in the book.

THE ABYSS

Abyss is a Greek word meaning "bottomless." The abyss is a prison where demonic creatures are restrained, but it is more than that.

The NIV Study Bible notes say that the Abyss is "conceived of as the subterranean abode of demonic hordes (see Rev.20:1; Luke 8:31). The Greek word means 'very deep' or 'bottomless.'"[k]

Many angels who defected are in this place of darkness and fire called the Abyss. Jude said, "And the angels who did not keep their positions of authority but abandoned their own home—these he has kept in darkness, bound with everlasting chains for judgment on the great day" (Jude 1: 6).

Demons on the earth know the terrors of the Abyss, and they hate it. When Jesus cast the demons out of a man ... "they begged him repeatedly not to order them to go into the Abyss" (Luke 8:31).

Once, when Jesus was about to cast the demons out of a man they shouted, "What do you want with us Son of God. Have you come to torture us before the appointed time?" (Matt. 8:29)

They know of the punishment that awaits them.

HADES IS HELL TOO

As we studied earlier, sinful people are also waiting in a place of torment.

We read, "For if God did not spare angels when they sinned, but sent them to hell, putting them into gloomy dungeons to be held for judgment ... if he condemned the cities of Sodom and Gomorrah by burning them to ashes, and made an example of what is going to happen to the ungodly ... if this is so, then the Lord knows how to rescue godly men from trials and to hold the unrighteous for the day of judgment, while continuing their punishment" (2 Pet. 2:4, 6, 9).

Fallen angels and people are held in gloomy dungeons until the final day of judgment. It appears that they are not kept in the same hell during this time. Angels are in the Abyss, and humans are in Hades.

From the cross, Jesus' went to Abraham's bosom or paradise. There he preached to the righteous captives as well as to those who had disobeyed long ago who were on the other side of the gulf. Those in Paradise received his message, and when Jesus rose from the dead they went with him. "When he ascended on high, he led captives in his train" (Eph. 4: 8).

Chapter Nineteen

Revelation Is About the First Woe: A Cloud of Demons

And out of the smoke locust came down upon the earth and were given power like that of scorpions of the earth. They were told not to harm the grass of the earth or any plant or tree, but only those people who did not have the seal of God on their foreheads. They were not given power to kill them, but only to torture them for five months. And the agony they suffered was like that of a sting of a scorpion when it strikes a man. During those days men will seek death, but not find it; they will long to die, but death will elude them.

The locusts looked like horses prepared for battle. On their heads they wore something like crowns, and their faces resembled human faces. Their hair was like woman's hair, and their teeth were like lions' teeth. They had breastplates like breastplates of iron, and the sound of their wings was like the thundering of many horses and chariots rushing into battle. They had tails and stings like scorpions, and in their tails they had power to torment people for five months.

They had as king over them the angel of the Abyss, whose name in Hebrew is Abaddon, and in Greek Apollyon. The first woe is past; the other two are yet to come. (Rev. 9:3–12)

Since Jesus died, the place of torment in Hades continues to fill u
but Abraham's bosom is now empty. Paul tells us, "To be absent fro
the body is to be present with the Lord" (2 Cor. 5:8).

Now when the redeemed die, their spirits go directly to God
throne room. There they wait for resurrection day when they wil
return to earth to be reunited with their bodies.

HE HAS THE KEYS

Jesus said, "I hold the keys of death and Hades" (Rev. 1:18).

He has all authority in heaven and earth, even authority over hell, and that includes Hades, the Abyss and the lake of fire.

Jesus uses the keys to unlock Hades and take the Old Testament saints to heaven. He will also unlock the Abyss at three important times in the future. He will choose one of the angels who came to earth during the angel battle we referred to in chapter 10 (see the section called "A Drop Zone for Angels"). To this angel, he will give the key to the Abyss. The angel will unlock the Abyss, and a horde of demons will be released. Among them, a demon king named Apollyon will come.

At the beginning of the millennium Jesus will send an angel to unlock the Abyss and Satan will be chained up and thrown into it (Rev. 20: 1-3).

After a thousand years have passed Jesus will send an angel to unlock the Abyss so that Satan can be released for a season before he is sent to the lake of fire (Rev. 20:7-10).

Whichever hell we speak of, it is never a kingdom where Satan is in control over other beings. It is a prison designed for punishment and that means that Satan is punished there. He will be bound in chains.

Since Jesus died, the place of torment in Hades continues to fill up, but Abraham's bosom is now empty. Paul tells us, "To be absent from the body is to be present with the Lord" (2 Cor. 5:8).

Now when the redeemed die, their spirits go directly to God's throne room. There they wait for resurrection day when they will return to earth to be reunited with their bodies.

HE HAS THE KEYS

Jesus said, "I hold the keys of death and Hades" (Rev. 1:18).

He has all authority in heaven and earth, even authority over hell, and that includes Hades, the Abyss and the lake of fire.

Jesus uses the keys to unlock Hades and take the Old Testament saints to heaven. He will also unlock the Abyss at three important times in the future. He will choose one of the angels who came to earth during the angel battle we referred to in chapter 10 (see the section called "A Drop Zone for Angels"). To this angel, he will give the key to the Abyss. The angel will unlock the Abyss, and a horde of demons will be released. Among them, a demon king named Apollyon will come.

At the beginning of the millennium Jesus will send an angel to unlock the Abyss and Satan will be chained up and thrown into it (Rev. 20: 1-3).

After a thousand years have passed Jesus will send an angel to unlock the Abyss so that Satan can be released for a season before he is sent to the lake of fire (Rev. 20:7-10).

Whichever hell we speak of, it is never a kingdom where Satan is in control over other beings. It is a prison designed for punishment and that means that Satan is punished there. He will be bound in chains.

Chapter Nineteen

Revelation is About the First Woe: A Cloud of Demons

And out of the smoke locust came down upon the earth and were given power like that of scorpions of the earth. They were told not to harm the grass of the earth or any plant or tree, but only those people who did not have the seal of God on their foreheads.
They were not given power to kill them, but only to torture them for five months. And the agony they suffered was like that of a sting of a scorpion when it strikes a man. During those days men will seek death, but not find it; they will long to die, but death will elude them.
The locusts looked like horses prepared for battle. On their heads they wore something like crowns, and their faces resembled human faces. Their hair was like woman's hair, and their teeth were like lions' teeth. They had breastplates like breastplates of iron, and the sound of their wings was like the thundering of many horses and chariots rushing into battle. They had tails and stings like scorpions, and in their tails they had power to torment people for five months.
They had as king over them the angel of the Abyss, whose name in Hebrew is Abaddon, and in Greek Apollyon. The first woe is past; the other two are yet to come. (Rev. 9:3–12)

CHAPTER TOPICS

1. The opening of the Abyss
2. The dreadful smoke
3. The demons that God uses to judge people
4. Torment for some and protection for others
5. The patience of God and the resolve of the Lamb

UNHOLY SMOKE

I WISH I DID NOT need to tell the story of these three woes. They are nightmarish. When the angel of God unlocks the Abyss, a cloud of smoke will billow forth like that from a huge furnace. The Abyss has an unusual entrance. It is like a chimney or shaft that reaches forever downward.

The smoke that will erupt from its fires will be sulfurous and black. The Abyss is a dungeon of pain like Hades, which we studied earlier (see Luke 16:24).

When the smoke comes, it will block the sun and sky. It is a literal smoke that will be seen in the earth's atmosphere, but it brings another kind of smoke—a spiritual darkness that will cover the globe. This will follow the great meteor shower, so the sky will already be dark with smoke and ash, and the malaise will only be worsened.

The spiritual darkness will be less recognizable, but far more severe, than the physical smoke. The light of God will be blocked out, and the sky, the provision of his grace, will be hidden from view. As is their mission, demons already blind the minds of people so they cannot see the light of God.

"The god of this age has blinded the minds of unbelievers, so that they cannot see the light of the Gospel" (2 Co. 4:4).

Fear, anguish, and torment are strongest when men lose sight of God. Demons block faith from reaching the hearts of people whenever and wherever they are able. Then hope is gone. Such will be the effect of the smoke that billows from the Abyss.

DEMONS LIKE LOCUSTS

Out of the smoke will come an army of demons. Evil spirits come in different forms, and these are like locusts. Spirits, are not usually visible; nevertheless, they are real.

Some theologians believe that the locusts spoken of by the prophet Joel were demon spirits that were sent as judgments upon Israel. Joel wrote, "What the locust swarms have left the great locusts have eaten; what the great locusts have left the young locusts have eaten; what the young locusts have left other locusts have eaten" (Joel 1:4).

Joel also prophesied to Israel that these judgments would be removed and God would restore their losses: "I will repay you for the years the locusts have eaten—the great locusts and the young locusts, the other locusts and the locust swarm—my great army that I sent among you" (Joel 2:25).

When Jesus walked the towns of Galilee or crossed the hills of Judea, he healed the sick and cast out demons. He restored to many the years that the locusts had eaten. He has done this many times since, through his servants. He will do it again, even more extensively, at the end of the age.

SCORPIONS

The Abyss demons will come with terrible power. Their mission will be to torment people with something like a scorpion's sting—designed not to kill, but to torture. Among approximately five hundred species of scorpions, many do not kill people; rather, they inflict a sting like that of a bee or wasp. Some scorpions have venom that is strong enough to kill a human.

According to the *Encyclopedia Britannica,* "Some are harmless. Not so with species whose poison is neurotoxic. Here the symptoms resemble poisoning with strychnine. The sting produces sharp pain, followed by numbness of the limb; speech becomes difficult; discharge of saliva is copious; the patient becomes restless; breathing is hard and death is not uncommon."[1]

Three times the scripture tells us that the locust demons will sting like scorpions. Perhaps the symptoms will be like those of the shingles or some other painful rash that attacks the human nervous system. People will writhe in agony and want to die, but they will be too afraid to commit suicide. They will live, but they will be in torment.

I WANT TO DIE

The plague of demonic torment will be absolutely dreadful. The Bible says, "During those days men will seek death, but will not find it; they will long to die, but death will elude them" (Rev. 9:6).

Many will lie in hospital beds or curl up on the floor of their homes wishing for death. The physical pain will be excruciating, but the spiritual torment will be worse. Demonic despair will grip the minds of those who do not have the seal of God on their foreheads. Those who do not have the mind of Christ will fall prey to lying spirits, nightmares, and horrible hallucinations. People will lose their minds, and mental and emotional breakdown will follow.

PROTECTION FOR THE FAITHFUL

So far in our verse by verse study of Revelation, we have found no mention of any Christians being raptured from the earth. The saints will be alive on earth when the locust demons invade; they will, however, have divine protection. The Lord will protect his people with his divine seal, and the locust demons will not harm them. The seal, which is a spiritual mark, will be placed on their foreheads.

Demons will know who has the seal and will not inflict those people with their poisons. Evil spirits will never be in charge during the time of the great tribulation; rather, they will be used by God to bring judgment.

In the same way, in the Old Testament, we learn that God used ungodly nations to judge his people. That is what happened when Israel was conquered by the Babylonians. We read: "And the nations will know that the people of Israel went into exile for their sin, because they were unfaithful to me. So I hid my face from them and handed them over to their enemies and they all fell by the sword" (Ezek. 39:23).

Likewise, God will use demons as judgments against ungodly people during the last days. The saints, however, will stay healthy while the rest of humanity suffers from disease and torment. This will stand as a testimony for the world to see. Many will not want to admit that God is with his people, but those who do will repent and come to Christ. Once again, the church will have an amazing opportunity to minister compassion to the world. God will have set the stage, and the battle lines will be clear; those who will be holy will be more holy, and those who will be unholy will be more unholy (see Rev. 22:11).

A DETAILED DESCRIPTION OF DEMONS

We do not know if people in the tribulation will be able to see these demons, but John saw them. He described them to us in great detail. The word *ghost* is the old English word for spirit. Some of Hollywood's depiction of ghosts or spirits may not be far from the truth. Spirits can take on various forms, and they can be visible. Luke 16:23 gives us an example of spirits recognizing each other in the afterlife. The spirits were talking with each other, and they felt comfort and pain. They had eyes and tongues. Some were hot and thirsty. Spirits or ghosts seem to have the shape and all of the parts that their physical bodies had when they were alive.

I have known a number of people who have seen demons, although I have never seen a being that I recognized as such. I have heard many unusual descriptions. Long before I wrote this book one friend told me that the demon they saw looked like a huge locust, and it moved across the ceiling of their room.

The demons John saw looked like horses covered in armor, prepared for war. They had human faces with long hair like a woman's. They had fanged teeth, golden crowns, and wings and tails like that of scorpions, complete with stingers. When the time comes, if people actually see these creatures, their trauma will be greatly increased.

When the demons come, scripture says that the sound of their wings will thunder like horses and chariots rushing into battle (Rev. 9:11). It will be dreadful.

FIVE MONTHS OF PAIN

The demons will torment people for five months and then their power will be removed. Each trauma of the great tribulation will have a limited time—each will start, complete its course, and stop. This is God's way of giving opportunity for repentance. Each event will be another warning, and people everywhere will be commanded to bow their knees to Jesus. This may seem to be cruel and inhumane, but in view of the eternal picture, it is extremely gracious. Momentary fear and pain is a gift if it leads to eternal life. Intermittent judgments are a demonstration of God's mercy and patience. He refuses to wipe out the world in one swift blow. His Spirit strives with man and, with amazing patience, he continues to reach humanity. Many who insist on stubborn rebellion during the tribulation will finally yield to Christ; too many, however, will still refuse.

APOLLYON

Leading the locust demons will be a dark lord who will, for a moment of time, rule the world. His name, which means "destruction," is Abaddon in Hebrew and Apollyon in Greek. He is the angel of the Abyss—the antichrist, the beast. Take note of Rev. 17:18: "The beast which you saw, once was, now is not, and will come out of the Abyss and go to his destruction."

Revelation has much to say about this evil creature. We will explain Apollyon, or the beast- which is his more common name- further in our study.

The attack of the demon cloud under the direction of Apollyon will be the first woe. The other two woes will also involve demonic creatures. That is why they are called the three woes and why they are singled out as such dreadful judgments.

The scripture says, "The first woe is past; two other woes are yet to come" (Rev. 9:12).

JESUS IS SERIOUS

At this point in our study, we have just passed the halfway point of the second campaign, and the armies of heaven are resolved to complete the judgments and to bless the people of God with their full reward.

After viewing the judgments thus far, it is hard to imagine that things on earth will become worse, but they will; then eventually, they will get much better. Jesus will be the conquering king. His rule and domain are not negotiable. The world has received his kindness for thousands of years, but justice and retribution must come as well.

Jesus spoke of himself when he said, "The stone the builders rejected has become the capstone" (Luke 20:17).

The next verse reads, "Everyone who falls on that stone will be broken to pieces, but he on whom it falls will be crushed" (Luke 20:18).

Chapter Twenty

Revelation is About the Second Woe

I heard a voice coming from the four horns … It said to the sixth angel who had the trumpet, "Release the four angels who are bound at the great river Euphrates." And the four angels who had been kept ready for this very hour and day and month and year were released to kill a third of mankind.

The number of the mounted troops was two hundred million. I heard their number. The hoses and riders I saw in my vision looked like this: Their breastplates were fiery red, dark blue and yellow as sulfur. The heads of the horses resembled the heads of lions, and out of their mouth came fire, smoke and sulfur. A third of mankind was killed by the three plagues of fire, smoke and sulfur that came out of their mouths. The power of the horses was in their mouths and in their tails; for their tails were like snakes, having heads with which they inflict injury.

They rest of mankind that were not killed by these plagues still did not repent of the work of their hands; they did not stop worshipping demons, and idols of gold, silver, bronze, stone and wood—idols that cannot see or hear or walk. Nor did they repent of their murders, their magic arts, their sexual immorality or their thefts. (Rev. 9:13–21)

CHAPTER TOPICS

1. Horns of power
2. The blowing of the sixth trumpet
3. The four demon lords
4. The world at war with Israel
5. A billion people dying
6. A description of the army and their weapons
7. The stubborn heart of humanity
8. The proliferation of the occult

THE HORNS OF THE ALTAR

"THE SIXTH ANGEL SOUNDED and I heard a voice coming from the horns of the golden altar that is before God" (Rev. 9:13).

The second campaign will be more than halfway complete when the sixth archangel blows his trumpet and the second woe is released. A voice will speak from the horns of the fiery altar. It is the voice of Jesus, who has gathered the prayers of his people, which were spoken long ago, but have waited patiently for the day when their answers would come. When the sixth angel blows the trumpet, he will be given further instructions.

Horns symbolize power; they are part of the altar because prayer has power. We read about horns of power throughout the scriptures. Revelation says, "The ten horns you saw were ten kings" (Rev. 17:12).

I that scripture, horns represent kings who wield great power and authority. The altar of prayer is a tool of power. Horns have been set on the corners of prayer altars since the days of the tabernacle in the wilderness. The altar in Solomon's temple, which was in Jerusalem, had similar horns.

Horns are the weapons of the bull and should not be taken lightly. Rodeo cowboys know how dangerous they are. I have a friend in Texas who almost lost his life while riding a bull. One of the bull's horns went through his face. Now he has a nasty scar and a steel plate in his skull.

Horns have long been a symbol of power. In ancient days, a man who feared for his life would run to the temple and grasp the horns of the altar to seek asylum. In 1 Kings 1:50, we read "But Adonijah, in fear of Solomon went and took hold of the horns of the altar."

The commentary on this scripture in the NIV Study Bible says, "The horns of the Altar were a final refuge for those subject to judicial action."[m]

Any man accused of a serious domestic crime could lay hold of the horns of the altar as a final court of appeal. Here the mercy of God Almighty was evoked. Protection was afforded until judgment could be made. The horns of heaven's altar speak of God's unquestionable authority. They are the final court of justice. The sound that comes from these horns will be merciful and just, but they will be final.

A voice will come from heaven's altar horns, saying that the time has come to release the four demon lords. This will be God's sovereign word, given at an exact time for an exact purpose. The directive, which will come from the horns, is an edict that is not negotiable.

FOUR DEMONIC LORDS – THE SECOND WOE

The angel who blows the sixth trumpet will be instructed to release four demonic generals, who are fallen angels. In eons past, these dark lords were bound in chains for crimes against their creator. They were not created for evil, but they turned from the Lord to serve Lucifer. God did not annihilate them, but kept them bound in chains for a day and a time when they would serve his purpose.

In eternity past, the great tribulation was planned, and these demons have been held in prison to wait for it. God will use them as a judgment against humanity. The scripture says, "And the four angels who had been kept ready for this very hour and day and month and year were released" (Rev. 9:15).

We learned that the first woe will be the release of tormenting demons who came out of the Abyss. The second woe will also be demonic. Four satanic generals will be released by God and commissioned by Satan to organize thousands of demons under their command. These demons will in turn influence and lead the armies of man to global warfare. They will also partner with Apollyon to attack the people of God.

WEAPONS OF MASS DESTRUCTION

The four dark angels will be able to windup the world until it spins into war. For years before their release, nations will have been at war, but their power will take war to another level.

Their strategy will be to kill one-third of the remaining people on earth. The death toll from this war will be about a billion (Rev. 9:14). Redeemed Jews and gentile Christians will be among those who die. Because of the number of people who will be killed, we can be certain that weapons of mass destruction will be employed. Nuclear, chemical, and biological weapons have been among mankind's greatest fears, and the nightmare will become a worldwide reality.

JEWISH OR MUSLIM TERRITORY

The demonic lords have been imprisoned along the river Euphrates, which runs through modern-day Turkey in the north and Iraq in the south. Their release will fire up a global war against Jews and Christians.

The global war at the beginning of the great tribulation will focus on dictatorships, especially those among the Islamic Arab nations, but the battles will take place on fronts all around the world.

This global war however, will focus on Israel. By this time in history, Jews will have possession of previously owned Muslim land and that, in part, will be justification for war. The land of Israel will extend from the Nile River in Egypt to the Euphrates River in Iraq. This is the promise that was given to them in Genesis when God made a covenant with their father Abram: "On that day the Lord made a covenant with Abram and said, 'To your descendants I give this land, from the river of Egypt to the great river, the Euphrates'" (Gen. 15:18).

The descendants referred to are the Israelites, not the descendants of Ishmael, for the Lord confirmed that the promises of the land would continue through Isaac: "The Lord appeared to Isaac and said ... 'To you and your descendants I will give all these lands and will confirm the oath I swore to your father Abraham'" (Gen. 26:2–3).

The Euphrates is the longest and most important river in western Asia, stretching one thousand, seven hundred and eighty miles. Baghdad, the capital of Iraq, is situated on the Tigris, just twenty-five miles from the Euphrates.

ARAB–JEWISH WAR

The historical and present day conflict between Arab Muslims and the state of Israel is a precursor to the evil work these fallen angels will orchestrate. The nations will come to defend the Arab peoples, who by this time will have lost much of their land to Israel.

Animosity between Muslims and Jews has a deeper application than a rivalry between two people groups. It represents a spiritual war between Satan and God. The issue is God's authority over all he has made. Demons, fallen angels, and many humans will resist God's rule. On the surface, ethnic strife between Jews and Muslims will appear to be the issue, but it is really a battle between God and demons, and at stake are the hearts of humanity. Although there are many good people who are Muslims, their religion is not from God and it is a tool of the antichrist/anti-God spirit. Likewise there are some Jews who are evil people; nevertheless, the faith of their fathers is born of God. These wars will erupt over arguments of Middle East land ownership, but it is really a spiritual battle.

In 1947, the United Nations agreed that Israel could repossess her homeland. Israel was given a section of land that was called Palestine. Over the fifty-five years that followed, Israel has been attacked by her Arab neighbors. The Arab peoples do not agree with the edicts of the United Nations or those of heaven. Their violent attacks have continued nonstop for all but ten of those fifty-five years. While defending herself, Israel has grown geographically. With God's help, she will continue to defend herself and, in so doing, she will continue to gain land. The growth that Israel gains through defensive retaliation will not stop until the eastern border of Israel extends to the banks of the Euphrates.

PROTECTION FOR ISRAEL'S LAND

The Lord promised to defend Israel with military might: "On that day when all the nations of the earth are gathered against her, I will make Jerusalem an immovable rock for all the nations. All who try to move it will injure themselves. On that day I will set out to destroy all the nations that attack Jerusalem" (Zech. 12:3, 9).

Throughout history, Jerusalem has been attacked, and the Jews have been driven from their homeland and scattered throughout the earth. The promise that Jerusalem will be unmovable has only been realized since 1948. That means this scripture in Zechariah refers to our present time period. Only since 1948 has Israel been an immovable rock among the nations.

Segments of the land may yet be ruled by Jewish or Arab leaders, but Israel, as a whole, will never be disposed of her land again. Just prior to, or during the early days of, the great tribulation she will possess all of the land that God promised Abraham.

TWO HUNDRED MILLION MOUNTS

"I heard their number," John recorded, as he reported the details of the war, "the number of mounted troops was two hundred million" (Rev. 9:16).

It must have been strange to report such a huge number of mounted soldiers preparing for battle. The population of the entire world—men, women, and children—at the time John was alive was only about two hundred and fifty million people.[n]

He described a battle that enlisted more people than the entire adult population of the world, during the time of the Roman Empire. Today, the idea two hundred million men in tanks and other military vehicles is still a phenomenon, but it is an attainable one.

STRANGE HORSES AND WEAPONS

John had never seen a tank or any motorized military vehicle. He had only seen men mounted on horses or riding chariots. He did remarkably well describing the mounts he saw, which appear to be tanks and other vehicles mounted with cannons, missile launchers, and machine guns. He wrote, "The horses and riders I saw in my vision looked like this: Their breastplates were fiery red, dark blue, and yellow as sulfur. The heads of the horses resembled the heads of lions, and out of their mouths came fire, smoke and sulfur ... The power of the horses was in their mouths and in their tails; for their tails were like snakes, having heads with which to inflict injury" (Rev. 9:17 19).

The men and so-called horses were brightly colored and wore armor plate. The flexible movement of modern machinery and weapons might have appeared more like living creatures than chariots. They seemed to have heads like lions, and out of their mouths and tails came fire, smoke, and sulfur. We can picture front- and rear-mounted guns fixed on huge turrets or cannons with protective shields. Some of these gun shields or fairings may have resembled lion's heads with large manes extending outward and upward. The power of these creatures was in their mouths and tails and carried three plagues of fire, smoke, and sulfur. Their tails were like snakes, having heads to inflict injury. How else would John describe a swivel-mounted machine gun or missile launcher?

STUBBORN REBELLION

One-third of the people on the earth, or about one billion people, will die because of this war. Suddenly, God's hand of judgment will be temporarily stayed. Once again the Lord will be giving opportunity for people to repent—waiting patiently as many vacillate in the valley of indecision. The warning will have reached the hearts of the two billion people who will remain on the earth, and the human race will quickly be running out of time, but the vast majority will still refuse to bow to their knees. Those more inclined to convert will have already turned to Christ during the first half of the tribulation, but God will not give up on those who remain. Unfortunately, the majority of sinners will continue to worship demons and materialism and to murder the innocent and steal for selfish gain (see Rev. 9:20-21).

OCCULT ACTIVITY

"The rest of mankind that were not killed by these plagues still did not repent of the work of their hands; they did not stop worshipping demons, and idols of gold, silver, bronze, stone and wood—idols that cannot see or hear or walk. Nor did they repent of their murders, their magic arts, their sexual immorality, or their thefts" (Rev. 9:20–21).

It may be difficult for scientific humanity to grasp the fact that modern, well-educated people are involved in witchcraft. We used to think that the magic arts were reserved for the more primitive peoples of the world. This is simply not true. Through many differing means and methods, the occult is running at top speed in the so-called civilized nations of the world.

Wherever and whenever an individual seeks spiritual counsel or help from any source but God, that person is in rebellion and is involved in a form of witchcraft. They have broken the first of the Ten Commandments: "You shall have no other gods before me" (Exod. 20:4).

The creator of heaven and earth—the creator of every human—will not allow his creation to worship and follow the very beings who rebelled against him. It is an act of treason and rebellion, which is detestable to the Lord, when anyone decides to align himself with the devil.

Deuteronomy gives a partial list of the witchcraft that God forbids. It says, "Let no one be found among you who sacrifices his son or daughter in the fire, who practices divination or sorcery, interprets omen, engages in witchcraft, or casts spells, or who is a medium or spiritist or who consults the dead. Anyone who does these things is detestable to the Lord" (Deut. 18:10–12).

Servants of Satan are very active in our nations. Some practice ritualistic sacrifices and the casting of devilish curses. They aim at destroying every good and godly virtue in society. Many dominate and manipulate others through the practice of witchcraft and sorcery.

Most people will not engage in such blatant evil, but will get involved in areas of the occult that appear more innocent.

The occult may be divided into three parts:

1. Divination: seeking spiritual information from any source other than God, which includes such things as fortunetelling, horoscopes, transcendental meditation, and séances
2. Sorcery: the use of physical objects to bring curses or to provide spiritual power and false blessing, which includes such things as charms, crystals, voodoo dolls, animal entrails, and symbols such as pentagrams and broken crosses
3. Witchcraft: the power branch of the occult, which includes human sacrifice, death threats, incantations, curses, ritualistic abuse and control of people's lives through spiritual manipulation, abuse, seduction or oppression

Many people stay far away from sorcery or witchcraft but still practice divination. Others, who would not knowingly indulge in these main forms of the occult, still participate by enjoying various forms of demonic entertainment. These include satanic video or board games that can open the spiritual doors of witchcraft, the role-playing of Dungeons and Dragons, and the use of Ouija boards. Many feast on demonic movies that are promoted under the guise of entertainment. New ones seem to come before the public more frequently than changes in the weather. People can become hooked on witchcraft by involving themselves in secret societies such as Free Masonry and the Ku Klux Klan. At first some of these societies may seem righteous in a weird sort of way, but many of them lead to satanic activities and rituals of witchcraft. They are an abomination to the Lord.

INCREASE OF THE OCCULT

As the events foretold in Revelation approach, Satan knows that his time is short. He is doing everything within his power to draw souls into his occult web. His demons blind the eyes of those who do not want to see the light of the Gospel. The demonic forces sugarcoat occult activity by making it pleasurable and entertaining. They even present it, in some cases, as being righteous. They wrap it in sensuality and seduce the world through sexual pleasures. They buy the souls of humanity with materialism and financial gain so people will compromise and throw godly behavior to the wind. Humankind's lust is the very thing that Satan uses to drag men and women into sin. People readily enjoy the occult and tell themselves that it is their privilege, their choice, and their right. Rebellion is the sin of witchcraft, and humankind's rebellion will lead people to that end.

Even before the tribulation period begins, the occult will run rampant throughout the modern world. It will be so popular during the days of the great tribulation that ungodly men and women will eagerly participate in devil worship. Even in the face of judgment, they will not repent and come to Christ. God, however, will not be finished calling people to salvation. The judgment of war will not be enough to turn the majority of hearts to God, but the Lord will continue to call humanity, and revival will come again.

Chapter Twenty-one

Revelation is About a Personal Scroll

He was holding a little scroll, which lay open in his hand … He gave a loud shout like the roar of a lion. When he shouted, the voices of the seven thunders spoke. And when the seven thunders spoke, I was about to write; but I heard a voice from heaven say, "Seal up what the seven thunders have said and do not write it down."
Then the angel I had seen standing on the sea and on the land raised his right hand to heaven. And he swore by him who lives for ever and ever … and said, "There will be no more delay! But in the days when the seventh angel is about to sound his trumpet, the mystery of God will be accomplished, just as he announced to his servants the prophets."
Then the voice that I heard from heaven spoke to me once more: "Go, take the scroll that lies open in the hand of the angel who is standing on the sea and on the land." So I went to the angel and asked him to give me the little scroll. He said to me, "Take it and eat it. It will turn your stomach sour, but in your mouth it will be as sweet as honey." I took the little scroll from the angel's hand and ate it. It tasted as sweet as honey in my mouth, but when I had eaten it, my stomach turned sour. Then I was told, "You must prophesy again about many peoples, nations, languages and kings." (Rev. 10:2-11)

SUGGESTED READING: REVELATION 10

CHAPTER TOPICS

1. More powerful angels
2. A personal scroll
3. The seven thunders speaking
4. No more delays
5. The mystery spoken to the prophets
6. The release in the days of the seventh trumpet
7. How John and all of us are called to prophesy

BEHIND THE SCENES

AT THIS POINT IN our study, the second campaign is almost complete. We have seen judgments and witnessed spiritual armies at war. It is time to gain a better perspective of the church's role during the first half of the tribulation. Revelation discloses powerful church activity. We see the call, the power, the ministry, as well as the struggle of the church. Revelation 10–12 gives us a glimpse of the assignment of the church. These chapters should inspire us and posture us prophetically. We have seen angels and demons, and now we will see the church's participation in the end-time battles.

God's people are not called to be an army of spectators: they are not now, and they certainly won't be during the tribulation period. Rather, we are coworkers with God in the destiny of the planet. Jesus calls us to be fishers of men, ambassadors of heaven, and prophets who wield the holy fire. We have been called to ministry.

Like John, we are commissioned to carry the word of God and the testimony of Jesus Christ. We have a personal prophecy to fulfill.

THE LION ANGEL

John saw a powerful angel plant his feet on the earth and shout with such authority that it reminded him of a roaring lion (Rev. 10:2-3). The angel will come like the Lord, himself. His face will shine like the sun, and his legs will be blazing pillars of fire. He will be clothed with a cloud, and a rainbow will glow brightly above his head.

This is one of the powerful cherubim. We know he is not the Lord, because he is called an angel. His lion's roar tells us that he may be one of the four living creatures. We saw one of them fly through midair as the eagle of prophecy. The eagle brought the warning of the three woes—the three judgments of demonic power. Two of the woes have been revealed, but the third woe is still coming.

This seraph embodies the character of the lion. He will call us to the high courts of heaven to prophesy and partner with God, and we cannot treat his words lightly, but must respond in faith. The lion angel will come with marching orders from King Jesus. That is why he will shine so brightly and shout with such authority.

HE COMES TO LAND AND SEA

The lion seraph will plant his right foot on the sea and his left foot on the land. (Rev. 10:2) This is not incidental. Earlier in our study, we identified the symbols of sea and land. The sea refers to a sea of people; the land speaks of earth's natural environment. Both the multitudes and the environment have suffered the judgments of God. In Rev. 13, we will see Satan take his stand on the shores of the sea, which symbolizes that he will be coming after the multitudes of humanity.

The church's involvement in Revelation is not a side issue; it is essential. The angel who addressed John was standing on the land and the sea, and his words to John were for the entire church. The saints affect earth's people and the environment. Man's sins have caused the environment to suffer great harm, and man's redemption will be used by God to restore it.

We read, "The creation waits in eager expectation for the sons of God to be revealed. For the creation was subjected to frustration, not by its own choice, but by the will of the one who subjected it, in hope that the creation itself will be liberated from its bondage to decay and brought into the glorious freedom of the children of God. We know that the whole creation has been groaning as in the pains of childbirth right up to this present time ... They and us, wait eagerly for our adoption as sons, the redemption of our bodies" (Rom. 8:19–23).

All of creation groans and waits for the completion of the resurrection when mankind will receive the redemption of their bodies. That will happen at the end of the great tribulation, not at the beginning. No animals receive a special blessing at a pre-tribulation moment. There is no rapture at that time. When the new millennium begins, Christians will walk in the full blessings of God, and creation will come into its glory. All of nature waits for resurrection day.

Before the great flood of Noah's day, when the earth was young, pollution was nonexistent. People lived for seven or eight hundred years. As sin increased, spiritual pollution led the way to physical and environmental pollution, and with it came death. It is prophesied that one day, after the tribulation period, men will live to be hundreds of years old: "He who dies at a hundred will be thought a mere youth; he who fails to reach a hundred will be considered accursed" (Isa. 65:20).

This long life will come before everyone is given immortality. It will come when the earth is renewed and replenished. God cares about people; he also cares for the environment and the animals. We will look at this in more detail when we study the new millennium.

SEVEN THUNDERS

John said that, after the lion seraph will set his feet on the land and sea, he shouted, and the seven thunders (the seven angels who are the generals of the Lamb, the seven spirits of God, the seven eyes of the Lord, and the angels who will blow the seven trumpets to release the judgments of the second campaign) spoke in unison. One can only guess what they said and what they will bring to the table. John was forbidden to write their words. "And when the seven thunders spoke, I was about to write; but I heard a voice from heaven say, "Seal up what the seven thunders have said and do not write it down" (Rev. 10:3).

I imagine they will call the people of God to specific purpose. Humankind's partnership with God is precious to him and hideous to the devil. It is of monumental significance. John was about to write the words of the seven thunders, but he was told to restrain his hand.

The commissioning of the church must wait for God's appointed time. If we were allowed to see our marching orders, we would definitely try to make the prophecies happen. The problem is that we do not have the necessary level of anointing or the authority for the task. During the tribulation, the glory of the Lord will rise upon the church as promised.

John was not the only man who was told to keep a heavenly revelation to himself. Both Daniel and Paul were forbidden to tell what they saw in heaven. One day, we will hear exactly what John heard and, if it is our commissioning, we will respond with zeal, obedience, and great anointing.

The reason I believe the words of the seven thunders are marching orders for the church is because of what followed: the angel gave marching orders to John. Multitudes in the church will receive a similar commissioning as the day of action arrives.

HE SWORE BY AN OATH

John saw the lion angel lift his right hand and speak an oath (Rev. 10:5-6). The right hand represents honesty, righteousness, and power. We must lift the right hand when making an oath in a court of law. Doing so signifies that we will tell the truth and it is legally binding. An oath should only be given in the most serious of situations and only by certain beings. The ramifications of such an act are that the oath taker will be held accountable before the courts of heaven.

The Bible instructs humans not to make such oaths, but just to speak truthfully. When we see the angel of Revelation swearing by an oath, we realize that the practice did not originate with man, but with God.

This is such a serious matter that the Bible says, "But above all, my brethren, do not swear, either by heaven or by earth or with any other oath; but let your yes be yes, and your no, no; so that you may not fall under judgment" (Judg. 5:12).

The angel will swear with an oath because he will have God's authority to do so. No matter what happens, he will be able to keep his word. Once the angel makes the oath it will be irreversible. The oath will be given for our sake, so we will know the seriousness of what is about to follow. God's people will have been waiting for thousands of years for this promise. The angel will declare emphatically that the time has come, and there will be no more delay.

NO MORE DELAY

"There will be no more delay! But in the days when the seventh angel is about to sound his trumpet, the mystery of God will be accomplished, just as he announced to his servants the prophets" (Rev. 10:7).

John will see a great impact event. It will happen during the days of the seventh trumpet (the last trumpet). It has been promised, but delayed until now. The sounding of the last trumpet will announce a short window of time when transitional and pivotal things will happen. That is why the scriptures speak of *the days* of the seventh trumpet. During *these days*, one event is more important than all others. It is called the mystery of God and it will come just as it was promised to the prophets of old.

THE MYSTERY OF GOD

The mystery of God is the second coming of the Lord and the resurrection of the saints. Note the language in 2nd Corinthians: "Listen, I tell you a *mystery*. We shall not all sleep, but we will all be changed—in a flash, in a twinkling of an eye, *at the last trumpet*. For the trumpet will sound, and the dead will be raised imperishable, and we will be changed. For the perishable must cloth itself with the imperishable and the mortal with immortality" (1 Cor. 15:51–53; italics added).

We find a similar account in Thessalonians: "For the Lord himself will come down from heaven, with a loud command, with the voice of the archangel and with the *trumpet call of God,* and the dead in Christ will rise first. After that we who are still alive and are left will be caught up together with them in the clouds to meet the Lord in the air. And so we will be with the Lord forever" (1 Thess. 4:16; italics added).

The mystery promised down through the ages is the resurrection of our bodies. It has been delayed through countless generations. It will happen at the second coming of Christ, and Christ's return will take place during the days of the last trumpet. The angel will swear by an oath, and there will be no more delay.

During the days of the seventh trumpet, the seven bowls of God's wrath will be poured out, and the resurrection of the dead and the second coming of Christ will happen. So much will take place in a short space of time.

THE LITTLE SCROLL

"'Go, take the scroll that lies open in the hand of the angel who is standing on the sea and on the land.' So I went to the angel and asked him to give me the little scroll. He said to me, 'Take it and eat it.'" (Rev. 10:8-9)

John saw a little scroll, which lay open, in the palm of the lion angel's hand, and he was instructed to ask the angel for it. Suddenly, John was not just a spectator or just a mere reporter of the events of Revelation. He was being called to active participation. He became like Moses who turned aside to look at the burning bush. God spoke out of the bush and commissioned him for service. The same amazing thing was suddenly happening to John.

The scroll was open so John could glance down and see what was written on it. It involved him. John must devour it and let it become part of him. The little scroll contained John's marching orders. He must accept it and own it for himself. He was told to eat it and then prophesy.

Revelation shows Jesus taking the larger scroll from the hand of God Almighty who sat on the throne—an act that will release the end of the age (Rev. 5:7-8). That scroll was the big scroll. John's scroll was called a little scroll. It revealed a small part of the big picture—the part that John himself would play.

OUR SCROLL

Each person who is called of God has a personal little scroll. Each will have a role to play in the end-time purposes of God. It will involve prayer, prophecy, acts of kindness, and carrying the testimony of Jesus.

Even now we can pray about the purposes of God for the end times. We may pray like this: "Come, Lord Jesus, come and fulfill all of the promises that you died for. Come, Almighty, come and receive the inheritance that Christ has purchased for you. Release your anointing on your people so they may partner with you to fulfill your end time plans."

Our specific marching orders may be brought to us through dreams, vision, scriptures, angels, the nudging of the Holy Spirit, signs and wonders, or the audible voice of the Lord. God is looking for partners and coworkers. When he gives us our personal scrolls, we must eat them and let their messages become part of us. It will take the entire church and myriads of angels to do the entire will of God.

Our response should be like that of the prophet Isaiah. He said, "I heard the voice of the Lord saying, 'Whom shall I send? And who will go for us?' And I said, 'Here am I. Send me'!" (Isa. 6:8).

BITTER SWEET

Every scroll designated for the tribulation is both bitter and sweet. The angel said to John, "Take it and eat it. It will turn your stomach sour, but in your mouth it will be as sweet as honey" (Rev. 10:9).

The tribulation will reveal the kindness and severity of God. The judgments of the Lord will be terrible. They will be difficult to watch and absolutely devastating to the ones on whom they fall. This will turn our stomachs bitter and make us feel sick. Even though we are aware that these events must happen, they will, nevertheless, be horrible.

Many, however, only see the doom and gloom of Revelation and fail to see the honey. God's people will rejoice with unspeakable joy as they see multitudes rescued and saved. Many who should have died will be delivered from death. Many will be born again as they finally bow to Christ. For them salvation will have come in the midnight hour because of the compassion of the saints and the fear of the Lord.

Such salvation is the victory of the Lord, and we will say, "It is sweet." As the old songwriter says, "Taste and see that the Lord is good. Oh, it tastes like honey in the rock."

Many will weep with uncontrollable joy as they see friends and relatives cross over into the Lord's camp. The answers to many prayers of supplication will bring amazing joy. A pent-up flood of happiness will burst inside the hearts of many people each time another soul is rescued. It is no wonder that the scripture says that Christ will wipe away every tear when his people finally stand before his throne. Many tears of sorrow and of joy will mingle together on that day.

The saints will play a dramatic role during the tribulation. Even those who go to heaven before the tribulation happens will stand with the heavenly host in aggressive prayer and worship. If you belong to Christ, you have a prophetic scroll that belongs to you alone. All of us must eat the scroll that is given to us. Be prepared: it will be both sweet and bitter.

PROPHESY TO THE NATIONS

Finally the angel spoke to John directly. John wrote, "Then I was told, 'You must prophesy again about many peoples, nations, languages, and kings'" (Rev. 10:11).

John was instructed to prophesy *again*. That means that he had already been prophesying before this Revelation scroll was given to him. John's scroll was a little scroll, but that is only from God's perspective. When each of us receives our full marching orders, they will be overwhelming. Our little scroll will be much bigger than what we are personally capable of. If the task that God has given you seems small and manageable, I doubt very much that you have discovered all of your marching orders. John was called to speak the word of the Lord over multitudes, nations, indigenous peoples, and kings.

Likewise, we will speak the prophetic message across the globe and around the world. No culture, peoples, or individuals will be outside of the prophetic words of heaven. Woe to the rebels of the world when the church breaks forth and prophesies. The kindness and severity of God will be released. This will produce the prayer of agreement. Earth will agree with heaven, and whatever the Spirit-led saints prophesy, it will surely come to pass.

These prophecies will not be made up, nor will they simply be good ideas. God's people will prophesy words from heaven. They will prophesy that which is written on the scrolls and given to them by holy angels.

THE WORD AND THE TESTIMONY

John—and in turn the entire church have received the book of Revelation for a specific purpose. It is for the word of God and the testimony of Jesus.

Let no one doubt it anymore—all are called to carry the word of God and the testimony of Jesus. John was told that he must prophesy, and so must we. The call to prophesy already came to John. He took hold of the baton and ran the race. He was trained, and he acted.

The book of Revelation is a training manual. Join with me in prayer, "Spirit of God, come and teach each of us to take the baton when it is our turn and then to run the race. Teach us to prophesy."

Chapter Twenty-two

Revelation is About the State of Israel

I was given a reed like a measuring rod and was told, "Go and measure the temple of God and the altar, and count the worshippers there.
But exclude the outer court; do not measure it, because it has been given to the Gentiles. They will trample on the holy city for 42 months. And I will give power to my two witnesses, and they will prophesy for 1,260 days, clothed in sackcloth. These are the two olive trees and the two lampstands that stand before the Lord of the earth." (Rev. 11:1–4)

CHAPTER TOPICS

1. The natural and the spiritual Jerusalem
2. Jews and Christians gathering in Jerusalem
3. A brief history of Jerusalem
4. Revival and renaissance in Israel
5. Rebuilding the Jewish Temple
6. Animal sacrifices
7. The beast infiltrating the Jewish temple
8. The book of Daniel
9. God's eight end-time promises for Israel

THE NATURAL AND THE SPIRITUAL

THE HOLY CITY, CALLED Jerusalem or Zion, has natural and spiritual counterparts. The natural city is the present capital of Israel; the spiritual one is called the New Jerusalem. Both are Zion, the city of the Great King.

The New Jerusalem is made up of all believers including redeemed Jews and true Christians. Both natural and spiritual Jerusalem will develop on parallel tracks as we approach the second coming of Christ.

In this chapter, we will attempt to give a brief overview of the natural state of Israel as it emerges in the first half of the great tribulation. In the next chapter, we will focus on the spiritual city, the New Jerusalem with its spiritual temple and worshippers.

ALL KINDS OF JEWS

In the early days of the great tribulation, revival will come to Israel. Millions of Jews will receive Jesus as Messiah. That does not mean that they will become gentile Christians. They will continue to be Jewish in every sense of the word. After receiving Jesus as Messiah, however, they will gain additional spiritual understanding concerning many of their religious customs and their Jewish religious law. They will receive the gift of the Holy Spirit and an anointing of God's supernatural power.

Like Nicodemus in Jesus' day, these born-again Jews will come into the New Covenant, which was designed for them (John 3:3, Hebrews 8:7–13). They will realize that most of their customs should still be celebrated, such as the feasts, but other aspects of Jewish history, such as animal sacrifices, will no longer be valid. They will understand that the Jewish religious law is holy and good, but it can never and will never make them righteous.

They will keep the law and much of their traditions as best they can, as a spiritual sign to the world. They will know, however, that keeping the law will not save them or bring them into righteousness.

The law is an illustrative teaching and a living parable that describes man's fellowship with God. Each detail of Jewish religious law and all of their God-given religious customs tell a story of God's involvement with, and his expectations of, humanity. The Jews have been called to embrace this symbolic lifestyle, and as a people, they fly like a banner for all the nations to see.

Jews who receive Jesus as Messiah will not be required to stop being Jews anymore than Jesus or his disciples stopped being Jews. They will simply need to walk with God in the fullness of the faith.

Not all Jews, however, will come to Christ during the great Jewish revival. Standing in opposition to undeniable evidence, many stubborn Jews will refuse to believe that Jesus is Messiah. Within this group, some Orthodox Jews and secular Jews will continue to resist the Lord.

The physical Jerusalem will be inhabited by a great mixture of redeemed, Messianic, Orthodox and non-religious Jews. It will remain that way until the Lord returns. When Jesus comes and his feet touch the Mount of Olives, there will still be many unsaved Jews in Israel. He will come and rescue them. This truth is developed in future chapters of the book. For quick verification, read Zech. 14. There you will see that when the Lord returns, some in Jerusalem have not received glorified bodies. That means they are not Christ's when he appears. They will run into the shelter that the Messiah provides, and they will be rescued.

JERUSALEM'S HISTORY IN BRIEF

Here is a brief history of the physical city of Jerusalem that stands in modern Israel today. It is situated on Mount Moriah, the site where God sent Abraham to sacrifice his son Isaac. A thousand years later, King David captured the site from the Jebusites and placed Israel's capital there. Nebuchadnezzar the Babylonian, invaded and captured it in 597 BC and subsequently razed it to the ground.

Then, the city was conquered by the Persian King Cyrus. Alexander the Great was the next conqueror. He overtook Jerusalem for the glory of Greece. Following his reign, it was briefly recaptured by the Jews under the leadership of the Macabees.

In AD 63, the Romans controlled it. The Catholics rose to power and dominated it for some time until in AD 635; Muslim armies invaded and captured Jerusalem. They Islamized the Temple Mount, first by constructing the al-Aqsa mosque, and then the Dome of the Rock. These were built on the exact Biblical site where Abraham's sacrifice and Solomon's temple were.

In 1099, European Crusaders invaded, mercilessly expunging all Muslims and Jews. Salah al-Din (Saladin), the Egyptian and Syrian sultan, recaptured the city for Islam in 1187. Then at the beginning of the [sixteenth] century, the Muslim Turks conquered and ruled the city until the disintegration of the Ottoman Empire in the early [twentieth] century.

The British liberated it in World War I and held it for 30 years. The United Nations agreed that the city be partitioned for Arab and Jewish interests in November of 1947 and the modern State of Israel was born in May1948. In the face of Arab attacks, they overtook the whole of the city of Jerusalem in 1967.

One day Christ will return to the city. He will cleanse it of its corruption, bring it into its full blessings and establish the headquarters of his earthly kingdom in this city of Jerusalem.

For a more detailed history of Jerusalem, go to the website, www.archpark.org.il Today, on the southern slopes of the Temple Mount there is a wonderful archeological park called the Davidson Center. The above website is theirs.

JERUSALEM IS FAVORED

Bible prophecies tell us that a time is coming when Jerusalem will be favored of the Lord. The Psalms read, "You will arise and have compassion on Zion, for it is time to show favor to her; the appointed time has come. For her stones are dear to your servants ... The nations will fear the name of the Lord ... For the Lord will rebuild Zion and appear in his glory ... Let this be written for a future generation, that a people not yet created may praise the Lord ... So the name of the Lord will be declared in Zion and his praise in Jerusalem when the peoples and the kingdoms assemble to worship the Lord" (Ps. 102:13–22).

THEY GATHER TO JERUSALEM

Throughout the tribulation period, Israel will be restored physically and spiritually. During this time, it will experience an ebb and flow of victories and defeats, like the coming and going of the tides. She will be attacked, she will grow in size and strength, and eventually she will be trampled on just before the return of the Lord.

Through it all, we will see the complete rebuilding of Israel, the expansion of her land, and the full institution of all of her religious traditions. During this Jewish renaissance, there will be a great mixture of religious activities. Not all of them will be desired or set in place by the Lord. Some of these activities will be the carry over of Old Testament Jewish life, which should have been adjusted or displaced by the New Covenant (Heb. 8:13). Some religious Jews, nevertheless, will hold on to all of the ways of the Old Covenant.

New Covenant Jews and Christians will support and encourage many Orthodox measures, but they will also resist some. God, however, will allow these Old Covenant, Orthodox Jews to do all that is in their hearts, even though they are somewhat misguided. As in the days of Paul, they have great zeal toward God, but they lack understanding (Rom. 10:1–4).

Christians from all nations will be excited as they see God's prophecies for the Jews being fulfilled. They will recognize God's favor on the land of Israel, and many will gather themselves to Jerusalem to be at the center of God's will. They will want to receive the anointing of God that has fallen on Israel. They will want to receive blessings from God's chosen people. They will also want to support the Jews and especially encourage those who have not yet been born again.

Just prior to the midpoint of the great tribulation, God will bring deliverance and peace to Jerusalem and to the entire world. We will study this in the next few chapters. Here we'll examine some of Zechariah's prophetic words regarding Israel's wonderful disposition during the end-times. These verses start by describing the scattering of Israel over the last two thousand years, but then we see the children of Israel being blessed in the promise land.

"When I called, they did not listen;' ... says the Lord Almighty. 'I scattered them with a whirlwind among the nations ... The land was left so desolate behind them" (Zech. 7:13, 14).

Zechariah also says: This is what the Lord says: "I will return to Zion and dwell in Jerusalem. ... I will save my people from the countries of the east and the west. I will bring them back to live in Jerusalem ... You who now hear these words spoken by the prophets, ... *let your hands be strong so that the temple may be built* ... As you have been an object of cursing among the nations, O Judah and Israel, so will I save you, and you will be a blessing ... Just as I had determined to bring disaster upon you ... So now I have determined to do good. ... Many people and the inhabitants of many cities will yet come ... And many peoples and powerful nations will come to Jerusalem to seek the Lord Almighty and to entreat him ..." In those days ten *men from all languages and nations will take firm hold of one Jew by the hem of his robe and say, "Let us go with you,* because we have heard that God is with you." (Zech. 8:1–23; italics added)

Christians of every language and nation will join themselves to a Jew and make their way to Jerusalem, where they will live and take a stand alongside the Jewish people. After a brief time of miraculous grace and political success, the nations will turn against Israel and attack her. Before that happens however, many Christians from many nations around the world will be extremely excited about her renaissance. We will explain this in the next chapters.

REBUILDING THE TEMPLE

The temple of the Lord will be rebuilt by the Lord himself. We have just read in Zechariah 8:9 that the Lord will encourage the building of his end-time temple.

He said, *"Let your hands be strong so that the temple may be built"* (Zech. 8:9; italics added).

We read of this also in Zech. 6. "This is what the Lord Almighty says: Here is the man whose name is Branch, and he will branch out from his place and *build the temple of the Lord. It is he who will rebuild the temple of the Lord,* and he will be clothed with majesty and will sit and rule on his throne. Those who are far away will come and help to *build the temple of the Lord,* and you will know that the Lord Almighty has sent me to you. This will happen if you diligently obey the Lord your God" (Zech. 6:12–15; italics added).

The rebuilding of the Jewish temple will happen during or just before the great tribulation. There is much discussion as to whether this new temple will be a physical one or just a spiritual one (comprised of the family of God around the world). The saints of God are indeed a spiritual temple of God. There is both a spiritual and a physical temple of the Lord that will be built in the last days. Just as Jerusalem, the city, is physical and yet it has a spiritual counterpart, so also does the temple. The Lord seems to mirror everything that is spiritual and give it a physical counterpart to it, in Israel.

The language in the prior verses causes me to believe that a physical temple, and not just a spiritual one, will be built. "Those who are far away will come and help to build the temple and this will happen if you diligently obey the Lord your God" (Zech. 6:15).

I do not think the words in Zechariah 6:15 would be spoken if the Lord was only planning to build a spiritual house. After all, the passage notes that people will be coming from far away to help and that it will only happen if people are diligent in obeying the Lord.

Orthodox Jews have already invested great sums of money to have the furniture of the temple created and crafted to the exact pattern in the scriptures. These furnishings are presently in storage in Jerusalem, waiting to furnish the temple.

The Lord used nonreligious Jews called Zionists to inspire the rebirth of Israel in 1948, but, still, it was an act of God. He could, in like manner, use non-messianic Jews to build a temple. In the end, whatever happens will happen because he has set the process in motion. He is able to perform his will through whomever he desires. The Lord himself is behind the building of his temple. He is the branch that branches out, as Zechariah mentions (Zech. 6:12). Those who do the actual work will be working for him.

ANIMAL SACRIFICES

One of the Old Covenant practices that will take place in the new temple will be animal sacrifices. Christ's death replaced the need for animal sacrifice. When Jesus, the Lamb of God, died on the cross two thousand years ago, he shed his blood for the sins of the world, once and for all. No other sacrifice is legitimate to justify a man before God. No other sacrifice can remove sin. Some Orthodox Jews, however, are stuck in the Old Testament. They are stubborn, and, thinking that they are serving the God of Abraham, they will reinstate animal sacrifices.

Orthodox Jews, although misguided, will offer these sacrifices with sincerity before God. They will be living in types and shadows rather than in the realities of Christ's provision. Their efforts will not make them righteous nor help them in any way.

They will continue offering these sacrifices until the midpoint of the tribulation when their sacrifices to God will be abolished by the beast. Before that time, the church and Israel will experience a great success. Then the beast will appear, and God will allow him to break the power of the church and Israel. "When the power of the holy people has been fully broken, all these things will be complete" (Dan. 12:7).

We will study this in the next couple of chapters.

Israel will continue to hold the Holy Land and defend it until Jesus comes, but it will suffer great upheaval. The beast will infiltrate and proceed to defile God's temple by bringing in a demonic sacrifice to replace the daily Jewish sacrifices.

This hideous counterfeit will be an antichrist sacrifice set in place to mock and blaspheme the sacrifice of Christ. It is called the abomination of desolation. The Antichrist takeover will come at a time when the Jewish renaissance and the church's glory will be at their highest levels. The beast will be allowed to squelch the power of God's people. The people of God will be finally broken due to persecution.

From that moment until the Lord returns, a further three and a half years will pass. That is the last half of the great tribulation. In the last chapter of the book of Daniel all of these events are clearly mentioned. This time period is described as a time (one year) times (two years) and half a time (half a year), totaling three and a half years. We read a powerful prophetic word that was given to Daniel from an angel. Their dialog reads as follows.

"At that time Michael, the great prince who protects your people, will arise. There will be a time of distress such as has not happened from the beginning of nations until then. But at that time your people—everyone whose name is found written in the book—will be delivered. Multitudes who sleep in the dust of the earth will awake: some to everlasting life, others to shame and everlasting contempt. Those who are wise will shine like the brightness of the heavens, and those who lead many to righteousness, like the stars for ever and ever ... close up and seal the words of this scroll until the time of the end. "How long will it be before these astonishing things are fulfilled? ... It will be for a time, times and half a time. When the power of the holy people has been finally broken, all these things will be completed."

I asked, "My lord, what will the outcome of all this be?"

He replied, "The words are closed up and sealed until the time of the end. Many will be purified, made spotless and refined, but the wicked will continue to be wicked. None of the wicked will understand, but those who are wise will understand. *From the time that the daily sacrifice is abolished and the abomination of desolation is set up, there will be 1, 290 days*. Blessed is the one who waits for and reaches the end of 1,335 days. As for you, go your way till the end. You will rest, and then at the end of the days you will rise to receive your allotted inheritance." (Dan. 12:1–13; italics added)

The 1,290 days, or approximately three and a half years, represents the last half of the great tribulation. I suggest that the 1,335 days marks the start of Christ's millennium kingdom, his thousand-year reign on earth. Blessed are those who reach that day without being killed. They will be among those who are alive and remain until the coming of the Lord.

STUDYING DANIEL

References taken from Daniel are often used to describe the end times. The entire book of Daniel, however, should not be used to describe the great tribulation. The NIV Study Bible notes, line up most of the events in Daniel with events that have already taken place in Jewish history.

They report things like, *"his large horn was broken off."* The death of Alexander the Great at the height of his power" and *"Another horn"* The horn that *"started small"* is Antiochus IV Epiphanes, who during the last few years of his reign (168-164B.C.) made a determined effort top destroy the Jewish faith."[o]

Many verses in Daniel are prophecies for sure, but most of them are for an earlier time period. If you look at a Zondervan Study Bible, you will discover that their commentaries reveal a precise fit with most of Daniel's prophesies and events that happened in such ancient empires as Persia, Greece, Egypt, and Asia Minor. The descriptions mentioned line up so accurately that one must be careful not to think that they automatically refer to the book of Revelation and the end of time. This is true for each of the Old Testament prophetic books. A careful study of Old Testament verses is recommended before assigning their contents to the end of the age.

Many scriptures and some parts of Daniel, like its last chapter, are definitely in reference to the last days. These end-time scriptures give such qualifying details as resurrection day, the coming of the Lord, the telltale three and a half years, or a direct mention of the end of time.

ISRAEL RECEIVES HER INHERITANCE

Between 1948 and the midpoint of the tribulation period, Israel will receive much her promised inheritance in systematic and incremental steps. All of these blessings will come before the Lord returns at the end of the great tribulation. (See Rev. 19.)

After the first half of the tribulation, Israel and the church will undergo severe persecution and battle. The end-time blessings will suddenly seem to fail. After a brief setback, the blessings will be fully restored and made complete for the new millennium: the thousand-year reign of Christ.

The scripture tells of eight end-time promises that are extended specifically to the Jews. These promises are Israel's inheritance. The church should pray passionately and assist the Jewish people in any way possible to cooperate with the plans of God for the end of the age.

Jerusalem is God's prophetic time clock. Only after seven of these eight promises are fulfilled for Israel will the Lord appear at his second coming. The eighth blessing will be fulfilled when he comes. Here are Israel's eight end-time blessings:

1. Israel will be given the ownership and the full extension of her land (Ezek. 20:42; Gen. 15:18).
2. The Jewish people will be regathered to their land (Isa. 11:12; Zeph. 3:20).
3. Israel's financial fortunes will be restored before her very eyes (Zeph. 2:7; 3:20; Joel 3:1).
4. Christian and Jewish intercessors around the world will stand on her spiritual walls and pray for Israel (Isa. 62:6).
5. A national revival will come to Israel as multitudes of Jews receive Jesus as their Messiah (Isa. 45:17; Zech. 12:10; Rom. 11:25–26).
6. God's glory and power will come upon Israel (Rom. 9:5; Isa. 60:1, 2).
7. The nations will give praise and honor to Israel (Zeph. 3:19; Isa. 60:2).
8. God's judgment will come upon the nations for how they have treated Israel (Joel 3:1–3).

Chapter Twenty-three

Revelation is About Identifying the Two Witnesses

I was given a reed like a measuring rod and was told, "Go and measure the temple of God and the altar, and count the worshippers there. But exclude the outer court; do not measure it, because it has been given to the Gentiles. They will trample on the holy city for 42 months.
And I will give power to my two witnesses, and they will prophesy for 1,260 days, clothed in sackcloth. These are the two olive trees and the two lampstands that stand before the Lord of the earth." (Rev. 11:1–4)

CHAPTER TOPICS

1. Recognizing the greatness of the church
2. Identifying the false church
3. Identifying the two witnesses
4. Identifying the olive branches
5. Identifying the lampstands
6. Recognizing the one new man
7. Powerful prophetic partners

THE PEOPLE OF GOD ARE MEASURED

IN THE ORIGINAL SCRIPTURES there were no chapter and verse divisions. That means there was no break between Revelation chapters 10 and 11. Immediately following John's instruction to prophesy, now found in chapter 10, he was asked to focus on Israel and the church, which is now found in chapter 11. He was told to measure the temple and the altar and to count the worshippers there. John was told to discover and evaluate the temple, which is a picture of God's people.

Ephesians reads, "Consequently, you are no longer foreigners and aliens, but fellow citizens with God's people and members of God's household, built on the foundation of the apostles and prophets, with Christ Jesus himself as the chief corner stone. In whom the whole building is joined together and rises to become *a holy temple* in the Lord" (Eph. 2:19–21; italics added).

John was told to measure the temple and the altar and count the worshippers. The altar was the spiritual place of sacrifice where worshippers present their bodies as living sacrifices to the Lord. Obedience and devotion to Christ is our sacrifice and our reasonable service of worship (Rom. 12:1–2).

John evaluated God's people and discovered that they were ready to play their part in the great tribulation. In a sense, God was showing off his glorious church. They are the saints on fire for Christ, ready to partner with him. The number of members in the tribulation church and their accumulated passion will be greater than the world has ever seen. God told John to measure the temple because he is proud of his people. It is as though God was saying, "John take notice of the worship of my people, behold their devotion and count them. They are ready, and I am about to use them as I said I would."

THE FALSE CHURCH

Like the Jewish temple, God's spiritual temple has an outer court. The Lord differentiates between his true church and those in the outer court. Outer court people are those who have a form of religion, even calling themselves Christians, but they are not God's people. They do not follow his directives or obey his will. Many false Christians are, in fact, enemies of God. They will trample on the people of God and the holy city for forty-two months, or three and a half years (Rev. 21:2). Throughout history these people have hindered the work of Christ. They have resisted the mandate of the true church, but they will experience a setback during the tribulation period. For a season, the true church will overcome them and rise with awesome power.

During the first three and a half years of the tribulation, two kingdoms will engage in open conflict. The people of God on one side will call the world to repentance and lift high the standards of biblical morality. They will minister compassion to the suffering and lead millions to salvation.

The false church, on the other hand, will be an ecumenical body of people, one comprised of individuals from all religions. They will undermine the message of Christ, mixing witchcraft and humanism in a pluralistic secular soup. This is the new world order. It is the inevitable outcome of societies merging together to make room for all without coming under the Lordship of Christ. On the surface, it sounds good, but there is only one true God, and he alone should be worshipped.

The governments of the world despise the claims of Christ and the narrow path of his devoted followers. The false church and modern secular societies will find themselves in a real dilemma as the tribulation unfolds. The world will experience severe judgments, and multitudes will wake up and turn to Christ.

THE TWO WITNESSES

"And I will give power to my two witnesses, and they will prophesy for 1,260 days, clothed in sackcloth. These are the two olive trees and the two lampstands that stand before the Lord of the earth." (Rev. 11:4)

The conflict between the two kingdoms will reach a critical level and, at that time, God will release supernatural power and authority upon his two witnesses. For centuries scholars have debated who the two witnesses are. While I greatly respect many of these teachers, I must differ from them on some points. I believe that the scriptures tell us clearly who the two witnesses are.

In Rev. 11, they are called prophets of the Lord. They are also called the two olive branches and the two lampstands that stand before the Lord of the earth. We read of them in Zechariah: "I see a gold lampstand with a bowl at the top. Also there are two olive trees. I asked the angel, 'What are these two olive trees, what are these two olive branches beside the two golden pipes that pour out golden oil?' So he said, 'These are the two who are anointed to serve the Lord of all the earth'" (Zech. 4:2, 11, 12, 14).

Notice that the terms olive trees and olive branches are interchangeable. These are the two anointed ones chosen to serve the Lord of all the earth.

The book of Romans tells us: "If some of the branches have been broken off, and you, though a wild olive shoot have been grafted in among the others and now share in the nourishing sap from the olive root, do not boast over the branches ... For if God did not spare the natural branches, he will not spare you either. And if they do not persist in unbelief, they will be grafted in, for God is able to graft them in again. After all if you were cut out of an olive tree that is wild by nature and contrary to nature were grafted into a cultivated olive tree, how much more readily will these, the natural branches, be grafted into their own olive tree!... I do not want you to be ignorant of this mystery, brothers, so that you may not be conceited. Israel has experienced a hardening in part until the full number of the Gentiles has come in. And so all Israel will be saved ... For God's gifts and his call are irrevocable" (Rom. 11:17–29).

We do not have to guess who the two olive branches are; scripture identifies them for us. They are Israel and the church, the natural and the wild branches of the olive tree. Some, but not all, of Israel's natural branches were broken off. They have experienced a hardening in part until a specific time when the full number of the gentiles will come in. Then revival will come to Israel, and she will be grafted in again. This is the great mystery concerning Israel that we read of in Romans 11:25.

Israel and the gentile church are the two anointed witnesses who serve the Lord of the whole earth. Throughout history God has ordained these two groups of people to represent him. They are the two who serve the Lord of all the earth. Both must embrace Jesus the Messiah before they can receive their full blessings. As the Bible says, they will come together to make one new man (Eph. 2:15). They will partner with God in the great end-time battles.

THE TWO PROPHETS

Within both groups, powerful, prophetic people will emerge. We may call these armies the prophetic church and prophetic Israel. They will be comprised of the ones who have received the small scrolls and embraced the word of God and the testimony of Jesus. The two witnesses will partner as God's end-time prophetic church.

We discovered the two groups in Rev. 7. The redeemed Jews were identified as the 144,000, and the gentile church was seen as the other multitude, the innumerable company of saints standing before the throne. Both groups will be present during the first three and a half years of the tribulation. They are evangelists, outspoken representatives of heaven, and compassionate ministers of God's grace. They will prophesy for one thousand two hundred sixty days, or just a little more than three and a half years.

The church is called the body of Christ; it is one new man. This is not a new teaching to call the church a man. Here we see redeemed Israel standing as a man, a prophet of the Lord. The gentile church is also seen as a man, the second prophet of the Lord. Now together they will become one new man.

THE LAMPSTANDS

"And I will give power to my two witnesses ... These are the two olive trees and the two lampstands that stand before the Lord of the earth." (Rev. 11:1–4)

The two witnesses are the two lampstands that stand before the Lord of the earth. Revelation tells us what lampstands represent. "And when I turned I saw seven golden lampstands, and among the lampstands was someone like the son of man. ... The seven lampstands are the seven churches" (Rev. 1:12, 20).

Lampstands in the book of Revelation represent churches. The two witnesses are churches, not two individual people. Israel was the Old Covenant church, and later redeemed gentiles joined them to form the New Covenant church, the church of the firstborn mentioned in Hebrews 12:23.

The book of Acts tells us of the Old Testament church. Jesus was with the Israelites, (in Spirit) in the church in the wilderness during the time of Moses. We read, "This is he, that was in the church in the wilderness" (Acts 7:38).

The church is not just a New Covenant entity. Before Jesus died on the cross, he taught his disciples to bring a believer before the church if their moral conduct was in question. He said, "And if he refuses to hear them, tell it to the church. But if he refuses to hear the church, let him be to you like a heathen" (Matt. 18:17).

Here, Jesus is talking about the first church, the Jewish church.

The two lampstands mentioned in Rev. 11 are the two olive branches, the two witnesses of the Lord of the earth and the two churches: prophetic Israel and the prophetic gentile church. The Lord of all the earth is calling for the participation of his two historical witnesses—the two will partner together in the last days.

It makes sense that the mighty signs and wonders that these witnesses are about to perform will be seen in every country around the world. Christians and redeemed Jews will infiltrate society, challenge the status quo, and release the power of God upon the earth. The church will shine exceedingly bright and, as promised, the glory of the Lord will come upon Israel before Christ returns (Isa. 60:1–2).

Jesus said, "He who believes in me, the works that I do he will do also: and greater works than these will he do, because I go to my Father" (John 14:12).Jesus did not die on the cross to produce an anemic church. He promised that his followers would perform greater miracles than he had performed, and this promise has not yet been fulfilled. The church and redeemed Israel will minister with a new level of anointing. One day when spiritual darkness is covering the earth God's glory will rise upon his people (Isa. 60:1–2).

In the next chapter, we will discover the miraculous power and anointing that is about to be displayed through Israel and the gentile church.

Chapter Twenty-four

Revelation is About the Power of the Two Witnesses

If anyone tries to harm them, fire comes from their mouths and devours their enemies. This is how anyone who wants to harm them must die.

These men have power to shut up the sky so that it will not rain during the time they are prophesying; and they have power to turn the waters into blood and to strike the earth with every kind of plague as often as they want.

Now when they have finished their testimony, the beast that comes up from the Abyss will attack them, and overpower and kill them. Their bodies will lie in the street of the great city, which is figuratively called Sodom and Egypt, where also their Lord was crucified. For three and a half days men from every people, tribe, language and nation will gaze on their bodies and refuse them burial. The inhabitants of the earth will gloat over them and will celebrate by sending each other gifts, because these two prophets had tormented those who live on the earth.

But after three and a half days a breath of life from God entered them, and they stood on their feet, and terror struck those who saw them. Then they heard a loud voice from heaven

> *saying to them, "Come up here." And they went up to heaven in a cloud, while their enemies looked on.*
> *At that very hour there was an earthquake and a tenth of the city collapsed. Seven thousand people were killed in the earthquake, and the survivors were terrified and gave glory to the God of heaven. The second woe is passed; the third is coming soon. (Rev. 11:4–14)*

CHAPTER TOPICS

1. The humility of the church
2. The world embracing democracy
3. The Bible ethic restored
4. The political and supernatural power of the saints
5. The rebel coup
6. The beast who comes from the Abyss
7. The death of the saints
8. Celebrations for the wicked
9. Resurrection and a rapture
10. Revival comes again

CLOTHED IN SACKCLOTH

GOD'S PROPHETIC GENTILES AND prophetic Israelites will be the frontline ministers of the end-time church. The two churches are the two witnesses, and they will minister the power of God at a level never before seen on earth.

One all-important quality must be present: humility. This is symbolically demonstrated because the witnesses are clothed in sackcloth. I do not believe that the churches members will literally wear sackcloth, although some might. Far more necessary will be the sackcloth on their hearts—the attitude of repentance, humility, and compassion. They will stand with a posture of humble piety and contrition. There can be no room for bravado or arrogance when one handles such godly power. The fear of God is the backdrop for this spiritual activity.

The saints have extended compassion and kindness to multitudes, but now they will demonstrate God's severity. They will rule with due diligence.

A DEMOCRATIC WORLD

As I write, the president of the United States, George W. Bush, is calling the entire world to embrace democracy. It is a slow process, but the western nations are influencing and even overpowering the eastern nations with the message of democracy. It is an appealing lure that will eventually be irresistible. Even Muslim nations and dictatorial regimes will ultimately yield to the democratic form of government. Dictatorships will topple, and violent fanatics will be subdued. The vote of the masses will eventually rule the world. It is a necessary political format for the end times. It will be democracy, not dictatorships that will unite the world for the end-time war against Israel and the church.

Before democracy unites the world against God, it will be used as a platform to usher in the church's finest hour. A phenomenon will surprise the world during the first three and a half years of the tribulation. As billions die because of God's judgments, multitudes will become disciples of Christ.

In a short time, the Christian and Jewish communities will grow with unprecedented numbers. They will even outnumber the enemies of God. Open political conflict will increase between the followers of Christ and humanists, but because there will be so many Christians, godly leaders will be voted to political power over the nations.

JUDEO-CHRISTIAN ETHICS RESTORED

For a short while the disciples of Christ will lead the political systems of the world. They will be so popular that they will hold an overwhelming majority of political power. They will change the laws of the nations and realign the morays of society to reflect a Judeo-Christian standard of civil practice and behavior. Some of the changes will include outlawing abortion and declaring homosexuality immoral. The nation's leaders will clamp down on drugs and stop the pornography trade from using the public marketplace. They will deal a deadly blow to organized crime and reinstate religious freedom. They will allow prayer, the teaching of creation, and other expressions of faith in the public place. They will make open statements from political platforms to declare that Jesus is Lord. They will not force Christianity on people, but they will legally change the laws of the nations to uphold a Christian standard of morality.

REBEL RESISTANCE

Although the new leaders will have come to power through legal political procedures, many will refuse to be governed by these disciples of Christ. The rebels will muster a strong resistance against their national governments, and guerrilla warfare will follow as they take up arms to overthrow the Biblical governments of the world.

Humanists will lose billions of dollars because their illegal or immoral trades have been shut down. The abortion trade and pornography industries will lose billions of dollars, the entertainment industry will be heavily censored, and the homosexual community will be irate because they have lost the ground of popularity that they held for so long. The world will become a boiling pot of demonic anger, and uprisings will be common.

TORMENTING EVILDOERS

Ungodly merchants will feel tormented by the two witnesses, because their evil merchandising has been forced underground. Their industries will lose billions of dollars Note the telltale words of Rev. 11:10: "The inhabitants of the earth will gloat over them [after the saints are killed] and will celebrate by sending each other gifts, because these two prophets had tormented those who live on the earth."

The two witnesses will be seen as tormenting the people of the earth because they will put an end to their evil liberties. They will halt evil merchandising and curb outward expressions of immorality. That is why many will react and call Israel and the church tormentors.

SUPERNATURAL POWER

Revelation says, "If anyone tries to harm them, fire comes from their mouths. This is how anyone who wants to harm them must die" (Rev. 11:5).

It will not be political and governmental speeches alone that will empower the two witnesses. They will have supernatural power from God. The rebel insurgencies will be frustrated as they are held at bay by the miraculous power of Christian governments, which will defend their communities with supernatural power. When Christian leaders speak the word, their enemies—the rebels—will fall dead.

This kind of power was demonstrated in the fifth chapter of Acts. Ananias and Sapphira fell on the floor dead when they resisted the word of the Lord, which was spoken by the apostle Peter (Acts 5:1-10).

The two witnesses will not kill people because those people refuse the gospel or speak out against the government. Rebels will be killed when they rise up with violent acts against the government and perpetrate terrorist activity within the community.

It would be wrong for the two witnesses to go out and kill unless they were exercising civil or military protection over the people; they cannot be self-appointed vigilante mercenaries. National and local governments, like all federal governments, will have a God-given mandate to keep the peace and protect the people from any harm that comes from without or from within their borders. To kill without federal or local civil authority may be murder, and the prophets of the Lord would not commit such acts. As governing rulers, they will function within God's laws and within the laws of their civil societies. In order for them to kill people as described in Rev. 11, they must have national authority, and that will be earned through national elections.

THIS WAS PROPHESIED FOR ISRAEL

Christian and Jewish leaders will have power to hold back the rain and to release plagues on the earth as often as they desire. This end-time power was prophesied over the Jewish people in the book of Micah.

Micah, representing Israel began to prophesy, "Do not gloat over me, my enemy! Though I have fallen, I will rise. Because I have sinned against him, I will bear the Lord's wrath, until he pleads my case and establishes my right. He will bring me into the light; I will see his righteousness. Then my enemy will see it and be covered with shame" (Mic. 7:8–10).

Then the Lord responded, "*As in the days when you came out of Egypt, I will show them my wonders*. Nations will see and be ashamed deprived of all their power. They will come trembling out of their dens; they will turn in fear to the Lord our God and will be afraid of you" (Mic. 7:15–17; italics added).

Then Israel responded back to the Lord: "Who is a God like you, who pardons sin and forgives the transgression of the remnant of his inheritance? You do not stay angry forever. You will be true to Jacob [Israel] and show mercy to Abraham, as you pledged on oath to our fathers in days long ago" (Mic. 7:18–20).

God will show the people of Israel the same wonders that he showed them when they came out of Egypt. Revelation says, "They have power to turn the waters to blood and to strike the earth with every kind of plague as often as they want" (Rev. 11:6).

Just like Micah prophesied, the plagues of Egypt's waters turning to blood and other deadly plagues will happen again. They will come during the great tribulation. This word of prophecy further supports our understanding that the two witnesses are the gentile church and Israel.

The saints will legally change the laws of nations and hold off violent uprisings with political protocol and supernatural might. The saints will come into political power during the first couple of years of the tribulation period.

Their reign among the nations will end at the midpoint of the tribulation—at the three and a half year mark. It will not extend beyond that season. Their reign of godly power may last for as much as two and a half years, but no longer.

BARBARIC SLAUGHTER

Then the beast from the Abyss will be ready. This beast is called Apollyon or Abaddon, as we learned from Rev. 9. He is the angel of the Abyss. We will learn more about him in upcoming chapters. He will use the four demon Lords who were released from the Euphrates River and he will launch an offensive against the two witnesses and come to the aid of the human rebels. He will add demons to their ranks and empower them with supernatural help. At the same instant, God will allow the Christian rulers to lose their supernatural powers. They will be overthrown and killed by Apollyon. This will be full-scale persecution; it will be a military coup against the saints, and the Lord will let it happen. God allowed his Son to be crucified in like manner. He removed his grace from Jesus and allowed his Son to be killed. He has good reason for the things he does.

Although many will not see the demonic forces at work, the power of Apollyon and the four demon Lords will enable the rebels to overpower the saints. In a worldwide coup, an all-out slaughter will allow the humanists to seize the thrones of the world. Multitudes of prophetic Christians and prophetic Jews will be slaughtered, and their bodies will be left on the ground to rot for three days—an act that is extremely barbaric and demonic. Even in ancient times, a slaughtered army would be buried or burned for health reasons alone, especially in tropical countries where dead bodies decompose quickly.

DEMONIC CELEBRATIONS

Multitudes of vile men will sell their souls to the devil for this victory. The demon spirits will be celebrating. So will the perverted and the criminal element of humanity. They will have become fully demonized, and many will be unaware of it. Evil people from every nation, tribe, and language will insist that these dead bodies are left where they lay, out in the open, as a show of distain and defeat.

Wicked men will celebrate and gloat over the dead bodies. They will throw expensive parties and send gifts of congratulations to one another. The news media will show pictures of the dead bodies on TV, on the front covers of newspapers, and on whatever means of communication they have.

Now the people will be able to return to their public orgies, their drug trade and to the craft of the abortuary. Homosexuals will be bolder than ever, demonstrating every vile thing in the streets. Hard-core pornography will be displayed openly. The wicked of the world will revel in lust and chaos, and the godly who are not killed will hide.

Not all Christians and Jews will be killed, but most of the prophetic leaders will be. The other saints who have not been on the frontlines will escape death and go into hiding. These are the more quiet Christians and Jews. They will not be targeted for death right away for they were not in the political forefront.

RESURRECTION AND A RAPTURE

Two thousand years ago Jesus was resurrected from the grave. After three days, death could hold him no more. A three-day period of lying dead and then a resurrection will happen again.

"After the three and a half days a breath of life from God entered them, and they stood to their feet, and terror struck those who saw them. Then they heard a voice from heaven saying to them, 'Come up here,' and they went up to heaven in a cloud while their enemies looked on" (Rev. 11:11–12).

This describes a rapture of saints. Jesus will not come into the sky to take his entire church to heaven, but many prophetic leaders will be resurrected from where their bodies lay and ascend to the throne room. Thousands, if not millions, will receive life in their bodies and be raised from the dead and taken up into heaven.

Orgies and vile parties will suddenly slam to a halt, as a rebellious world experiences a new terror. People will be jolted back to their senses. Many will cry out in fear, others will run to get away from the crowds, repenting as best as they can as they go.

THE WORLD IS STUNNED

The media will change its course. The resurrections will be caught on tape, and the world will be stunned. The demonized will not care, but many ungodly people will be shaken to the core. Within the hour, an earthquake will hit a major city killing seven thousand people. Even ungodly newscasters will make the connection. The two events will just be too powerful and too well timed to be coincidental. People who previously were enemies of God will fall on their faces in repentance.

THE HONOR OF THE REVIVAL

"The survivors were terrified and gave glory to the God of heaven" (Rev. 11:13).

God will not let so many people go to hell. The powerful blood of Jesus will prevail, and, even at this stage of the tribulation period, another revival will break forth. Multitudes of sinners will give glory to God when they see those who were slaughtered come to life and rise into the heavens. Some of them will have been guilty of murdering the saints, but the cross of Jesus will cover their sins just as he has covered ours.

It took the death of Christ to save a lost world, and God will use the death of the two witnesses (prophetic gentiles and Jews) to draw such hardcore sinners to repentance. It will be such an honor to be a member of the two-witness church; to help God reach the unreachable and bring them to salvation; and to die for Christ, to be raised, and raptured at such a time as this.

THE SECOND WOE IS NOW COMPLETE

This portion of scripture ends with these words. "Seven thousand people were killed in the earthquake, and the survivors were terrified and gave glory to the God of heaven. The second woe is passed; the third is coming soon." (Rev. 11:14)

The first woe was demon hoards, like locusts being released from the Abyss to torment non-believers for five months. They had a king over them named Apollyon. The second woe was four demon Lords who came up from the Euphrates River. They brought the world into war. At the mid-point of the tribulation period, these two forces will be led by Apollyon to overthrow the two churches and kill a multitude of saints. They will not do the killing directly, but they will empower wicked people to achieve this evil act. Once this has been done the second woe will be complete.

Woe to the earth! The third woe is still to come. It will also involve a demonic creature being released on the planet.

Part Four
The Third campaign

Chapter Twenty-five

Revelation is About the Last Trumpet

The seventh angel sounded his trumpet, and there were loud voices in heaven which said: "The kingdom of the world has become the kingdom of our Lord and of his Christ, and he will reign for ever and ever."

And the twenty-four elders, who were seated on their thrones before God, fell on their faces and worshipped God, saying: "We give thanks to you, Lord God Almighty, the One who is and who was, because you have taken your great power and have begun to reign.

The nations were angry; and your wrath has come. The time has come for judging the dead, and for rewarding your servants the prophets and your saints and those who reverence your name, both small and great—and for destroying those who destroy the earth."

Then God's temple in heaven was opened, and within his temple was the ark of his covenant. And there came flashes of lightning, rumblings, peals of thunder, an earthquake and a great hailstorm. (Rev. 11:15–19)

CHAPTER TOPICS

1. The seventh trumpet
2. Loud prophetic voices
3. The seven events of the last trumpet
4. The temple opening in heaven
5. The covenant and the ark
6. New faith for God's people

CRITICAL MASS

REVELATION 10–12 SHOWS US what the church will be doing during the tribulation period. We know thus far that, although she will suffer persecution, she will have risen to political power over the nations. Under the anointing of the Holy Spirit, she will show the world God's standards for society and will rule the nations, but her reign will be short-lived. The power of the two churches cannot be sustained until Satan is completely removed and Jesus sits on the throne. The kingdom of God will never be complete without the presence of the king.

Jesus will not return, however, until Israel experiences revival and the gentile church has partnered with Israel in the power of the Spirit. When these two prerequisites have been accomplished, the kingdom of God will reach the point of critical mass. It is fitting that the twenty-four elders are given the role of proclaiming this breakthrough moment.

THE SEVENTH TRUMPET IS PROPHESIED

Following God's pattern—his plans are always prophesied before they happen. When the seventh trumpet is sounded, the third campaign will begin. Learning that this is God's pattern is an important step in partnering with God. Intercessors and servants of the Lord take note; we must prophesy God's plans into existence. We must not be passive onlookers, but active participants in the day of God's power by praying the prayer of agreement and speaking the word of faith. When God's plans come to pass, they will be the exact outworking of those prayers and prophecies. This demonstrates God's foreknowledge, his sovereignty, and his plan to partner with his people.

LOUD VOICES

Loud voices from heaven will prophesy, "The kingdom of the world has become the kingdom of our Lord and of his Christ, and he will reign for ever and ever" (Rev. 11:15).

When the time is right, pray and prophesy with a loud voice. If it is a true word from God, it will be all the more powerful. If it is a word of your own making or given at an inappropriate time, it will be just a loud noise, empty of power. When a prophecy or prayer is given in a loud voice, it exposes its power level. Its source becomes evident very quickly.

A prophecy is linked to two decisive moments: the time of its proclamation and the time of its fulfillment. This prophecy of the seventh trumpet will be fulfilled in the days of the sounding of the seventh trumpet. This is last trump and it will come with monumental significance.

THE EVENT LIST FOR THE LAST TRUMP

During the days of the seventh trumpet, seven catastrophic things will happen. They were prophesied by the angel in Rev. 11. They are as follows:

1. The kingdoms of the world will become Jesus' kingdom.
2. God will begin to rule on earth, by releasing great power in his people.
3. The ultimate wrath of God—the worst judgments—will come.
4. God will judge the dead—the saints will be judged before Christ, and sinners will receive judgment because they will not be included in the first resurrection.

5. The first resurrection and the second coming of Christ will occur together.
6. Prophets, saints, and those who reverence God's name will be rewarded with resurrected bodies and an amazing inheritance.
7. As the judgments of God are poured out from the seven bowls of wrath, those who have destroyed the earth will be destroyed. Wicked men, the devil, and his demonic army will all receive their judgments.

Seven is the number of completion. The days of the seventh trumpet will usher in and complete the seven goals of the tribulation period.

AN OPEN TEMPLE

Events on earth will reach the point of critical mass, and this will trigger a new event in heaven—the temple will be opened. We discovered earlier that the Lamb will open the scroll to reveal and release the great tribulation. Now we learn that heaven's temple will be opened to reveal new blessings for the church. It is always open in heaven, but at the sounding of the last trumpet, it will open so the saints on earth can receive new faith. For the first time in history, the entire church will see inside the heavenly temple. Paul, Ezekiel, and Daniel saw it in their day and were empowered by what they saw. They were told, however, not to share the vision until the time of the end. When the temple moment has come, the heavenly vision will be open for all of God's people to see.

Seeing inside the temple will raise the vision and faith of the saints to an amazing new level. It will be a special gift for saints on the planet. The coming judgments will be worse than the judgments of the past, but seeing inside the temple will give grace, dignity, and strength to the church for what lies ahead.

THE ARK OF HIS COVENANT

The Lamb and the Almighty are the light of the temple. In their light, many amazing things will be revealed, and we cannot know all of them until when the temple is open. One of the secret temple blessings is the ark of God's covenant. The ark is a reminder to the saints that the covenant of God extends over them. In other words, God is letting the saints know that his covenant continues, that he is with his people, and all that he promised will come to pass."

The ark represents God's presence, power, and mercy. It represents God's promise for his people. For forty years, Moses led the children of Israel through the wilderness. A magnificent cloud rose before them during the day, and a blazing pillar of fire rose before them each night; both came from the ark of the covenant. They gave Israel shade by day and warmth at night. They reminded the Israelites of God's presence and power. Furthermore, these signs caused the nations round about to fear the Israelites. No army wanted to attack a people who manifested such supernatural power. Once the temple was built in Jerusalem, the fire and the cloud went inside the holy of holies. The presence of God was known because of the fire and the cloud that came from the ark.

When the temple in heaven is opened, the covenant and the power that is connected with it will be revealed. This is a sample of the many temple blessings that will be seen by the church.

THE LAST TRUMPET WILL BE ACTIVATED

Every act of judgment or provision of mercy, from the moment that the temple doors open until the millennial reign, will be part of the seven-trumpet package. As the last trump sounds, the earth will be rocked with storms and earthquakes.

"And there came flashes of lightning, rumblings, peals of thunder, an earthquake and a great hailstorm" (Rev. 11:19).

These traumas will be hurled from the altar of prayer like those in Rev. 8.

"He was given much incense, together with the prayers of the saints, on the golden altar ... Then the angel took the censer, filled it with fire from the altar, and hurled it on the earth. And there came peals of thunder, rumblings, flashes of lightning and an earthquake" (Rev. 8:3, 5).

The days of the last trumpet are the grand finale of the tribulation. They will be prayed into existence, prophesied over, and proclaimed by saints in heaven and earth. The angel will gather the prophetic prayers and hurl them to the earth. Physical storms and earthquakes will mark a new chapter in God's end-time book. God answers prayer. That is included in his covenant of blessing.

Chapter Twenty-six

Revelation is About a Woman Clothed with the Sun

A great and wondrous sign appeared in heaven: a woman clothed with the sun, with the moon under her feet and a crown of twelve stars on her head.
She was pregnant and cried out in pain as she was about to give birth.
Then another sign appeared in heaven: an enormous red dragon with seven heads and ten horns and seven crowns on his heads. His tail swept a third of the stars out of the sky and flung them to the earth. The dragon stood in front of the woman who was about to give birth, so that he might devour her child the moment it was born.
She gave birth to a son, a male child, who will rule all the nations with an iron sceptre. And her child was snatched up to God and to the throne.
The woman fled into the desert place prepared for her by God, where she might be taken care of for 1,260 days. (Rev. 12:1–6)

CHAPTER TOPICS

1. God's people in history, including the Jews and the gentile church
2. A review of the great tribulation as it has been revealed so far
3. A different kind of rapture
4. The uncontrollable anger of the devil
5. A special anointing for the saints who are left behind

SIGNS AND SYMBOLS

THE BOOK OF REVELATION is written in symbols. The twelfth chapter is one of the most encrypted in the book. Many different interpretations have been given. This is what I see.

THE FIRST THREE AND A HALF YEARS

The first six verses of Rev. 12 are a review of the first half of the great tribulation. John received amazing details of these three and a half years. Now, at this stage of the vision the Lord gave him, and us, a word picture to summarize what had happened. John had seen angels, demons, deadly judgments, revivals, heaven's glorious courts, and the awful decimation of the earth's environment. It was time to review the most important detail, what will happen to the church?

IDENTIFYING THE WOMAN

John called this word picture a great and wonderful sign. It is easy to identify it because it is someone, a woman, clothed with the sun. The sun is a symbol of Christ.

Galatians says, "All of you who were baptized into Christ have clothed yourselves with Christ" (Gal. 3:27).

Romans says, "Clothe yourselves with the Lord Jesus Christ," (Rom. 13:14).

To be clothed with Christ is to be made righteous before God. No one is righteous because of their own efforts. Only when we are clothed with Christ are we justified in God's sight. Who clothes themselves with the sun? The answer is simple: only the people of God do.

We know the woman belongs to God for the son she births goes to heaven, and God protects her by giving her a hiding place. Who does God care for in this way? The answer is clear: he cares for his people in this way (Rev. 15:5–6).

The dragon described in the opening verses of Rev. 12 has seven heads and ten horns. This represents Satan and his army. He is ready to eat the woman's baby. Whom does Satan want to devour? The answer is the people of God.

These details are enough for us to draw a clear conclusion: the wondrous woman represents the people of God.

TWO DEFINING DETAILS

The woman represents God's people, but there is more to tell about her. Her feet and head are given special mention (Rev.12:1). The symbol on her head represents her beginnings; the symbol at her feet represents her completion. A twelve-jeweled crown is on her head, and the moon is under her feet. The twelve-jeweled crown on the woman's head refers to Israel and the twelve tribes. Scripture teaches that twelve jewels represent the twelve tribes of Israel: "Mount four rows of precious stones on it … a ruby, a topaz, a beryl, a turquoise, a sapphire, an emerald, a jacinth, an agate, an amethyst, a chrysolite, an onyx and a jasper. Mount them in gold settings. There are to be twelve stones, one for each of the names of the sons of Israel, each engraved like a seal with the name of one of the twelve tribes" (Exod. 28:17–22).

We have already discovered that the moon represents the church, for it reflects the sun as the church reflects Christ. Redeemed Jews and gentiles are both included as part of the people of God. Redeemed Jews and the gentile church are the two anointed ones who serve the

Lord of the whole earth. These two entities make up the wondrous woman clothed with the sun. One is at her head, and the other at her feet.

THE BRIDE

It is no surprise that God refers to the woman as great and wondrous. God loves her; Jesus died for her. Here are the Jews (the twelve-jeweled crown) and the gentile church, (the moon) partnering together at the end of the age. Together, they make up the bride of Christ.

Ephesians five says that a married couple is like Christ and his church. Revelation tells us that the city of God (his people) is the bride of Christ. "One of the angels said to me, 'Come, I will show you the bride, the wife of the Lamb' ... He showed me the Holy City, Jerusalem" (Rev. 21:2, 9).

The Lord is married to his people (Isaiah 62:4–5). This is not just a New Covenant reality. Throughout the Old Testament the Jews are seen as God's bride. Jeremiah tells us that God married the people of Israel even though they were unfaithful. He said, "Return, faithless people, declares the Lord, for I am your husband" (Jer. 3:14).

The fact that this crowned woman with a moon under her feet represents the people of God is not a new concept. She has existed for thousands of years; she is God's bride: the people of God.

THE WOMAN IS PREGNANT

The woman in John's vision is about to give birth. Jesus prophesied that a miraculous birth would take place at the end of the age. He said, "Nation will rise against nation, and kingdom against kingdom. There will be famines and earthquakes in various places. All of these are the beginnings of birth pains" (Matt. 24:8).

Birth pains come when a woman is birthing. The woman in the opening of Rev. 12 cries out in pain for she is about to give birth. Revelation tells us that the woman gives birth to a "male child." The people of God will have a special baby at the end of the age.

THE MAN CHILD

This word picture is a review of what has happened so far in the great tribulation. We have already discovered who the child is. The child is the prophetic church that emerges during the first half of the tribulation. We identified the prophetic church as the two witnesses, the two anointed ones, made up of Jews and gentiles. The churches will prophesy for one thousand two hundred sixty days, just a bit more than three and a half years. Not all the members of the church will prophesy, but only the prophetic outspoken leaders. The prophetic witnesses will be born out of the church, the people of God.

The rest of the church members are the rest of the woman's offspring, who are described later in the chapter. They will remain on earth after the prophetic ones are gone. Satan will be so angry that he will attempt to destroy the Christians and Jews who remain.

"Then the dragon was enraged at the woman and went off to make war against *the rest of her offspring*—those who obey God's commandments and hold to the testimony of Jesus" (Rev. 12:16; italics added).

Pain accompanies birth, and we are told that the woman cried out in pain. Israel and the church will suffer great pain as they enter the tribulation period. They will be mocked and ridiculed by the world. They will be persecuted, and many will be killed. Recall from our earlier studies that the moon turns to blood? There will be much pain during those days—labor pains. In the midst of that pain, the people of God will cry out and the prophetic end-time church will be born.

A PARALLEL TO JESUS

Illustrations in the scriptures often parallel many things at the same time. The woman in this vision parallels Mary and the birth of the male child parallels the birth of Jesus in Bethlehem and Herod's attempt to kill him.

Revelation 12 however, is not about Jesus, for the parallels soon break down as we examine the entire story. One day Jesus will rule with an iron sceptre, but that will happen in the millennium, not at this point in the tribulation period. Furthermore, following the male child's ascent to heaven, the rest of the woman's offspring run to a special hiding place to be taken care of for one thousand two hundred sixty days. That did not happen after the resurrection of Christ; but it will happen in the tribulation period. The male child is not Jesus, but the prophetic church at the midpoint of the tribulation.

TWO FIRSTS FOR THE CHURCH

As we review the amazing works of the prophetic church, two notable things stand out; the male child (the prophetic Church) will do two things that have never happened before.

First, he will rule all of the nations with an iron sceptre. For a very brief period of time, the church and Israel will rule the world after they are voted into power democratically.

Secondly, the male child is caught up to God and to his throne: "She gave birth to a son, a male child, who will rule all the nations with an iron sceptre. And her child was snatched up to God and to the throne" (Rev. 12:5).

Here are the two firsts for the church:

1. Never before have all the nations of the world been ruled by God's people.
2. Although a few individuals have experienced resurrection before this time, there has never before been a major rapture to the throne room of God, before now.

The church (redeemed Jews and gentiles) will be outstanding in the first half of the tribulation. Even though persecution and judgment will be common, they will lead multitudes to Christ. This will happen so extensively that for a moment, Christians will become a majority in the world. The church, the two witnesses (prophetic Jews and gentiles) will do exactly as their name suggests: they will witness. They will evangelize the world: "And this Gospel of the kingdom will be preached in the whole world as a testimony to all nations, and then the end will come" (Matt. 24:14).

In every nation, new Christians will vote the leaders of God's people into positions of political power, and they will rule the nations with an iron sceptre. Once in power, they will take a strong stand. They will clamp down on corruption and immorality, changing the laws and bringing civil righteousness to the world.

The second amazing phenomenon that will take place is a massive resurrection and rapture. The Lord will strategically lift his hand of protection from the prophetic church. He will release the Antichrist, the beast from the Abyss. Satan will be ready and waiting to devour the child that was born of the woman. After the beast from the Abyss is released, violence will erupt. Only a couple of years after the Christians come to power, they will be removed from office. All around the world, God's prophetic people who at that time will rule the nations, will be attacked and killed, and their bodies will be left on the streets. After three days, God will breathe life into them, and they will be snatched up to heaven.

THE SUMMARY

Revelation paints a perfect picture, the woman is the bride of Christ made up of redeemed Jews and gentiles. Her special baby is the prophetic church, the two witnesses. Satan hates them and wants to destroy them. For a brief period of time, they will rule the nations in righteousness. Satan, with the help of the beast, will eventually gain ground and kill them. Satan's plan will backfire, for God is the one who has orchestrated all of these events. Through the death and resurrection of the prophetic church, multitudes of rebellious sinners will be snatched from hell. These events will lead to the salvation of many souls. The greatest revival in history is still to come.

The review of Rev. 12 keeps us from losing sight of God's big plan. It shows us that God is in control and everything that happens is a fulfillment of his prophetic word.

THE LEFT BEHIND CHURCH

John wrote, "The woman fled into the desert to a place prepared for her by God, where she might be taken care of for 1,260 days" (Rev. 12:6).

A few verses later, he wrote, "Then the dragon was enraged at the woman and went off to make war against the rest of her offspring—those who obey God's commandments and hold to the testimony of Jesus" (Rev. 12:16).

When the prophetic church is martyred and subsequently raptured to heaven, the rest of the church will be left behind. The saints will run into hiding. The church that remains will have witnessed a full-scale slaughter of thousands of her most dynamic members. She will be feeling weak and helpless, but God will do a great work with these remaining saints.

First, God will provide a place of protection for them for the three and a half years that will follow the slaughter. Second, he will soon anoint these saints who have not been on the frontlines and release them to the work of the ministry.

At this point, God is not finished with the earth, nor with the people who live on it. His judgments and mercies will be more demonstrative than ever before. He will shake the world to find more who might be saved.

He will not be finished with the woman offspring. The hiding church will come into her own. These more feeble saints will soon find new strength and anointing. They will rise to champion the cause of Christ in the very end.

Some Christians feel that the days of high profile heroes are over. They say that God will take his anointing away from the superstars so that all in Christ's body will be equal. Nothing could be further from the truth. In the days ahead, the most gifted saints will become even more powerful. Their anointing will not be reduced; rather the weaker saints will rise in the Spirit and posses a new release of authority.

Chapter Twenty-seven

REVELATION IS ABOUT THE THIRD WOE

And there was war in heaven, Michael and his angels fought against the dragon, and the dragon and his angels fought back. But he was not strong enough, and they lost their place in heaven. The great dragon was hurled down—that ancient serpent called the devil or Satan, who leads the whole world astray. He was hurled to the earth, and his angels with him. (Rev. 12:7–9)

SUGGEST READING: REVELATION 12:7–17

CHAPTER TOPICS

1. Identifying the three woes
2. Michael finally receiving permission to attack Satan
3. Satan being thrown out of the heavens
4. The devil being cast down to the earth full of anger
5. An amazing expression of power in the church

THE THREE WOES

WE WERE WARNED IN Rev. 8:13, "Woe! Woe! Woe to the inhabitants of the earth because of the trumpet blasts by the other three angels."

This reference points to the fifth, sixth, and seventh trumpets. Their sounding will release the three woes, and all three will involve demonic creatures.

We learned that the first woe will be the release of demons from the Abyss along with their king, Apollyon. They will torture and torment people, and Apollyon will lead the army that will kill the two witnesses, the prophetic church.

John wrote, "The sun and sky were darkened by the smoke from the Abyss. Out of the smoke locusts came down upon the earth and were given power like that of scorpions" (Rev. 9:2–3).

In chapter 11 he wrote, "Now when they [the prophetic church] have finished their testimony, the beast that comes up from the Abyss will attack them, and overpower them and kill them" (Rev. 11:17).

"The first woe is past; two other woes are yet to come" (Rev. 9:12).

We discovered that the second woe will be the release of four satanic generals from prison, somewhere along the Euphrates. They will activate two hundred million soldiers to a world war, and one-third of the earth's already decimated population (about a billion people) will die.

John wrote, "The sixth angel sounded his trumpet … 'Release the four angels who were bound at the great river Euphrates … to kill a third of mankind. The number of the mounted troops was two hundred million." … "The second woe has passed; the third woe is coming soon" (Rev. 9:13-16, Rev. 11:14).

The third woe will be the release of another demonic force upon the earth. Satan himself will be cast down upon the earth, and he will be full of anger.

"The seventh angel sounded his trumpet" … "But woe to the earth and the sea, because the devil has gone down to you … When the dragon saw that he had been hurled to the earth, he pursued the woman who had given birth to the male child. The dragon was enraged at the woman and went off to make war against the rest of her offspring—those who obey God's commandments" (Rev. 11:12, Rev. 12:13–17).

SATANIC ARMIES

Since before the creation of man, Satan has lived in rebellion against Almighty God. He has gathered around him a highly organized army of fallen angels and demons who are with him in his pursuit of evil. There are many types of demons and many levels of fallen angels who serve under his command.

Demons are evil spirits or in the old English language, ghosts. The Bible speaks of them often. Demons trouble humanity by deceiving, tempting, and hurting people in any way possible. They control behavior in people and often live inside of them. When they come from without, scripture exhorts us to resist them. When they live inside a person, they must be driven out. When Jesus walked with his disciples through the regions of Galilee, he cast demons out of many people. This was a regular part of his ministry.

Fallen angels spend much of their time in the heavens. They rule with demonic intent over geographical regions of the earth. They are called the rulers of the darkness of this age (Eph. 6:12 NKJV).

Recall the story in the book of Daniel. Gabriel fought a battle with demonic angels in the heavens, somewhere above the earth. Daniel said, "The prince of the Persian kingdom resisted me twenty-one days. Then Michael, one of the chief princes, came to help me ... Soon I will return to fight against the prince of Persia, and when I go the prince of Greece will come; (No one supports me except Michael, your prince. And in the first year of Darius the Mede, I took my stand to support and protect him.)" (Dan. 10:12–21).

These angels fought somewhere between heaven and earth. Their battle took place in either the first or second heaven. The archangel Michael is called Israel's prince. He came and helped Gabriel, enabling him to get through to Daniel. These ruling angels, both good and evil ones, are called princes and they lead massive troops of warrior angels, called principalities (Eph. 6:12 KJV).

It is interesting to note that the angel Gabriel was assigned to watch over king Darius. He said, "I took my stand to support and protect him" (Dan. 10:21).

Angels are assigned to watch over and protect people.

SATAN ON THE PROWL

"And there was war in heaven, Michael and his angels fought against the dragon, ... and they lost their place in heaven. The great dragon was hurled down—that ancient serpent called the devil or Satan, who leads the whole world astray. He was hurled to the earth, and his angels with him. (Rev. 12:7–9)

Before Satan is cast out of the middle heaven by Michael, he is able to move freely between heaven and earth, visiting earth to kill, steal, and destroy.

Peter warned, "Be alert. Your enemy the devil prowls around like a roaring lion looking for someone to devour. Resist him" (1 Pet. 5:8).

Satan was seen in the Garden of Eden, and he has troubled millions of people since. He even troubled Jesus in the wilderness. We know that Satan moves upon the earth.

He is also called the ruler of the kingdom of the air (Eph. 2:2). In the book of Job, Satan is seen in heaven arguing with God: "One day the angels came to present themselves before the Lord, and Satan also came with them. The Lord said to Satan, 'Where have you come from?' Satan answered the Lord, 'From roaming through the earth and going back and forth in it'" (Job 1:6–8).

He is trouble. He is the accuser of our brothers, accusing them before God day and night (Rev. 12:10). An example of his slander was revealed when Satan came before God to accuse Job. He accused Job of spiritual infidelity, saying that Job would reject God and curse him if forced to endure enough hardship.

He said to God, "Stretch out your hand and strike everything he [Job] has, and he will surely curse you to your face" (Job 1:11).

Satan slanders people, attempting to tear them down and discredit them. He does this to mock God by emphasizing the failures of his children He attempts to (as it were) rub these human failures in God's face before the courts of heaven. This is only one of Satan's many tactics to bring down humanity.

For thousands of years, Satan has led demon armies in rebellion against God. They trouble the human race because man is created in the image of God. Humans were made for partnership with God; if Satan inflicts humanity, he indirectly inflicts the Almighty.

Speaking of the devil, Jesus said, "The thief comes only to steal and kill and to destroy" (John 10:10).

MICHAEL ATTACKS THE DEVIL

For thousands of years prior to the midpoint of the tribulation period, Satan will have had diplomatic immunity. He has had license to come and go at will through all the kingdoms of heaven and earth. He was not personally attacked or restrained from sending his troops into battle during this time.

Before now, "even the archangel Michael ... did not dare to bring a slanderous accusation against him, but said, 'The Lord rebuke you'" (Jude 1:9).

He has done his evil work for centuries, but finally, the hour of his demise will come.

Many Bible teachers espouse that Michael cast Satan out of heaven thousands of years ago. They take this 12th chapter of Revelation out of the book and allocate it's events to an era that existed some ten thousand years ago. There is no reason that I can see, to make such a textual maneuver. Furthermore, I do not think that such a treatment fits with the rest of scripture.

I suggest we keep Revelation chapter 12 right where it is. Keep it in the context of the book. Like the rest of the book of Revelation these events are still before us. They will happen during the great tribulation. God will speak, and Michael will go to war against the devil. There will be war in the heavens, the likes of which have not happened since the creation of man. Michael and his angels will fight Satan and his angels. They will overpower the devil, but they will not destroy him. Instead, Satan will be hurled down to the earth to be exposed, defrocked, and defeated before the sons of men.

He and his angels had a place in heaven where they were left alone. It was their safe house. That privilege will be taken from them. Revelation says, "They lost their place in heaven" (Rev. 12:8).

A HUGE PARADIGM SHIFT

A massive paradigm (pattern or standard) shift will explode in the universe. Satan's activities will change and be curtailed. He will be exiled to the planet's surface to serve the Lord, and then he will be judged. He will continue to deceive and destroy whomever he can, but all his evil actions will serve the purposes of God. He will come to the earth full of anger for he will know his time is short.

Most likely, the elders in heaven will announce the paradigm shift, because the prophecy refers to saints on earth as brothers. The proclamation will be given in a loud voice. Demons, angels, and faithful followers of the Lamb will hear the powerful words, and they will release celebration in heaven, but dread upon the earth. The words of the prophecy will cut the atmosphere like a knife.

John said, "Then I heard a loud voice in heaven say: "Now, have come the salvation and the power and the kingdom of our God, and the authority of his Christ. For the accuser of our brothers, who accuses them before our God day and night, has been hurled down. They overcame him by the blood of the Lamb and by the word of their testimony; they did not love their lives so much as to shrink from death. Therefore rejoice, you heavens and you who dwell in them! But woe to the earth and the sea because the devil has gone down to you! He is filled with fury, because he knows that his time is short." (Rev. 12:10–12)

THE SAINTS WILL HELP PULL DOWN SATAN

God does nothing on earth without requiring prayer and agreement from his people.

We read, "Surely the Sovereign Lord does nothing without revealing his plan to his servants, the prophets" (Amos 3:7).

Even in this monumental event of throwing Satan down to earth, God will enlist the help of humans. Michael and his angels will execute the battle plan and forcibly overpower Satan, but they will do it with the help of the church. The saints will overcome the devil by the blood of the Lamb and the word of their testimony.

The two end-time witnesses, the prophetic churches, will accomplish their essential assignment. They will rule the planet, restore righteousness among the nations, and evangelize the world. From that position of authority they will pray the prayer of agreement and finish their testimony (Rev. 11:7).

They will obtain the political authority of the kingdoms of earth, and because of that, God will obtain the prayer agreement he is looking for from those who hold the legal government of the earth. While the saints govern the earth they will pray, "Thy kingdom come, thy will be done on earth as it is in heaven." (Matt. 6:10).

When that prayer is spoken by the rulers of the earth, God will proceed to cast Satan out of heaven to be exposed and judged. God does nothing without prayer agreement from his people on earth. When the legitimate government on earth agrees with God in prayer, he will release the final stages of the tribulation period.

It will be because of the efforts of Spirit-led saints that Satan will be hurled down. They (the Christians) will overcome him by the blood of the Lamb and by the word of their testimony; they did not love their lives so much as to shrink from death. Their prayers and prophetic words, empowered by the blood of Jesus, will become their testimony. This will release the power of heaven and break the back of thousands of years of satanic rule. Adam gave Satan legal rights in the Garden of Eden, but the male child born of the woman, at the end of the age, will take those rights away by the blood of the Lamb and the word of their testimony.

Chapter Twenty-eight

Revelation is About Satan's Anger

When the dragon saw that he had been hurled to the earth, he pursued the woman who had given birth to the male child. The woman was given the two wings of a great eagle, so that she might fly to the place prepared for her in the desert, where she would be taken care of for a time, times and half a time, out of the serpent's reach.
Then from his mouth the serpent spewed water like a river, to overtake the woman and sweep her away with the torrent.
But the earth helped the woman by opening its mouth and swallowing the river that the dragon had spewed out of his mouth.
Then the dragon was enraged at the woman and went off to make war against the rest of her offspring—those who obey God's commandments and hold to the testimony of Jesus.
And the dragon stood on the shore of the sea. (Rev. 12:13–17)

CHAPTER TOPICS

1. Protection for left behind saints
2. Satan's campaign of slander against the church
3. Scientific facts that back Christian teaching
4. Satan's anger causing him to show his hand

PROTECTION FOR THE WOMAN'S OFFSPRING

IN EARLIER CHAPTERS OF Revelation, we saw that God will place his protective mark on the forehead of believers. Once again, during the time of the great tribulation, God will extend his protection. For a further three and a half years, God will provide a shield against mental and spiritual attacks on Christians.

The protection for the woman's seed (the church that will remain) is not protection against physical death. In the next chapter of Revelation we will discover that many saints will be killed.

"He [the beast, antichrist or Apollyon] was given power to make war against the saints and to conquer them ... If anyone is to be killed with the sword, with the sword he will be killed. This calls for patient endurance and faithfulness on the part of the saints" (Rev. 13:7, 10).

The beast will kill many Christians, but he will not be able to hurt them spiritually or tarnish their souls. They will be divinely protected from temptation, sin, defilement, and backsliding.

MY VIEWS

Revelation 12:13–17 may be the book's most difficult to interpret passages because they give us little information. My suggestions fit the context, timing, and scope of the book of Revelation. The following sections summarize what I believe the scriptures are saying. Others may come up with a more definitive argument, and I would like to hear them. Until then, I present to you, my personal view on these verses.

A PLACE PREPARED

In two separate passages, we read that God provided a desert place for the woman to flee to. I do not think this is a literal geographical hiding place, but a place of spiritual protection beyond the serpent's reach. It is a spiritual hiding place where a person's mind is guarded by the angels of God. Satan and his demons cannot penetrate that barrier.

Demons are infamous for attacking the minds of people. Through lies and lusts, they lure humanity away from God to sin and eternal damnation.

Jesus said, "Do not be afraid of those who kill the body but cannot kill the soul. Rather, be afraid of the One who can destroy both body and soul in hell" (Matt. 10:28).

Warfare of the mind is a serious battle for Christians, and many fall prey to the devil's devices. They are enticed to doubt their faith and entertain sinful thoughts. Doubt and sin can lead dedicated Christians away from God. I see this happening to many young Christians who are attending a secular university. Many lose the strength of their faith even within the first month of university life.

Recall the verses that we mentioned from 2 Corinthians: "The weapons we fight with are not weapons of the world. On the contrary, we have divine power to demolish strongholds. We demolish arguments and every pretension that sets itself up against the knowledge of God, and we take captive every thought to make it obedient to Christ" (2 Cor. 10:4–5).

I have observed that many of those young people will come back to Christ once they leave university, get married, and begin to raise a family.

Christians are commissioned to fight the good fight of faith. They are instructed to put on the armor of God in order to stand against the attacks of the devil (Eph. 6:10–18). Many however, will be caught off guard and backslide.

Backsliding will not happen to any true Christian during the second half of the tribulation period. They will be protected in a spiritual place out of Satan's reach.

EAGLE'S WINGS

In these difficult-to-interpret passages of Revelation, we read that the woman was given the two wings of a great eagle to fly to the place of protection for three and a half years. I think these two wings are exactly what a Christian will need to stay beyond the devil's enticing reach. I think they refer to faith and self-control, two of the nine fruit of the Holy Spirit (Gal. 5:22).

Faith keeps one walking in fellowship with God. The shield of faith is part of our spiritual armor, and it extinguishes the flaming arrows of the devil (Eph. 6:16).

Self-control is the other wing of the eagle. It keeps our flesh from wandering into sin. If we have self-control, Satan cannot control us. He finds nothing in us to entice.

The eagle in Revelation refers to one of the four living creatures. A seraph will be commissioned to lead an army of angels to guard the people of God against demonic influence and penetration. Satan will pursue the woman and her offspring, but he will not oppress her, posses her, or defile her. His armies will be stopped by the eagle seraphim. No creature can defeat a seraph in battle. Their protection over the saints will not be compromised.

MALICIOUS SLANDER

Since Satan will not be able to entice the saints to sin as he has done for centuries, he will try to destroy them through other means.

Violent uprisings will have removed the saints from political power. The two witnesses (the prophetic church and Israel) have been killed, resurrected to life, and raptured to heaven. Nonbelievers have usurped legitimate authority and taken political power around the globe. With newly acquired positions of government, they will be busy reorganizing the world to suit their humanistic agenda. At this time, they will have no reason to kill the rest of the woman's seed. Satan, however, hates the church, and he will want to destroy her immediately.

The riots will have stopped because the remaining Christians will not present an immediate threat to the new politic. Satan will try a new tactic; he will not be able to tempt Christians to sin, and it will not be the right time to kill them, so he will slander them.

"Then from his mouth the serpent spewed water like a river, to overtake the woman and sweep her away with the torrent" (Rev. 12:15).

The devil will strike with slander. The smoothest talkers will be enlisted to hurl venom at the church. They will speak on behalf of medical, social, scientific, and civil rights lobby groups. They will fabricate persuasive information that seems undeniable. Satan's lies and propaganda against the church will be spewed out like verbal vomit through the media. The devil will launch an extensive media campaign like the world has never seen, which will pour over the nations like a powerful river and gush upon society with unimaginable force. It will squeeze the remaining saints, discredit the claims of the church, render God's people vulnerable, and attempt to sweep them away.

The slander will portray Christians as deceivers and produce evidence to show that their doctrines are scientifically impossible. The slanderers will even suggest that Christians are ruthless enemies of society—shysters and manipulators who prey on weak, suffering people. They will accuse Christians of mind control and brainwashing and give examples of people who have been hurt and killed because of Christian activity. They will use footage from the recent rule of Christians around the world comparing theirs with Hitler's rule. The world will once again shift toward anti-Christian sentiment, and persecution against the church will rise.

THE EARTH HELPS

Suddenly and unexpectedly, the natural world will be used by God to help the church: "Then from his mouth the serpent spewed water like a river, to overtake the woman and sweep her away with the torrent. But the earth helped the woman by opening its mouth and swallowing the river that the dragon had spewed out of his mouth" (Rev. 12:15–16).

At this time, the earth itself will help remove the slander. To everyone's surprise, scientific breakthroughs will erupt around the world. New information involving nature will come to light exposing the devil's lies. Categorically, the new research will confirm the scientific truth of Judeo-Christian teachings. I suggest that the following will suddenly come into view; evolution will be proven scientifically wrong, the life of a fetus will be seen as human and homosexual unions will be scientifically shown as abnormal. When this happens, thousands of scientists will believe in God, and simultaneously, multitudes will come forward to defend the saints. They will tell countless stories of Christian compassion and heaven-sent miracles. The devil's propaganda plan will backfire.

The lies of Satan that will come like a mighty rushing river, but they will be swallowed up by scientific facts that prove the Bible to be scientifically correct. These scientific breakthroughs will became a platform of testimony that will open the door for many expressions of appreciation for the church.

SATAN DECLARES WAR

Satan will be furious. He will stand on the shore of the sea and look out across the world. He will conjure and scheme, and all of his hatred will focus on the church. Outraged with his failed attempts at destroying the remaining seed of the church, the dragon will declare outright war against the rest of the woman's offspring.

But Satan's anger will soon expose his hand. Unable to stop himself and against reasonable judgment, he will employ his most powerful forces openly. His most wicked weapons of witchcraft will be unleashed to defile mankind and crush the church.

Satan will rally fallen angels, demons lords, and wicked men. He will stretch forth his arm to demonize the world and kill every Christian on the planet. He will use all of the weapons in his arsenal to achieve his quest, but he will not be able to escape his humiliation and judgment. He will soon be drawn out and seen for what he is. All his plans are destined to backfire, and he knows it.

Many who had followed him through the tribulation period will turn away from him in the end. The seven bowls of wrath will soon be released. The remainder of the woman's seed (the church) will rise with new evangelistic anointing. Revival will sweep the earth again. Beyond all of this, Satan's most dreaded moment will be drawing near; the return of the king will devastate him.

Chapter Twenty-nine

Revelation is About the Identity of the Beast

And I saw a beast coming out of the sea. He had ten horns and seven heads, with ten crowns on his horns, and on each head a blasphemous name ... The dragon gave the beast his power and his throne and great authority ...
The whole world was astonished and followed the beast. Men worshipped the dragon because he had given authority to the beast, and they also worshipped the beast and asked, "Who is like the beast? Who can make war against him?"
The beast was given a mouth to utter proud words and blasphemies and to exercise his authority for forty-two months. He was given power to make war against the saints and to conquer them.
And he was given authority over every tribe, people, language and nation. All inhabitants of the earth will worship the beast—all whose names have not been written in the book of life belonging to the Lamb that was slain from the creation of the world.
He who has an ear, let him hear ... This calls for patient endurance and faithfulness on the part of the saints. (Rev. 13:1–10)

If anyone has insight, let him calculate the number of the beast, for it is man's number. His number is 666. (Rev. 13:18)

CHAPTER TOPICS

1. Satan's champion
2. Identifying the beast
3. The ruling spirit of humanism
4. Paul's insight on the Antichrist
5. Why the world will worship the Antichrist

SATAN'S POWER GRID REVEALED

REVELATION 10–12 SHOWS US the church and Israel and their rise to power under the anointing of the Holy Spirit during the tribulation.

Chapter 13 gives us a glimpse of Satan's army. In it, we are introduced to the beast and the false prophet, and we discover the power grid of demonic angels.

In this chapter, we identify the beast. In accordance with God's plan, the beast will emerge at the midpoint of the great tribulation, and once he is revealed, the battle against God's people will intensify. Satan will be forced to use his most vile demons at the end of the age. This will serve the purposes of God; as Satan's evil is exposed, more people will ultimately come to Christ.

WHO IS THE BEAST

For centuries people have assigned the identity of the beast to one individual or another. Some have said he was a Catholic pope from the dark ages; others have prophesied that he was a more contemporary world leader, like Hitler. Down through the ages, many evil men have manifested the spirit of the Antichrist, but until now, the beast has not emerged.

I have great respect for many who teach on this subject. Some suggest that the beast will soon arise from one group of people or another. I have a different perspective, and although my suggestion is controversial, I ask the reader not to dismiss it quickly.

I do not believe the beast is a man at all, although his influence will control the minds of millions, and powerful men will distinguish themselves and champion his evil cause. The beast is introduced to us as an evil spirit, a fallen angel. He has an extensive army of demons and fallen angels under his command. His army has been at work influencing mankind since the beginning of time, but the beast himself has been restrained.

John wrote, "And I saw a beast coming out of the sea. He had *ten horns and seven heads*, with ten crowns on his horns" (Rev. 13:1; italics added).

He continued, "The whole world was astonished and followed the beast. Men worshipped the dragon because he had given authority to the beast, and *they also worshipped the beast* and asked, 'Who is like the beast'?" (Rev. 13:4; italics added).

"All inhabitants of the *earth will worship the beast*" (Rev. 13:8; italics added).

"The beast ... has *seven heads and ten horns*. The beast, which you saw, once was, now is not, and will come up *out of the Abyss*" (Rev. 17:7–8; italics added).

"They had a king over them the *angel of the Abyss*, whose name in Hebrew is Abaddon, and in Greek Apollyon" (Rev. 9:11; italics added).

All of these scriptures refer to the same beast. The beast is Apollyon, which means destroyer. He will come from the Abyss where he has been restrained.

The angel of the Abyss is also one of eight spirit kings who rule the dark angels:

"The beast who once was, and now is not, is an eighth king. He belongs to the seven and is going to his destruction" (Rev. 17:11).

If we connect the facts from these verses we discover:

1. The beast or Antichrist is a fallen angel, an evil spirit
2. The beast comes from the Abyss
3. He was on earth during the early days of early man because *he was*
4. He was restrained for thousands of years including during the days of the early disciples, because John was told, *he is not*
5. He will be released for the last half of the great tribulation because *he yet will be*
6. Satan will give him great authority
7. The whole earth, except the saints, will worship him
8. He is a king, one with the other seven fallen angels

THE SPIRIT OF HUMANISM

The beast is called Apollyon; he is the angel of the Abyss. He is the Antichrist, whom the world will worship. To identify him better, I will give him another name, a name that identifies his mission. His prime directive is the propagation of humanism. Recall the number of the beast. It is 666—the number of man.

John wrote, "If anyone has insight, let him calculate the number of the beast, for it is man's number. His number is 666" (Rev. 13:18).

Revelation instructs us to find insight and contemplate his number. Humanism, which teaches that through evolution man will eventually become God, is man worshipping himself, and 666 is the number for humanism.

In *A Christian Manifesto,* Francis Schaeffer wrote, "The Humanist Manifestos I and II both state that humanism is a religion, a faith. The Humanist Manifestos not only say that humanism is a religion, but the Supreme Court has declared it to be a religion."[p]

Humanism attempts to remove God from the throne of the universe and put humankind in his place. That is why the beast (Apollyon) is called the Antichrist; he is against Christ and takes the place of God in people's lives. Humanism says that man will become the answer to all problems.

Humanism rejects God as creator, salvation through Jesus, and eternal judgment. It declares that man does not need an outside force such as God to tell him how to live. Humanism says there are no moral absolutes, no sins, no right or wrongs, and every disposition of man must be tolerated—short of murder, hurting living things, and theft.

Humanism believes the way to utopia lies inside man. Communism believes this, socialism believes this, Hinduism believes this, and secular capitalism believes this. Only the three monotheistic religions (Judaism, Christianity, and Islam) in their purest forms, do not subscribe to humanism. They believe that a supreme being is man's only salvation and hope. Humanism says that evolving man is the sum of all things. It is the created (man) not the creator (God) whom humanism would have us worship.

APOLLYON'S TASK

This is Apollyon's task: to get man worshipping himself by subscribing to humanism. The beast is the ruling spirit of the religion of humanism. Many university professors are the high priests of this religion. They renounce the God of Abraham and put human kind on the throne. Evolution is their number one doctrine. It is a doctrine of devils (1 Tim. 4:1).

Apollyon's first task will be to kill the saints who will be leading the governments of the world at the midpoint of the tribulation. We described that event when we studied Revelation eleven: "Now when they [the people of God] have finished their testimony, the beast that comes up from the Abyss will attack them, and overpower and kill them" (Rev. 11:7).

Revelation 17 gives more insight to help us determine the identity of the beast. Again, he is identified as Apollyon. He has seven heads and ten horns and comes from the Abyss. He has been restrained; he was, now is not, and yet will come. This confirms that the beast, the Antichrist, is an evil spirit and not a man. Only a spirit can come up out of the Abyss. Only a spirit was, now is not, and yet will be.

An angel said to John, "I will explain to you the mystery of the woman and of the beast she rides, which has the seven heads and the ten horns. The beast, which you saw, once was, now is not, and will come up out of the Abyss and go to his destruction. The inhabitants of the earth whose names have not been written in the book of life from the creation of the world will be astonished when they see the beast, because he once was, now is not, and yet will come" (Rev. 17:7–8).

"The beast who once was, and now is not, is an eighth king" (Rev. 17:11).

KEYS FROM THE EARLY CHURCH

In the days when the New Testament was written a false rumor was troubling the church. Some thought the second coming of Christ had already come. They thought this not because any friends had been raptured and gone to heaven. We know from history that their fellow Christians were still present. They thought that the Lord had come and that some had met him in the air; were perfected; and, in a twinkling of an eye, had returned to the earth, ready to fight the final battle. They feared they had missed this gathering to the Lord. Of course they hadn't.

Paul explained that the second coming of Christ will not take place until after the Antichrist has appeared. In the teaching, Paul identifies the Antichrist:

"Concerning the coming of the Lord Jesus Christ and our being gathered to him, we ask you, brothers, not to become easily unsettled or alarmed by some prophecy, report or letter supposed to have come from us, saying that the day of the Lord had already come. Don't let anyone deceive you in any way, for that day will not come until the rebellion occurs and the man of lawlessness is revealed, the man doomed to destruction. He will oppose and will exalt himself over everything that is called God or is worshipped, so that he sets himself up in God's temple, proclaiming himself to be God. Don't you remember that when I was with you I used to tell you these things? And now you know what is holding him back, so that he may be revealed at the proper time. For the secret power of lawlessness is already at work; but the one who now holds it back will continue to do so till he is taken out of the way. And then the lawless one will be revealed, whom the Lord Jesus will overthrow with the breath of his mouth and destroy by the splendor of his coming. The coming of the lawless one will be in accordance with the work of Satan displayed in all kinds of counterfeit miracles, signs and wonders, and in every sort of evil that deceives those who are perishing" (2 Thess. 2:1–10).

HE WAS, NOW IS NOT, YET WILL COME

"The inhabitants of the earth whose names have not been written in the book of life from the creation of the world will be astonished when they see the beast, because he once was, now is not, and yet will come" (Rev. 17:8).

Once again we read that the Antichrist will be restrained until the tribulation. Perhaps the beast spoke through the serpent as the spirit of humanism in the Garden of Eden. Eve said that God told her not to eat from the tree in the middle of the garden or she would die.

'"You will not surely die,' the serpent said to the woman. 'For God knows that when you eat of it your eyes will be opened, and *you will be like God,* [that's the teaching of humanism] knowing good and evil'" (Gen. 3:4–5; italics added).

Humanism was in the beginning tempting Eve to reject God's word and become like God. *The teaching of the beast was* (in the garden). Then at some point, he was imprisoned in the Abyss, for perhaps thousands of years. *The beast was not* during the days of Paul and the other disciples. The spirit of humanism *will be released* from the Abyss to sit on the throne, and man will worship the beast. *He will yet be.*

A human being does not fit this description. A spirit has the ability to be, then not to be, and then to return to the scene of human history once again. That is the description that Paul gave of the Antichrist.

THE SPIRIT OF LAWLESSNESS

Apollyon, the ruler of humanism, is the spirit of lawlessness described in 2 Thess. 2. Humanism is the embodiment of lawlessness. It defies God's laws and instructs people to break them. It entices people to please themselves. Laws will become twisted, and logic will be lost under Apollyon's government.

That is why abortion, homosexuality, and sexual promiscuity are commonplace. They are naturally, logically, and morally wrong, but modern societies say they are not only permitted, but they are right. The humanist religion has intensified over the past fifty years; it has become popular in most societies. The stage is set for the controller of humanism to emerge. In the next chapter, we will study the work of the beast. His mandate is to lure humanity away from God and then destroy it.

Chapter Thirty

Revelation is About the Work of the Beast

And I saw a beast coming out of the sea. He had ten horns and seven heads, with ten crowns on his horns, and on each head a blasphemous name.

The beast I saw resembled a leopard, but had feet like those of a bear and a mouth like that of a lion. The dragon gave the beast his power and his throne and great authority.

One of the heads of the beast seemed to have a fatal wound, but the fatal wound had been healed.

The whole world was astonished and followed the beast. Men worshipped the dragon because he had given authority to the beast and they also worshipped the beast and asked, "Who is like the beast? Who can make war against him?"

The beast was given a mouth to utter proud words and blasphemies and to exercise his authority for forty-two months.

He was given power to make war against the saints and to conquer them.

And he was given authority over every tribe, people, language and nation.

All inhabitants of the earth will worship the beast—all whose names have not been written in the book of life belonging to the Lamb that was slain from the creation of the world.

He who has an ear, let him hear. If anyone is to go into

captivity, into captivity he will go. If anyone is to be killed with the sword, with the sword he will be killed.
This calls for patient endurance and faithfulness on the part of the saints. (Rev. 13:1–10)
He ordered them to set up an image in honor of the beast who was wounded by the sword and yet lived. He was given power to give breath to the image of the first beast, so that it could speak and cause all who refused to worship the image to be killed.
He also forced everyone, small and great, rich and poor, free and slave, to receive a mark on his right hand or on his forehead, so that no one could buy or sell unless he had the mark, which is the name of the beast or the number of his name.
This calls for wisdom. If anyone has insight, let him calculate the number of the beast, for it is man's number. His number is 666. (Rev. 13:14–18)

CHAPTER TOPICS

1. The mandate of the beast
2. The activity of the beast
3. The ten spirit kings
4. The seven spirit kings
5. The worship of the beast
6. The abomination that causes desolation
7. The mark of the beast

HUMANISM

APOLLYON, THE BEAST, IS a fallen angel and an evil spirit. He is the Antichrist and the ruling spirit of humanism. He will accomplish his goal- to displace God and cause the world to worship him- by getting the world to worship humanism. On the surface humanism appears harmless and even beneficial, but it is the deception of all deceptions.

He has three initiatives in place to accomplish his goals:

1. He will promote humanism.
   In the name of tolerance and equality for all, the beast will promote humanism in every society on earth. Any contrary philosophy will be unacceptable. Because they will not embrace humanism, true Christians and Jews will be deemed unacceptable by society. Christians will tolerate other philosophies, but not when those philosophies break God's laws for life or morality or personal worship. Accepting humanism would require the saints to embrace false religions and worship the image or philosophy of humanism. Society will allow Christians and Jews to keep their religion as long as they will embrace all other religions. In other words they will have to renounce the exclusivity or Lordship of Christ and reject the one Almighty God. That will be unacceptable.
2. The beast will kill Christians and Jews and any people who will not embrace humanism.
   Jews and Christians will be seen as enemies of the global family. Many groups have been killed through the centuries. History tells of thousands of communities that were decimated because of nationality, race, religious class, or color of skin. It is happening as I write this book, and it is not difficult to believe that it will happen again in the tribulation period.
3. The beast will make purchases of food and products conditional.
   To complete his plan and weed out those who have kept their faith quiet, the beast will make the purchase and sale of all food and merchandise conditional. Only those who give open and unqualified allegiance to humanism will be able to buy or sell. To have food and property one will have to be a citizen of the world, and that will require cooperation with the global agenda. Those who refuse

will be killed. Those who hide will starve, and those who help them will be branded as traitors and receive the death penalty as well.

DEMONS ON THE THRONE

The beast will accomplish his task through fallen angels, demons, and the people they influence.

John wrote, "He had ten horns and seven heads, with ten crowns on his horns and on each head a blasphemous name" (Rev. 13:1).

The heads, horns, and crowns are spirit rulers. They are spirit kings with myriads of demons under their charge. The beast is an evil spirit, and so are his rulers. Each of the seven or ten will have responsibility over a continent, a nation, or a system of government. Although they will not be visible on the natural plane, their demonic armies will be very active. They will work in and through people to accomplish their goals. They are evil spirits who will rule by demonic influence.

"The seven heads ... are seven kings. The beast who once was, and now is not, is an eighth king. He belongs to the seven and is going to his destruction. The ten horns you saw are ten kings who have not yet received a kingdom, but who for one hour will receive authority as kings along with the beast. They have one purpose and will give their power and authority to the beast" (Rev. 17:9–13).

Daniel 10:20–32 depicts demonic angels who rule. One is called the Prince of Persia, and another the Prince of Greece. They are spiritual heads of state, or horns of power. They have crowns on their heads, and each has an army of demons under his command.

They infiltrate government, groups of people, and political systems. They are not independent warlords; they carry an agenda from higher up. Because people sin, these spirit leaders gain access into their lives. Once they find access, they influence, bribe, coerce, and control people. That is how they expedite their evil schemes.

Ephesians describes this spiritual warfare: "For our struggle is not against flesh and blood, but against the rulers, against the authorities, against the powers of this dark world and against the spiritual forces of evil in the heavenly realms. Therefore put on the full armor of God, so that when the day of evil comes, you may be able to stand your ground" (Eph. 6:12).

The demonic rulers are already here unleashing evil in society. We are told to put on the armor of God, which provides truth, righteousness, hope, salvation, peace, faith, and the word of God (Eph. 6:2–18).

The armor of God keeps us from sin and stops demons from having inroads or influence in our lives, and donning it is the only way we can stand against demon forces. Sin is a legal invitation for their involvement in our world. The more we sin, the more they will influence our minds and our emotions. Once they have a stronghold in a human being, they will rule through that person to perpetuate evil.

Most of this happens in such a way that the person involved is oblivious. Often a sinner does not think consequentially, but damage always follows sin. Sin mars and destroys the lives of individuals, families, communities, and nations. We battle against a highly sophisticated and well-organized army of subversive demons. They are called, the rulers of the darkness of this world (Eph. 6:12).

Evil spirits have been spreading the lies of humanism for countless generations. Their efforts have intensified greatly over the past century. With every passing decade, they take more ground. Presently, they have enormous influence in every nation and every section of society.

Apollyon will return to lead his army, and Satan, the dragon, will give Apollyon the authority he needs. Apollyon's horns, heads, and crowns are already at work, even though he has not yet arrived on the scene.

We cannot be sure of the horns and heads specific designations and responsibilities, but their assignments will be similar to the format that I will lay out in the following section. This will help us grasp the big picture.

SUGGESTED DEMONIC DESIGNATIONS

The ten horns are demon kings who will be positioned over ten geographical areas of the planet. They will infiltrate the peoples within their realm, following their assignments—to promote humanism in their geographical areas. Here are ten areas of the earth that could be the ten regions designated to the ten horns (ruling spirits):

1. Central and South America
2. North America
3. Europe
4. Countries that were part of the Soviet bloc
5. China and surrounding countries
6. Africa
7. The Middle East
8. Israel
9. India and surrounding countries
10. Australia, New Zealand, and surrounding countries

The ten horns have ten crowns. They will be kings over their geographical areas. They will have authority over the demonic beings within their realm.

Like the ten horns, the seven heads are also spirit kings. I think each one will have influence over a specific system of government. The seven heads will rule demonic armies who infiltrate such systems as the military, medical systems, and the media in every community of the world. Because these demons will be working under the authority of Apollyon, their goal will be to bring humanism to the systems of the world. They will release millions of dark spirits to infect these systems. Using strategic deception, they will manipulate each system. They will infiltrate each community in a manner fitting its culture and ethnicity.

Here are the seven suggested systems that already are, and will be, infiltrated by these demonic kings (heads):

1. The media and entertainment arena
2. The political arena at both local and federal levels
3. The education system from kindergarten to university, including venues of scientific research and analysis
4. The medical system, including areas of practice and research
5. The judicial system, including local civil courts, supreme courts and international courts
6. The military and law enforcement systems
7. The religious front, including both freelance mysticism and tradition religions

The scriptures say that one of the heads seemed to have a fatal wound: "One of the heads of the beast seemed to have a fatal wound, but the fatal wound had been healed" (Rev. 13:3).

I believe this head that has the fatal wound is the political system. This speaks of the rise of power by the Christian and Jewish right when they will be voted into power and rule the world for a season. Apollyon's first mission after being released from the Abyss was to kill those biblical rulers. The political head of the beast had been fatally wounded, but the system was healed when he regained political control of the world.

THE POWER OF THE BEAST

The extent of Apollyon's power will be far reaching. He will exercise his authority for forty-two months, or three and a half years, which represents the last half of the tribulation period. During this time, he will speak blasphemous words at God, heaven, and God's dwelling place on the earth (God's Holy Spirit dwells inside his people).

For a season, the devil will give the beast unequalled power over the earth. He will make war against the saints and conquer them, taking many captive and killing millions around the world.

John wrote, "He was given power to make war against the saints and to conquer them. And he was given authority over every tribe, people, language and nation. All inhabitants of the earth will worship the beast … If anyone is to go to captivity, into captivity he will go. If anyone is to be killed by the sword, with the sword he will be killed. And cause all who refused to worship the [his] image to be killed. This calls for the patient endurance and faithfulness on the part of the saints" (Rev. 13:7, 8, 10, 12).

THE WORSHIP OF THE BEAST

The demonic infiltration, media hype, and forced compliance through the mark of the beast will cause the whole world to worship him. The work of the false prophet will also inspire the world to worship the beast. We will study the work of the false prophet in the next chapter.

"All inhabitants of the earth will worship the beast—all whose names have not been written in the book of life belonging to the Lamb" (Rev. 13:8).

Worship of the beast is not difficult to imagine, if we realize that the beast is not a man, but a spirit who promotes the philosophy of humanism. The world will not worship the evil spirit Apollyon directly, but will worship his image—the philosophy of humanism.

Here again is another reason why I do not believe the Antichrist is a man. It is too much of a stretch to imagine Russians, Americans, Israelis, Chinese, Koreans, Iranians, and Europeans all worshipping the statue of a man. In our modern world, most people will not worship an idol made of metal or stone. It is not likely that people of different nations will worship a man either, especially if he comes from a strange and different country then they are used to.

All, however, whose names are not recorded in the book of life, are already worshipping humanism at some level. Through education, media hype, and political power, humanism will rise to a level of global control.

THE ABOMINATION THAT CAUSES DESOLATION

The image of the beast will be set up in the holy place, and this will be the straw that will break the proverbial camel's back. When we study the pouring of the seven bowls of God's wrath, we will realize that his wrath will bring absolute desolation. The desolation was planned by God ages ago, but so was the abomination that will precede it. The abomination is the setting up of the image of the beast in the holy place. The Bible mentions the abomination that will cause desolation in several places.

We find references to the abomination in three passages in the book of Daniel. In Daniel 9:27 we read, "In the middle of the 'seven' he will put an end to sacrifice and offering. And on a wing of the temple, he will set up an abomination that causes desolation."

Then in Daniel 11:31–32, scripture tells us, "His armed forces will rise up to desecrate the temple fortress and will abolish the daily sacrifice. Then they will set up the abomination that causes desolation. With flattery he will corrupt those who have violated the covenant, but the people who know their God will firmly resist him."

In Daniel 12:12, we read, "From the time that the daily sacrifice is abolished and the abomination that causes desolation is set up, there will be 1,290 days. Blessed is the one who waits for and reaches the end of the 1,335 days."

The book of Matthew records Jesus mentioning the abomination: "So when you see standing in the holy place the abomination that causes desolation, spoken of by the prophet Daniel—let the reader understand—then let those who are in Judea flee to the mountains" (Matt. 24:15–16).

We find yet another reference in 2 Thessalonians: "He will exalt himself over everything that is called God or is worshipped, so that he sets himself up in God's temple, proclaiming himself to be God" (2 Thess. 2:4).

In Revelation we read, "He ordered them to set up an image in honor of the beast who was wounded by the sword and yet lived. He was given power to give breath to the image of the first beast, so that it could speak and cause all who refused to worship the image to be killed" (Rev. 13:14–15).

Throughout history, various abominations have been set up in the temple in Jerusalem, and desolation has followed. Zeus, foreign rulers, pigs, an Islamic mosque, and the Dome of the Rock, have each in turn, been set up in the holy place. Each was an abomination to the Lord, and each caused desolation. Each time, Jews were killed and forced to flee to the mountains as invasion and judgment came. It happened before and after the time of Christ, but Jesus makes reference to the words of Daniel and points to the future. In 70 AD desolation came to Jerusalem and this could have been a fulfillment of Christ's words. However, Matt. 24 speaks of the very end of time, that of the great tribulation and the second coming of Christ. He says that Christ will come after the setting up of the abomination in the holy place. All prior events will pale in comparison to the abomination and the desolation that is yet to come.

The image or philosophy of the beast being set up in the Jewish Temple will happen at the midpoint of the tribulation, just after the beast kills the prophetic Jews and gentiles, the two witnesses who rule the nations. Jerusalem alone will be strong enough to resist the beast, but she will be engaged in war from then to the coming of Christ.

The armies of Israel will firmly resist the beast, but he will accomplish his essential goal and gain access to the new temple in Jerusalem, and a symbol of humanism will be set up in the holy place. It will be an anti-God, anti-Christ symbol. It will announce man's divinity and man's sovereignty, and it will speak and perform with supernatural ability. The media will set up and broadcast from the temple, and the world will see the abomination that will cause desolation. It will epitomize the spirit and philosophy of humanism and be backed by the spirit of witchcraft. The world will worship humanism because it will be seen as the savior of the world. Humanism will be man's hope for peace, global cooperation, the uniting of resources, care for the nations of the poor, survival of the planet, sexual and moral freedom, and most of all financial prosperity under the one-world monetary fund. These promises have been extended before, under the banners of socialism, communism and Nazism. They are not new, but for the first time they will be global.

Utopian hope for man's future can only be realized when Christ returns and the new millennium begins. Before then, the judgments of God will bring absolute desolation.

THE MARK OF THE BEAST

The physical mark on one's hand or forehead is not as serious as what is in one's heart and mind. Christians will have the seal of God and the name of God on their foreheads (Rev. 7:3, 9:4, 14:1). That does not mean that Christians will have an implant or tattoo, they will simply have the mind of Christ and God's protection from demonic infiltration.

Likewise, the mark of the beast will first and foremost be a persuasion of the mind. Those who have the mark of the beast will have the mind of the Antichrist, a conviction of humanism, in their thoughts (forehead). In other words, people with the worldview of the Antichrist will have his mark, and the mark will be reflected in their lifestyles, activities, and actions (the right hand).

I am sure that there will be a literal mark inserted or branded on one's hand or forehead, but that is simply an indicator of a much deeper mark. The evil mark of Apollyon will be on the souls and spirits of humanity.

Chapter Thirty-one

Revelation is About the False Prophet

Then I saw another beast, coming out of the earth. He had two horns like a lamb, but he spoke like a dragon. He exercised all the authority of the first beast on his behalf, and made the earth and its inhabitants worship the first beast, whose fatal wound had been healed.

And he performed great and miraculous signs, even causing fire to come down from heaven to earth in full view of men. Because of the signs he was given power to do on behalf of the first beast, he deceived the inhabitants of the earth.

He ordered them to set up an image in honor of the beast who was wounded by the sword and yet lived. He was given power to give breath to the image of the first beast, so that it could speak and cause all who refuse to worship the image to be killed. (Rev. 13:11–15)

CHAPTER TOPICS

1. The false prophet
2. The rise of the occult
3. The New Age movement
4. Humanism and witchcraft working together
5. The image of the beast

6. Democratic dictatorships
7. Trouble stirring in Satan's camp

THE FALSE PROPHET

THREE DIFFERENT PLACES IN the book of Revelation identify the second beast as the false prophet. They are Rev. 16:13; 19:20, and 20:10.

In chapter 19 we read, "But the beast was captured, and with him the *false prophet* who had performed the miraculous signs on his behalf. With these signs he had deluded those who had received the mark of the beast and worshipped his image" (Rev. 19:20; italics added).

Like Apollyon, the second beast is a fallen angel of the spirit world. He has two horns like that of a lamb, which are the spirit generals under his command. He is like a lamb because he wants to appear gentle and innocent, but the false prophet speaks like a dragon because he carries the words of the devil. He is the devil's puppet and the ruling spirit of witchcraft, and he will be given supernatural power to deceive the world on behalf of the beast.

THE RELIGIOUS BEAST

This false prophet is not the prominent beast of the two because most secular people in the modern world are not religious. They demand separation of church and state. Their gods are money and pleasure, so humanism is the main theme the devil will use to capture most people. The false prophet, however, will play an important role: he will be the backup for the first beast.

He and his team will have the job of creating and perpetuating occult activity on the earth. He will exercise all the authority of the first beast, weaving his witchcraft into every culture and system on the planet. This has happened since the beginning of time, but technology has given rise to the proliferation of spiritism on a much broader scale.

THE NEW AGE MOVEMENT

Although the term, *New Age movement* is not as popular as it was in the 1960s, '70s, and '80s, it is probably the best way to describe the modern phenomena of witchcraft. The New Age movement is an umbrella term that describes all spiritual activity that does not come from the God of the Bible. It became popular in western society after the Beetles went to India in the 1960s in search of spirituality, opening a door for Hinduism to infect the world. Since then Hinduism has adapted to western culture. It has changed its terminology and made itself seeker-friendly for the western mind. Witchcraft in educational, fun, and friendly forms is now popular around the world.

The Ten Commandments forbid the worship of any spiritual entity except God himself. Whenever man looks for spiritual help or spiritual pleasure from any source other than God, he seeks help from an evil spirit. That is the worship of a false god. Evil spirits hide behind a thousand different faces, but they are all part of the new age movement.

People's fascination and involvement with witchcraft is the number one reason for demonic strongholds in the lives of so many. The New Age movement is massive, and all of its activities and branches cannot be listed in this paragraph. The following is a sample of modern witchcraft at work.

Witchcraft has been popularized and made society-friendly through movies and TV shows such as *Bewitched, Star Wars, Harry Potter, Charmed,* and *Buffy* to name only a few. Hundreds of horror movies involve the occult. Many magicians, rock groups, Gay pride parades, and celebrities promote spiritism, pagan rituals, and even the more obvious forms of witchcraft, such as Satan worship itself. Fortune telling, horoscopes, séances, power crystals, pyramid power, and mother-earth worship are all forms of modern day witchcraft. Transcendental meditation, mind reading, reincarnation, spiritual yoga, hypnotism, hallucinatory drugs, astral projection, and spirit guides all have their deceptive places in the New Age movement. Even some traditional religions and some secret societies that inspire newcomers with good works of community service will draw their members into forms of witchcraft, satanic ritual, and demon worship. God forbids all activities of the New Age movement because they are demonic lures, teaching doctrines of demons that lead to devilish activities.

The biggest lure to witchcraft is black magic, supernatural phenomena, miraculous signs, and wonders. These signs will become prevalent when the false prophet appears. Miracles will seemingly authenticate the false prophet and legitimize his message. With his amazing charismatic appeal, he will inspire the world to worship humanism, the first beast. People will love him because he will perform amazing acts of magic and because he will speak of equality for all—the wisdom of humanism.

IDENTIFYING THE FALSE PROPHET

The false prophet is the ruling spirit of the New Age movement. The New Age movement is the religious force behind humanism. Deep in the human psyche is a propensity for spirituality. Although many deny it, human beings are drawn to worship. If a person does not worship God he or she will inadvertently worship something else.

Humankind's growing spirituality is also seen as part of his evolution. It is falsely said that tapping the inner spiritual potential leads one to be more like God. It lifts humankind into the supernatural realm. All of this is a carefully crafted deception. Unless these powers come from God, they are the works of demons.

The false prophet, a fallen angel will likely be in visible to the world, but everyone will see his effects. At that time the New Age movement, will likely be promoted under a different name.

A BEASTLY TEAM

Humanism and the New Age movement will team up during the latter half of the tribulation. Humankind worshipping humankind (humanism) and reveling in witchcraft (the new age movement) at the same time seems to be a contradiction. It is just the formula, however, that Satan will concoct to control the world. Humanism will draw the materialistic scientific types, and the New Age movement will draw the more intuitive, spiritual types. Everyone on the planet who does not have God's worldview will become part of this new world order.

WORSHIPPING THE IMAGE

"He ordered them to set up an image in honor of the beast who was wounded by the sword and yet lived. He was given power to give breath to the image of the first beast, so that it could speak and cause all who refuse to worship the image to be killed. (Rev. 13:15)

The world will worship the image of the beast—the philosophy of humanism. The philosophy of the beast will not just be policy on paper or laws written on computer screens. Computers and other high-tech devices talk, so the image will speak.

When John received this revelation, he could not imagine such technology. He saw a vision of a talking image and to him the image came to life. Modern technology alone can explain the life-like function of the image of the beast, but still, I think it will be more than technology at work.

The false prophet is a spirit with supernatural power. He can perform great and miraculous signs, even causing fire to come down from heaven. Whatever his magic is, it will be persuasive enough to deceive the world. That makes me believe that his acts will indeed be supernatural.

Magicians, psychics, and religious gurus will become more popular as we approach the tribulation. We already accept them as entertainment in our modern society. On stage and on TV, they thrill the masses and wow the world, and many of their activities are unexplainable.

The false prophet will lift this present magic show to a new level. With amazing supernatural acts, he will promote humanism around the world. Picture a different kind of fireworks on the Fourth of July, one with the theme of humanism. The celebration of many national holidays will take on new humanistic themes. One world in peace and humanism will cause the nations to rejoice. The miraculous demonstrations at these events will seal the humanistic agenda and bring the devil to the height of his glory.

TROUBLE IN SATAN'S CAMP

People will worship the beast (humanism) because of the power of the false prophet, and indirectly they will worship the devil. Something, however, will eat away at the hearts of humanity. The death of millions of Christians and Jews will not have gone unnoticed, and it will trouble many people.

At this point, the world will have seen the elimination of tyrannical dictators early in the tribulation period, but people replaced them with a new dictator named democracy. The one world order will become a democratic tyrant, and the tyranny of the new majority will be hideous. Those who do not conform to the majority will be removed. It will be no different from Nazi Germany or communist Russia under Stalin.

Conformity to an evil ideology will not last, no matter how logical or appealing it seems to be. Once again, God will reach the deep, hidden places in the hearts of humankind, and many who have previously championed the cause of atheism will find a last-minute faith in God. We will discover the greatest revivals in history in the next few chapters.

Chapter Thirty-two

Revelation is About a Powerful New Anointing

Then I looked, and there before me was the Lamb, standing on Mount Zion, and with him 144,000 who had his Father's name written on their foreheads.
And I heard a sound from heaven like the roar of rushing waters and like a loud peal of thunder. The sound I heard was like that of harpists playing their harps. And they sang a new song before the throne and before the four living creatures and the elders.
No one could learn the song except the 144,000 who had been redeemed from the earth. These are those who did not defile themselves with women, for they kept themselves pure. They follow the Lamb wherever he goes. They were purchased from among men and offered as first fruits to God and the Lamb. No lie was found in their mouths; they are blameless. (Rev. 14:1–5)

CHAPTER TOPICS

1. A six-part plan
2. Standing on Mount Zion
3. The intercessors' anointing
4. The holiness anointing

5. The ministry anointing
6. The greatest revival ever

MORE OF THE BIG PICTURE

REVELATION 10–12 DESCRIBED THE people of God in the first half of the tribulation.

Chapter 13 pointed to the last half of the tribulation; it described the agenda of the beast and the false prophet.

Chapter 14 gives us a picture of God at work during the second half of the tribulation. It begins with four prophecies, after which two actual events unfold very quickly. The first event is a revival that makes all previous revivals look small. The second event is the launch of the final campaign, which unleashes God's wrath.

Here is a six-part overview of Rev. 14, including the four prophecies and two enormous events:

1. A prophecy will say that saints will receive a powerful new anointing (Rev. 14:1–5).
2. A prophecy will say that the gospel will be preached to all remaining people on the earth (Rev. 14:6–7).
3. A prophecy will say that Satan's kingdom is about to fall (Rev. 14:8–11).
4. A prophecy will declare that, following the revival, it will be better for the saints to die then to remain on earth during the final judgments of wrath (Rev. 14:12–13).
5. Heaven will activate the world's greatest revival (Rev. 14:14–16).
6. Heaven will initiate God's wrath, the worst judgments to fall on earth (Rev. 14 14–20).

In this chapter we will focus only on the first part of this six-part drama.

A NEW PHENOMENON

Following the first half of the tribulation, John saw an amazing new thing happen to God's people. He saw that they would receive three supernatural empowerments, which together would be part of the new anointing.

The saints will receive a special anointing:

1. for intercession
2. to live pure and holy lives
3. to hear and follow the directives of the Lamb

It is not that these three dynamics have been unavailable through the centuries. The saints have always had the option of walking in the Spirit and fulfilling the will of God. This, however, is greater. A new anointing will come upon the earth, perhaps because the battle and the stakes are so intensified. The saints will be given a level of sanctification and power that none on earth have known before.

STANDING ON MOUNT ZION

Mount Zion refers to both the physical mount in present day Jerusalem and also to the New Jerusalem. It is the spiritual dwelling place of God and his people. The book of Hebrews tells us that Christians and redeemed Jews, even before they die and go to heaven, have already arrived at Mount Zion. They were already included in the family of God the day they are saved.

The scripture says, "But you have come to Mount Zion, to the heavenly Jerusalem, the city of the Living God" (Heb. 12:22).

God is omnipresent, and each person who receives him is with him. Spiritually speaking, we sit on the throne of heaven with him, partnering and fellowshipping with him through prayer and worship.

"By grace you have been saved. And God raised us up with Christ and seated us with him in the heavenly realms" (Eph. 2:5–6).

Now we read in revelation; "Then I looked and there before me was the Lamb, standing on Mount Zion" (Rev. 14:1).

Revelation 14 begins with a picture of Jesus standing with his family. He is about to give them a new anointing.

144,000 HAVE THE FATHER'S NAME

"before me was the Lamb, standing on Mount Zion, and with him 144,000 who had his Father's name written on their foreheads" (Rev.14:1).

Recall that in Rev. 7 the 144,000 were clearly described as Jews (Rev. 7:4). Here in chapter 14 we see no such distinction—although it is possible that these are the same 144,000, and, as such, they would be Jews.

I think, however, they are saints of every nation. God's number for a great family is 144,000. Twelve is the number for family, as we see with the twelve tribes of Israel or the twelve disciples of Jesus. Twelve times twelve, times one thousand equals 144,000. I think this number is symbolic. In fact, I believe there will be many more than 144,000 people around the world who will experience this new anointing.

The 144,000 (family) are standing with Jesus, and they have the name of the Father written on their foreheads. God will not put a tattoo, a visible brand, or some physical mark on the heads of Christians; this is a spiritual mark. It means that his family is called by his name, and the family belongs to him. They are marked people in that they have the mind of Christ.

THE INTERCESSOR'S SOUND

"And I heard a sound from heaven like the roar of rushing waters and like a loud peal of thunder. The sound I heard was like that of harpists playing their harps. And they sang a new song before the throne and before the four living creatures and the elders." (Rev. 14:3)

A sound of harps from heaven is very loud, but it can only be heard by the family of God. It comes from the elders and the millions of saints in heaven who all play harps (Rev. 15:2). The sound of the harps resonates through earth's atmosphere and into the ears of the intercessors. It brings with it God's plans for the salvation of sinners and the defeat of Satan.

God will not release his prophetic plans on the earth without agreement from his people in prayer. Many will be woken from sleep; others will be driving in their cars or standing at the sink, washing dishes. In their hearts, they will hear the sounds of the harps, and they will pray and intercede. They will come into agreement with God as the Holy Spirit directs them.

A NEW SONG

The prayers will flow like new songs. I am sure that some will pray in tongues. Some will sing with a heavenly prayer language. The Holy Spirit will pray through them and secret details and godly anointing will rise to heaven. Many saints will be shocked by the power of the words that will break forth from their mouths and overwhelm their emotions.

They will sing these songs and pray these prayers before the throne of God and before the four living creatures and before the elders of heaven. The heavenly host will be totally focused on the prayers of the saints for this spiritual agreement from earth will not be underestimated. These prayers will become the most important action in the universe. The super angels and human leaders who stand in heaven will be enthralled with this long awaited day. Finally earth has learned to cooperate with heaven.

END-TIME SANCTIFICATION

A special anointing for prayer will not be the only outstanding feature of the day. The saints on earth will be given a special dispensation for righteous living as well. Some disciples have known the provision of the Holy Spirit to walk in day-to-day holiness before this time, but many have fallen to temptation and walked in compromise. God's grace covers us when we fall, if we repent and turn back to him.

In the second half of the tribulation, it will be nearly impossible for saints to sin. In the middle of judgment, unprecedented persecution, and supernatural miracles from heaven, God's people will receive a holiness anointing. During this season, the 144,000 (God's family on earth) will be covered by the sanctifying power of the Holy Spirit. Listen to John's testimony of the church in those days: "These are those who did not defile themselves with women, for they kept themselves pure. No lie was found in their mouths; they are blameless" (Rev. 14:4–5).

Modern statistics tell us that presently, the church does not hold to this holy standard of living. Although chastity, fidelity, and integrity are desired, sin is prevalent in the church. That will change as we enter the tribulation period, and it will move to a whole new level when the tribulation period is halfway complete. It will not be human zeal or personal efforts that cause such a level of holiness; it will be an empowerment from heaven that counters the deception of demonic enticements.

Once this anointing is given to the saints, those who sin will be severely judged. There will be no excuse for sin in God's house during that dispensation. That is why any who receive the mark or philosophy of the beast will go to hell. It is also the reason why the cowardly, the unbelieving, the vile, the murderers, the sexually immoral, all those who practice magic arts, the idolaters, and all liars will have their place in the fiery lake of burning sulfur (Rev. 21:8).

I do not think that all cowards or any who tell any kind of lie during this time period will go to hell. That would mean that multitudes of Christians would automatically go to hell, which does not fit the message of God's grace as I understand it.

During the last half of the tribulation period, however, things will be different because of the new anointing. In those days, it will be difficult for saints to sin, and they will have no excuse if they do.

SAINTS ON ASSIGNMENT

"They follow the Lamb wherever he goes. They were purchased from among men and offered as first fruits to God and the Lamb." (Rev. 14:4)

The third empowerment that will come to the saints in the second half of the tribulation will be an amazing propensity to work for God. Believers will follow the Lamb wherever he goes. Most Christians today desire to be used of God, and many put forth serious efforts to follow him.

Knowing the times and the season of the tribulation, saints will set their entire focus on ministering for Christ. Even more than the disciples of the early church, they will go everywhere preaching the gospel. With power and authority, they will even minister under pain of death.

With sanctified lives and heaven-sent intercession, they will serve the Lord in remarkable ways. They will escape the clutches of their oppressors and find their way into the homes and communities of those who are spiritually hungry.

The saints on fire for God will be the reason for the revival that will soon cover the earth. It will be so powerful that it will be called the harvest of the earth. In a time of great judgment and horrific persecution, multitudes of saints will be thrilled to be on earth partnering with the Lord in his victory harvest.

Let God's excitement rise within you and pray into the book of Revelation. Be led by the Holy Spirit. Pray and prophesy so that the will of God will unfold and the magnificent day of the Lord will come quickly.

Chapter Thirty-three

Revelation is About the Eternal Gospel

Then I saw another angel flying in midair, and he had the eternal gospel to proclaim to those who live on the earth—to every nation, tribe, language and people. He said in a loud voice, "Fear God and give him glory, because the hour of his judgment has come. Worship him who made the heavens, the earth, the sea and the springs of water." (Rev. 14:6–7)

CHAPTER TOPICS

1. The angels that prophesy
2. The work of angels
3. How angels help spread the gospel
4. The warnings that accompany the gospel

AN ANGEL AND A PROPHET

AMONG OTHER THINGS, ANGELS are prophets. They carry words of God from heaven to man. Prophets proclaim the future. They call us to the blessings of Christ and warn us of impending danger.

There are four main reasons why God sends prophets to announce his plans:

1. *In case we are dull of hearing*: In case we ignore the gentle voice of the Holy Spirit or fail to take note of the subtle messages given through signs and wonders, God speaks to us directly through prophets.
2. *To prove that God is sovereign*: All of God's plans must be spoken through his servants the prophets before the Lord releases them into action. By so doing, he tells men, angels, and demons what he is about to do. Once the word is released, it will not return to him without being fulfilled. Because prophecies always come to pass, they confirm God's sovereignty. No one in heaven or earth can stop his plans.
3. *To inspire faith*: Prophetic men and angels inspire the armies of God, giving them hope when they are surrounded with darkness. A true prophetic word is an anchor to hold one on course when difficulty comes.
4. *To instruct us how to partner with God*: Prophetic words are signals that tell the angels when to act. When the word comes, they go. For them a prophecy is a marching order. The saints who hear the prophetic word also receive marching orders. They come into agreement with God by praying the prophecies. Then they act by preaching, ministering, and exercising kindness.

MIDAIR

John sees another prophetic angel and like other angels before, this one will announce his word in midair, which is the second heaven. In the next verse, John said that when the angel spoke, he cried in a "loud voice." That does not mean that people, even with modern technology, will be able to hear the sounds. When things are proclaimed in midair, they are heard in the spirit realm. Intercessors will hear these words deep in their spirits. Angels and demons will hear these words as well. To them, the angelic prophecy will sound like a freight train roaring past.

Most nights I am aware that God speaks to me in my dreams. On the rare occasion, I have heard the voice of loud prophetic angels in my dreams. When I hear them, their voices are so loud that I am shaken in my bones. I bolt upright in bed, aware that heaven has allowed me to hear an important word. These words are of highest importance to me. They never leave me. They are eternal. I am so drawn to God when he speaks to me like this. Although I look for confirmations, prophetic words like these are mile markers in my life.

THE ETERNAL GOSPEL

This angel that John described will proclaim the eternal gospel. The word *gospel* means "the good news." The eternal gospel has a personal application and a global application. Firstly, it refers specifically to the salvation of the human race that was paid for when Jesus died for man's sins on the cross.

Secondly, the gospel brings redemption to the environment, the animals, and the planet. It means that the kingdoms of the world will become the kingdoms of God.

The personal aspect of the gospel has the power to take souls who are in Satan's kingdom and bring them into God's kingdom. For many in the world, the gospel is foolishness, but Satan does not think it is foolish; he hates it. He knows that it is the power of God unto salvation. Salvation saves souls from judgment and hell and puts them on the path of sanctification, the process by which one changes to be like Christ. The gospel not only frees a soul from hell, but ultimately changes people through the power of the Holy Spirit. That ultimately means that Satan will have no access, possession, or affect on their lives. The gospel becomes the doorway for one to receive all the riches of God's blessings.

On the cross, a massive exchange took place. Jesus took on himself all that was bad to give us everything that was good. That is the gospel, and as we walk in fellowship and harmony with God, we take all of these blessings unto ourselves.

Here is a partial list of the gospel exchange:

1. Jesus became sin that we might receive righteousness.
2. Jesus was punished that we might be forgiven.
3. Jesus was cursed that we might receive blessings.
4. Jesus was rejected that we might be accepted.
5. Jesus received shame that we might receive glory.
6. Jesus was wounded that we might receive healing.
7. Jesus became poor that we might become rich.
8. Jesus died that we might have eternal life.
9. Jesus was humiliated that we might be exalted.

The global application of the gospel will result in another great process. The environment will be freed from decay, pollution, and corruption. All animals will live in peace one with another and will no longer suffer the normal processes of death and decay (Rom. 8:19–22).

When the full gospel comes to earth, the government of the planet will be under the rule of King Jesus, and we will live in a kingdom of righteousness. The nations will be called the nations of the saved (Rev. 21:24). The world will be filled with the glory of the Lord. We will study the new heavens and the new earth in more detail in a later chapter.

The good news of the gospel is about full personal salvation, and on the global scale, it will mean a new heaven and a new earth: "Then I saw a new heaven and a new earth, for the first heaven and the first earth had passed away" (Rev. 21:1).

TO EVERY NATION

The angel's prophecy of a fresh release of the eternal gospel will send millions of angels to visit the nations of the world. They will partner with God's people for the proclamation, extension, and success of the gospel. They are presently engaged in all of these activities today and will be, on a much greater scale, during the tribulation period.

Here are some of the angel's activities:

1. *Angels will fight against demons and fallen angels*. Demons blind the eyes of unbelievers and control the spirit world over systems of government and communities of people. We may recognize these demonic strongholds as heaviness, confusion, depression, foul thoughts, wicked thinking, rebellion and hardness in people, failure in business, strife in families, poor health, and even technical failure with electronics or machinery. A discerning person will detect an oppressive atmosphere where one feels claustrophobic, fearful, or constantly tired or a where there is a sense of impending doom or entrapment. These are not always caused by demons, but they may be the work of demons. Angels drive the demons back, freeing the air and removing the malaise of darkness, opening door for the message of the gospel.
2. *Angels will instruct God's people*. Angels may show up in a person's dream. They bring messages of all sorts. It may be a warning, a prophecy of an upcoming scenario, or a direct call for a person to come to Christ for salvation. They may appear in the dreams of both saints and sinners. They also bring godly instruction to saints to help them act in accordance with the purposes of God. They bring dreams to sinners that will cause them to listen to the Holy Spirit. In this way they help draw people to the Lord.
3. *Angels will orchestrate circumstances*. Angels arrange things in the lives of people so they will find supernatural direction. They provide miraculous signs and wonders for the non-expecting. They catch people's attention and point them in the direction of the Lord. People then listen more intently to the Holy Spirit. The more angelic involvement in a person's life, the more likely it is that he or she will yield to the drawing of the Lord.
4. *Angels will commit dynamic acts*. Some of the angels' acts are amazing rescues, protecting those in harm's way. Angels also release natural disasters as judgments. This usually comes because of major sins at a national level.

THE MESSAGE

In Rev. 14 John saw that angels will be deployed to the nations to release the eternal gospel. Here is the message: "Fear God and give him glory, because the hour of his judgment has come. Worship him who made the heavens, the earth, the sea and the springs of water" (Rev. 14:7).

The message has three parts:

1. *Fear God and give him glory*. The gospel will be a warning to the world to fear God and give him glory. In other words, it is a wake up call. The traumas that will have come to earth during the tribulation will not simply be natural disasters or wars over differing ideologies. The world will be in God's furnace. He is God, and this message will tell people that it is time to pay attention to him.
2. The hour of judgment has come. The gospel will bring a final warning that the hour is at hand. In other words, people will be told that this is their last chance to bow on their knees and make things right with God. They will be warned not to waiver in the hour of salvation, for it will be an emergency situation, and they must not delay repentance.
3. Worship the creator. In other words, the gospel will call everyone to give his or her allegiance to the living God, who made all things including the springs of water, which will be the only source of drinking water on the planet during the last half of the tribulation (notice the reference to springs of water at the end of verse 7). Water will be the most valuable natural commodity, and God will be the only one who can help people survive. He will also let people drink from the other spring of water, the one that bubbles up and gives eternal life.

A PROPHECY

The prophecy will be given by an angel flying in midair. It will not be long before the prophetic word becomes reality. God's people will pray the prayer of agreement that will release the word of God into action.

Here are the words of Jesus regarding the eternal gospel: "And this gospel of the kingdom will be preached in the whole world as a testimony to all nations, and then the end will come" (Matt. 24:14).

Chapter Thirty-four

Revelation is About the Fall of Babylon

A second angel followed and said, "Fallen, fallen is Babylon the Great, which made all the nations drink the maddening wine of her adulteries."

A third angel followed them and said in a loud voice: "If anyone worships the beast and his image and receives his mark on the forehead or on the hand, he, too, will drink the wine of God's fury, which has been poured full strength into the cup of his wrath. He will be tormented with burning sulfur in the presence of the holy angels and of the Lamb. And the smoke of their torment rises forever and ever. There is no rest day or night for those who worship the beast and his image, or for anyone who receives the mark of his name. (Rev. 14:8–11)

CHAPTER TOPICS

1. Three prophetic angels
2. Babylon the Great
3. The seductions of Babylon
4. The fall of Babylon
5. Hell fires

THREE PROPHETIC ANGELS

REVELATION TELLS US THAT three angel prophets will announce the choices that man has at the midpoint of the tribulation. In the last chapter, we discussed how the first angel will announce the eternal gospel. Here, by examining Rev. 14:8–11, we learn that the second and third angels will prophesy the fall of Babylon.

All will choose God or the beast, blessings or curses, Zion or Babylon, and heaven or hell. The contrast has never been so obvious. God will help humankind make the right choice. God will use every means possible to reach humanity. With the work and skill of heaven's army and the radical forces of saints on earth, God will call every soul on the planet to join his Son. The results will be phenomenal; before the events foretold in the fourteenth chapter of Revelation are complete, the greatest revival in human history will take place.

As with all major initiatives, the Lord will incorporate the work of the prophets, both angelic and human. He will also include the prayers of the saints, and with agreement and unity, his predetermined plans will unfold.

BABYLON THE GREAT

Babylon is the evil counterpart to Zion. Zion is the dwelling place of God, his angels, and his people. Babylon is the dwelling place of Satan, the beast, the false prophet, and all of their armies, which includes people of darkness and demon spirits.

Mankind was not made for evil, but many choose to reject God and do the works of the Antichrist. They receive superficial rewards as compensation for demonic loyalties. The wage of sin, however, is death; sinful pleasures are short-lived, and eternal judgment and hell will become sinners' final reward.

THE GREAT HARLOT

Babylon is vast, well organized, and enticing. She is the mother of spiritual prostitutes, because she draws the world away from God with sensual pleasures.

Revelation says, "Babylon the Great ... made all the nations drink the maddening wine of her adulteries" (Rev. 14:8).

Satan's schemes include tempting people to partake of damnable pleasures. These sins are not only harmful to those who commit them, but they also destroy families, friends, and communities.

Being drunk with alcohol and sex outside of marriage are two vices used to illustrate the enticements of Babylon. Both have been snares of destruction throughout history. Presently they are normal activities in most societies. The entertainment media illustrates and promotes these pleasures with powerful allurements. Sexual immorality and the overindulgence of alcohol are two of the most common reasons for divorce and family dysfunction. These activities will only increase before and during the tribulation. People will be controlled by the power of these pleasures until they are unable to resist them. Only God's grace will enable people to be free from the demons that will drive them.

People will have one passion or the other; they will either be impassioned with Jesus or they will be impassioned with sexual perversion and other lusts. Multitudes from every nation will commit spiritual adultery with the Great Harlot (Babylon). People will sell their souls to the devil for the pleasures of forbidden sex, financial gain and political control.

SEDUCTIONS GALORE

Immoral sex and intoxication are only two of the many vices used by the devil to control people. Any device, action, or philosophy that causes a person to reject God becomes an idol. The worst and most destructive of these idols are the ones that send us to hell. When we persist in evil vices such as adultery, witchcraft, thieving, murder, violence, oppression of others, continuous lying, sordid gain, and deviant sexuality we are on the pathway to hell.

FALLEN, FALLEN

Before Babylon's actual demise and fall, the angel will prophesy it. Babylon's failure is irreversible, it is not negotiable. The fall of Satan's kingdom is one of the two main themes of Revelation; the other is the fulfillment of God's blessings upon Israel and the church.

The next six chapters of Revelation describe, in great detail, the complete fall and destruction of Babylon. Deception will cease, sin will stop, demons will be judged, and Satan will be dethroned and cast into hell. Then truth will come, love and peace will be the norm, and angels and men will enjoy full fellowship with each other and with God. Then the saints will reign with Christ throughout eternity.

PEOPLE IN HELL

It is God's desire that no human will end up in hell, but he leaves the choice to us. I believe that, in the end, God's grace will cover more people than we could imagine. I expect a lot more people to be in heaven than in hell. I say this because of God's great love. God is patient beyond measure and fair beyond fair. He is called in scripture the God of all grace (1 Pet. 5:10), and I think he will surprise us with the extension of his mercy and the power of his love.

Even though hell was designed for the devil and his angels, some people who persist in being a part of the devil's kingdom, will end up there. God alone will decide who goes to hell and who will be saved from it. The Bible indicates the basic guidelines for salvation, but God is the judge and he would have us pray that mercy triumphs over judgment. God will find a way for that to happen for multitudes of people.

HELL IS HORRIBLE

During the tribulation, anyone who dies as a worshipper of the beast or a carrier of his mark will drink the wine of God's wrath. The full dose of that wrath will end with hell fires. Although many will be converted and freed from the beast, others will still embrace evil.

They will suffer the full consequences of their final choice: "[They] will be tormented with burning sulfur. And the smoke of their torment rises forever and ever. There is no rest day or night for those who worship the beast and his image, or for anyone who receives the mark of his name" (Rev. 14:10–11).

The pain and continuance of hell are inconceivable to me. Both, however, are clearly described in God's word. God alone can properly justify this degree of punishment.

His desire, combined with the efforts of countless angels and men will rescue as many as possible from such a dreadful destiny.

May all who read this book fear God and give him glory. Follow Jesus, not the Antichrist. Every person has the ability to enter the safety of Zion. Babylon the Great is destined and doomed to failure. Whatever it takes, do not go down with her.

Chapter Thirty-five

Revelation is About Saints Who Die

There is no rest day or night for those who worship the beast and his image, or for anyone who receives the mark of his name. This calls for patient endurance on the part of the saints who obey God's commandments and remain faithful to Jesus. Then I heard a voice from heaven say, "Write: Blessed are the dead who die in the Lord from now on." "Yes," says the Spirit, "they will rest from their labor, for their deeds will follow them. (Rev. 14:11–13)

CHAPTER TOPICS

1. Unavoidable war
2. The trauma of the saints
3. The saints who welcome death
4. The death of the saints being precious
5. The saints receiving rest
6. The saints receiving rewards

THE WORST OF WAR

WAR RUINS LIVES, SEPARATES families, maims innocent people, and kills many. During war, the inheritance and cultures of ancient families and historical communities are decimated. War is a last resort, but good people must not yield to tyranny. When terror comes, it must be resisted.

The war predicted in Revelation will be a war against demonic terror. In fact, the war will be the cessation of demonic terror. This really will be the war to end all wars.

There will be a point in the war when the fighting becomes most intense and loss of human life is at its highest. The tribulation wars will be worse than any the world has known. The devastation will become so horrible that God will no longer want his people present on earth.

He says, "Blessed are the dead who die in the Lord from now on" (Rev. 14:13).

NOT WITHOUT PURPOSE

As demons and evil men are driven back, God will empower his saints to save the world, and millions will come to Christ. His strategy is perfect, and it will bring about the world's greatest revival. This, however, will call for patient endurance of the saints (Rev. 14:12). It will require a level of endurance that reaches through pain and is prepared for death.

In a desperate struggle to solidify his hold on the world, Satan will employ every possible tactic. Even though his time will be short, he will abuse humanity to the very end. In the few years remaining, evil will be at its worse. The reign of evil will produce three things:

1. It will expose the devil's true nature and remove the pretense of lies that he hides behind.
2. Simultaneously, the Lord will call the world to a great revival.

3. The saints will suffer greatly as the beast overpowers them.

Unprecedented persecution is only one side of the trauma the saints will be called to endure. More judgments will fall in the form of natural disasters. They will be so bad they will make the previous ones appear much tamer. Unbearable calamities will come, and all on the planet will suffer.

A MAJOR SHIFT

The tide will have turned and a major shift will occur. Before now, saints will have been part of a glorious adventure. Although the world will have suffered pain, the servants of God will have been heroes. They will have witnessed providential protection, seen countless miracles, rescued multitudes from hell, and driven back darkness. They will have fought evil, lifted high the name of Christ, and even ruled the world in righteousness for a brief period of time.

At this point, the greatest evangelistic explosion in the history of the world will be yet to come. Following that, however, the beast will pressure the world into witchcraft. Then God's unrelenting judgments will fall, and those who die in the Lord will be considered blessed.

GOING TO THEIR REST

Even at this point, all of the saints will not die, for scripture informs us that, when the Lord returns, *those who are alive and remain* shall be caught up to meet him in the air (1Thess.4:17). Then God's family will reign on the earth, and a kingdom of righteousness will be established.

Perhaps a billion souls will be saved in the last revival. Not all of them will die before the Lord returns, but multitudes will die and go to their reward.

The first reward is rest: "They will go to their rest" (Rev. 14:13).

The battle will have been so intense that many will welcome death. This happens with seniors who do not fear death. In their final days, their bodies are frail and they are weary. Many family members and friends who are predeceased are waiting for them. These elderly people linger as those around them say their good byes, but they have already given up life in this world and it is time to let them go. They look for rest and reward. The last half of the tribulation will be such an endurance-course that many will be like the elderly who look for higher skies.

GOING TO THEIR REWARD

It is not just rest that weary saints will look for; it is also the promised rewards. Their payment will be extravagant. Even those who have hated God all their lives and persecuted his people will receive amazing rewards if they come to Christ before they die.

Jesus told a parable of last minute conversions. He said:

A landowner went out … to hire men to work in his vineyard. He agreed to pay them a denarius for the day … About the eleventh hour he went out and found still others standing around … He said to them …"You go and work in my vineyard …" Those came who were hired first, they expected to receive more [reward]. But each one of them also received a denarius … "These men who were hired worked only one hour." They said, "and you have made them equal to us who have borne the burden of the work and the heat of the day." (Matt. 20:1–12)

Whether we have championed the cause of Christ all of our lives or accepted him with our last breath, we will receive great rewards. Every soul who repents and receives Christ will inherit all things. Eternal life, incorruptible bodies, Christ-like character, and pleasures forevermore are the rewards that will be given to all who become part of God's family. Jesus paid the full price for all of these benefits, and we can receive them by receiving him.

"He who did not spare his own Son, but gave him up for us all—how will he not also, along with him, graciously give us all things?" (Rom. 8:32).

SPECIAL REWARDS

Special rewards will be given to those who serve the Lord with distinction. They will receive crowns, thrones, and authority to be kings and rulers in his kingdom. Our present afflictions, though horrible, will be brief. They cannot be compared to the glories of the eternal rewards that wait for us in the kingdom of our Lord.

"I consider that our present sufferings are not worth comparing with the glory that will be compared in us" (Rom. 8:18).

Chapter Thirty-six

Revelation is About the Greatest Revival

I looked, and there before me was a white cloud, and seated on the cloud was one "like a son of man" with a crown of gold on his head and a sharp sickle in his hand.
Then another angel came out of the temple and he called in a loud voice to him who was sitting on the cloud, "Take your sickle and reap, because the time to reap has come, for the harvest of the earth is ripe." So he who was seated on the cloud swung his sickle over the earth, and the earth was harvested. (Rev. 14:14–16)

CHAPTER TOPICS

1. The two sickles
2. Angel prophets
3. The greatest revival
4. The latter rain
5. The testimony to the nations

TWO SICKLES

PROPHECY IS LIKE A bow pulled back. It waits for perfect timing, a proper focus on the target, and the action of release. Four prophecy themes were recorded in the first half of Rev. 14. Our last four chapters highlighted these prophecies, which will be about

1. a new anointing for the saints;
2. the eternal gospel;
3. the fall of Babylon;
4. final judgments and the death of the saints.

In the time spoken of in Rev. 14, these prophetic arrows will be released from the bow. Two great events will also happen and they will involve sickles.

The first is the sickle of salvation. It will harvest those who turn to the Lord. God will extract the precious fruit of the earth.

The second is the sickle one of cleansing. It will cut away the evil from the earth. It is the sickle of judgment like the one held in the hands of the grim reaper.

In this chapter, we will focus on the first sickle. It is a harvest tool, an instrument of blessings.

LIKE THE SON OF MAN

"I looked, and there before me was a white cloud, and seated on the cloud was one "like a son of man" with a crown of gold on his head and a sharp sickle in his hand (Rev, 14:14).

A new picture appeared on the Revelation screen. John saw a white cloud and someone like the son of man sitting on it. The term, "Son of Man," is a title used in scripture to describe Jesus. The "son of man" in this portion of Revelation is not the Lord, but someone like him. John said that he was glistening white and shinning like the sun.

We know he is an angel for we read, "Then another angel came out" (Rev. 14:15).

God's awesome glory will shine through the angel. Two things about his attire stood out to John: he had a golden crown on his head and a sharp sickle in his hand. He was poised over the earth, waiting among the clouds ready to bring in the biggest harvest yet.

COMMANDING OFFICER

Suddenly, John saw another angel come out of the temple, which is God's throne room. The angel will come from the presence of God Almighty, the Lamb, and the congregation of heaven; he is an officer of the throne room. He will receive instructions from Jesus and proclaim it in a loud voice to the angel who sits on the clouds. His order will not be a secret; the entire spirit realm will hear him. He will shout "Take your sickle and reap, because the time to reap has come, for the harvest of the earth is ripe" (Rev. 14:15).

Three simple phrases will initiate the greatest revival in history:

1. The time has come
2. The fruit is ripe
3. Take your sickle and reap

GOD IS PATIENT

Harvesting the earth was in God's heart even before the world was formed. God wants his human family (his harvest) at his side. He waited patiently as man was created. Then he waited as humankind, who had free will, faltered and fell. According to plan, God sent his son, redeemed the world, and began to harvest a family for eternity.

He has drawn mankind to himself through the cross of Christ. The message of God's grace has gone around the world, and people of every nation have responded. No human needs go to hell because God's mercy overcomes judgment. Christ paid for man's sin to bring us to God.

Each man will be judged according to what he knows and what opportunities he has had to receive or reject the Lord. Those who understand more about the Lord will be judged more severely than those who understand little. There are billions of people who have been saved throughout history. A steady harvest of souls has come to Christ. Only God knows how these souls came, who they are, and how many souls there have been. God has been patient.

At the end, the majority of people on the planet will come to Christ in a brief season of time.

THE FRUIT IS RIPE

At no previous time in history have all the nations come to such a corporate valley of decision as they will during the final portion of the tribulation period. Never before has the veil of secrecy drawn back to expose both the kingdom of darkness and the kingdom of God as it will at that time. Nor has the anointing on God's people to evangelize the world ever reached such a powerful level. There has never been so many who are ready to receive the Lord—the fruit has never been so ripe.

The spiritual environment of the great tribulation will have brought the scorching heat and the heavy rains. Droughts, winds, and calamity will help prepare the harvest, and then it will come.

THE LATTER RAIN

The end-time harvest of the earth is known in scripture as the latter rain. In the twentieth century, a powerful season of revival was called the Latter Rain Movement. The participants saw miracles, thousands were saved, and the leaders of the movement thought they would usher in the great harvest of souls and see the return of the Lord.

The Latter Rain Movement came and went. It was a foreshadowing of the great one, and we can expect many more foreshadows before the coming of the real latter rain. Scripture talks about the former and the latter rains. Here are just a few verses:

"Therefore be patient, brethren, until the coming of the Lord. See how the farmer waits for the precious fruit of the earth, waiting patiently for it until it receives the early and latter rain" (James. 5:7 NKJV).

"Be glad then you children of Zion, And rejoice in the Lord your God; for he has given you the former rain faithfully, And he will cause the rain to come down for you—The former rain, And the latter rain" (Joel 2:23 NKJV).

"Ask the Lord for rain in the time of the latter rain. The Lord will make flashing clouds; He will give them showers of rain, Grass in the field for everyone" (Zech. 10:1 NKJV).

"Let us pursue the knowledge of the Lord. His going forth is established as the morning; He will come to us like the rain, Like the latter and the former rain to the earth" (Hosea 6:3 NKJV).

"Then I will give you the rain for your land in its season, the early rain and the latter rain, that you may gather in your grain, your new wine and your oil" (Deut. 11:14 NKJV).

The latter rain is so powerful that the Lord uses it to describe his blessings and favor.

"In the light of the king's face is life, and his favor is like a cloud of the latter rain" (Prov. 16:15 NKJV).

The latter rain will come, and the greatest of harvests will follow.

THE EARTH WAS HARVESTED

John wrote, "So he who was seated on the cloud swung his sickle and the earth was harvested" (Rev. 14:16).

The end-time revival will be so massive that it deserves the title, "the harvest of the earth." The harvest does not mean the removal of people off of the earth, although many will die soon after they are saved, and their souls will go to heaven. The harvest means that souls will be collected into God's family; multitudes will be saved. Some of them will not die, but will be present on earth for the second coming of Christ. Both those who die and those who remain until the coming of the Lord will be part of the harvest.

Shortly after the halfway point of the tribulation, the massive revival will come. It will happen so quickly that it will be compared to the single stroke of a farmer's sickle. Millions of evangelists, many of them Jews, will share the testimony of Christ in every land. Miracles of healing and deliverance will follow the preaching of the gospel. The result will be the greatest harvest of souls in human history.

During the first half of the tribulation, many non-committed souls will have become believers, so only the toughest of sinners will still be on earth at the halfway mark. It seems impossible for these to be saved, but not so; God will have been working on them. The power of Jesus' blood and the anointing of the Holy Spirit will still save vast multitudes this late in time. The hardest of hearts will be softened, and they will turn to God in an instant.

We should never say that our community is too difficult for the gospel. We should never think that he or she is so defiled or stubborn that they are beyond God's grace. God will prove that they are not.

While millions upon millions will be converted to Christ, still many will refuse, and they are the ones who will choose to serve the beast. Even many of them will eventually come to Christ before the very end. Oh the wonders of the riches of Christ. Even when times get their very worst, Christ's victorious cross will still be saving souls.

A TESTIMONY TO THE NATIONS

The Lord Jesus said, "And this gospel of the kingdom will be preached in all the world *as a testimony to all nations* and then the end shall come" (Matt. 24:14; italics added).

It is not just the salvation of souls that will be at stake when it comes to this final revival; the testimony of the revival will also be significant. This one-time global harvest will be the high-point victory of the cross. The darker the evil, the brighter will be the works of God. Where sin abounds, grace does much more abound. The testimony of the cross will be seen by all. Heaven will see it, the nations will see it, and Satan and his demons will see it as well. Heaven will rejoice and the earth will be glad, but Satan will be angry and completely frustrated.

Chapter Thirty-seven

Revelation is About the Wrath of God

Another angel came out of the temple in heaven, and he too had a sharp sickle.
Still another angel, who had charge of the fire, came from the altar and called in a loud voice to him who had the sharp sickle, "Take your sharp sickle and gather the clusters of grapes from the earth's vine, because its grapes are ripe."
The angel swung his sickle on the earth, gathered its grapes and threw them into the great winepress of God's wrath.
They were trampled in the winepress outside the city, and blood flowed out of the press, rising as high as the horses' bridles for a distance of 1,600 stadia. (Rev. 14:17–20)

CHAPTER TOPICS

1. The two sickles
2. The extent of God's mercy
3. The angel of fire
4. The winepress of God's wrath
5. Metaphors that illustrate the devastation
6. The extent of human loss
7. The most dreadful time of judgment prior to hell

THE SECOND SICKLE

THE FIRST SICKLE WILL be for harvesting souls for salvation, but the second one will have an opposite purpose—cutting down the wicked for judgment. Notice the words in Paul's letter to the Romans. He speaks of the kindness and the sternness of the Lord: "Consider therefore the kindness and sternness of God: sternness to those who fell, but kindness to you, provided that you continue in his kindness. Otherwise, you also will be cut off" (Rom. 11:22).

THE MERCY OF GOD

Like the angel of salvation, the angel who carries the sickle of judgment will come from the temple in heaven—from the presence of God and the Lamb. As there will be a perfect time for the harvest revival, so there will be a time for judgment. God is merciful and patient, but not negligent. If a human being were sitting on the judgment seat, judgment would have come much sooner.

Before looking at the wrath of God, it is important to remember God's amazing mercy. We have seen that God will delay judgment when it appears to be due, not as an emotional afterthought, but as a predetermined plan that is consistent with his mercy. He waits long and is patient as only God can be. He is just, but his mercy far exceeds his judgment. Look at the following scripture that calls us to be merciful as God is merciful.

"Love your enemies, do good to them, and lend to them without expecting to get anything back. Then your reward will be great, and you will be sons of the Most High, because he is kind to the ungrateful and wicked. Be merciful, just as your Father [God] is merciful" (Luke 6:35–36).

There seems to be two opposing views in the church as to how to deal with sin. One group in the church today would never judge anyone for even the worst sins. They are not able to defend those who have been victimized. There is another group of Christians who make judgment and legalism the theme of church life. They are more like police than saints.

This second group is just as wrong as the first. God hates legalists; they lack compassion and mercy. On the whole, I believe that the Christian community should be far more forgiving of those who stumble and fall.

Several parables highlight God's attitude toward the uncompassionate and the unforgiving.

In Matthew 18:32–35, we read, "Then the master called the servant in. 'You wicked servant,' he said, 'I cancelled all that debt of yours because you begged me to. Shouldn't you have mercy on your fellow servant just as I had on you?' In anger his master turned him over to the jailer to be tortured, until he should pay back all he owed. This is how your heavenly Father will treat each of you unless you forgive your brother from your heart."

Matthew 6: 14–15 reads, "If you forgive men when they sin against you, your heavenly Father will also forgive you. But if you do not forgive men their sins, your Father will not forgive your sins."

Paul wrote to the Corinthian church:

"If anyone has caused grief ... not to put it too severely. The punishment inflicted on him by the majority is sufficient for him. Now instead, you ought to forgive and comfort him ... so that he will not be overwhelmed by excessive sorrow. I urge you, therefore, to reaffirm your love for him. The reason I wrote you was to see if you would stand the test and be obedient in everything. If you forgive anyone, I also forgive him. And what I have forgiven—if there is anything to forgive—I have forgiven in the sight of Christ for your sake, in order that Satan might not outwit us. For we are not unaware of his schemes." (2 Cor. 2:5–11)

Notice that when we judge so much that we fail to forgive, comfort, and love, we allow the devil to outwit us. One of his schemes is to use legalistic people to hurt and break weak members of the church through excessive judgments. While thinking they are holy, they are actually doing the devil's work.

God is not like that; he is compassionate. Even in the Old Testament, we read of his amazing attitude of mercy toward the sinner:

"The Lord is compassionate and gracious, slow to anger, abounding in love. He will not always accuse, nor will he harbor his anger forever; he does not treat us as our sins deserve or repay us according to our iniquities. For as high as the heavens are above the earth, so great is his love for those who fear him; as far as the east is from the west, so far has he removed our transgressions from us. As a father has compassion on his children, so the Lord has compassion on those who fear him; for he knows how we are formed, he remembers that we are dust". (Ps. 103:8–14)

God alone can balance kindness and severity, mercy and judgment, but two things are certain: first, the Lord's mercy is greater than his judgment; and second, we should be just as merciful as he is.

ANGEL OF FIRE

"Another angel came out of the temple in heaven, and he too had a sharp sickle" (Rev. 14:17–20).

Now that we have duly noted the power of God's grace, we turn to the fact that judgment must eventually come. The angel with the sickle of judgment has been instructed to position his sickle to strike the earth, and he is waiting for orders.

"Still another angel, who had charge of the fire, came from the altar and called in a loud voice to him who had the sharp sickle, "Take your sharp sickle and gather the clusters of grapes from the earth's vine, because its grapes are ripe" (Rev. 14:18).

In the next verse, John saw another senior angel come forth. He is the angel in charge of fire, and he has come from the altar of heaven, which is the altar of prayer positioned before God's throne.

PROPHETIC PRAYERS

Prayers are like prophecies in that they connect heaven and earth, except they travel in the opposite direction. Prophecies go down from

God to people. They announce what God will do. Prayer on the other hand goes up from people to God. They also announce what God will do. The elders of heaven work with this back and forth, heaven to earth, communication system. All saints in heaven participate in this activity as well. Our parents and friends who have preceded us into God's presence are actively praying and prophesying in heaven. The kingdom of God is a kingdom of unity, and in that unity God releases authority.

The angel in charge of the altar will take the fire and hurl it to the earth, and at that moment our prayers will be answered.

THE RELEASE OF POWER

I understand that the procedure for the release of a nuclear missile involves at least two people. Two officers must work in tandem to fire it. Keys are turned, codes are typed into keyboards, and buttons are pushed simultaneously so that one person may not launch a nuclear device on his or her own.

Heaven seems to operate in similar fashion when it comes to major events. Commands come from the throne, prophecies are spoken, and only then will angels and elders release the answers to prayer.

All of heaven will be in agreement as heaven's army releases the wrath of God during the final stages of the tribulation.

The angel in charge of answered prayer, the angel of fire, will call out in a booming voice, "Take your sharp sickle and gather the clusters of grapes from the earth's vine, because it's grapes are ripe" (Rev. 14:18).

THE WINEPRESS

The winepress is the metaphor for the last campaign. And as a winepress is devastating to the grapes within it, so the last campaign will be to demons and sinners who are still on the earth at the end of the great tribulation. It will be absolutely devastating.

The ancient winepress was a large open pit lined with flat rocks. Hundreds of pounds of grapes would be cut from the vines once they were fully ripe and bursting with juice and thrown into the pit. Then several workers with bare feet would wade into the winepress. They would begin to trample the grapes with their feet. The dark red juice would squirt in every direction. Often they would have ropes hanging from overhead tree branches or poles to hold on to because the soupy mixture would become slippery. They would trample for hours on end, squishing, breaking, and totally pulverizing each grape. By the time their job was complete, every grape would be crushed, and every skin would be emptied of its fleshy jelly. Everything would be liquefied.

That is the picture Revelation gives of the final judgments that will fall during the last campaign. As we study the next chapters of Revelation, we will discover that the winepress is a very accurate illustration of God's wrath.

THE SICKLE

Suddenly the angel with the sickle will swing it upon the earth, gather the grapes (the wicked people and demons) and throw them into the winepress of God's wrath, and they will be trampled by the angels of heaven. The hour of judgment will have come.

It is no wonder that the Lord says, "Blessed are the dead who die in the Lord from now on, they will rest from their labor" (Rev. 14:13).

No one will want to be on the planet to witness or to be part of this judgment.

THE BLOODY METAPHOR CONTINUES

The two sickles, one of evangelism and the other of judgment, emphasize the finality and the speed of angelic action at the end of the tribulation. They are illustrations. It would be silly to think they are literal sickles. Here are the metaphors used to illustrate the final series of judgments and a list of what each image represents:

1. *The sickles* illustrate the speed and finality of God's wrath.
2. *The winepress* is the planet earth.
3. *The bowls* ready to be poured illustrate that judgment is overdue.
4. *The crushing of grapes* illustrates the force of the judgments.
5. *The grapes* are the people and demons who will receive judgment.
6. *The thrashers of the grapes* are the angels.

A further metaphor illustrates the extent of human loss that will occur because of the judgments. The scripture says, "They [wicked people] were trampled in the winepress outside the city, and blood flowed out of the press, rising as high as the horses bridles for a distance of 1,600 stadia" (Rev. 14:20).

According to the Zondervan Study Bible, "It [the distance of 1600 stadia] is approximately the length of Palestine from north to south."[q]

The illustration tells of blood flowing about five feet deep for a distance of one hundred and eighty miles, or three hundred kilometers. That was the entire length of Palestine in Bible times. It is not logical to think that blood will actually flow this deep for this distance. The number of dead bodies needed to produce that amount of blood is inconceivable. The blood would first drain and saturate the land and then cause a flood beyond our imagination.

In keeping with the previous six metaphors, this is an illustration. It tells us that the loss of human life will be enormous. So many will die during the final judgments that it will be like a flood of blood. It will be as if the blood poured out from a winepress to a depth of five feet deep covering an area one hundred and eighty miles long. The bowls of God's wrath will produce the most dreadful time of judgment.

Chapter Thirty-eight

Revelation is About Seven Last Plagues

I saw in heaven another great and marvelous sign: seven angels with the seven last plagues—last, because with them God's wrath is complete.

And I saw what looked like a sea of glass mixed with fire and, standing beside the sea, those who had been victorious over the beast and his image and over the number of his name. They held harps given them by God and sang the song of Moses the servant of God and the song of the Lamb: "Great and marvelous are your deeds, Lord God Almighty. Just and true are your ways, King of the ages. Who will not fear you, O Lord, and bring glory to your name? For you alone are holy. All nations will come and worship before you, for your righteous acts have been revealed."

After this I looked and in heaven the temple, that is, the tabernacle of the testimony, was opened. Out of the temple came the seven angels with the seven plagues. They were dressed in clean, shining linen and wore golden sashes around their chests.

Then one of the four living creatures gave to the seven angels seven golden bowls filled with the wrath of God, who lives for ever and ever.

And the temple was filled with smoke from the glory of God and from his power, and no one could enter the temple until the seven plagues of the seven angels were complete. (Rev. 15:1–8)

SUGGESTED READING: REVELATION 15

CHAPTER TOPICS

1. The seven angels
2. The seven plagues
3. The war song of heaven
4. The tabernacle of testimony
5. The dwelling of God is with man
6. Honoring the justice of God
7. An end of grace

THE GROUP OF SEVEN

AT THE BEGINNING OF Rev. 15, John tells us that he saw seven angels standing ready to release the seven last plagues (Rev. 15:1). The angels will come from the throne room, the temple of heaven. Their mission is frightening, for their plagues will be the worst judgments the earth has ever seen. The plagues will be so destructive that with them God's judgments will be complete.

Heaven will be sober as the angels emerge. Already the demons and fallen angels will sense the impending doom. They know what will befall them, and they will be terrified and angry. The seven angels, on the other hand, will not lose their composure. They will be dressed in white linen with golden sashes across their chests. They are angels of war, and they will administer the judgments of God with technical precision. They will be passionate for their mission, which is for the Almighty and for the Lamb, has been anticipated from before the foundations of the world.

SEVEN PLAGUES

The angels will release seven plagues. They will be like the plagues of Egypt, only they will cover the entire planet. They will include painful sores, toxic water, flesh-scorching heat, darkness, global war, earthquakes, and hundred pound hailstones. They will come quickly, but when they are finished, the earth will be uninhabitable, and most people on it will be dead.

THE WAR SONG

"And I saw what looked like a sea of glass mixed with fire and, standing beside the sea, those who had been victorious over the beast and his image and over the number of his name. They held harps given them by God and sang the song of Moses the servant of God and the song of the Lamb:" (Rev. 15:1–8).

John recognized another great and marvelous sign in heaven. As soon as he saw the seven angels, he saw the sea of glass. This sea is the multitude of human spirits from every generation in history standing in heaven. They are mixed with fire, for they are bursting with unbroken intercession. Prayers of supplication, dedication, proclamation, and thanksgiving are flaming fires that pour out from God's holy people in heaven. Standing with this great company are those who have died during the great tribulation. They are those who were victorious over the beast, his image, and the number of his name (Rev.13, 14).

This group is probably more than two billion in number, and each is given a harp. They play the song of the intercessor. The twenty-four elders have harps, and along with the great multitude, they lead humanity in prayer. They are playing a war song. It is the song of Moses, the servant of God, and the song of the Lamb:

"Great and marvelous are your deeds, Lord God Almighty. Just and true are your ways, King of the ages. Who will not fear you, O Lord, and bring glory to your name? For you alone are holy. All nations will come and worship before you, for your righteous acts have been revealed" (Rev. 15:4).

The battle hymn is exactly what is needed for the troops who will march to war. The song of Moses declares that God is great and his deeds are marvelous, that his acts are justified and true. It announces that everyone will ultimately fear the Lord and bring him glory because he is holy and without blame. It concludes with a prophecy that all nations will come and worship the Lord because they will see and understand that all his acts are righteous.

This is not an embellished war chant designed to bolster a weary army. It is not wishful thinking; it is in fact, the truth. The message is not negotiable or stoppable. This is the war cry of victory that will be sung before the battle is even fought. Heaven will know it, demons will know it, and the saints on earth will be learning it.

This song is about the victory of the king, the victory of the Lamb. Each military maneuver will be orchestrated by him. The book of Revelation is about Jesus; about his army, his angels, and his kingdom advancing on the earth. Angels move at his command, saints rise up according to his will, and the Father's plans are released through him. When all is complete, he will hand the kingdom back to his Father, but first his enemies must become his footstool.

THE TABERNACLE OF TESTIMONY

The war song of Moses and the Lamb will open the tabernacle of testimony. This is so important. The tabernacle of testimony was the dwelling place of God when he journeyed with Israel in the wilderness during the time of Moses. The plans for the tabernacle were given to Moses from God. He was commanded to build it exactly as instructed.

Like hundreds of directives given to the Jewish people, the details of the tabernacle spoke of God living with his people. Every part symbolized some aspect of the relationship between God and the Jews. The tabernacle is a metaphor, a testimony of God living with man.

The surrounding nations could look at the tabernacle of testimony and discover the amazing phenomenon of God with man. For forty years, the nations could see a permanent cloud rising by day and a pillar of fire coming from it by night. When the cloud or fire moved, the children of Israel moved.

The throne room in heaven has the same purpose. It was there before the tabernacle in the wilderness. This is amazing. It is a testimony of God and man living together. It is all about fellowship, love, peace, joy, worship, righteousness, goodness, and honor.

It is not just for Jewish saints, but for all mankind who hold to the testimony of Jesus. It is a testimony not to a few surrounding nations to see, but for every creature in the universe.

Later in Revelation, John wrote, "I heard a loud voice from the throne saying, 'Now the dwelling place of God is with men, and he will live with them. They will be his people, and God himself will be with them and be their God'" (Rev. 21:3).

Let wicked men and atheists attempt to deny the testimony; let demons try to hinder it; their efforts will be to no avail. The testimony of God with man is unstoppable. God will live with people. The final act at the end of the Bible is all about this. After the new millennium, God will move his throne room to planet earth. There he will live in fellowship with humanity (Rev. 22:3). The seven angels will come and perform the acts that make the testimony possible.

THE FOUR CREATURES PARTICIPATE

One of the four living creatures will be involved. He will give the seven golden bowls to the seven angels. Each will be filled with the wrath of God. As if he is handling plutonium—a weapon of mass destruction—the seraph will carefully dispense the bowls. The wrath of God will be passed from the seraph to the angels. It will be extremely potent. It should be labeled, "handle with caution" or "handle with fear."

EXTREME GLORY

"And the temple was filled with smoke from the glory of God and from his power, and no one could enter the temple until the seven plagues of the seven angels were complete. (Rev. 15:1–8)

Suddenly the temple of God will be filled with smoke because the glory of God will be released. From that point until the plagues are completed, no one will be allowed to enter the temple.

I am reminded of the half hour of silence in heaven when the eternal prayers of the saints are about to be answered. The reverence and holiness of the moment will demand complete attention. Heaven's silence honors the followers of the Lamb (Rev. 8:1–5).

This will be a similar moment. As Jesus releases the wrath of God and the worst judgments are set in motion, the power and glory of God will be manifest. All movement in and around the throne room will be halted. It will be an awesome moment; full attention and concentration will be aimed at the equitable justice of the Almighty. It will be an awful time for lost humanity, and God will not have entered upon it lightly. He will have come to it with perfect righteousness. His grace for the rebels will be coming to an end. Who will be able to bear such a moment?

Chapter Thirty-nine

Revelation is About Bowls of Judgment

Then I heard a loud voice from the temple saying to the seven angels, "Go, pour out the seven bowls of God's wrath on the earth."

The first angel went and poured out his bowl on the land, and ugly and painful sores broke out on the people who had the mark of the beast and worshipped his image.

The second angel went and poured out his bowl on the sea, and it turned into blood like that of a dead man, and every living thing in the sea died.

The third angel poured out his bowl on the rivers and springs of water, and they became blood. Then I heard the angel in charge of the waters say: "You are just in these judgments, you who are and who were, the Holy One, because you have so judged; for they have shed the blood of your saints and prophets, and you have given them blood to drink as they deserve." And I heard the altar respond: "Yes, Lord God Almighty, true and just are your judgments" (Rev. 16:1–7)

CHAPTER TOPICS

1. The pouring of the bowls
2. The plague of painful sores
3. Protection for the saints
4. Genocide in the oceans
5. Poison in the rivers
6. The angel of the water
7. Revenge for the martyrs
8. God's judgments are just

POURING THE FIRST BOWL

JUSTICE AND PATIENCE WILL meet, and the time for God's wrath will come. Those who receive punishment will be more than guilty; they will have been shown what is right and given multiple opportunities to repent, and still they will have turned toward the devil. They will have refused the Lord, embraced evil, and taken a decisive stand against the people of God. None who are judged will receive eternal penalties for minor infractions or simple mistakes. They will be well aware of their choices and will have spat in the face of God's mercy.

"The first angel went and poured out his bowl on the land, and ugly and painful sores broke out on the people who had the mark of the beast and worshipped his image" (Rev. 16:2).

An angel will cry from the temple, commanding the seven to pour the judgments of God upon the earth. The first angel will pour out his bowl on the land and everyone who has the mark of the beast will contract painful sores all over their bodies. They will writhe in pain.

PROTECTION FOR THE SAINTS

The saints on earth will experience supernatural protection. Because the scripture reports that the sores will break out on those who have the mark of the beast, we know that those who do not have the mark—the followers of the Lamb—will not receive the lesions that will cover the bodies of God's enemies. Naturally it will be unexplainable, but by this time in the tribulation period, the spiritual curtain will be drawn back, and people will understand the supernatural. Even the naturalists and the materialists will no longer deny the existence of the spiritual realm and the power of miracles.

Those infected will not find an easy solution. Strong pain killers will bring temporary relief, but the drugs will cause those taking them to be weary and lethargic. Many will not have money or access to the drugs. No disease has ever affected the world on as large a scale as this one will.

Christians will once again minister to the wounded. They will love their enemies, bless and forgive those who have persecuted them, and they will pray even at this hour for God's mercy to continue.

THE SECOND BOWL

"The second angel went and poured out his bowl on the sea, and it turned into blood like that of a dead man, and every living thing in t he sea died" (Rev. 16:1–7).

The first angel will pour his bowl on the land; the second will pour his bowl on the sea. The oceans of the world will turn into blood like that of a dead man. The water will become a deadly toxin, and everything in the oceans will die. It is not that the water will literally turn to blood, but the poison in it will be so vile that it will be like that of a dead man. The water will actually be worse than a dead man's blood for the scripture says that every living thing in the sea will die. There are many creatures that feed off of rotten blood, but not on this kind of poison.

Many times I have visited the Dead Sea in the land of Israel. The water is so salty that no living thing exists in it. That is how it will be in every sea and every ocean when the second bowl is poured out.

Harvesting the sea is a huge part of the food quota that the world depends on for survival. That will come to an abrupt end. There will be no saltwater fish, mammals, shrimp, or even seaweed to eat. All will be destroyed. Millions of businesses will shut down, and people will starve. The world will be scrambling to survive.

THE THIRD BOWL

"The third angel poured out his bowl on the rivers and springs of water, and they became blood" (Rev. 16:1–7).

The second angel will pour his bowl on the sea; the third will pour his on fresh surface water. Every lake, river, and spring of water will become polluted. Only subterranean sources will still provide drinkable water. All surface water will become vile and unusable.

People who drink it will die, and the procedures necessary to clean the water will not be able to keep up with the demand. People will go to special drinking stations, and many will die of thirst or be poisoned from drinking foul water. This will be especially true in the warmer places of the earth.

THE WATER ANGEL

John said that the angel in charge of water declared that God's justice was appropriate: "Then I heard the angel in charge of the waters say: 'You are just in these judgments'" (Rev. 16:5).

It seems that an angel has had responsibility for the water sources of the earth. This angel has a great army of angels under his command who have cared for certain aspects of earth's environment. The water angel has protected and stewarded the waters of the world. Because of his leadership, men and animals have had food from the oceans and water from the rivers.

When the third bowl is poured out, the saltwater will become toxic, and fresh surface water will be undrinkable. The angel of water will have reason for concern for this has been his responsibility. He has fought defiling spirits and unscrupulous men who have acted to pollute the waters of the world. The creator, who initially gave him this responsibility, will destroy the environment.

It is important that the water angel will be in agreement with the judgments of heaven. More important than the task, is the one who gave it to him. He will not only step aside to let the waters be fouled, he will agree with God's judgments.

John heard him speak these words: "You are just in these judgments, you who are and who were, the holy one, because you have so judged; for they have shed the blood of your saints and prophets, and you have given them blood to drink as they deserve" (Rev. 16:5–6).

The Lord looks for agreement and unity. He desires agreement from angels and from men. Jesus will be accomplishing the work of Revelation with the partnership of angels and men. He will continue to stand in the middle of his church, the lampstand, and he will continue to hold the angels in his right hand. Unity and participation will prevail.

THE MARTYRS ARE AVENGED

Unity will be further emphasized by the voice of man. The souls of the martyrs will have patiently waited. They died for the testimony of Christ, and many will have seen no justice. They will not have been avenged, and they will have witnessed many unanswered crimes against the innocent, not to mention Satan's corruption of the earth and wicked men taking advantage of the righteous.

In the sixth chapter of Revelation the martyrs cried out, "How long, Sovereign Lord, holy and true, until you judge the inhabitants of the earth and avenge our blood?" (Rev. 6:10).

In that early moment of the tribulation, the martyrs will be comforted and given instruction, but they will not experience justice. If God could wince, I think it would happen at moments like those. The time for resolve must wait. God will continue to reach out to the souls of lost humanity. If judgment had preceded his appointed time, untold millions would go to hell. That has never been God's desire.

God, however, will not forget the martyrs. The time of reckoning will come. As the bowls of God's wrath are poured out, the souls from under the altar will agree with his judgments. Without hesitation, they will verbalize their agreement.

John said, "And I heard the altar respond: 'Yes, Lord God Almighty, true and just are your judgments'" (Rev. 16:7).

The earth will become all but unlivable because of the judgments of God, but no one who walks with God will be in disagreement. No one will think that God is unreasonable or too harsh.

No one in the universe has shown more mercy and grace to humanity than God has. None could have been more merciful, and humankind will be without excuse. Heaven will be thrilled. Its inhabitants will have found it hard to wait so long, but finally justice will come.

Oh, the amazing wonder of love that comes from the Almighty and from his Christ. Let the heavens rejoice.

Chapter Forty

Revelation is About Extreme Defiance

The fourth angel poured out his bowl on the sun, and the sun was given power to scorch people with fire. They were seared by the intense heat and they cursed the name of God, who had control over the plagues, but they refused to repent and glorify him.

The fifth angel poured out his bowl on the throne of the beast, and his kingdom was plunged into darkness. Men gnawed their tongues in agony and cursed the God of heaven because of their pains and their sores, but they refused to repent of what they had done.

The sixth angel poured out his bowl on the great river Euphrates, and its water was dried up to prepare the way for the kings of the East.

Then I saw three evil spirits that looked like frogs: they came out of the mouth of the dragon, out of the mouth of the beast and out of the mouth of the false prophet. They are spirits of demons performing miraculous signs, and they go out to the kings of the whole world, to gather them for the battle on the great day of God Almighty.

"Behold, I come like a thief! Blessed is he who stays awake and keeps his clothes with him, so that he may not go naked and be shamefully exposed."

Then they gathered the kings together to the place that in Hebrew is called Armageddon. (Rev. 16:8–16)

CHAPTER TOPICS

1. Men and demons being defiant
2. The sun burning people's flesh
3. Satan loosing diplomatic immunity
4. The Euphrates River drying up
5. The armies mustering for Armageddon
6. The eight end-time promises for Israel
7. Jesus coming will not be a surprise

BOWLS OF WRATH

I PICTURE LARGE BOWLS OF boiling hot stew on a kitchen table. Suddenly the bowls are tipped, throwing the boiling concoction all over the laps of those around the table. The recipients are instantly burned, but suddenly they discover that this is not a healthy stew, but a lethal chemical blend that produces irreversible, catastrophic, and violent death.

Some chemicals weapons cause flesh to dissolve, internal organs to erupt, and blood to thin and pour out of bodies. Others will instantly coagulate one's blood into a hardened gel. While those traumas are not the specific symptoms that will accompany the devastation of these bowls, they are not far removed. The end of the tribulation will be as chaotic and as traumatic as the kitchen of death that I described. Please grasp the seriousness of the hour. God's wrath is caustic. It is lethal.

THE FOURTH PLAGUE

"The fourth angel poured out his bowl on the sun, and the sun was given power to scorch people with fire. They were seared by the intense heat and they cursed the name of God, who had control over the plagues, but they refused to repent and glorify him" (Rev. 16:8–9).

We learned that first the land and water will be violated, and then the air will become deadly as well. The fourth angel will pour his bowl upon the sun and its rays will operate like burning lasers. The ozone layer around the earth will be destroyed, and anyone exposed to direct sunlight for any length of time will be scorched. Human skin will burn, bubble, and blister, and no amount of sun block cream will protect it.

The combination of the bowls will be unbearable. All food from the sea will be rotting along the coasts, causing outbreaks of plague and disease. All fresh surface water on the globe will be poisonous, and people will be dying of hunger and thirst. Painful boils will cover the bodies of all of those who worship the Antichrist. With death and suffering on every side, people will be confined to homes and shelters during daylight hours, because direct contact with the rays of the sun will rip into their skin and eat their flesh.

DEFIANT SINNERS

Many sinners will remain defiant in the face of God's wrath. It is not as though people will be unaware that the plagues are judgments from heaven. They will know that the calamities are not just natural disasters caused by pollution or neglect of the environment. They will be fully aware that death has come and that it is a punishment from God. They will also understand that the judgments are irreversible, and the problems the earth is facing cannot be fixed. This will be the end of the world, and it will be hard to understand that people with this level of understanding will still align themselves with the kingdom of Satan.

Scripture says, "They cursed the name of God, who had control over the plagues, but they refused to repent and glorify him … Men gnawed their tongues in agony and cursed the God of heaven because of their pains and their sores, but they refused to repent of what they had done" (Rev. 16:9–11).

Throughout history, men have defied the Lord even in the face of certain death. At this point in the tribulation God will have given humankind every opportunity to accept redemption. He will have used every righteous plan to win the hearts of men and women, but some will still refuse to bow their knees.

The second Psalm says it like this:

"Why do the nations conspire and the peoples plot in vain? The kings of the earth take their stand and the rulers gather together against the Lord and against his Anointed One. "Let us break their chains," they say, "and throw off their fetters." The One enthroned in the heavens laughs; the Lord scoffs at them. Then he rebukes them in his anger and terrifies them in his wrath, saying, "I have installed my King on Zion, my holy hill. Therefore you kings, be wise; be warned you rulers of the earth. Serve the Lord with fear and rejoice with trembling. Kiss the Son, lest he be angry and you be destroyed in the way, for his wrath can flare up in a moment. Blessed are all who take refuge in him." (Ps. 2:1–6, 10–12)

THE FIFTH BOWL

"The fifth angel poured out his bowl on the throne of the beast, and his kingdom was plunged into darkness. Men gnawed their tongues in agony and cursed the God of heaven because of their pains and their sores, but they refused to repent of what they had done" (Rev. 16:10–11).

The fifth angel will pour out his bowl on Satan's kingdom and the beast and the demons will plummet into darkness. Before this time, Satan and his armies will have possessed diplomatic immunity and will have been allowed to hassle humankind without being hurt or cast into hell.

Protection for demons against serious reprisals will be over. This will cause every demon on the planet to suffer confusion. Their supernatural strength will be weakened, and they will feel the pain of impending doom. Like human beings, demons will know terror. They will be frustrated and angry.

The demons will vent their frustrations on their human coworkers. Humans who have been abused often carry emotional and psychological baggage, and they hurt those closest to them. This will happen with the demons. Unsaved and unprotected men will be beaten and ravaged by angry demons set on tormenting and terrorizing whoever they can before they are cast into hell.

THE SIXTH BOWL

"The sixth angel poured out his bowl on the great river Euphrates, and its water was dried up to prepare the way for the kings of the East" (Rev. 16:12).

The sixth bowl will cause the river Euphrates to once again be the focus of world attention. It will be the border of Israel during the tribulation. The Lord sets the boundaries of the nations and gives the nations their appointed time so that the people of those nations might seek him (Acts 17:26–27). That is especially true for Israel. It is one of the ways that the Lord demonstrates his sovereignty over the world. Ungodly nations will not comply with God's blessings for Israel. They will never accept the nation of Israel owning the land that God has promised her.

When the sixth angel pours out his bowl, the water of the river Euphrates will dry up. This will prepare the way for the kings of the east to attack Israel.

"Then I saw three evil spirits that looked like frogs: they came out of the mouth of the dragon, out of the mouth of the beast and out of the mouth of the false prophet. They are spirits of demons performing miraculous signs, and they go out to the kings of the whole world, to gather them for the battle on the great day of God Almighty" (Rev. 16:13–14).

At this time, three war-mongering demons that look life frogs will emerge. They will come from the mouth of the devil, the beast, and the false prophet. They will go to the nations of the world performing supernatural signs and wonders. Their trickery will have a specific purpose. It will be used to deceive the nations into thinking that they have enough supernatural power to fight against God and his people. These people and the demons will be so defiant that they will be predisposed to attack the kingdom of God. They will especially hate the Jewish people, who will have led the recent wave of revivals.

THE GREAT WAR

"Then they gathered the kings together to the place that in Hebrew is called Armageddon" (Rev. 16:16).

This will be the mustering for the Great War. The kings of the east referenced in Revelation will likely include the rulers of China, North Korea, India, and other surrounding nations, but we are told that the whole world will come and participate in this battle as well. The nations will be gathering for the battle of Armageddon. Troop deployment takes time, but this will be the largest gathering of troops in the history of mankind.

God will dry up the Euphrates and initiate war, although Satan, the beast and the false prophet will think that the war is their idea. The battlefield will be Israel, and the nations will stream toward it. The battle will end with the second coming of Christ, but before that happens violence and devastation will erupt around the world.

A RECKONING ON ISRAEL'S ACCOUNT

As the battle begins, one of the eight end-time promises for Israel will be fulfilled. As promised, God will gather the nations and judge them for how they have treated Israel. This will happen at the great battle, the battle of Armageddon. God will gather the nations for judgment because they have hurt Israel.

"In those days and at that time, when I restore the fortunes of Judah and Jerusalem, I will gather all nations and bring them down to the Valley of Jehoshaphat. There I will enter into judgment against them concerning my inheritance, my people Israel, for they scattered my people among the nations and divided up my land. They cast lots for my people and traded boys for prostitutes; they sold girls for wine that they might drink" (Joel 3:1–4).

"Prepare for war! Rouse the warriors! Let all the fighting men draw near and attack. Beat your ploughs into swords and your pruning hooks into spears. Let the weakling say, 'I am strong!' Come quickly all you nations from every side, and assemble there. Bring down your warriors, O Lord! 'Let the nations be roused; let them advance into the Valley of Jehoshaphat, for there I will sit to judge all nations on every side'" (Joel 3:9–12).

The very next verses in Joel clearly illustrate the last campaign of the great tribulation. They speak of the sickle, the harvest, and the winepress of God's wrath, which we know to be the pouring out of the seven bowls of judgment.

"Swing the sickle, for the harvest is ripe. Come, trample the grapes, for the winepress is full and its vats overflow—so great is their wickedness!" ... Multitudes, multitudes in the valley of decision! For the day of the Lord is near in the valley of decision. ... The Lord will roar from Zion and thunder from Jerusalem; the earth and the sky will tremble. But the Lord will be a refuge for his people, a stronghold for the people of Israel." Joel 3:13-14, 16

The Valley of Jehoshaphat is likely the Valley of Armageddon. There is no place in Israel called the Valley of Jehoshaphat, but Jehoshaphat in Hebrew means "God's judgment." In other words, God will gather the nations to the valley of his judgment—Armageddon.

PROMISES FOR ISRAEL

For interest and instruction I have listed God's eight end-time promises for Israel:

1. God will choose Israel again (Zech. 2:12).
2. Israel will be given her land (Ezek. 20:42).
3. International intercessors will pray for Israel until she becomes the praise of the whole world (Isa. 62:6).
4. The people of Israel will be gathered back to their land from

among the nations. (Isa. 11:12).
5. Israel's fortunes will be restored before her very eyes (Zeph. 3:20).
6. Revival will come to Israel (Zech. 12:10; 13:1).
7. God's Glory will come upon Israel (Isa. 60:1–2).
8. Nations who have hurt the people of Israel will be judged (Joel 3).

LIKE A THIEF

'"Behold, I come like a thief! Blessed is he who stays awake and keeps his clothes with him, so that he may not go naked and be shamefully exposed." Then they gathered the kings together to the place that in Hebrew is called Armageddon" (Rev. 16:15–16).

Jesus prophesied his second coming. He will come as a thief in a time when the sinner does not expect him. The saints who are alive during the tribulation will not be taken unawares. They will have been warned to be watchful. They will stay awake and will be fully clothed with the linen of God's righteousness.

The Lord will come as a thief to sinners. A momentary display of supernatural signs from demons and the gathering of huge international armies will not sway the faithful. The teachings and unveiling of the book of Revelation will be studied and preached so that those saints who are present during the tribulation will know the times and the season. They will be ready for the return of the Lord.

Chapter Forty-one

Revelation is About Completing the Judgments

The seventh angel poured out his bowl into the air, and out of the temple came a loud voice from the throne, saying, "It is done!"
Then there came flashes of lightning, rumblings, peals of thunder and a severe earthquake. No earthquake like it has ever occurred since man has been on earth, so tremendous was the quake. The great city split into three parts, and the cities of the nations collapsed.
God remembered Babylon the Great and gave her the cup filled with the wine of the fury of his wrath.
Every island fled away and the mountains could not be found.
From the sky huge hailstones of about a hundred pounds each fell upon men. And they cursed God on account of the plague of hail, because the plague was so terrible. (Rev. 16:17–21)

CHAPTER TOPICS

1. The worst earthquake in history
2. The devil's camp being divided
3. Man's security being totally removed
4. One hundred pound hailstones

5. Man's pride being his greatest enemy

IT IS DONE

WHEN THE SEVENTH ANGEL pours the seventh bowl, a loud voice from the temple says, "It is done" (Rev. 16:17).

The announcement is like the seventh day of creation when God completed his work. He said it was very good and rested from his labor. The task was over; it was announced and remembered.

It is like the awful but glorious day of the cross. Jesus was drained of life. It was the most terrible moment of injustice because the cost of sin fell on the most innocent. Just before Jesus died, he yelled, "It is finished" (John 19:30). The awful job was done, but immeasurable rewards have followed.

The final bowl will be poured, and heaven will announce, "It is done." The awful, but necessary judgments will be over. Eternal rewards will follow. This will be the completion of earth's judgments and the completion of the work of the cross. With it, the door will open for Jesus to receive the full reward for which he died.

THE WORST EARTHQUAKE

Lightning and thunder will rock the earth. This will happen every time heaven releases judgments. It is the power of pent-up prayer rocketing through earth's atmosphere.

With such prayer will come a massive earthquake. John wrote, "No earthquake like it has ever occurred since man has been on earth … the cities of the nations collapsed" (Rev. 16:18-19).

At times terrifying earthquakes have decimated major cites around the world. The tribulation will bring record-breaking earthquakes. This one, however, will be worse than any previous; it will strike every major city on the planet. It will not just be one fault line shifting; the entire world will quake.

Skyscrapers will crumble and be disintegrated, and humble homes will be flattened to rubble. The trauma will come to an already dying world. The death toll will be immeasurable.

People who are already dying from hunger, thirst, depression, tormenting darkness, plague, scorching heat, and infection will suffer the collapse of their homes. Most will be sheltered in them when the earthquakes hit. They will already be struggling, but suddenly their private hiding places will be gone. Those who are not crushed will be left with no refuge or comfort. They will be out in the open, exposed to the lethal rays of a burning sun, and the essentials of life will be unavailable.

THE GREAT CITY IS SHAKEN

The earthquake will hit the spirit world as well. It will strike at the heart of the Satan's camp.

John wrote, "The great city split into three parts" (Rev. 16:19). The mystical "great city" is mentioned throughout the book of Revelation. It always refers to the kingdom of Satan. The great prostitute sits as queen over it. In Revelation, the holy city, or the beloved city, refers to the kingdom of God, but the great city refers to the demonic kingdom of darkness.

It is called great because its evil influence is so pervasive in the world. In antiquity, when civilization developed, darkness began to grow and permeate every society. By the time the great tribulation comes, darkness will have reached critical mass. God will judge the demon world. First the great city will be divided into three parts.

The great city is listed nine times in the book of Revelation, and each time it is referring to the mystical city of evil called Babylon, Sodom or Egypt. Notice, each time this evil city is called, "The Great City." Here are the listings:

- "The *great city*, which is figuratively called Sodom, and Egypt, where also their Lord was crucified" (Rev. 11:8; italics added).
- "Babylon is fallen, is fallen, that *great city*" (Rev. 14:8 NKJV; italics added).
- "The *great city* split into three parts ... Babylon the Great" (Rev. 16:19; italics added).
- "The woman you saw is the *great city* that rules over the kings of the earth" (Rev. 17:18; italics added).
- "Woe! Woe, O *great city*, O Babylon" (Rev. 18:10; italics added).
- "Woe! Woe, O *great city* ... In one hour has been brought to ruin" (Rev. 18:16; italics added).
- "When they saw the smoke of her burning, they will exclaim, Was there ever a city like this *great city*?" (Rev. 18:18; italics added).
- "Woe! Woe, O *great city* ... In one hour she has been brought to ruin" (Rev. 18:19; italics added).
- "The *great city* of Babylon will be thrown down never to be found again" (Rev. 18:21; italics added).

The choice of mystical cities will be given to man, but too many will choose the city of darkness. God will embrace those who follow him, but he will judge the devil, the demons, and all in the city of darkness. The great prostitute is the queen of the great city. She has seduced and will continue to seduce the nations with her adulteries. We will study her in the next chapter.

THE DARKNESS SPITS IN THREE

The mystical great city will split into three parts as a spiritual earthquake coincides with the physical one. Satan's kingdom has never been divided like it will at this time. God will cause it. The dark kingdom, which until that point, has been unified in purpose, will begin to fall apart from the inside.

First, as God will have orchestrated, the beast will attack the great prostitute and bring her to ruin.

"They [the beast and his demons] will bring her [the great harlot] to ruin and leave her naked ... For *God has put it in their hearts to accomplish his purpose*" (Rev. 17:16–17; italics added).

Second, the great prostitute, the queen of darkness, will be cut off from the people of darkness who she ruled. They will be afraid and will no longer partner with her. They will "stand far off" and abandon her.

"When the kings of the earth ... [the human rulers] see her [the great prostitute] burning ... they *will stand far off* and cry" (Rev. 18:9–10; italics added).

"The merchants ... [the business people] who gained their wealth from her [the great prostitute] *will stand far off*, terrified at her torment" (Rev. 18:15; italics added).

"Every sea captain ... *will stand far off*. When they see the smoke of her burning" (Rev. 18:17–18).

The mystical evil city will be split into three parts; the beast, the great prostitute, and wicked people will no longer work in unity. They will be divided. They will stand far off and even attack each other. Violence and division will erupt within Satan's camp.

"God remembered Babylon the Great, and gave her the cup filled with the wine of the fury of his wrath" (Rev. 16:19).

We will study the confusion in Satan's kingdom in more detail in the following chapters. We will also identify the great prostitute in our present world. She has been active on the planet since the early days of man.

ISLANDS AND MOUNTAINS DISAPPEAR

In earlier chapters, we identified the islands and mountains as high places and secret holdings for financial security. They are mentioned here again in chapter 16: "Every island fled away and the mountains could not be found" (Rev. 16:20).

The mountains of wealth and the offshore banks have provided security against monetary weakness and financial collapse. In Rev. 6:14, we read that these mountains and Islands will be removed from their place. Many, however, who sell their souls to the devil, will still manage black market business for a while, but even that will come to an end when God judges Babylon. All financial enterprise will be finished. This devastation is shown with amazing detail in Rev. 17. We will discuss those details in the next chapters.

HUGE HAILSTONES

"From the sky huge hailstones of about a hundred pounds each fell upon men. And they cursed God on account of the plague of hail, because the plague was so terrible" (Rev. 16:17–21).

The climate of the earth will become extreme. Adding to the already lethal environment, deadly storms will ravage the world. Roaring hurricanes and tornadoes will frequent the planet, and with the storms will come massive hailstones. The blocks of ice that will fall from the sky will weigh about one hundred pounds each and be about three feet in diameter. Like cannonballs they will pound and pulverize everything in their paths.

Cannonballs used in war come in volleys and are launched to hit specific targets. They inevitably miss large areas of the landscape. That is not so with hailstones. They drop on everything and cover every inch during the storm. Everything in the path of these storms will be demolished, and every person who is above ground level will be crushed to death. We are not told that these storms will hit every city, but whichever areas they hit, will be pulverized. The earthquakes will have ruined most shelters, and the hailstones will fall on unprotected people.

DEADLY PRIDE

The end of all things is prophesied, and people who still rebel against their creator will curse him. No love, compassion, trauma, or threat of death or hell will cause these people to yield. Even when the sinful pleasures of life no longer available, some will still defy God.

As a pastor serving in the ministry for over thirty-five years, I have seen a few men and women die in their sins. Even though Christian relatives have endeavored to persuade their loved ones to receive Christ, pleading with the dying in the final hours of life, a few have blatantly refused God's grace. It has always been difficult for me to understand such defiance. People's will and their pride are their greatest enemies. It is the saddest commentary, but some will hang onto their pride even if it kills them.

"And they cursed God on account of the plagues of hail, because the plague was so terrible" (Rev. 16:21).

Chapter Forty-two

Revelation is About Identifying the Great Prostitute

One of the seven angels who had the seven bowls came and said to me, "Come, I will show you the punishment of the great prostitute, who sits on many waters. With her the kings of the earth committed adultery and the inhabitants of the earth were intoxicated with the wine of her adulteries."
Then the angel carried me away in the Spirit into the desert. There I saw a woman sitting on a scarlet beast that was covered with blasphemous names …
The woman was dressed in purple and scarlet, and was glittering with gold, precious stones and pearls.
She held a golden cup in her hand, filled with abominable things and the filth of her adulteries. This title was written on her forehead: Mystery, Babylon The Great, The Mother Of Prostitutes And Of The Abominations Of The Earth.
I saw that the woman was drunk with the blood of the saints, the blood of those who bore the testimony to Jesus.
When I saw her, I was greatly astonished. Then the angel said to me: "Why are you astonished? I will explain to you the mystery of the woman …
Then the angel said to me, "The waters you saw, where the

prostitute sits, are peoples, nations and languages ... The woman you saw is the great city that rules the kings of the earth." (Rev. 17:1–8, 15–18)

CHAPTER TOPICS

1. The spirit of seduction
2. Why the Catholic Church is not the great prostitute
3. The identity of the great prostitute
4. The biblical teaching of lust
5. Godly desires that are good
6. Legalisms in religions that will not protect people
7. Lust ruling the world

SEDUCING THE WHOLE WORLD

REVELATION 17 IS ABOUT the great prostitute. The great prostitute will have spiritual power over the entire world. She will rule the kings and the merchants of the earth (Rev. 17:18).

"And the merchants of the earth grow rich from her excessive luxuries" (Rev. 18:3).

Every nation, people group, and language will be under her influence and control. She will sit on all nations and communities: "The waters you saw where the prostitute sits, are peoples, multitudes, nations, and languages" (Rev. 17:15).

She will control every nation in the world with the exception of Israel. She will do this through the power of seduction: "All the nations have drunk the maddening wine of her adulteries" (Rev. 18:3).

Earlier in Revelation we read, "With her the kings of the earth committed adultery and the inhabitants of the earth were intoxicated with the wine of her adulteries" (Rev. 17:2).

NOT THE CATHOLIC CHURCH

Some scholars think that the Catholic Church is the great prostitute. I do not think that the Catholic Church fits the description. There are many godly people in the Catholic Church. Multitudes of Catholics are moral, God-fearing people who are totally devoted to Jesus. Furthermore, while I do not agree with every teaching or practice of the Catholic Church, its doctrines embrace the God of the Bible as Almighty God, and the church acknowledges the Lordship of Jesus Christ. The fundamental doctrine of Catholicism does not in any way embrace the spirit of Antichrist or humanism.

Furthermore, while the Catholic Church is popular in many nations of the world, there are many large regions of the globe where her influence is weak. The Catholic Church is not powerful enough to rule the entire world. She has almost no power in the nations of Islam, such as Iran, Syria, Iraq, Afghanistan, and others. India, China, and many of the surrounding nations in the Far East are by no means under the control of the Catholic Church. Europe, at one time was controlled by Catholics, but that dominating influence has long passed. Russia and the nations that were once part of the Soviet Communist Block have not been controlled by the Catholic or Orthodox Church for ages. Those churches are tolerated, but they are not center stage.

While the Catholic Church is very large, carrying great political and domestic influence in many parts of the globe, it does not control the passions of men around the world. It will never again dominate the majority of nations and certainly not rule over merchants, kings, and the multitudes of people in every part of the planet.

A TEMPTRESS SPIRIT

The activity of the metaphorical prostitute is that of a temptress who leads the entire world into great abominations and sin: "She held a golden cup in her hand filled with abominable things and the filth of her adulteries" (Rev. 17:5).

Later we read, "Come out from her my people, so that you will not share in her sins, for her sins have piled up to heaven and God has remembered her crimes" (Rev. 18:5).

What power on earth is seducing all of humanity? What force has infiltrated every level of society in every nation and is gaining more control with every passing season? The great prostitute will be sexually perverse, greedy, arrogant, proud and shameless and will drive humanity into the sins of sexual perversion and financial greed. Leading up to, and during the first half of the great tribulation, the great prostitute will be the queen of spiritual Babylon.

"Babylon the Great ... has become a home for demons and a haunt for every evil spirit, a haunt for every unclean and detestable bird. For all the nations have drunk the maddening wine of her adulteries" (Rev. 18:2–3).

The great prostitute is a ruling spirit who dominates hordes of lesser demons (detestable birds). She commands a massive army that uses the power of seduction. In every community, she orchestrates and leads multitudes of lusty demons.

Like Jezebel, who seduced Ahab and the people of Israel, the great prostitute's home is filled with the servants of Satan. Around her table sit the demon lords of Baal and Ashterah (1Kings 16:33; 18:19). Her home is the kingdom of darkness. It is filled with every wicked spirit and every demonic bird.

The great prostitute is the mother of seducing spirits; she is the mother of harlots and the mother of abominations. In other words, her children are demons of prostitution, pornography, perversion and spirits of abominations, such as greedy murderers and those who love to shed innocent blood. These demons go to the nations to deceive men and women. They promise pleasure, but bring destruction and abomination. They draw the nations into adulterous filth.

THE RULING SPIRIT OF LUST

Her identity is all but given. She is the great prostitute—the ruling spirit of lust in the world. Lust, seems too simple an answer. We naturally look for a secret society or a political system, like the Illuminati, the World Monetary Fund, Islam, the Ecumenical Church, communism, or capitalism.

When I look at the prostitute's description and the scope of her reign, I realize she has the ability to dominate all these groups. She affects grassroots humanity, and no group except the redeemed of the Lord will be safe from her. She is the ruling spirit of lust. She is lust incarnate.

Lust is the driving and controlling desire to satisfy ones inner urges. Its seductions are so strong that people yield to them even when they know it will harm them. It is the proverbial ring in the bull's nose that leads people where they do not want to go. With enough pulling, people become compliant rather than resistant.

GOD GIVEN DESIRES

It is not wrong to have passions and desires; they are God given. God made us with cravings. With godly boundaries in place, desires and pleasures are meant to be fulfilled. Passions that pull us beyond godly boundaries, however, are lusts. Following after lust is sin; it brings destruction.

UNGODLY PASSIONS

Feeding on ungodly passions is like taking addictive drugs. The more people indulge, the more they crave. Soon they are controlled by their desires. Like with drug addicts, lust addicts are drawn to stronger doses and more powerful fixes. Before long they are hooked, and they are beyond the point of easy return. They are slaves to lust, and demons of lust are waiting to participate. They will gorge on these lusts, using human bodies to fulfill their own passions.

DEMONS TEMPT PEOPLE

At some point of human lust feasting, demons get involved. They find a person indulging in reckless sin and enter that person to help perpetuate the process. They act as though they have received a personal invitation to a party. They are lust providers and pleasure facilitators. They will seduce, tempt, and draw people deeper into a destructive web of filth. Ultimately they draw people away from God. They rob people of godliness and take them far from the principles of healthy living.

Demons live inside people. They are skilful with seduction and mind control. They work with the emotions of one person to arouse, tempt, and control another. Lust is a hideous deception. It starts with pleasure, it but finishes in disease, corruption, and entrapment. Temptation is not a sin, but following after it is.

"Each one is tempted when he is drawn away by his own desires and enticed" (James. 1:14 NKJV).

Temptation has two parts: (1) a drawing away from godliness by our own desires and (2) being enticed. The enticement is the work of seducing demons.

BIBLICAL TEACHING ON LUST

I feel it is appropriate, with all we are studying, to examine what the Bible says about lust. The Bible teaches that all sin is a form of lust and can be categorized under three headings: (1) the lust of the flesh, (2) the lust of the eyes, and (3) the pride of life.

Lust is the most pervasive of demonic activities in the world. We cannot love the operations of the demonic world and love God at the same time. The system of the demonic world is opposite to the kingdom of God. You can love evil or goodness, but not both at the same time.

Here is what the Bible says about demonic lust: "Do not love the world or the things in the world. If anyone loves the world, the love of the Father is not in him. For all that is in the world—the lust of the flesh, the lust of the eyes, and the pride of life—is not of the Father but is of the world. And the world is passing away, and the lust of it; but he who does the will of God abides forever" (1 John 2:15–17 NKJV).

1. The lust of the flesh is the controlling desire to satisfy the cravings of the body. This includes, among other things, sexual perversions, adultery, laziness, gluttony, and habitual drunkenness.
2. The lust of the eyes is the controlling desire to have things we see. It includes covetousness, the uncontrollable lust to have materialistic things, and the love of money, which is the root of all kinds of evil (1 Tim. 6:10).
3. The pride of life is the controlling desire to be seen as a great person. Pride is the passion to be worshipped—to have people elevate and idolize us—and it drives us to dominate others and promote ourselves. People will do almost anything to become celebrities. As I write, the most popular TV show in America is *American Idol*. Viewers are asked to vote for their favorite singer on the show. More people vote for one of these want-to-be idols than for their choice of president for the United States in the national elections. It is not wrong to sing or to be famous, but it may lead to a level of pride that becomes a controlling lust.

The Bible teaches that all corruption exists in the world because of lust: Corruption … is in the world through lusts" (2 Pet. 1:4).

THE GRACE OF GOD

Everyone falls into sin, from time to time (1 John. 1:10), but a godly person is known by God. The fruit of his or her life will be good. Even though godly people fall, they repent and are washed by the sanctifying blood of Jesus and thus are forgiven. If people remain in fellowship with God, they will not be rejected.

Scripture says, "The steps of a good man are ordered by the Lord, And he delights in his way. Though he fall, he shall not be cast down; For the Lord upholds him with his hand" (Ps. 37:23–24).

QUEEN OF BABYLON

The Queen of Babylon is lust, and she has multitudes of cohorts who work for her. She is the mother (the source) of lust and immoral pleasure on the planet. She puts a lust time bomb in every one she can, and her demons light the fuse. She is bent on wickedness, but she packages every bomb with candy-coated enticements.

She will drive people mad. She controls politicians, celebrities, business leaders, professionals, and every day people, with pride, perversion and profit. She infects every soul who has not made Jesus his or her Lord.

The media flaunts the queen's wares. Merchants use lust to sell goods. Kings are in bed with her because they use people's passions to hold influence over them. Under the guise of liberty for all and freedom of speech, lust popularizes pornography, perversion, and capitalistic greed. Lust in all of its forms is the main reason for crime in society.

EVEN IN RELIGIOUS NATIONS

The great prostitute drives people to lust for money, sexual perversion, and exaltation of self. In nations were strict religious rules are enforced, lust functions differently. The countries of Islam, for example, may not be inundated with overt sexual perversion, but monetary greed and male pride rank among the highest in the world. Lusting pride causes men to dominate others, especially the women in society. They will often treat women as slaves, forbid them to interact in society, and disqualify them from fulfilling their destinies. Wealthy sheikhs are among the worst for hoarding riches and living in ivory towers while those around them live in poverty and squalor.

Lust is just as powerful in religious nations as it is in secular ones; it just functions differently. All the perversions of other nations are alive in Muslim nations. They are hidden from public view and kept predominantly for the males of society.

Islam is an abomination to the Christian and Jewish God. It is an expression of Antichrist, and Satan does not need to indulge them in other distractions such as overt sexual perversion. Those people are already far from the Christ. Many will, nevertheless, come to salvation during the tribulation.

The great prostitute has her armies at work in every nation and among every group of people. She fashions her adulteries for each nation individually. She sits on them and controls them with arrogant ease.

Recall that John wrote, "The waters you saw, where the prostitute sits, are peoples, multitudes, nations and languages" (Rev. 17:15).

Her wickedness is so vile that God will judge her first, even before the beast and the false prophet.

Chapter Forty-Three

Revelation is About the Rider of the Beast

Then the angel carried me away in the Spirit into the desert. There I saw a woman sitting on a scarlet beast that was covered with blasphemous names and had seven heads and ten horns.

The woman was dressed in purple and scarlet, and was glittering with gold, precious stones and pearls. She held a golden cup in her hand, filled with abominable things and the filth of her adulteries.

This title was written on her forehead: Mystery, Babylon The Great, The Mother Of Prostitutes And Of The Abominations Of The Earth.

I saw that the woman was drunk with the blood of the saints, the blood of those who bore the testimony to Jesus. When I saw her, I was greatly astonished.

Then the angel said to me: "Why are you astonished? I will explain to you the mystery of the woman and of the beast she rides, which has the seven heads and ten horns …

"This calls for a mind of wisdom. The seven heads are seven hills on which the woman sits. They are also seven kings … The beast who once was, and now is not, is an eight king. He belongs to the seven and is going to his destruction.

The ten horns you saw are ten kings who have not

yet received a kingdom, but who for one hour will receive authority as kings along with the beast. (Rev. 17:3–7, 9–12)

CHAPTER TOPICS

1. The prostitute who rides the beast
2. Demons who abuse their power
3. Humanism needing lust
4. The confessions of those who believe in Darwinism
5. The queen who murders saints
6. The beast who hates the queen

SHE RIDES WHOEVER SHE CAN

IN REVELATION, JOHN WROTE that the great prostitute was riding a beast. She was holding a golden cup full of "the filth of her adulteries"—she is the spirit of lust. John noticed that "mystery" was one of the labels written on her forehead. Perhaps she is a mystery because of her control over humanity and because of her control over the beast. It is hard to understand how this woman can actually ride the beast.

The beast John saw had seven heads and ten horns: he is Apollyon, the Antichrist who will come up from the Abyss. How can lust, the Queen of Babylon, be riding the one who will be worshipped by the whole world?

She is a control freak; she manipulates, seduces, and deceives to gain power over anyone she can. She overpowers demons and boasts her proverbial title, "queen of the castle."

Scripture says, "In her heart she boasts, 'I sit as queen'" (Rev. 18:7).

In the demonic realm, spirits will step on one another to position themselves higher. They will grasp whatever authority they can. The fact is, the most hideous character flaws of fallen men are normal behavior for demons.

When Satan allows, one will gather as much pride, pleasure, and political standing as possible. Demons will dominate, control, and ride each other. They are abusive. Instead of co-laboring, walking in unity, or being a support to each other, they gain advantage and make those around them subservient. Demons get excited when they are given control.

Demon abuse is tolerated by Satan and demons are submitted to him. They are forced to conform. Satan loves the great queen of prostitutes because she is so effective in fouling humanity. Throughout history Satan has used the prostitute well and will continue to use her as long as she performs well. By the time of the tribulation, he will gladly give her free reign, and she takes full advantage of her favor. That is how she will come to ride the beast. She is so proud; she rides him with bravado. She flaunts her position with arrogance. The supernatural world, including powers and principalities, are witness to her dominance over the beast.

WHY THE BEAST NEEDS HER

"The seven heads are seven hills on which the woman sits. They are also seven kings" (Rev. 17:9–10).

The beast needs the great prostitute. He is the ruling spirit of humanism. He has ten horns, which are demon kings who rule over areas of the globe. He also has seven heads, the demon kings who will rule society. They will infiltrate the political structures of society. The great prostitute rides the beast and sits like a hen on his seven kings.

The beast is humanism. He will remove God from the place of worship and lift man into that position. As man worships humanism, he inadvertently worships the beast and his philosophy or image. In earlier chapters, we noted that humanism's main doctrine is evolution. It is that doctrine that eliminates the need for God. Who needs a creator if man is a product of evolution? The doctrine further supports the idea that man is still developing. In time, he will become God.

The beast, humanism, has a partner—the false prophet, who brings supernatural power to his plan. Humanism and witchcraft alone are still not enough however, to sway the entire world. To gain full control of man, the beast will need lust. The lust of the flesh (adulteries), the lust of the eyes (the love of money), and the lust of pride (self idolizing) are stronger forces than humanism or witchcraft. The beast must titillate and satisfy the base desires of humankind in order to possess people's hearts. He has the intellectual hook and the supernatural hook, but that is still not enough to hold man's attention. He needs lust, so he will employ the services of the wicked queen. Only the great prostitute has the power to keep humankind in the devil's net.

The great prostitute will agree to partner with the beast, but only if she can be in control. She wants the upper hand, and the beast will be forced to acquiesce. Lust does not need humanism to seduce the world, but humanism needs lust. Most people will not go the mile for philosophy alone. Sinful people must satisfy their passions or they will eventually abandon intellectual reason. The beast hates this, but he is powerless to refuse, and the woman dressed in purple will grasp the opportunity.

CONFESSIONS OF DARWINISTS

Look at these writings. They are listed in Frank Turek's book, "I don't Have Enough Faith to be an Atheist."[r]

Dostoevsky wrote, "Finally, and perhaps the most significantly, by admitting God, Darwinists would be admitting that they don't have the authority to define right and wrong for themselves. By ruling out the supernatural, Darwinists can avoid the possibility that anything is morally prohibited. For if there is no God, everything is lawful."[s]

Julian Huxley, a Darwinists, also agreed that sexual freedom is one of the reasons why the evolution teaching is so popular. Merv Griffin, an American talk show host, once asked Huxley the pointed question, "Why do people believe in evolution?"

Huxley honestly answered, "The reason we accepted Darwinism even without proof, is because we didn't want God to interfere with our sexual mores."[t]

Lee Strobel had the same immoral motive when he was a Darwinist. He wrote, "I was more than happy to latch onto Darwinism as an excuse to jettison the idea of God so I could unabashedly pursue my own agenda in life without moral constraints."[u]

Theologian and public speaker Ron Carlson has talked with Darwinists who concur. Once, after speaking at a well known university on Darwinism verses Intelligent Design, Carlson met with a biology professor who attended the lecture.

"So what do you think of my lecture?" Carlson asked.

"Well, Ron," began the professor, "what you say is true and makes a lot of sense. But I'm gonna continue to teach Darwinism anyway."

Carlson was baffled. "Why would you do that?" he asked.

"Well, to be honest with you, Ron, it's because Darwinism is morally comfortable."

"Morally comfortable? What do you mean?" Carlson pressed.

"I mean if Darwinism is true—if there is no God and we all evolved from slimy green algae—then I can sleep with whomever I want," observed the professor. "In Darwinism, there's no moral accountability."[v]

I am sure that not every Darwinist is one because of the motivation of immorality, but it is evident that some are. At the end of the age, immorality and lust will ride humanism. The lust of the flesh, the lust of the eyes, and lusty pride will be the backdrop for resisting God and embracing humanism.

SHE KILLS GOD'S PEOPLE

During the tribulation, the spirit of lust will be unbridled. Today, multitudes around the world are already consumed with self-indulgence and lust. The planet is already intoxicated with the wine of the great prostitute's adulteries. The maddening trend will grow much worse. The only voice that will resist the great prostitute in the last days will be the unified voice of Judaism and Christianity. Therefore, the great prostitute will kill saints.

Christians and redeemed Jews will stand against ungodly lust and humanism. They will fight against the queen and the beast with prayer, faith, political speeches, and godly counsel. They will expose the evils of sexual perversion, greed, pride, and the idolization of man. They will influence souls for Christ.

Today, the voice in the west that opposes sexual perversion, abortion, and human atrocities around the world is predominantly, the Christian voice. Bible-believing Christians and Jews are often hated by the liberal left. This hatred will ferment and escalate until it becomes murderous. The spirit of lust will kill Christians and Jews during the tribulation. She will be drunk with their blood.

John wrote, "I saw that the woman was drunk with the blood of the saints, the blood of those who bore the testimony to Jesus. When I saw her, I was greatly astonished" (Rev. 17:6).

APOLLYON THE ANGRY

The great prostitute is not the only one who will commit murder. The beast hates the people of God, and he will murder millions as soon as he comes up from the Abyss. He will be frustrated, however, with his inability to control the rest of humanity without the help of the wicked queen, and his eyes will be red with hatred toward her. "The beast and the ten horns you saw will hate the prostitute'" (Rev. 17:16).

Besides his hatred for God's people, the beast despises the prostitute who rides him. He has murder in his heart for her. When the time comes that he no longer needs her lusty ways, he will turn on her with vengeance. He is in competition with her and is humiliated because she rides him. He will watch for his opportunity to turn on her.

The beast's scientific façade will be unraveling and then the full violence of the beast will emerge (Rev.19:19). He will have been somewhat of a humanist gentleman to win the minds of ungodly men. That will change, and he will soon destroy whomever he can. Then God will judge him, and he will go to his destruction.

Chapter Forty-four

REVELATION IS ABOUT THE PUNISHMENT OF THE PROSTITUTE

"Come, I will show you the punishment of the great prostitute, who sits on many waters…"
There I saw a woman sitting on a scarlet beast that was covered with blasphemous names and had seven heads and ten horns …
This title was written on her forehead: Mystery, Babylon The Great, The Mother Of Prostitutes And Of The Abominations Of The Earth …
Then the angel said to me: "Why are you astonished? I will explain to you the mystery of the woman and of the beast she rides, which has the seven heads and ten horns. The beast, which you saw, once was, now is not, and will come up out of the Abyss and go to his destruction"…
"The seven heads are seven hills on which the woman sits. They are also seven kings. Five have fallen, one is, and the other has not yet come; but when he does come, he must remain for a little while. The beast who once was, and now is not, is an eight king. He belongs to the seven and is going to his destruction" …
The beast and the ten horns you saw will hate the prostitute.

They will bring her to ruin and leave her naked; they will eat her flesh and burn her with fire. For God has put it into their hearts to accomplish his purpose by agreeing to give the beast their power to rule, until God's words are fulfilled. The woman you saw is the great city that rules the kings of the earth." (Rev. 17:1–8, 9–11, 15–18)

SUGGESTED READING: REVELATION 17:1–11; 15–18

CHAPTER TOPICS

1. Demons who go to hell
2. The punishment of the queen
3. The beast, who hates her
4. The demons, who hate her
5. Survival displacing the passion of lust
6. The world's fallen infrastructure
7. The one world army
8. The eating of the prostitutes flesh

HELL IS FOR THE DEVIL

THE BOOK OF REVELATION is about judgment for the wicked and blessings for the righteous. God does not wish any human to perish, but for all to come to life in him. He will take every step necessary to save every soul who can be saved. No one is more forgiving, gracious, inclusive, or longsuffering than God Almighty. Some, however, will insist on aligning themselves with Satan.

"He [God] is patient with you, not wanting anyone to perish, but everyone to come to repentance" (2 Pet. 3:9).

Punishment is designed for demons and fallen angels. They have rebelled against God and usurped his kingdom. They will be punished. Humans have come to this drama, after the fact. It is horrible to think that some have joined the devil's evil scheme. Hell was made for the devil, but some people will be sent there also. That is not God's desire; it is not what he wants.

"Then he will say to those on his left, 'Depart from me, you who are cursed, into the eternal fire prepared for the devil and his angels'" (Matt. 25:41).

THE FIRST TO BE PUNISHED

All demons, fallen angels, and rulers of darkness will be punished, each in their appointed time. The great prostitute will be first. Lust has stolen the hearts of people like no other enemy. God will make it possible for the beast and his ten kings to turn on her—they will be used to punish the mother of harlots.

THE BEAST HATES HER

Apollyon, Antichrist, humanism, and the beast are all one and the same. The beast *once was*, when humanity was young and Adam walked in Eden. He *now is not*—he has been held captive in the Abyss for thousands of years; even during Bible times he was not free to roam the earth. And John was warned that he is yet to *come - up out of the Abyss*.

His under lords have led the charge of humanism over the centuries. When he is released from the Abyss, he will champion humanism with a skill the world has not yet seen. The inhabitants of the earth will be amazed at his appearance and power. Probably, they will not see him in the flesh, but they will see many world leaders champion his cause and realize a significant paradigm shift in man's thinking. Humanism will become the express philosophy of the world.

With the help of the false prophet, the world will worship Apollyon and his philosophy of humanism. He will be able to do this because of his partnership with Lust. Although the partnership will be necessary for a time, the beast hates her. Her pomp and arrogance is more than he wants to bear. When things in the world of humanity change, he will need her no more. Then he will assassinate her.

THE DEMON KINGS HATE HER

The great prostitute will sit on seven hills and seven kings. The hills are the political systems of society, and the kings are the demon personalities that rule over them with the philosophy of humanism. They will function like a fifth column, infiltrating the infrastructure of civilization and culture. Although they will be under the rule of the beast, lust will be needed to complete their mission. She sits on the hills and manipulates the demon kings. She rides them all. She will control them and steal their allegiance away from the beast. All of these kings will hate her.

SURVIVAL DISPLACES LUST

The third campaign will release God's final judgments. Disease, scorching sun, earthquakes, starvation, toxic water, darkness, and huge hailstones will render the world near uninhabitable. All of man's energies will turn toward survival. Like a deviant person who contracts a disease, the world will be too tired to pursue lustful passions. The world will not be looking for sexual activity anymore, but will be fighting for life itself.

COLLAPSING INFRASTRUCTURES

All societies fall when their infrastructure fails. The seven hills and the seven demon kings will become dysfunctional because their systems will be gone. They will be destroyed by the seven bowls of wrath.

As a reminder, here are the seven systems of society (hills) that will have been infiltrated by the seven demonic kings (heads):

1. The media and entertainment system
2. The political system
3. The education system
4. The medical system

5. The judicial system
6. The military and law enforcement system
7. The religious system

FIVE HAVE FALLEN

"The seven heads are seven hills on which the woman sits. They are also seven kings. Five have fallen, one is, and the other has not yet come; but when he does come, he must remain for a little while" (Rev. 17:10).

The last judgments will crush five of the infrastructures in society rendering the demonic strongholds over those systems dysfunctional. The following is a suggested list of the five structures that will fall.

1. The medical system will collapse due to insufficient facilities, workers, and supplies.
2. The religious systems will shut down due to lack of resources and workers.
3. Much of the media will shut down and be turned off due to the destruction of high tech facilities and equipment. It will be completely dysfunctional.
4. The judicial systems will be discontinued due to an overload of crime and no functional prisons to house criminals. Whatever control is maintained will be maintained by marshal law.
5. The education system will fall because school buildings will have been destroyed and the world will be focused on survival, not learning.

ONE REMAINS

"The seven heads are seven hills on which the woman sits. They are also seven kings. Five have fallen, one is, ..." (Rev. 17:10).

The system that will still be functional around the world will be the political one. Ungodly governments will guard their right to rule.

They will employ military rule where possible, and national leaders will gather to conspire against the Lord and his people.

ONE HAS NOT YET COME

"Five have fallen, one is, and the other has not yet come; but when he does come, he must remain for a little while" (Rev. 17:10).

The system that will start to emerge and remain for a while is the new military. A united global army will come together. The military will operate under the united government of the world. They will join together and produce a worldwide military force. Never before have all of the armies of the earth come together like they will. In earthly terms, they will be formidable.

They will be commissioned by the united world government, led by the beast and his ten horns, the demon kings. Soon they will march against Jerusalem, against the Lord and his people. They will amass at strategic fronts around Israel, in such places as the eastern shore of the Euphrates River.

THE BEAST DOESN'T NEED HER

When the infrastructures of society collapse, the beast will no longer need the philosophy of humanism to dope people. Arguing over philosophies will be meaningless when everyone is just trying to survive. Therefore he will not need the services of lust either. He will begin to control humanity with military might alone.

He will not be concerned anymore with the seven kings because their infrastructures no longer function. He will give full authority to his ten horns, and they will enforce military rule (Rev. 17:12). The ten horns are the demon kings who will rule over the geographic regions of the world. Finally the beast will be in charge, and he and his kings will turn on the great prostitute.

PUNISHING THE PROSTITUTE

"The beast and the ten horns you saw will hate the prostitute. They will bring her to ruin and leave her naked; they will eat her flesh and burn her with fire. For God has put it into their hearts to accomplish his purpose by agreeing to give the beast their power to rule, until God's words are fulfilled." (Rev. 17:16–17)

Lust will no longer be needed to control humanity, and civil war will break out within the enemy's camp. Satan will not get in the way, for the great prostitute will not be able to serve him anymore. The senior demons of lust under her will rally around her, but their military strength will be feeble compared to the strength of the beast and his ten war-demons.

The beast and the ten horns will bring the great prostitute to ruin. They will strip her naked to rob her of dignity and pride. Then they will eat her flesh and burn her with fire. God will give the beast the power and authority to accomplish this judgment. God will put this judgment into their hearts and they will inadvertently fulfill his plan.

THE HARLOT'S FLESH

Lust is not just a spirit, but a demon with a body of flesh. The beast and his hoard will commit cannibalism by eating their own kind. This is the vilest expression of a public court-martial. Before principalities and powers, the great prostitute will be stripped of her colors. Her pride will be removed; her ruin will be seen by all. She will be absolutely and eternally wasted.

Some heathen armies have historically eaten their fallen enemies to demonstrate their superiority. Some obliterate their foes by eating them. In this way, they drive fear into all who might still oppose them. Some believe that devouring the flesh of their foes transfers their enemy's power to them. It supposedly gives them the highest level of victory, and it desecrates their enemies forever.

Now we know where such cannibalistic behavior originates. These demon creatures have been in existence long before man. Cannibalism is a doctrine of demons. Their possession and influence over the minds of men provides a pathway of activity for all of their perverted and filthy ways.

The flesh of the great prostitute will be devoured, and she will be burned. Her spirit will suffer in the fires of hell for all eternity. That is the punishment of the great prostitute. Others will follow.

Chapter Forty-five

Revelation is About the Beast at War with Jesus

The beast who once was, and now is not, is an eighth king. He belongs to the seven and is going to his destruction. The ten horns you saw are ten kings who have not yet received a kingdom, but who for one hour will receive authority as kings along with the beast. They have one purpose and will give their power and authority to the beast. They will make war against the Lamb, but the Lamb will overcome them because he is Lord of lords and King of kings—and with him will be his called, chosen and faithful followers. (Rev. 17:8–14)

CHAPTER TOPICS

1. God's sovereign plan
2. The importance of eternity
3. Satan's second in command
4. Ten demon kings
5. Hatred toward Jews and Christians
6. The beast who makes war with Jesus
7. The Lamb and his faithful followers

GOD'S PLAN

THE BEAST WILL BE released from the Abyss to serve God's plans. Just as Satan will be released to tempt the nations at the end of the new millennium. He will have great authority, for no creature has ruled over so many people before. All authority is God-given, but the beast will flaunt his. God will give people the choice to serve whomever they wish and, unfortunately, many will rally around the beast.

The popular songwriter and entertainer, Bob Dylan, wrote a song on this theme. One line in the song reads, "Well, it may be the devil or it may be the Lord, but you gonna have to serve somebody."[w]

Remember, soon after his appearance, the beast will come as an angel of light, promising equality for all and human utopia. As the beast advertises his ever-popular image of humanism, humankind will be given a choice. People will be in the valley of decision.

ETERNITY

A look at eternity will help us understand the need for struggles on earth. Earth is a place of testing and these tests decide our eternal well-being. People face an enormous amount of pressure in their lifetimes, but if their heart is true, they will be rescued for eternity. Our present lives are like a vapor; they come and go in an instant. While our mortal lives are important, God values our eternal lives much more. He will even allow us to lose our mortal lives prematurely if the loss solidifies eternity for us and others. Spiritually mature people learn to value eternity with God's perspective.

AN EIGHTH KING

Apollyon, the beast is called an eighth king, and he belongs to the seven. Satan has organized his government and appointed Apollyon as his second in command. Satan appointed seven kings over the society of man. He will position the beast over the other seven. He gave him the number 666 and assigned him the mandate of humanism.

Ten other spirit kings are placed under Apollyon's command. They are the ten horns of military power. They will rule over the geographical areas of the world.

The function of these two groups of spirit kings is very different. The seven are infiltrators with skills of deception and persuasion. They are more cunning than mighty. They are demonic intellectuals and are called "heads."

The ten military commanders are enforcers. They are mighty creatures who direct massive armies. Their boast is power. That is why they are called horns. They lead angelic strongmen, spirits of violence, and reckless demons of blood and battle.

THE TEN HORNS RECEIVE POWER

A paradigm shift will set the ten kings in motion. The judgments of the last campaign will erase the need for the seven, and five of them will fall into the background of ineffectiveness. When this happens, the ten horns will rise to their potential.

They will have previously led armies against the angels of God as they came with messages for humanity. Each will have guarded a region of the earth (Daniel 9). Before now these ten kings did not have kingdoms on earth. They were warring kings, fighting in the heavens. They will have also sent demonic forces to help wicked men lead their nations to war.

For one brief hour (perhaps a year or two), the ten kings will gain military control over the nations. John wrote, "The ten horns you saw are ten kings who have not yet received a kingdom, but who for one hour will receive authority as kings along with the beast" (Rev. 17:13).

They will be given earthly kingdoms, which will be conglomerates of nations that divide the world into ten parts. The one who was previously over Israel will now be assigned to another group of nations because Israel, as a nation, will not be vulnerable to the commands of the beast. God will give the Jews supernatural power to defend themselves (Zech. 12). Israel will be the only remaining stronghold for God's people on earth.

The ten horns will be given new power and will increase their military initiatives. For their first maneuver, they will destroy the great prostitute and her commanding officers. The temptress of lust will be no match for the warmongering horns and their armies. The easy victory over the Queen of Babylon will embolden them to muster the armies of man.

The nations will not understand that they are being led by evil spirits. They will have human leaders administrating their politics. However, they will be influenced, controlled, and even embodied by demons who are under the command of the ten horns. The nations will be looking to the beast to lead them in battle against the Jews and Christians. They will look toward the land of Israel with distain.

HATING JEWS AND CHRISTIANS

Throughout history, Jews have been blamed for national calamities and worldwide propaganda will once again paint the saints in a very poor light. They will be blamed for all of earth's traumas.

In his book, *The Anguish of the Jews: Twenty-three Centuries of Anti-Semitism*, Edward H. Flannery wrote, "When the Black Death (1347–1350) broke out in Europe, the Jews were held responsible: they had poisoned the wells. In southern France, northern Spain, Switzerland, Bavaria, Rhineland, eastern Germany, Belgium, Poland and Austria the charge was believed—and over 200 Jewish communities throughout Europe were destroyed.

The extent of the tragedy can best be gauged by the reported 10,000 casualties in Poland—where the Jews escaped comparatively lightly. Considerably more than 10,000 were killed in three German towns (Erfurt, Mainz, and Breslau) alone" (109, 111).[x]

In 1481, the Jews were blamed for desecrating religious life in Spain and Rome. The governments incited the masses to riot, and they [the masses] turned on the Jews and killed them by the thousands. For further details on these events see Brown's book "Our Hands are Stained With Blood."[y]

The Jews were blamed for economic failure in Russia and Germany before World War II. Hitler blamed the Jews for all of the problems in Germany and around the world. Propaganda like that has been promoted against the Jews repeatedly for almost two thousand years, and it will happen again during the great tribulation.

For a brief but informative study on anti-Semitism in Europe over the past 2000 years, see "The Guilt of Christianity Toward the Jewish People" by Sister Pista.[z]

During the great tribulation, Jews and Christians will congregate in Israel and make a stand to defend themselves. All other nations will blame them for the demise of the world. Some will no-doubt say, "The Jewish and Christian God has caused this worldwide devastation."

Others who are steeped in witchcraft will promote the idea that the gods are angry because of Israel's non-compliance with the occult.

Some will likely claim that Christians and Jews have caused the environment to collapse because of greed. They will even suggest that right-wing Christians and Jews have orchestrated the failure of earth's environment. They will say that in the name of their God, Jews and Christians are manipulating the world to kill every non-believer and then they will have the earth for themselves. They will notice that the plagues did not affect the saints and conclude that they must be using a secret antidote.

Many will just hate the saints because of their moral lifestyles. Their standards for godly living will stand out as judgments against a perverted world. That is what happened in Noah's day.

To worsen the soupy mix, demons will put murder in the hearts of people toward Jews and Christians. Their aim will be to finish what Hitler started. They will attempt to annihilate the people of God and eradicate them from the earth. Because of such malice against the Jews and the Christians, the people of the world will gladly embrace the military rule of the ten horns.

"The ten horns you saw are ten kings who have not yet received a kingdom, but who for one hour will receive authority as kings along with the beast. They have one purpose and will give their power and authority to the beast" (Rev. 17:13).

THE BEAST MAKES WAR

"They will make war against the Lamb, but the Lamb will overcome them because he is Lord of lords and King of kings—and with him will be his called, chosen and faithful followers" (Rev. 17:14).

The beast and his ten horns will make war against Jesus, his angels, and his people. He knows that when he attacks the people of God, he will be attacking Jesus himself. He is like Saul on the Damascus Road, who was knocked to the ground.

The Lord said to him, "Saul, Saul why do you persecute me? ... I am Jesus whom you are persecuting" (Acts 9:4–5).

Saul did not persecute Jesus directly; he had never even seen Jesus. Saul was persecuting God's people, and Jesus took it personally. If you hurt the people of God, you hurt the Lord himself. When the beast mounts an assault against the people of God, he will be attacking Jesus.

JESUS OVERCOMES

Before the battle takes place, the prophetic word will go out. John wrote, "The Lamb will overcome them because he is Lord of lords and King of kings—and with him will be his called, chosen and faithful followers" (Rev. 17:14).

Jesus is the Lord over all of the lords of heaven and earth. He is king over all demon and human kings. There are none who rival his power. It is not a difficult thing for Jesus to conquer his enemies; he has all authority and power at his disposal. He will make a quick end of all who oppose him.

Although Jesus needs no help, he will not fight the final battle alone. With him are his called, chosen, and faithful followers. From the beginning of Revelation to the end, Jesus has called and will call his angels and saints to partner with him. It is endearing to hear him refer to his people as his "called, chosen, and faithful." All included in those accolades may lift their heads with honor and dignity. They are the Lord's.

Chapter Forty-six

Revelation is About Judging Evil

After this I saw another angel coming down from heaven. He had great authority, and the earth was illuminated by his splendor. With a mighty voice he shouted: "Fallen! Fallen is Babylon the Great!
She has become a home for demons and a haunt for every evil spirit, a haunt for every unclean and detestable bird. For all the nations have drunk the maddening wine of her adulteries. The kings of the earth committed adultery with her, and the merchants of the earth grew rich from her excessive luxuries." (Rev. 18:1–3)

CHAPTER TOPICS

1. Zion and Babylon
2. The three voices who announce Babylon's fall
3. God's judgments being assessed
4. The guilt of Babylon
5. The judgment of demons and men
6. The removal of Babylon

ZION AND BABYLON

ZION AND BABYLON, THE mystical two cities, represent the two spiritual camps at the end of the age. The Zion represents the city of God—the entire government of God on earth. Included in Zion is God the Judge, Jesus, angels of all government levels, and all the people of God.

Babylon is the composite of all that is evil on the earth—the entire government of darkness on the planet. This includes Satan, the beast and false prophet, the great prostitute who is the queen of Babylon, fallen angels, demons, and all wicked people.

THREE VOICES

Revelation 18 reveals a monumental announcement, given in triplicate. Each part proclaims the fall of Babylon. Babylon's queen will be first; then all Babylon will fall with her.

The first voice to make the announcement will justify Babylon's judgment. His words will be brief, but powerful.

The second voice will give a more detailed announcement. That voice will report the extent of Babylon's fall and the effects it will have on the world's economy. He will also describe the response of her people when they realize that Babylon is no more. We will hear their cries, but the saints will be called to rejoice.

The third voice will dramatize the prophecy with an object lesson. He will seal Babylon's doom by casting a millstone into the sea.

THE FIRST VOICE

In this chapter, we will focus on the first voice. A mighty angel will tell the world that permanent change has come. As the angel descends from heaven, his splendor will light up the planet.

The angels who brought the message of Christ's birth to the shepherds long ago lit up the hillside (Luke 2:9). This angel will illuminate the whole world. He will bring a different announcement than the one given to the shepherds. They spoke of peace; he will speak of judgment.

A MIGHTY VOICE

When the time comes, this angel will not herald a prophecy of future events; he will give an announcement of what has just happened. Never before has anyone reported the ruin of Babylon. This is monumental. He will shout the message so all can hear it.

Angels can appear in dreams and visions, but they can also materialize in physical form and stand before us as a man stands before a man. A huge company of the heavenly host appeared before the shepherds of Bethlehem (Luke 2:8–14). People will turn to see the angel. They will hear and be afraid.

JUSTIFICATION FOR JUDGMENT

"With a mighty voice he shouted: "Fallen! Fallen is Babylon the Great! She has become a home for demons and a haunt for every evil spirit, a haunt for every unclean and detestable bird. For all the nations have drunk the maddening wine of her adulteries. The kings of the earth committed adultery with her, and the merchants of the earth grew rich from her excessive luxuries" (Rev. 18:2–3).

Like on a news report, the angel will give seven headlines:

1. Babylon has fallen.
2. It is a home for evil spirits.
3. It is a place for every unclean bird.
4. Babylon is adulterous.
5. All nations have drunk the wine of her adulteries.
6. The kings of earth have committed adultery with her.
7. The merchants of earth have grown rich from her excesses.

BABYLON IS GUILTY

Here are the accusations that bring judgment against Babylon:

1. The demons are guilty because they partner with Babylon's schemes.
2. The demons are guilty because they seduce and beguile mankind with perversions.
3. The nations are guilty because they drink the wine of Babylon; they embrace evil.
4. The kings are guilty because they fail to lead with righteousness. They commit adultery and indulge the nations in sin.
5. The merchants are guilty because they employ the methods of Babylon. They sell vile things in vile ways for ill-gotten gain.

THE CRIMES REQUIRE JUSTICE

Babylon the Great will be the safe house for darkness on the planet. All evils and abominations will have come from this city. Vast multitudes of people will have been corrupted, abused, and murdered because of the adulteries of Babylon. Innocent children and multitudes of good people will have been ravaged because of Babylon. This malaise requires justice. It will not be left unanswered. Justice is required:

1. The gross darkness of demonic filth must be removed from the earth.
2. The demonic embrace on humanity must end.
3. Men of good intention deserve a world of righteousness, peace, and joy.
4. The anti-God and Antichrist spirits must be removed from the earth.
5. The saints require justice for all of their pain.
6. Heaven's angels need to see justice.

7. Jesus deserves the full rewards for which he died.
8. The Almighty requires all things to be made right, and he will not ignore injustice.

Billions of people will have suffered because of Babylon. Every single man and woman on the planet will have been hindered or victimized, at some level, because of her evil. The human race will have had enough. They will have been robbed, some will have lost their blessings, and many will have been killed. God's kingdom will have been delayed. Babylon must go.

For a season, God will have allowed Babylon to entice the world so that humankind would have a choice. If humankind had refused her evil, she would have had no place on earth. But people embraced Babylon and gave her a legal right to perpetuate wickedness. As technology advanced, the ways of evil men and women spread more quickly. Sins increased, and many more people fell into darkness.

Some people will have escaped the entrapments of Babylon because they walked with God. Multitudes, however, will have ruined their lives or incurred great injury because they did not resist the devil. They will have suffered excessive loss. Most of them will be found by God's grace and will be rescued in the end.

The fall of Babylon will inspire celebrations throughout the universe. Her collapse will open the door for the kingdom of God, which has three stages of development.

The first stage began when Jesus came to earth two thousand years ago. His kingdom has been growing since then.

The second stage of God's kingdom will be enjoyed during Christ's thousand-year reign on earth. The joys and blessings will be amazing, but some final refinements are still needed.

The third stage of God's kingdom will come at the end of the new millennium. That is when Satan will be cast into hell, the final dregs of sin will be removed, and we will reign with God Almighty and the Lamb for all eternity.

Chapter Forty-seven

Revelation is About Jesus the Judge

Then I heard another voice from heaven say: "Come out of her, my people,… for her sins are piled up to heaven, and God has remembered her crimes.
Give back to her as she has given; double for what she has done …
In her heart she boasts, "I sit as queen; I am not a widow, and I will never mourn." Therefore in one day her plagues will overtake her …
When kings … see the smoke of her burning, they will weep … they will stand far off and cry: "Woe! Woe, O great city, O Babylon, city of power! In one hour your doom has come!"
The merchants of the earth will weep … because no one buys their cargoes any more—cargoes of gold, silver, precious stones and pearls; fine linen, purple silk, and scarlet cloth; every sort of citron wood, and articles of every kind made of ivory, costly wood, bronze, iron and marble; cargoes of cinnamon and spice, of incense, myrrh and frankincense, of wine and olive oil. Of fine flour and wheat; cattle and sheep; horses and carriages; and bodies and souls of men.
The merchants who sold these things … will stand far off … and mourn and cry out: "Woe! Woe, O great city …In one hour such great wealth has been brought to ruin!"

Every sea captain ... will stand far off. When they see the smoke of her burning, they will exclaim, "Was there ever a city like this great city?" ... "Woe! Woe, O great city ... In one hour she has been brought to ruin!"
Rejoice over her, O heaven! Rejoice, saints and apostles and prophets! God has judged her for the way she treated you." (Rev. 18:4–20)

SUGGESTED READING (REV. 18:4-20)

CHAPTER TOPICS

1. The second voice from heaven
2. The details of Babylon's fall
3. The voice of Jesus, the judge
4. Jesus the Lion
5. Seven themes that Christ announces
6. Judgment for sinners and rejoicing for saints

A FALLEN CITY

BESIDES DEMONS, BABYLON WILL include earthly kings, merchants, and all people who oppose God. The leading lady of the city, the great prostitute, will have been unrestrained as she lured humanity with her seductive lusts and many will have followed her. At the end of the tribulation, she will be no more. Then the whole city of Babylon will fall. The entire infrastructure of the world will collapse, and people will be shocked.

Three times the earth will cry out "Woe! Woe, O great city, O Babylon, city of power! In one hour your doom has come!" (Rev. 18:10, 16, 19).

Three times, we read that the people of earth will stand back and watch. Kings, merchants, and shippers will witness the chaos as though they are in a dream. They will watch the world crumble and their treasures disintegrate, and a knife will be thrust into their hearts.

In Rev. 18:9–17, we read that the "kings," the "merchants," "all who travel by ships," and "all who earn their living from the sea" will stand "far off."

Three times we read that God Almighty will remember the crimes of Babylon and will judge her.

THE SECOND VOICE

Three voices from heaven will announce the fall of Babylon. The first will give reason for the judgments and the second will detail the fall.

The second voice is Jesus speaking. We know this because the record starts, "Then I heard another voice from heaven say: 'Come out of her, *my people*'" (Rev. 18:4; italics added).

Only a member of the Trinity calls the saints, "my people."

The pronoun *my* is used a total of twenty-four times by Jesus in the book of Revelation. Jesus' voice will be the second voice to declare the fall of Babylon. He will call his people to separate themselves from her.

ANNOUNCING SEVEN THEMES

In his announcement of Babylon's fall, Jesus will make seven statements. Here are the themes of Christ's statements:

1. Separation—He will call saints to separate themselves from the world's systems.
2. Retaliation—He will call for retaliation on those who have joined Babylon.
3. Judgment—He will announce judgments for Babylon.
4. Response of kings—He will report the response of the world's political leaders.
5. Response of business—He will report the response of

merchants.

6. Response of shippers—He will report the response of the shipping industry.
7. Joyful resolve—He will call for heaven and the righteous on earth to rejoice.

SEPARATION

Jesus will call his people to distance themselves from the economic systems of the world.

He will say, "Come out of her, my people, so that you will not share in her sins, so that you will not receive any of her plagues; for her sins are piled up to heaven, and God has remembered her crimes" (Rev. 18:4).

As Jesus prepares for his return to earth, he will caution his disciples to be separate from the world. Today we live in a world of mixture; we have both good and evil leaders and merchants. It will not be so in the last of days. In the end, all business and politics will turn evil. Jesus will call his people at the end of the tribulation period to have no dealings in politics or business. The sins of civilization will have reached heaven, and God will judge those involved.

RETALIATION

In the second theme of this dossier, Jesus will pronounce retaliation upon Babylon, saying that Babylon will be punished severely. Like an eye for an eye and a tooth for a tooth, she will receive due judgment. The Lord will go further by saying that Babylon will be paid double for all the torture and grief she has caused. She has lived in luxury at the cost of human lives and now it is payback time.

We read, "Give back to her as she has given; double for what she has done. Mix her a double portion from her own cup. Give her as much torture and grief as the glory and luxury she gave herself" (Rev. 18:5).

JUDGMENT

The sins of Babylon and her evil queen will not have been hidden acts. They will have been the focus of arrogant boasting. Sinners will not have been ashamed; rather, they will have celebrated evil. Jesus says that this attitude has only served to seal their judgment. In a moment of time, plagues will overtake them; famine, fire, mourning, and death will consume them. Then they will wait for judgment.

John wrote, "In her heart she boasts, 'I sit as queen; I am not a widow, and I will never morn.' Therefore in one day her plagues will overtake her: death, morning and famine. She will be consumed by fire, for mighty is the Lord God who judges her" (Rev. 18:6).

RESPONSE OF KINGS

Jesus looked into the future and observed the response of the world's political leaders as they watched Babylon fall. These people had been given positions of leadership and responsibility, but they had committed spiritual adultery to gain personal luxuries. Now they saw the smoke of Babylon burning, and they were terrified. John wrote that they cried: "O Babylon, city of power! In one hour your doom has come!" (Rev. 18:10).

RESPONSE OF BUSINESS

Following his report of the kings, Jesus reported on the demonized business community. He said that the merchants will be grieving because no one will be buying their products anymore. A great list of manufactured goods, agricultural commodities, and natural resources will have been bought and sold. At the end of the list, two commodities will stand out in contrast to the others. Shamelessly, the bodies and souls of men and women will have been bought and sold by these merchants. God will hold them accountable for their heinous crimes against humanity.

They will yell to their coworkers, "The fruit you longed for is gone … your riches have vanished, never to be recovered … O great city, dressed in fine linen, purple and scarlet, and glittering with gold, precious stones and pearls! In one hour such great wealth has been brought to ruin!" (Rev. 18:14–17).

RESPONSE OF SHIPPERS

Jesus then showed us the third group within the business community—the shippers. They will not be innocent. They will have partnered with the merchants. Although they will not have initiated the crimes, they will have been accomplices.

They are like the captains who carried black slaves from Africa to be sold in the west, hundreds of years ago. Their blood guilt was just as real.

The judgments will include those who will have shipped by boat, plane, truck, train, the media, the internet, and other electronic devices.

When they see Babylon burning, they will throw dust on their heads and cry "Woe! Woe, O great city, where all who had ships on the sea became rich through her wealth! In one hour she has been brought to ruin!" (Rev. 18:19).

JOYFUL RESOLVE

The seventh theme that Jesus communicates is for the saints. Speaking of Babylon's fall he will say, "Rejoice over her, O heaven! Rejoice, saints and apostles and prophets! God has judged her for the way she treated you" (Rev. 18:20).

Jesus will posture us. He will address the angels and saints in heaven first. They will have waited a long time for this day. He will call to the saints on earth. He will specifically address three groups of people: apostles, prophets, and saints. Here we see the importance of apostles and prophets. Jesus will call for a celebration, for the one who mistreated the saints will have been judged.

WEEP NO MORE

The Lord will exhort the saints to weep no more. Many will have grieved at the financial success of the wicked. Many who served the Lord will have seen their own families living in sacrifice.

Back in the day, they laid up treasures in heaven, and now their reward is at hand. The day of reckoning has come and the righteous will weep no more. Come, the night has passed. Rejoice and celebrate for evil will soon be over.

Chapter Forty-eight

Revelation is About Eliminating Babylon

Then a mighty angel picked up a boulder the size of a large millstone and threw it into the sea, and said: "With such violence the great city of Babylon will be thrown down, never to be found again.
The music of harpists and musicians, flute players and trumpeters, will never be heard in you again.
No workmen of any trade will ever be found in you again. The sound of a millstone will never be heard in you again.
The light of a lamp will never shine in you again. The voice of the bridegroom and bride will never be heard in you again.
Your merchants were the world's great men. By your magic spell all the nations were led astray.
In her was found the blood of prophets and of saints, and of all who have been killed on the earth." (Rev. 18:31–34)

Chapter Topics

1. The third voice
2. An act of violence
3. A massive boulder being hurled into the sea
4. Heaven's judgment on Babylon
5. The removal of Babylon's simple pleasures

6. Isaiah's description of judgment

THE THIRD VOICE

AS WE HAVE DISCUSSED, the fall of Babylon will be announced by three voices, the first and last of which belong to angels and the middle of which is Jesus' voice.

Scripture says, "Every matter must be established by the testimony of two or three witnesses" (2 Cor. 13:1).

The third voice will be more than words; it will be a demonstration of power.

AN ACT OF VIOLENCE

Before the third angel speaks, he will perform a violent act. He will pick up a massive boulder and throw it into the sea. I expect it to be the Mediterranean. The eyes of the world will be on Israel, and if one were to choose a large body of water for this purpose, the waters along the shores of Israel would be fitting.

The angel will hurl the rock with great emotion. He will release it with holy rage and pent-up indignation. The angel will come like an explosion of fire from the throne room, and Babylon will take notice and be afraid.

Babylon will already be cowering because of the first angel and the judgments spoken by Jesus. Like a shockwave that follows a nuclear blast, the third angel will remove any hope for survival. Wicked men and demons will tremble.

"You believe that there is one God. You do well. Even the demons believe—and tremble" (James 2:19).

WORDS OF NO RETURN

Five times the angel will say that the pleasures of Babylon will never return. Like the rock that is cast into the sea, Babylon will be thrown to her destruction. She will sink into oblivion.

1. Music will never be performed in Babylon again.
2. Trade workers will never work under this regime again.
3. Machines for manufacturing will never serve Satan's plans again.
4. Even a lamp or a light will never again shine in any room where demons rule.
5. Marriage will never be celebrated in Babylon again.

Babylon will be finished, not for a season, but for eternity; her judgments will be final. The people of Babylon will have enjoyed life's pleasures, but all they will have left is punishment. Babylon will be judged for high treason and for crimes against humanity. The angel will conclude his announcement with three statements.

He will say:

1. The merchants of Babylon were the world's great men.
2. Babylon led the world astray through her magic spells.
3. Babylon is responsible for the death of God's prophets and for every godly and innocent person who has been killed on the earth.

ISAIAH 24

Isaiah 24 gives such a detailed description of these judgments.

It reads:

"See, the Lord is going to lay waste the earth and devastate it; he will ruin its face and scatter its inhabitants—It will be the same for priests as for people, for masters as for servants, for mistress as for maid, for seller as for buyer, for borrower as for lender, for debtor as for creditor. The earth will be completely laid waste and totally plundered. The Lord has spoken this word. The earth dries up and withers, the world languishes and withers, the exalted of the earth languish. The earth is defiled by its people; they have disobeyed the laws, violated the statutes and broken the everlasting covenant. Therefore a curse consumes the earth; its people must bear their guilt. Therefore earth's inhabitants are burned up, and very few are left. The new wine dries up and the vine withers; all the merry makers groan. The gaiety of the tambourines is stilled, the noise of the revelers has stopped, the joyful harp is silent. No longer do they drink wine with a song; the beer is bitter to its drinkers. The ruined city lies desolate; the entrance to every house is barred. In the streets they cry out for wine; all joy turns to gloom, all gaiety is banished from the earth. The city is left in ruins, its gate is battered to pieces. So will it be on the earth and among the nations, as when an olive tree is beaten, or as when gleanings are left after the grape harvest." (Isa. 24:1–13)

The description continues:

"The floodgates of the heavens are opened, the foundations of the earth shake. The earth is broken up, the earth is split asunder, the earth is thoroughly shaken. The earth reels like a drunkard, it sways like a hut in the wind; so heavy upon it is the guilt of its rebellion that it falls—never to rise again. In that day the Lord will punish the powers in the heavens above and the kings on the earth below. They will be herded together like prisoners bound in a dungeon. They will be shut up in prison and be punished after many days. The moon will be abashed, the sun ashamed; for the Lord Almighty will reign on Mount Zion and in Jerusalem, and before its elders gloriously. (Isa. 24:18–23)

May all who read this book answer the call to follow Christ. Be sure not to embrace the darkness of Babylon.

Part Five
The Millennium and Beyond

Chapter Forty-nine

Revelation is About the Hallelujah Chorus

I heard what sounded like the roar of a great multitude in heaven shouting: "Hallelujah! Salvation and glory and power belong to our God."
And again they shouted: "Hallelujah! The smoke from her goes up for ever and ever."
The twenty-four elders and the four living creatures fell down and worshipped God … And they cried: "Amen, Hallelujah!"
Then a voice came from the throne, saying: "Praise our God, all you his servants!"
Then I heard what sounded like a great multitude, like the roar of rushing waters and like loud peals of thunder, shouting: "Hallelujah! For our Lord God Almighty reigns.
Let us rejoice and be glad and give him glory! For the wedding of the Lamb has come, and his bride has made herself ready." [Fine linen stands for the righteous act of the saints.]
At this I fell at his [the Angel's] feet to worship him. But he said to me, "Do not do it! I am a fellow servant with you and with your brothers who hold to the testimony of Jesus. Worship God! For the testimony of Jesus is the spirit of prophecy." (Rev. 19:1–10)

CHAPTER TOPICS

1. The kingdom in chorus
2. Precision in the heavens
3. The angels giving praise
4. The seraphim giving praise
5. The humans giving praise
6. The hallelujah chorus
7. The amazing wedding
8. John's important lesson

THE KINGDOM IN CHORUS

AFTER JESUS COMPLETES HIS announcement of Babylon's fall, he will call the faithful to rejoice and give glory to God (Rev. 18:20). Revelation 19 is heaven's response to that call.

In church liturgy, we find a call to worship. People ask God for mercy and praise him for who he is and what he has done. The basis for liturgy is found here in the scriptures. Responsive readings in churches may be stoic or at best enthusiastic. Heaven's call to worship, however, will be explosive. Angels and men will shout and cry with all they have as they praise God. The noise will be almost deafening.

John was amazed at the volume and intensity of the worship. It was louder and carried more emotion than anything he had heard. He described it as a roar of a multitude, shouting (Rev.19:1)

My mind goes back to some sports events that I have attended where tens of thousands of fans rose in triumphant exaltation. I have taken my eyes off the field to look at the cheering crowd. The noise and excitement was a spectacle in itself.

I am sure that John had an experience like that as he witnessed heaven in praise. Instead of tens of thousands, however, he saw billions united in extravagant praise.

HOLY PRECISION

Harmony and synchronization will fill the heavens. As soon as one group is finished, another will take its turn, breaking in with spontaneous praise. One would think the holy symphony was well rehearsed. The chorus will unfold with amazing precision. Millions will speak the same words at the same time. No preliminary practice will be necessary, however, as each group will be led by the Holy Spirit.

If the Holy Spirit orchestrates his perfect timing in the lives of believers here on earth, how much more will he accomplish in heaven? On earth, he directs people in one continent so that their efforts serve saints on the opposite side of the earth. We recognize his impeccable timing, often in answer to prayer. In heaven, everyone is led by the Holy Spirit.

THE GREAT MULTITUDE

John heard the judgments of Babylon; then suddenly he heard heaven shouting. He had heard the first of a four-part chorus, and each part would be given by a different choir.

Praise will resonate around the throne. It will break the sound barrier and skip to the furthest reaches of the universe. The first choir will be of angels, the second will be the twenty-four elders and the four living creatures, the third voice will be Jesus' voice and the fourth choir will be a massive multitude of saints.

ANGELS GIVE PRAISE

The angels will begin the praise; one hundred million will circle high above the throne shouting praises to God (Rev. 5:11). They will start with "Hallelujah!"

John wrote, "After this I heard what sounded like the roar of a great multitude in heaven shouting: 'Hallelujah'!" (Rev. 19:1).

The Zondervan Study Bible notes that, "the word 'Hallelujah!' occurs four times in verses one to six [of Rev. 19], but nowhere else in the Bible. 'Hallelujah,' is derived from two Hebrew words meaning, 'Praise the Lord.'" [aa]

The two Hebrew words that bring us "Praise the Lord" are mentioned separately in the Psalms. They are not combined anywhere in the Bible to make the word "Hallelujah," except in the book of Revelation. This is the highest expression of praise, and it is reserved for the victory shout at the end of the age.

The angels will declare that salvation, glory, and power belong to God.

Glory belongs to God because beyond God's kingdom there is no glory; yet all within his kingdom will receive glory.

Power belongs to God because all power in heaven and earth comes from God.

Salvation belongs to God because there is no other name under heaven whereby a man can be saved except by the name of Jesus, God's son.

The angels herald God's salvation, glory, and power over the great prostitute, their archenemy. Of all fallen angels, she has been the most obnoxious. The angels had not been allowed to stop her terror before the fall of Babylon. They will praise God for avenging on her the blood of his saints. They will praise him with Hallelujahs, for her smoke rises forever.

SERAPHIM AND ELDERS GIVE PRAISE

The angels will complete their chorus of praise, and suddenly, without missing a beat, the twenty-four elders and the four living creatures will fall down and worship God.

They will cry, "Amen, Hallelujah!" (Rev. 19:4).

The "amen" is their signature agreement. It will empower the proclamation of the angel's chorus and release it like an arrow sent from a bow. While the angels are circling high above the throne, the elders and four living creatures will fall prostrate on the ground. Their worship will be wonderful.

A SECOND CALL TO WORSHIP

Immediately, the voice of Jesus will come from the throne. He who called heaven and earth to worship will call a second time.

The Lord will say, "Praise our God, all you his servants, you who fear him, both great and small!" (Rev. 19:5).

Jesus will beckon all to praise God the Father. One member of the Trinity will encourage us to praise the other. Praise will go back and forth between Father, Son, and Holy Spirit.

The second call to worship will be to every creature who serves God. Everyone will hear the call, and the praise will soar higher than before.

HUMANS GIVE PRAISE

Billions of human souls in heaven will be impatient. They will be anxious to join in, and their turn will finally come. John's description of the next part of the chorus is extremely dynamic. He noted the vastness of the multitude, the roar of rushing waters, and the loud peals of thunder. He said that the people were shouting louder than the angels. He heard shouting that sounded like loud peals of thunder. The people will praise God because he reigns, and he will be fulfilling his kingdom promises. The humans will shout the Hallelujahs.

"Hallelujah! For our Lord God Almighty reigns. Let us rejoice and be glad and give him glory! For the wedding of the Lamb has come" (Rev. 19:7).

They will shout, for the Lord reigns. They will shout, for the wedding has come; the Lord will be ready to receive his bride. This amazing promise is not for angels or the four living creatures, it is only for God's people.

THE AMAZING WEDDING

The wedding of God's Son with his people is the greatest mystery of all. God loves people so much that they will be betrothed to his

Son. They will be one with him. I have been to many wedding feasts, but this one will be the party of parties. It will last for one thousand years.

The saints will explode with excitement as they proclaim, "his bride has made herself ready. Fine linen, bright and clean, was given her to wear" (Rev. 19:7–8).

God will have brought each person to the marriage, and he will have given them marriage garments, yet scripture says, "The bride has made herself ready" (Rev. 19:7).

The fine linen is the righteous acts of the saints. While salvation cannot be earned, God expects us to put on the garments. He expects us to do the works of righteousness. Godly actions will become our marriage garments.

During the tribulation, a special sanctifying grace will be afforded God's people. Many throughout history have served God, but godly acts will be much greater during the tribulation. Today many flounder, but then they will shine in white linen.

What hilarity will fill the hearts of God's people as they praise the Lord and announce the wedding. They will be on the threshold of God's eternal promises. Uncontainable excitement will flood the air.

John must have been ready to explode. I imagine his face was flush and his heart was pumping like the heart of a racehorse.

JOHN EMBARRASSES THE ANGEL

John watched the Hallelujah chorus continue as Jesus rallied his team. John looked at the angel who was beside him.

The angel nodded and said, "Write: 'Blessed are those who are invited to the wedding supper of the Lamb'!" And he added, "These are the true words of God" (Rev. 19:9).

John was so excited. The euphoria was more than he could handle, and he made a mistake. He fell before the angel to worship him. The Lord forbids the worship of angels, but John saw the ancient blessings unfolding before his eyes and he could not contain himself.

The moment was awkward and somewhat humorous. The angel was taken off guard. He knew that he must never receive worship from humans, nor did he want to. He certainly hoped that no one in heaven was watching. If angels can be embarrassed, it happened here.

With a knee-jerk reaction, the angel blurted out, "Do not do it!" (Rev. 19:10).

Without taking so much as a pause, he explained, "I am a fellow servant with you and with your brothers who hold to the testimony of Jesus" (Rev. 19:10).

THE ANGEL TEACHES JOHN

Teaching John, the angel continued: "Worship God! For the testimony of Jesus is the Spirit of prophecy" (Rev. 19:10).

I am sure that John rose to his feet, but he was taken aback by the words of the angel. He remembered them and wrote them down later. The teaching is insightful: as we worship God, the Spirit of prophecy is released. Prophecy is sharing the words that God gives us. That is the testimony of Jesus; that is how we know that Jesus is present with us.

Worship releases prophecy, and prophecy is the testimony of Jesus. This applies to church meetings. When genuine prophecy happens in meetings, we know that the Spirit of Jesus is manifest among us.

The day is fast approaching when all who love him will prophesy. The day is coming when all saints will join in the greatest of all symphonies: the amazing Hallelujah Chorus.

Chapter Fifty

Revelation is About the Return of the King

I saw heaven standing open and there before me was a white horse, whose rider is called Faithful and True.
With justice he judges and makes war. His eyes are like blazing fire, and on his head are many crowns. He has a name written on him that no one knows but he himself. He is dressed in a robe dipped in blood, and his name is the Word of God.
The armies of heaven were following him, riding on white horses and dressed in fine linen, white and clean.
Out of his mouth comes a sharp sword with which to strike down the nations. He will rule them with an iron scepter. He treads the winepress of the fury of the wrath of God Almighty.
On his robe and on his thigh he has this name written: KING OF KINGS AND LORD OF LORDS." (Rev. 19:11–16)

CHAPTER TOPICS

1. An open heaven
2. The white rider
3. Jesus and justice
4. A robe dipped in blood
5. The judgment of Jesus
6. Undercover saints
7. The unknown name
8. Israel at Christ's coming

AN OPEN HEAVEN

"I SAW HEAVEN STANDING OPEN and there before me was a white horse, whose rider is called Faithful and True" (Rev. 19:11–16).

The heavens are open to receive the prayers of the saints. The heavens are open, and multitudes of angels bring revelations to God's people. The heavens are open to release the white horse. The saints are in step with the Lord, and an open heaven is above them.

Men like Ezekiel, Isaiah, Stephen, Peter, and Paul saw heaven open, and each received a vision. At the end of time, visions will come frequently and this moment will bring more than a vision. The King and his armies will soon come through those open gates. The time of the King will have come.

THE WHITE RIDER

John saw a white horse. A white horse was ridden at the start of the tribulation, and a white horse will be ridden to finish it. In folklore, white unicorns and white, winged horses have filled the imagination of storytellers. Whether those stories have some basis in truth is unknown, but this white horse is the most famous of them all, and he is real, although he has a supernatural quality.

It is not beyond the scope of heaven to have horses. God made them. This horse possesses supernatural qualities for it will fly through the heavens and make the journey all the way to earth.

There are horses in heaven. Recall that Zechariah speaks of spirits riding horses: "The first chariot had red horses, the second black, the third white, and the fourth dappled—all of them powerful. I asked the angel who was speaking to me, 'What are these, my lord?'

"The angel answered me, 'These are the four spirits of heaven, going out from the presence of the Lord'" (Zech. 6:2–5).

I find it interesting that we do not see Jesus accompanied by wheels within wheels like the seraphim. Nor do these creatures fire sulfur through their tails as some earthly mounts were described earlier. This horse is not a spaceship, a jet fighter, or a mechanical vessel. It reminds me of the famous Lipizzaners of Spain.

The white rider is Jesus. Our initial picture of him in Revelation is bright like the sun. He has a robe reaching to his feet and a golden sash around his chest. His hair is like wool, white as snow, and his eyes are like blazing fire. His feet are like burnished bronze, his voice is like a rushing river, and his face shines like the sun in all its brilliance (Rev. 1:13–16).

HE BRINGS JUSTICE

Revelation 1 shows Jesus, the Warrior King. Now we see the same king coming to execute judgment.

"In that day the Lord will punish the powers in the heavens above and the kings on the earth below" (Isa. 24:21).

Jesus is called "'Faithful and True." He is faithful and true to his Father. He has never run ahead of time nor failed to execute the smallest detail of his Father's wishes.

Jesus was there at creation; thousands of years later, he humbled himself and become a man. He died for the sins of the world and has waited patiently while the covenant of his blood drew men and women to God. The time of grace has all but ended. He will be coming in faithful obedience to make war.

This war will not be like any before it. There will be no drawn-out battles. It will be totally one-sided. This war will be an execution of judgment. Jesus will strike the nations with the word of his mouth, and his enemies will fall like pieces of kindling struck by an axe, like pieces of pottery dashed to pieces.

"You will rule them with an iron sceptre; you will dash them to pieces like pottery" (Ps. 2:9).

THE BLOOD IS COMING

"He is dressed in a robe dipped in blood, and his name is the Word of God" (Rev. 19:13).

John noted that the rider's robe was dipped in blood—perhaps the blood was his own or perhaps it was the blood of the martyrs or maybe it was both; the shedding of blood is the reason why justice will be due. The blood will call for justice, and the Lord will wear it unashamedly. The blood must be answered; there will be a reckoning.

WHEN JUDGMENT FALLS

Jesus will tread the winepress of the fury of the wrath of God. Throughout the tribulation, God's wrath, which will be aimed at the devil and his followers, will come with increasing intensity. Earlier on many tribulation judgments will have fallen on humanity. Many will have repented and come to the Lord, and all who could be saved will have been saved. To our surprise, we will discover an amazing extension of God's grace—a hope beyond hope. The nation of Israel and even some gentiles in distant lands will yet be drawn to Christ in the days ahead.

For the ultimate rebels, the Lord says:

"Woe to them! They have taken the way of Cain [He murdered his brother]; they have rushed for profit into Balaam's error [The error of lustful greed]; they have been destroyed in Korah's rebellion [He attacked God's appointed leadership] ... They are clouds without rain, blown along by the wind; autumn trees, without fruit and uprooted—twice dead. They are wild waves of the sea, foaming up their shame; wandering stars, for whom the blackest darkness has been reserved forever. Enoch, the seventh from Adam, prophesied about these men: "See, the Lord is coming with thousands upon thousands of his holy ones to judge everyone, and to convict all the ungodly of all the ungodly acts they have done in the ungodly way, and of all the harsh words ungodly sinners have spoken against him." These men … follow their own evil desires; they boast about themselves. (Jude 1:11–16)

People who will receive this judgment are evil. They love wickedness rather than good, and all efforts to turn them will have expired. Jesus will bring the wrath of God. His word is a sharp sword. It will come with amazing speed. No one will be able to escape it.

UNDERCOVER SAINTS

In the end, except for Israel, all nations and most people will be demonized. While many saints will still be alive, none of them will have a leading role in managing the nations. They will now be undercover. Like many European Jews during the Second World War, they will be incognito.

These saints will be waiting to welcome the king. They will look to the skies in anticipation of his arrival. Before Jesus strikes, they will be raptured into the air, changed in a twinkling of an eye, and will descend back to earth as part of Christ's army.

THE NATION OF ISRAEL

The nation of Israel will have a special dispensation. During the tribulation, she will defend herself, and God will empower her (Zech. 12). Many Christians and redeemed Jews will congregate in the Holy Land. By the end of the tribulation, it will be the only nation on earth that will retain moral integrity. Many of the Jews will be saved, but many will not have received Jesus as Messiah. They will believe that their Messiah (other than Jesus) is still coming. The traditional Jewish faith, however, does not believe that Messiah is God's Son or that he will come from heaven. They believe he is a spiritual man, a political figure who will bring restoration and stability to Israel. The Jews who believe this will have a great shock when Jesus arrives.

Persecution will cause Orthodox Jews to work and stand side by side with Christians and Messianic Jews, but many will still refuse to believe that Jesus is Messiah. The Lord will reveal himself to them in the end (Zech. 14).

JESUS IS KING

Jesus will come, not only as executioner, but also as king. He will come to establish the kingdom of heaven on earth. This is in answer to his own prayer.

"Your kingdom come, your will be done on earth as it is in heaven" (Matt. 6:10).

When Jesus comes: "His eyes are like blazing fire, and on his head are many crowns " (Rev. 19:12).

John said that Jesus had many crowns on his head. No doubt this is symbolic. It means that he is king of every realm.

"On his robe and on his thigh he has this name written: KING OF KINGS AND LORD OF LORDS" (Rev. 19:16).

John also said that the rider had a name written on his thigh: "KING OF KINGS AND LORD OF LORDS." That is because he is not just king; he is king of all other kings. All angel kings, spirit kings, and human kings will bow the knee before King Jesus. He is the king of the Jews, the king of the world, and the king of the universe.

The Almighty tells us in the Psalms: "I have installed my King on Zion, my holy hill" … "I will make the nations your inheritance, the ends of the earth your possession. You will rule them with an iron sceptre; you will dash them to pieces like pottery.' Therefore you kings be wise; be warned, you rulers of the earth. Serve the Lord with fear and rejoice with trembling. Kiss the Son, lest he be angry and you be destroyed in your way, for his wrath can flare up in a moment. Blessed are all who take refuge in him" (Ps. 2:4; 2:12).

THE UNKNOWN NAME

"He has a name written on him that no one knows but he himself " (Rev. 19:12). Our picture of Jesus is still incomplete, for "he has a name written on him that no one knows but he himself." I would not attempt to guess this name, for I would not want to suggest that I, or anyone else, could know the full scope and measure of who Jesus is.

We know he is God, and since his time on earth, he is also man; still he remains a mystery. There is an aspect of his nature that stretches beyond our comprehension. Therefore he has a name that no one knows but himself. Perhaps this name is so magnificent that it cannot be spoken in any human language, and any earthly attempt to define it would fall short of its magnitude. It is enough to know there are aspects of Jesus that are beyond us.

When thinking of this, I am reminded of one of the scenes in the C. S. Lewis story, *The Lion, the Witch and the Wardrobe*. Speaking of Aslan the Lion, who represents Jesus, we read the words of Mr. Beaver:

"Mr. Beaver had warned them, 'He'll be coming and going,' he had said. 'One day you'll see him and another you won't. He doesn't like being tied down, and of course he has other countries to attend to. It's quite all right. He'll often drop in. Only you mustn't press him. He's wild, you know. Not like a tame lion.'"[ab]

Jesus is not in and cannot be put in our human box of understanding. He is king of kings and Lord of lords, and that is enough for me.

Chapter Fifty-one

Revelation Is About the Second Coming

I saw heaven standing open and there before me was a white horse, whose rider is called Faithful and True. With justice he judges and makes war.
His eyes are like blazing fire, and on his head are many crowns. He has a name written on him that no one knows but he himself. He is dressed in a robe dipped in blood, and his name is the Word of God.
The armies of heaven were following him, riding on white horses and dressed in fine linen, white and clean.
Out of his mouth comes a sharp sword with which to strike down the nations. He will rule them with an iron scepter. He treads the winepress of the fury of the wrath of God Almighty.
On his robe and on his thigh he has this name written: KING OF KINGS AND LORD OF LORDS. (Rev. 19:11–16)

CHAPTER TOPICS

1. An introduction to the chapter
2. The second coming of Christ
3. The last trumpet
4. The saints descending to earth
5. The resurrection of the saints
6. The fear of not being ready
7. Being caught up in the air
8. The Mount of Olives
9. One taken, the other left
10. Vultures feeding on the dead carcasses
11. The thief in the night

INTRODUCING THIS CHAPTER

AT CHRIST'S SECOND COMING, the final battle before the millennium will take place. This final battle will include many dynamics. Many things will happen simultaneously or within a very brief period of time.

The battle will involve:

1. Christ coming in the clouds at the end of the great tribulation
2. The armies of heaven, including the spirits of the saints, descending from heaven with Christ
3. The saints being instantaneously resurrected, glorified, and returned to earth
4. The death and removal of most of Christ's enemies, whose souls will be taken away—two will be in the field, and the sinner will be taken
5. The judgment of nations who gather in the valley of Armageddon
6. Vultures eating the dead bodies of the sinners after their spirits are taken

Parts of this chapter will be explained in greater detail in subsequent chapters.

THE SECOND COMING

Revelation 19 tells of the second coming of Christ.

"There before me was a ... rider ... called Faithful and True ... And his name is the Word of God. The armies of heaven were following him" (Rev. 19:11, 14).

Although I honor many of those who teach a pre-tribulation rapture, I do not agree with their findings or their reasoning. I find no third coming of Christ in the scriptures. Before these verses in Rev. 19, there is no account of Christ's second coming. Neither is there any record in scripture where Jesus comes into the air and takes his people away to heaven.

In this chapter, we will look at the verses that refer to Christ's second coming and point out that he comes at the end, not at the beginning, of the great tribulation. We will further see that when he does come, Jesus will appear in the clouds, and then he will descend and stand on the Mount of Olives. He will not appear in the clouds, receive the saints, and go back to heaven.

In fact, the scripture says that Christ must remain in heaven until the time comes for God to restore all things. That will only happen at the end of the tribulation when the new millennium is about to begin.

"He may send the Christ who has been appointed to you—even Jesus. He must remain in heaven until the time comes for God to restore everything as he promised" (Acts 3:20–21).

THE DAYS OF THE LAST TRUMP

Revelation records seven trumpets, which are blown by angels. The return of Jesus will happen during the days of the seventh and last trumpet. The coming of Jesus and the resurrection of the dead are *the mystery* of the seventh angel as foretold by Old Testament prophets.

Remember Rev. 10: "In the days when the *seventh angel* is about to sound his trumpet, *the mystery of God* will be accomplished, just as he announced to his servants the prophets" (Rev. 10:7; italics added).

The second coming of Christ will come at the *last trump*. It is also recorded in 1 Corinthians: "So in Christ will all be made alive. But each in turn: Christ the firstfruits; then, when he comes, those who belong to him ... Listen, *I tell you a mystery*: We will not all sleep, but we will all be changed—in a flash, in a twinkling of an eye, *at the last trumpet*. For the trumpet will sound, the dead will be raised imperishable, and we will be changed" (1 Cor. 15:22–23, 51–52; italics added).

Some say that at the second coming, Christ will return in the air, that he will resurrect the saints and go back to heaven. Then he will come back at the sound of the last trumpet. This cannot be true, for Corinthians tells us that the resurrection happens during the days of the last trumpet. It is clear that the second coming, the resurrection, and the last trump all happen at the same time.

COMING WITH HIS SAINTS

John wrote, "The armies of heaven were following him, riding on white horses and dressed in fine linen, white and clean" (Rev. 19:14).

By the end of the tribulation, heaven will be inhabited with billions of humans. Some will be without bodies and some will have bodies. The ones without bodies are the spirits of righteous men, mentioned in Hebrews 12:23. These human spirits will descend with Jesus to be joined to their bodies. That is resurrection.

There are also humans in heaven who already have resurrected bodies. Some of them were resurrected at the time of Christ's resurrection (Matt. 27:51–53).

There will also be others in heaven with resurrected bodies, like those who will have been brought to life after being murdered and left on the streets for three days at the midpoint of the great tribulation. "But after the three and a half days a breath of life from God entered them, and they stood on their feet and terror struck all those who saw them. Then they heard a loud voice from heaven saying to them, 'Come up here.' And they went up to heaven in a cloud while their enemies looked on" (Rev. 11:11).

PEOPLE DESCENDING WITH CHRIST

The armies of heaven will descend with Christ at the second coming (Jude 14). Humans, angels and seraphim will be included for Scripture says that the armies of heaven will be riding to earth on white horses. Humans with bodies, some without, the twenty-four elders, myriads of angels, and the mighty seraphim will be riding with Jesus to battle.

What a sight that will be! It has long been seen by prophets of old. Enoch, who was the seventh generation after Adam, received a vision of this event thousands of years ago.

"Enoch, the seventh from Adam prophesied ... See, the Lord is coming with thousands upon thousands of his holy ones to judge everyone, and to convict all the ungodly of all the ungodly acts they have done" (Jude 14:15).

The descending armies will include our relatives who have preceded us into heaven. If the Lord tarries and we die as believers, then we also will be part of this great descending army.

THE RESURRECTION OF THE DEAD

As Jesus breaks into earth's atmosphere, the dead bodies of the saints will stir. In a nanosecond, they will wake from sleep; body parts will come together and lift into the sky. The God of creation who formed the first man from dust will do it again. Human molecules that have been dispersed into the environment will fly from hidden places until they find their initial host. Bodies will come together and receive an instant upgrade; they will be perfected. They will rush with lightning speed to meet their souls and the spirits that ride toward them from heaven.

This is how the Bible describes the scene:

"God will bring with Jesus those who have fallen asleep [died] in him ... we who are still alive, who are left till the coming of the Lord, will certainly not precede those who have fallen asleep [died]. For the Lord himself will come down from heaven, with a loud command, with the voice of the archangel and with the trumpet call of God, and the dead in Christ will rise first. After that, we who are still alive and are left will be caught up together with them in the clouds to meet the Lord in the air. And so we will be with the Lord forever" (1 Thess. 4:14–17).

The Lord will return with archangels at the sound of the trumpet call. The dead will be raised and caught up into the clouds to be reunited with their spirits as they come down from heaven. Immediately, the believers who are still living will be caught up together with them in the clouds. Both groups will be given new glorified bodies and from that time on they will remain with the Lord.

The question is: where will the Lord be? We will soon see that he will not return to the throne room, but will come down to earth. That is why he has an army with him. He will be poised to defeat his enemies. The army will come, first for the resurrection of their bodies, then to defeat the armies of Satan.

John wrote, *"This is the first resurrection.* Blessed and holy are those who have part in the *first resurrection*. The second death has no power over them, but they will be priests of God and of Christ and will reign with him for a thousand years" (Rev. 20:6; italics added).

It is no mistake that this resurrection that takes place at the end of the tribulation is called the first resurrection. It will be the first resurrection to include all of the saints who have died since Adam.

THEY DIDN'T MISS HIS COMING

Paul wrote the saints in Thessalonica a second time regarding the resurrection and the second coming of Christ. Some thought that Jesus had already come and they had missed him.

Recall what Paul said:

"Concerning the coming of the Lord Jesus Christ and our being gathered to him, we ask you, brothers, not to become easily unsettled or alarmed by some prophecy, report or letter supposed to have come from us, saying that the day of the Lord has already come. Don't let anyone deceive you in any way, for that day will not come until the rebellion occurs and the man of lawlessness is revealed, the man doomed to destruction ... He will oppose God ... proclaiming himself to be God ... And now you know what is holding him back, so that he may be revealed at the proper time ... the Lord Jesus will overthrow [him] with the breath of his mouth and destroy [him] by the splendor of his coming" (2 Thess. 2:1–8).

This scripture is about the second coming. Paul exhorted the saints not to be alarmed; they had not missed the coming of the Lord. He told them that Christ will destroy the Antichrist when he comes. We know that the Antichrist is destroyed at the end of Revelation, not at the beginning; therefore, the second coming is at the end of the tribulation.

Furthermore, Paul explained that Christ will not come until after the Antichrist is released and revealed. We have learned that the Antichrist will not be released or revealed until halfway through the tribulation period (Rev. 13).

He is the beast, the lawless one who was alive, but was restrained (in the Abyss) even back in Paul's time. He is being held in prison until the angel who has him in captivity releases him. Remember, he will come up from the Abyss where he has been restrained (Rev. 9). Then he will appear with the false prophet to deceive the nations. Paul said that only after this happens will Jesus return and destroy the Antichrist (the beast) with the breath of his mouth. Jesus will not come at the beginning of the tribulation; he will come at the end.

Another amazing detail in this scripture reveals information regarding the second coming. Paul told the church not to be alarmed by any letter supposed to have come from him saying that Christ has already come. He said "Concerning the coming of the Lord Jesus Christ and our being gathered to him, we ask you, brothers, not to become easily unsettled or alarmed by some prophecy, report or letter supposed to have come from us, saying that the day of the Lord has already come" (2 Thess. 2:1-2)

Now, if Christ had come and taken Paul to heaven in a rapture, how could he supposedly have sent a letter to the saints in Thessalonica? (He said, "Don't be alarmed if you receive a letter that seems to come from us.") There is no postal service between heaven and earth.

The theology of early Christians is clear; they believed that when Jesus returns, believers will meet him in the air. Then, in a twinkling of an eye, they will be back on the earth with glorified bodies. Only then could anyone send a letter. The church did not eliminate the possibility of letters coming from glorified saints. This further confirms that the second coming is not to take people away to heaven, but to bring Jesus and his kingdom to earth.

THE MOUNT OF OLIVES

When Jesus comes, he will land on the Mount of Olives. If you go to Jerusalem, you will see thousands of graves covering the entire side of the Mount of Olives. They are mostly Jewish tombs. The Jews read the scriptures and know that when the Lord comes, he will land on the Mount of Olives, and at that time the resurrection will take place. That is why their tombs are there. They want to be ready when he comes. They want to be first in line for the resurrection. Bible theology does not teach that the Lord will come in the clouds, resurrect the righteous, and then go back to heaven. Jews know the book of Zechariah. They know that the resurrection will happen when the Lord comes down to the Mount of Olives.

"Then the Lord will go out and fight against those nations, as he fights in the day of battle. On that day *his feet will stand on the Mount of Olives*, east of Jerusalem, and the *Mount of Olives* will be split in two from east to west, forming a great valley, with half of the mountain moving north and half moving south. You will flee by my mountain valley, for it will extend to Azel. You will flee as you fled from the earthquake in the days of Uzziah king of Judah. Then the Lord God will come, and all his holy ones with him" (Zech. 14:4–5).

In another chapter, we will study the special disposition of unsaved Jews in the city of Jerusalem at the time of Christ's return.

Angels, present at Christ's ascension, also made this inference concerning the Mount of Olives. About five hundred people were present when Jesus ascended into heaven, forty days after his resurrection. The ascension happened on the Mount of Olives. After Jesus disappeared in the clouds, two angels spoke to the crowd.

"Men of Galilee," they said, "why do you stand here looking up into the sky? This same Jesus, who has been taken from you into heaven, will come back in the same way you have seen him go into heaven" (Acts 1:11).

They saw him ascend from the Mount of Olives, and in the same way, he will return to them on the Mount of Olives.

TAKEN FROM THE FIELD

When Jesus comes back, one will be taken and another will be left on the earth. We read this in Matthew and in Luke.

"As it was in the days of Noah, so it will be at the coming of the Son of Man ... they knew nothing about what would happen until the flood came and took them all away. That is how it will be at the coming of the Son of Man. Two will be in the field; one will be taken and the other left. Two women will be grinding with a hand mill; one will be taken and the other left" (Matt. 24:37–41).

It is obvious that one is taken and the other left, but which one is taken? In Noah's day, judgment came, and the sinner was taken away by the flood. The sinners knew nothing until the flood came and took them all away. If the coming of the Son of Man will be as it was in the days of Noah, then the sinner will be taken away in the judgment. The sinners will know nothing until the fire of the Lord comes and takes them away. The saints will know what is happening.

A PARTNER PARABLE

That the sinners will be taken and the saints will be left is further substantiated in a compatible parable—the story of the weeds and the wheat.

"The owner's servant came to him and said, 'Sir, didn't you sow good seed in your field? Where did the weeds come from?'

"'An enemy did this,' he replied.

"The servant asked him, 'Do you want us to go and pull them up?'

"'No,' he answered, 'because while you are pulling the weeds, you may root up the wheat with them. Let both grow together until the harvest. At that time I will tell the harvesters: *First collect the weeds and tie them in bundles to be burned*; then gather the wheat and bring it into my barn'" (Matt. 13:27–30; italics added).

Notice that the weeds were taken first. Starting in Matthew 13:36, Jesus explains the parable. The wheat represents believers, the weeds are evil people, and the harvesters are the angels. The weeds are pulled up first to be burned in the fire.

As with the story of Noah, the ones that are taken away are not the saints, but the sinners. I think it is very plain, but even if you still believe that the saints are taken from the field or the bed first, the question remains, where are they taken to? When the saints go, they meet the Lord in the air and immediately return to earth for a great battle. They are not taken to heaven.

When Jesus comes," one taken and the other left," means that the sinners (weeds) will be taken away to Hades to suffer in its fire. The wheat will be gathered into God's barn to enjoy the new millennium.

VULTURES GATHER TO EAT SINNERS

At the second coming, the soul of the sinner will be taken, and the one left is the believer. This is emphasized even more so in Luke's Gospel. Luke recorded the words of Jesus as follows: "On that night, two people will be in one bed; one will be taken and the other left. Two women will be grinding grain together; one will be taken and the other left.'

'Where Lord?' They asked.

"He replied, 'Where there is a dead body, there the vultures will gather' (Luke 17:34–37).

Where will one be taken? Wherever there is a dead body—a sinner. When Jesus comes, the sinners will be killed; their souls will go immediately to Hades, the place of torment. Their bodies, as gross as it sounds, will be left for the vultures. This is not only recorded in the Gospels, it is exactly what happens in the very next verses of Rev. 19. It is also recorded in Ezekiel 39:12–19.

Immediately following the return of the Lord, an angel calls the birds to gather so that they may eat the flesh of men: "And I saw an angel … who cried … to all the birds, 'Come, so that you may eat the flesh of kings, generals, and mighty men … and the flesh of all people free and slave, small and great'" (Rev. 19:17–18).

In Ezekiel we read:

"On the mountains of Israel you will fall, you and all your troops and the nations with you. I will give you as food to all kinds of carrion birds … For seven months the house of Israel will be burying them in order to cleanse the land … And so they will cleanse the land … Son of man, this is what the sovereign Lord says: Call out to every kind of bird … You will eat the flesh of mighty men and drink the blood of princes of the earth … I will display my glory among the nations, and all the nations will see the punishment I inflict. (Ezek. 39:4, 12, 16, 18, 21)

Read another portion of Matthew's report on the second coming. These are the words of Jesus: "So if anyone tells you, 'There he is, out in the desert,' do not go out: or, 'Here he is, in the inner rooms,' do not believe it. For as the lightning that comes from the east is visible in the west, so will be the coming of the Son of Man. Wherever there is a carcass, there the vultures will gather" (Matt. 24:26–28).

It is clear: at the time when Christ comes, one will be taken, and the other will be left, and a dead body will remain for the vultures to eat. It is not the dead bodies of the saints that vultures will eat, but of sinners. Just like after the flood in Noah's day, the souls of sinners will be taken from the earth, and their bodies will be left to decay. In a global flash, Jesus will come, and sinners will be killed by the words of his mouth. Wherever a carcass is, wherever a dead body is, the vultures will gather and feed. The saints will be very much alive. They will remain on the earth to reign with Christ for a thousand years. We will study this further in the next chapter.

THE THIEF IN THE NIGHT

The thief in the night is a thief to sinners, not to saints, and as was the case in Noah's day, the sinner will not be ready (Matt. 24:43–44). Jesus will not be a thief to his children. He will not snatch us away like a thief. Angels will be like thieves to sinners, for suddenly, without warning, the sinners will lose their lives and their souls will be stolen away.

The scriptures are clear about these five things:

1. Christ's second coming will happen at the end of the tribulation.
2. When he comes, he will kill his enemies and their souls will be taken away.
3. The saints will have glorified bodies and remain on the earth.
4. Vultures will eat the bodies of the sinners whose spirits were taken.
5. A season of cleaning up, restoration, and transition will take place before the new millennium begins.

Chapter Fifty-two

Revelation is About Judging the Beasts

And I saw an angel standing in the sun, who cried in a loud voice to all the birds flying in midair, "Come, gather together for the great supper of God, so that you may eat the flesh of kings, generals, and mighty men, of horses and their riders, and the flesh of all people, free and slave, small and great."
Then I saw the beast and the kings of the earth and their armies gathered together to make war against the rider on the horse and his army.
But the beast was captured, and with him the false prophet who had preformed the miraculous signs on his behalf. With these signs he deluded those who had received the mark of the beast and worshipped his image.
The two of them were thrown alive into the fiery lake of burning sulfur. The rest of them were killed with the sword that came out of the mouth of the rider on the horse, and all the birds gorged themselves on their flesh. (Rev. 19:17–21)

CHAPTER TOPICS

1. An angel in the sun
2. The desecrated bodies of the dead
3. The beast who makes war against Christ

4. The capture of Jerusalem
5. The salvation of Jerusalem
6. A unique day
7. A weapon of mass destruction
8. The beast and false prophet judged
9. Survivors

ANGEL IN THE SUN

JOHN SAW AN ANGEL standing in an elevated place above the earth. John said the angel was "standing in the sun," so we know he will be in our solar system. He will be difficult to look at, for the blinding sun will be behind him.

He will give a loud announcement that can be heard both on earth and in heaven. The cry will be directed to the birds in midair. In Rev. 8:13 we discovered an eagle that was flying in midair. We determined that midair was middle heaven—the area between the throne room of God and earth's atmosphere. It is a place of fallen angels. In Rev. 18:2 we read that evil spirits are called detestable birds. It is likely that the angel standing in the sun will be speaking to both natural birds on earth and spiritual birds or evil spirits above the earth.

The angel will cry, "Come, gather together for the great supper of God, so that you may eat the flesh of kings, generals, and mighty men, of horses and their riders, and the flesh of all people, free and slave, small and great" (Rev. 19:17–18).

DESECRATION OF BODIES

Throughout the tribulation period, the natural scavengers of earth will be feeding heartily on dead carrion, including human remains. Scavengers are the only creatures on the planet who will be surviving well. They have stomachs that can ingest the water that would kill a human, and there will be no shortage of dead bodies to gorge on.

There are tribal groups in India who purposely place their dead ancestors on hilltops for vultures to eat. They believe in reincarnation and suppose that an ancestor cannot return in another form until his or her body has been broken down to its base components. When a bird such as a vulture eats their flesh and then defecates, the human body has a head start toward the next life.

This desecration of human remains, however, is a judgment in most cultures. In ancient times, when enemies were seen as hideous or perverse, their fallen bodies were given no dignity. They were left as carrion by their conquerors. This was extreme and barbaric, but was due treatment for an army who deserved to be dishonored.

For a more complete study of the fallen being eaten as carrion at the end of the great tribulation, read Ezek. 39.

SPIRITUAL VULTURES

Besides natural vultures, spiritual ones exist. Both eat flesh. Recall from Rev. 17:16 that the beast and his cohorts will eat the flesh of the great prostitute. Demons are foul creatures, and God pulls back his protection off of people when they persist in choosing a demonic lifestyle.

God uses demon spirits to punish people (Rev. 9:5). Those spirits torment and control humans who oppose God. Now, it seems that a specific kind of scavenger spirit will be called from the heavens to feed on the dead bodies of ungodly people.

The Bible teaches that death is our last enemy (1 Cor. 15:26). Satan hates humans. He enjoys the corruption of our bodies as a final humiliation before we enter the joys of heaven. That is why Satan was angry when he could not find the dead body of Moses. There was an argument between the archangel Michael and the devil over this matter.

The scriptures read, "But even the archangel Michael, when he was disputing with the devil about the body of Moses, did not dare bring a slanderous accusation against him, but said, 'The Lord rebuke you'" (Jude 1:9).

God afforded Moses the special honor of bodily protection, for he was such a good friend. Satan would get no satisfaction from seeing Moses' body come to decay.

The angel will call the evil spirits in midair to feast on the bodies of dead sinners at the end of the great tribulation.

THE BEAST MAKES WAR

The beast will instruct the kings of the earth to gather their armies in a massive assault against Israel. The armies of the world will surround Jerusalem, and the entire valley of Armageddon will be filled with enemy soldiers. This was foretold in Rev. 16:12–17. Led by three evil spirits that look like frogs, the kings of the east will cross the Euphrates River and march on Jerusalem.

With the help of the false prophet, they will perform miracles to deceive the nations. The world will be focused on Israel's destruction, and the armies will attack before the second coming of Christ.

They will not realize it, but Jesus has planned their gathering. He will judge the nations for how they have treated Israel (Joel 3). God has brought the nations down to the valley of Jehoshaphat, (judgment) to judge them: "I will gather all nations and bring them down to the valley of Jehoshaphat. There I will enter into judgment against them concerning my people Israel, for they scattered my people among the nations and divided up my land" (Joel 3:2).

JERUSALEM IS CAPTURED

Israel will be inhabited by Christians and Jews of every type. There will be Messianic Jews, Hassidic Jews, Orthodox Jews, and even liberal, reformed and secular Jews living in Jerusalem. The world will be demonically inspired to hate Jews.

Jesus will come and rescue Israel and Jerusalem, but many Jews who have not yet received salvation will suffer in the early stages of the battle. I think that most non-believing Jews will become believers as soon as they see King Jesus. God-fearing Jews will accept Jesus as Messiah when he comes. Most will repent and confess him as Lord.

Before Christ's coming, Jerusalem will be captured and half of its people will be incarcerated. The nations will plunder Jerusalem. Jesus will come to a war-torn, chaotic mess. He will descend to the Mount of Olives with his holy ones and he will rescue the people of Jerusalem. Here is biblical prophecy that describes the scene.

JESUS SAVES JERUSALEM

In Zechariah 14 we read:

"A day of the Lord is coming when your plunder will be divided among you. I will gather all the nations to Jerusalem to fight against it; the city will be captured, the houses ransacked, and the women raped. Half of the city will go into exile, but the rest of the people will not be taken from the city.

Then the Lord will go out and fight against those nations, as he fights in the day of battle. *On that day his feet will stand on the Mount of Olives* east of Jerusalem, and the Mount of Olives will be split in two from east to west, forming a great valley, with half of the mountain moving north and half moving south.

You will flee by my mountain valley, for it will extend to Azel. You will flee as you fled from the earthquake in the days of Uzziah king of Judah.

Then the Lord my God will come, and all the holy ones with him. On that day there will be no light, no cold or frost. It will be a unique day, without daytime or nighttime—a day known to the Lord. When evening comes there will be light.

On that day living water will flow out of Jerusalem, half to the eastern sea and half to the western sea, in summer and winter.

The Lord will be king over the whole earth. On that day there will be one Lord, and his name the only name" (Zech. 14:1-9).

Shortly after the beast captures Jerusalem, the second coming will occur. Jesus will come and land on the Mount of Olives, and the mountain will split from east to west. A huge traffic tunnel has recently been built under the Mount of Olives, which runs from east to west, exactly where the split will take place. The people of Jerusalem will run for cover in the crevice that the Lord has made. There they will be safe while the armies of heaven fight the enemies that are stationed around Jerusalem.

A UNIQUE DAY

"It will be a unique day, without daytime or nighttime—a day known to the Lord. When evening comes there will be light" (Zech. 14:6).

This day will be like no other in history. It will be a day without time, without day or night, as if the sun was gone and a supernatural glow has taken its place. There will be no light from the sun during the day, but at evening time it will be light. Perhaps the light will come from the splendor of the Lord.

The Bible record says that there will be no cold or frost, which leads one to believe that it might take place in winter; otherwise we would not expect frost.

The battle will involve the entire world. The Lord will not only destroy all who are invading Jerusalem but many around the world who hate him. The solar system will hold its breath as the king of kings eliminates his enemies. (That is when two will be in the field and one will be taken. Around the world, there will be saints living alongside sinners, incognito. The sinners will die, but the saints will live with glorified bodies, and the bodies of the sinners will become the vultures' feast.)

WEAPONS OF MASS DESTRUCTION

Those armies that have gathered around Jerusalem will face a horrible end. As we continue reading in Zech. 14, we find details regarding their deaths:

"This is the plague with which the Lord will strike all the nations that fought against Jerusalem:

Their flesh will rot while they are still standing on their feet, their eyes will rot in their sockets, and their tongues will rot in their mouths. On that day men will be stricken by the Lord with great panic. Each man will seize the hand of another, and they will attack each other. Judah too will fight at Jerusalem.

The wealth of all the surrounding nations will be collected—great quantities of gold and silver and clothing. A similar plague will strike the horses and mules, the camels and donkeys, and all the animals in those camps.

Then the survivors from all the nations that have attacked Jerusalem will go up year after year to worship the King, the Lord Almighty, and to celebrate the Feast of Tabernacles. (Zech. 14:12–16)

The judgment of the Lord will not hit everyone, but whomever it hits will die instantly. Their flesh, eyes, and tongues will begin to rot before they fall to the ground. Even animals in the enemies' camp will be struck. The effects on the human body will be like that of a nuclear blast or of chemical warfare. This plague will be amazing, however, in that it will not strike every person. It will be a weapon of mass destruction that the world has never seen. Those who are not immediately hit will begin to panic and fight one another.

The people of Jerusalem will fight against their aggressors, and the armies of heaven will fight. We are not given details of their maneuvers. Perhaps angels and saints, mounted on flying horses, will circle the globe destroying the enemies of God.

The final part of Zech. 14 points to the upcoming millennium. It tells us that Jesus will allow some sinners to survive the battle. We will talk about them in our study of the new millennium. Israel will not only be rescued, but she will become wealthy because of the riches she collects from the surrounding nations.

THE BEAST AND FALSE PROPHET JUDGED

The beast and the kings of the earth will fight against the Lord, but their efforts will be futile. The beast and the false prophet will not be destroyed, only captured.

The two of them will be thrown alive into the final hell—the lake of fire. This is the place that has been prepared for the devil and his angels.

After a further thousand years in Hades, some people will be thrown into that lake of fire with them. The people must first stand before the throne of the Lord God Almighty. This point fits our understanding that the beast and false prophet are fallen angels and not men. No human being will go to the final hell until after the great white throne judgment is complete.

THE REST OF THE PEOPLE

All wicked people who have continued to worship the philosophy of the beast will be killed. John wrote, "The rest of them were killed with the sword that came out of the mouth of the rider on the horse, and all the birds gorged themselves on their flesh" (Rev. 19:21).

God, nevertheless, will not throw innocent children or ignorant people into hell to be tortured forever. (For a more complete study on there being no children in hell, see chapter 59.) Those who go to hell will have consistently rebelled against the Lord. God is just. Every person has had or will have ample opportunity to be forgiven of their sins and receive salvation because of the blood of Jesus Christ.

God's character is such that he is gracious, merciful, compassionate, just, and fair. We do not fully understand the ways of salvation, but in the end, God will judge every man. If there is a way that a soul may be eternally saved, God will see that it happens.

One of his ways to see that every eligible soul is saved - is to allow those who are still undecided into the millennium. The Bible teaches that unborn infants, children, some unsaved survivors, and other mortals will enter the new millennium. They will be invited to join Jesus and his holy ones in his millennium kingdom. We will learn more about these people as we study the Lamb's thousand-year reign on earth. Some of these people may yet be saved.

Chapter Fifty-three

Revelation is About the Binding of Satan

And I saw an angel coming down out of heaven, having the key to the Abyss and holding in his hand a great chain.
He seized the dragon, that ancient serpent, who is the devil, or Satan, and bound him for a thousand years. He threw him into the Abyss, and locked and sealed it over him, to keep him from deceiving the nations anymore until the thousand years were ended.
After that, he must be set free for a short time. (Rev. 20:1–3)

CHAPTER TOPICS

1. The roaring lion
2. Satan's wicked ways
3. The essence of Satan's power
4. Why we have pain
5. The angel who binds the devil
6. The devil's jail
7. One thousand years in jail

THE ROARING LION

AT THE BEGINNING OF Rev. 20, the devil is called by a few names. He has many names including "the dragon," the "ancient serpent," Lucifer, "the devil," and "Satan." Since the beginning of man, the devil has deceived and corrupted society. People feared him for he roamed the earth like a roaring lion seeking to devour people. He is the ruler of the darkness of the world.

Man's lusts are evil, and Satan's plans are evil. When the two connect for pleasure and power, death and destruction follow. The lives of billions of people have been defiled because of Satan and his demons.

When people give themselves to Satan, they become his servant. Directly or by association, with or without understanding, those people will then perform the devil's plans. Murder, horror, rape, oppression, abuse, ritualistic sacrifice, tyranny, and corruption are among the terrors that follow. The more people submit to the ways of the serpent, the more they bring pain to themselves and to those around them.

Many in the west do not believe that demons exist, but those in more primitive cultures need not be convinced. The demonic strategy in advanced nations has gone underground. It is clandestine, but still multitudes suffer from torment, fear, rejection, hallucinations, horror, devastating curses, sleepless nights, terrorizing nightmares, mental illness, physical wounds, accidents, technical and mechanical interference, sickness, criminal activity, and death. Not every accident, sickness, bodily wound, sleepless night, or technical hindrance is caused by a demon, but many are.

The paranormal is all around us. Demons are active in the lives of many people who do not know they exist. While many refuse to believe that the devil exists, many others know he is real. They know his power.

People need protection from Satan, and common grace, prayer, salvation, and righteous living before God provide it. Willful participation in Satan's plans, however, removes God's protection.

SATAN HAS NO POWER

Seemingly without restraint, Satan has done much harm to humankind. Many think that his power is almost equal to God's, as if he is the antithesis of God—equal but opposite. To those people, it seems that God and good stand on one side of the road, and Satan and evil stand on the other, and that the two have been in an epic battle throughout the ages. Sometimes God seems to get the upper hand and sometimes Satan does.

This is a complete misunderstanding. God and the devil are not equal in power. The serpent is just a fallen angel. Satan has no power in and of himself. Unlike God, he is not omnipresent, omniscient, or omnipotent. All of his power comes from God. He has more power than humankind, but his power is ineffective unless somehow people open a door for him to enter into their lives.

Although God sees the future and knows every person's heart, he still gives people a choice. In the end, those who choose to reject God will have no excuse. It is not for us to say who is on the Lord's side; only he can make that judgment. We know that many will ruin their lives on earth, but by God's grace they will still arrive in heaven.

Scripture says, "If it [what a man builds] is burned up, he will suffer loss; he himself will be saved, but only as one escaping through the flames" (1 Cor. 3:15).

WHY SUCH PAIN

Why is there such pain for so many in this life? Only God can adequately answer such a question. He sees things from eternity, and we see from a finite perspective. Our journey on earth is just a vapor and our affliction here, no matter how severe, is over in a blink, compared to eternity.

For many who suffer on earth, life is like a surgeon's operation or a root canal at the dentist office. After momentary pain, the problem is fixed, and we are restored to health for all eternity. Without the hope of eternity and our place in it, none of earth's traumas can make sense.

Those who know that their eternal future will be spent with Christ however, have faith to rejoice in the present.

JUST ONE ANGEL

God is all-powerful, and Satan is just a tool used for his purpose. Satan's role in the plan of God will soon be over. In Rev. 20 he is about to be judged, and, when that happens, only one angel will be sent to apprehend him.

"An angel ... out of heaven, having the key to the Abyss and holding in his hand a great chain ... seized the dragon, that ancient serpent, who is the devil, or Satan, and bound him for a thousand years. He threw him into the Abyss, and locked and sealed it over him" (Rev. 20:1–2).

An angel will come from heaven, carrying a key in one hand and a chain in the other. I have often wondered which angel will be chosen. Perhaps every angel will want the task. Perhaps God will give the job to the most insignificant angel to show the entire universe that even one of his smallest can overpower the devil—that once the ban not to harm Satan is lifted, he will be fair game and there will be no contest. That is only my imagination, but the fact remains that just one angel will be sent to seize the devil.

SATAN IS CHAINED

The angel will seize the devil and bind him in chains. He will cast him into the Abyss. That is the place where the beast and the locust demons will have come from at the midpoint of the tribulation. The Abyss is a holding pen for evil spirits and fallen angels. It is a jail, and the final lake of fire is a maximum security prison.

Satan will be cast into the Abyss, and the gate will be sealed and locked by the same angel who captured him. There will be no procession, no great crowd to accompany them on their journey. We envision one solitary soldier dragging the serpent along the lonely pathway. He will take him down the great chimney, past the smoke encrusted gates.

He will throw Satan headlong into the dark hole, close the gate and seal it up behind him.

BOUND FOR A THOUSAND YEARS

Satan will stay in the Abyss for one thousand years. The thousand years is probably a real number, delineating real time. We are given no reason to believe that the thousand years is a symbolic number representing an abstract period of time. With all we know about the coming reign of Christ on earth it is logical and reasonable that it will last for a thousand years.

The thousand-year reference is repeated at least six times in the Bible and I believe that helps to substantiate it as an authentic period of time and not a symbolic time period. A thousand years will be needed for all that must happen.

1. The souls of sinners will be in Hades for a thousand years before they face their final judgment (Rev. 20:5).
2. The saints will rule on the earth with Jesus for a thousand years during the same period of time (Rev. 20:4).
3. We will discover actual details of aging that apply to the thousand-year reign as we study the great millennium in a future chapter (Isa. 65:20).
4. Satan is bound in the Abyss for a thousand years and will be unable to deceive the nations (Rev. 20:2).
5. After the thousand years are over, Satan will be released momentarily. God has still one purpose for him and that purpose will soon become clear (Rev. 20:7).

Chapter Fifty-four

Revelation is About the First Resurrection

I saw thrones on which were seated those who had been given authority to judge.
And I saw the souls of those who had been beheaded because of their testimony for Jesus and because of the word of God. They had not worshipped the beast or his image and had not received the mark on their foreheads or their hands. They came to life and reigned with Christ a thousand years.
(The rest of the dead did not come to life until the thousand years were ended.) This is the first resurrection.
Blessed and holy are those who have part in the first resurrection. The second death has no power over them, but they will be priests of God and of Christ and will reign with him for a thousand years. (Rev. 20:4–6)

CHAPTER TOPICS

1. Saints that help judge
2. The judgment seat of Christ
3. Generous rewards
4. Martyrs ending well
5. The first resurrection
6. The second death

WE WANT TO KNOW

REVELATION 20–21 TRANSITIONS US to a new heaven and earth. These chapters cover six major things. They:

1. fill in information gaps about the eternity;
2. enhance our understanding of the resurrections;
3. include Christ's thousand-year reign;
4. include rewards for saints;
5. describe the judgment of sinners;
6. show us Satan's final destination.

That is a massive amount of information to cover in two chapters. Most everybody would like more details. Although Revelation reveals little on the theme of eternity, we will look to other parts of the Bible to enhance the picture.

I will present several chapters to help us gain a workable understanding of these themes. While the seven-year tribulation period is explained in amazing detail, eternity is not. Still, what we are told of eternity is absolutely fabulous.

SAINTS WILL HELP JUDGE

A select group of saints will help judge the rest of God's people: "I saw thrones on which were seated those who had been given authority to judge" (Rev. 20:4).

The Lord will give authority to a special group of people. These men and women will sit on thrones to help judge the saints. They will not judge sinners, nor will they determine the eternal destination of believers. Only God has that right. They will, however, judge the behavior and the works of other believers. They will allocate to them roles of service and responsibility in Christ's millennium kingdom according to what they did when they lived on the earth.

THE JUDGMENT SEAT OF CHRIST

There is a judgment seat of Christ. In the original Greek language, it is called the *bema* and it is different from the great white throne judgment. The Almighty alone presides over that. The great white throne judgment will be reserved for all sinners and for mortals who are alive during the new millennium. Many who stand before this judgment will be sentenced to hell. The fact that Jesus will not raise unbelievers from the dead when he comes means they are judged already.

PERSONAL CONSIDERATION

Billions of saints will be judged at the judgment seat of Christ, the *bema*. Following the resurrection, each believer will be given personal consideration. Perhaps this is why the Lord will delegate much of this to special disciples. They will help him judge the nations.

Many will be given special rewards to serve in the coming millennium. The *bema* will reveal Christ's gracious assessments, not his harsh judgments. It will be a time of wonderful restitution. The saints will receive all that was promised to them. Even the most failing saint will receive great rewards. Those who have served the Lord with distinction during their lifetime will be given extra special blessings.

"For we must all appear before the judgment seat of Christ, that each one may receive what is due him for the things done while in the body, weather good or bad" (2 Cor. 5:10).

"I the Lord search the heart and examine the mind, to reward a man according to his conduct, according to what his deeds deserve" (Jer. 17:10).

JESUS EXPLAINS REWARDS

Jesus told a parable of a man who went on a journey and returned to see how his servants had behaved in his absence. The Lord put us on earth, and he will return to see how we have behaved in his absence. Here is the judgment the Lord gives one of those servants: "Well done, good and faithful servant! You have been faithful with a few things; I will put you in charge of many things. Come and share your master's happiness!" (Matt. 5:21).

Notice that the man served well and was given great authority, great responsibility, and wonderful blessings.

MARTYRS END WELL

John had a vision of special people who will come to life and receive special honor to rule with Christ. They are the martyrs. John wrote, "And I saw the souls of those who had been beheaded because of their testimony for Jesus and because of the word of God. They had not worshipped the beast or his image and had not received the mark on their foreheads or their hands. They came to life and reigned with Christ a thousand years" (Rev. 20:4).

Special honor will be given to those who are martyred for Christ. During the tribulation they will not receive the mark or philosophy of the beast. They will refuse to worship him. They will be killed, but they will be raised from the dead to reign with Christ for a thousand years.

THE FIRST RESURRECTION

"This is the first resurrection. Blessed and holy are those who have part in the first resurrection" (Rev. 20:5–6).

The resurrection of the saints is called the first resurrection to distinguish it from the resurrection of sinners that will take place a thousand years later. Here, at the end of the tribulation, the first resurrection will take place. Whoever is raised in the first resurrection will be blessed. They are holy unto the Lord and will be given new, glorified bodies.

"But someone may ask, 'How are the dead raised? With what kind of body will they come'?" (1 Cor. 15:35).

"The body that is sown is perishable, it is raised imperishable; it is sown in dishonor, it is raised in glory; it is sown in weakness, it is raised in power; it is sown a natural body, it is raised a spiritual body" (1 Cor. 15:42–44).

"For the trumpet will sound, the dead will be raised imperishable, and we will be changed ... When the perishable has been clothed with the imperishable, and the mortal with immortality, then the saying that is written will come true: Death has been swallowed up in victory" (1 Cor. 15:52–54).

"Dear friends, now we are the children of God, and what we will be has not yet been made known. But we know that when he appears, we shall be like him, for we shall see him as he is" (1 John 3:2).

Our resurrected bodies will be like the body of the Lord Jesus. The resurrected body is imperishable, incorruptible, glorious, immortal, and mature. It will exist without getting older, without falling apart. It will be free from the process of decay.

I am sure that each will be brought backward or forward to their prime age before permanence sets in. It would be no good to have a ninety-year-old body that is worn thin to be one's final state. The ninety-year-old will have their body as it was in their twenties, only perfected. A newborn will be fully mature like a twenty-year-old and glorified.

Everyone's body is irregular or deficient. Some are deformed, crippled, or in some way handicapped. Their resurrected bodies will be perfect. They may have elements of dishonor now, but then they will be glorious (1 Cor. 15:40).

THE SECOND DEATH

Those who are called to the first resurrection will never die again. They will have died once and been raised back to life. They will never experience a second death because their bodies will be immortal. To understand this more fully, here is a simple Bible definition of death: "As *the body without the spirit is dead*, so faith without deeds is dead" (James 2:26; italics added).

Physical death is the separation of the spirit from the body. When we die, our spirits go to Hades or heaven, and our body is buried in the ground or suffers decomposition in some other place. Resurrection happens when the body parts are gathered together again and the person's spirit comes inside the restored body.

A second death is when the spirit leaves the body a second time and the body decomposes again. This will happen to sinners who are resurrected after the thousand-year period has passed. Their spirits will rise from Hades to join their re-gathered bodies. Their bodies, however, will not be raised imperishable, immortal, or incorruptible. Sinners will be brought back to life in their old bodies. The scripture does not say that unbelievers will receive a glorified body.

After being judged at the great white throne, the sinners will be cast into the final hell. Their bodies will once again suffer decay and dishonor. That is the second death. Their spirits will be separated from their bodies. From then on they will live in eternity without bodies once again. As in Hades, they will still be recognizable and they will still suffer.

The second death has no power or place in the lives of believers. They will reign with Christ for a thousand years and then throughout eternity. They will be glorified and be supernatural in body, soul, and spirit.

"The second death has no power over them, but they will be priests of God and of Christ and will reign with him for a thousand years" (Rev. 20:6).

Chapter Fifty-five

Revelation is About the Millennium

They came to life and reigned with Christ a thousand years. (The rest of the dead did not come to life until the thousand years were ended.)
This is the first resurrection. Blessed and holy are those who have part in the first resurrection. The second death has no power over them, but they will be priests of God and of Christ and will reign with him for a thousand years. (Rev. 20:4–6)

CHAPTER TOPICS

1. The great restoration
2. Refreshing the environment
3. People cleaning up the earth
4. Animals becoming immortal
5. Mortals and immortals in the millennium
6. Children being born in the millennium

AFTER THE SECOND COMING

ONCE SATAN AND HIS armies are removed, the thousand-year reign will begin. The process of earth's restoration will be both natural and supernatural. Supernatural elements will be released into the air, sea, and land, but the administration and management of the world will be a process of Christ's rule.

A NEW GARDEN OF EDEN

During the millennium, the earth will be like the Garden of Eden.

"This land that was laid waste has become like the Garden of Eden" (Ezek. 36:35).

Jesus will not just speak the word to instantly renew the earth and give us a completed paradise. The earth will *become* a Garden of Eden; however, there will be a time of cleaning up the mess and developing the new world. There will be a time of transition, a time of building and of restoration of all things. Scripture speaks of the tribulation and of the clean up that follows:

"On the mountains of Israel you will fall, you and all your troops and the nations with you. I will give you as food to all kinds of carrion birds and to wild animals ... Israel will go out and use the weapons for fuel and burn them up ... For seven years they will use them for fuel ... On that day I will give Gog a burial place in Israel ... for seven months the house of Israel will be burying them in order to cleanse the land ... Men will be regularly employed to cleanse the land ... at the end of the seven months they will begin their search. As they go through the land and one of them sees a human bone, he will set up a marker beside it until the gravediggers have buried it" (Ezek. 39:4–15).

Jesus will be personally in charge. The first Eden was left in Adam's charge, and he did not complete his task. We will see what is possible when King Jesus rules. The second Adam, Jesus, will cause the world to become all that it was intended to be from the beginning. At the end of the thousand-year reign, Jesus will finish his task and release the entire kingdom back to his Father.

Adam was immortal when he walked in the garden with Eve. The animals lived in harmony with them. Adam was commissioned to be fruitful; he was to have children, fill the earth, manage it, and eventually rule the entire planet (Gen. 1:28–30).

In those early days before Adam fulfilled his mandate, the Lord God would come and fellowship with him. They would walk together in the cool evenings. Adam was God's friend (Gen. 3:8–9).

This will happen again. Peace and righteousness will be the order of the day. We will enjoy harmony and fellowship with God and with one another, all things will become new, and our joy will be complete.

THE ENVIRONMENT

When the Lord returns to earth at the end of the great tribulation, the planet will be uninhabitable. The environment will be totally devastated. Man's pollutants and the judgments from heaven will have flattened most cities, burned up most of the vegetation, and killed everything in the seas. Ground water will be undrinkable, and most animals will have died. The planet will be a mess.

Instinctively, the animals and all of creation have an eager expectation. It has waited for the return of Jesus and the resurrection of the saints.

Paul wrote:

"The creation waits in eager expectation for the sons of God to be revealed. For the creation was subjected to frustration, not by its own choice, but by the will of the one who subjected it, in hope that the creation itself will be liberated from its bondage to decay and be brought into the glorious freedom of the children of God. We know that the whole creation has been groaning as in the pains of childbirth right up to this present time. Not only so, but we ourselves, who have the firstfruits of the Spirit, groan inwardly as we wait eagerly for our adoption as sons, the redemption of our bodies" (Rom. 8:19–23).

FIRSTFRUITS OF THE SPIRIT

Today, believers receive the firstfruits of the Holy Spirit when they receive Christ as Savior. This has happened to men and women since the day Jesus rose into heaven following his death on the cross. At that time he released the Holy Spirit to the earth, and now God's Spirit lives inside his people. This is the firstfruits of the Spirit, the down payment of their inheritance. The saints' adoption process has begun, but it is not complete. Their souls are redeemed, but not their bodies. When Jesus returns, and his people are resurrected, they will experience the redemption of the body.

That is the moment creation is waiting for. Whatever curse came upon creation at the fall will begin to lift. The environment will begin a process of renewal. It will replenish itself in quick order. We have never seen plants grow so fast or grow to be as beautiful as they will be then.

Jesus will supernaturally clean up the water and the air, and all pollution will vanish. The Lord will heal the cracks in the earth due to the massive earthquakes. He will recreate animals and plants, even some that have become extinct. Maybe we will see dinosaurs. That detail is yet to be discovered. Soon the oceans will team with life, and the wilds of the world will once again be filled with all manner of creatures.

"Behold, I will create new heavens and a new earth. The former things will not be remembered, nor will they come to mind" (Isa. 65:17).

THE ANIMALS

During the transition between the tribulation and the new millennium, animals will feast on flesh and remain wild, but once the *bema* is complete and the sons of God are revealed, then a transformation will occur in the animal kingdom. During the thousand-year reign, people and animals will be vegetarian. There will be no killing of animals.

Having said that, I cannot determine the outcome of insects or fish. I imagine that many insects will be stepped on as larger animals move around. When animals eat plants, insects on the underside of leaves will be consumed. After giving the matter a bit of thought, it would seem that insects may be eaten by animals.

Fisheries will also exist, for the Dead Sea will team with fish and we are told that fishermen will be catching them (Ezek. 47:9–10). Even today, Jews do not consider fish in the same category as meat from land animals. Jewish kosher laws will not allow them to eat chicken, beef or lamb at the same meal where dairy products are present. They may however eat fish with dairy products.

When God destroyed the world in the flood during the days of Noah, he said that every living thing that moved on the ground and every bird would be destroyed. The fish in the sea were not destroyed. Notice the description in Genesis: "Everything on the dry land *that had the breath of life* in its nostrils died. *Every living thing* on the face of the earth was wiped out: men and animals and the creatures that move along the ground and the birds of the air were wiped from the earth. Only Noah was left and those with him in the ark" (Gen. 7:22–23

The fish were not considered as living things because they did not have the breath of life in them. That is the Jewish understanding, and it fits the picture we are given of the new millennium.

With pollutants gone, the plant life reenergized, and fish available, no one will lack the nutrition that has been supplemented through the consumption of land animals. Before Noah and his family entered the ark, Noah and his family were vegetarian. Only after they departed from the ark did God invite them to eat meat (Gen. 9:2–3).

FRIENDLY ANIMALS

In the new millennium, the world will not only return to life as it was before the flood, but to life as it was before the fall. That was a time when all animals were friendly. In the millennium, massive grizzly bears, killer whales, Siberian tigers, and king cobras will be as gentle and sociable as the most loving pet.

Read the prophetic words of Isaiah:

"The wolf will live with the lamb, the leopard will lie down with the goat, the calf and the lion will yearling together; and a little child will lead them. The cow will feed with the bear, their young will lie down together and the lion will eat straw like the ox. The infant will play near the hole of the cobra and the young child will put his hand in the viper's nest. They will neither harm nor destroy on all my holy mountain, for the earth will be full of the knowledge of the Lord as the waters cover the sea. In that day the root of Jesse will stand as a banner for the peoples; the nations will rally to him, and his rest will be glorious. In that day the Lord will reach out his hand a second time to reclaim the remnant of his people" (Isa. 11:6–11).

At that time, animals *will not suffer decay*. Romans 8:21 says they will be *liberated from the bondage of decay*. They will not have wisdom, higher intelligence, or the level of understanding that man has; they are not made in God's image. They will be more like pets that roam freely throughout the earth. Little children will lead them. It will be a wonderful sight to see a little boy or girl lead a black panther or a wolf through the streets of a city. The animals will have babies and their young will get along together. No animal will be carnivorous; in fact, lions will eat straw like an ox. Nothing and no one will destroy an animal or a person in God's new world. There will be a new understanding in the world, for the knowledge of the Lord will be everywhere.

MORTALS AND IMMORTALS ARE THERE

There will be different kinds of people living on earth as well. Mortals and immortals will live side by side. Different races and nationalities will retain their identities. The Jewish nation will especially be identifiable.

We know that billions of people will be immortal and will posses glorified bodies. They will include all believers who died and went to heaven throughout history. Some will already have received new bodies while in heaven, but most in heaven will have been waiting for resurrection day when their spirits will be reunited with their bodies.

Also included in this number are those believers who will be alive at his coming. They will be caught up into the air, and in a flash they will receive new bodies and return to earth with the Lord. The scripture says they will forever be with the Lord.

These glorified, resurrected people are not the only ones who will be alive on earth during the millennium; mortals will be there as well. We know this is true because at the end of the millennium, Satan will be released to tempt the nations once again. A great multitude of mortals will join his army, and the Lord will kill them (Rev. 20:9). If they can be killed, they are not immortal.

SURVIVORS

The mortals will be made up of different groups of people, some of whom will be survivors of the battle of Armageddon.

"Then the survivors from all the nations that have attacked Jerusalem will go up year after year to worship the King, the Lord Almighty, and to celebrate the Feast of Tabernacle" (Zech. 14:16).

The survivors are some of those who attacked Jerusalem. For reasons unknown, the Lord will not destroy every individual who fights against him at his coming. Perhaps he will extend grace to those who might have been dragged or forced to follow the beast. We do not know, but we do know that there will be survivors. The Lord is gracious, and he will be giving them another chance to escape eternal damnation.

There will be babies and unborn children who will be alive at his coming. God will not send children to hell. There are also a large group of Jews in Jerusalem who do not believe that Jesus is their Messiah. The Lord will rescue them when he returns, but many of them will not receive a glorified body (Zech. 14:1–2).

For reasons only known to God, he will give many people another chance to believe in him. He will welcome them into the millennium with his holy ones, but they will not have glorified bodies. In the next chapters, we will look more closely at the life of the Jews and the life in the gentiles during the thousand-year reign on earth.

MORTALS IN THE MILLENNIUM

Whether you have a glorified body or a mortal one, it will be absolutely amazing to live under the rule of King Jesus in the new millennium. Mortals will be married and have children during this time. We are told that people will bear children during these days, and children of various ages are mentioned playing with the animals (Isa. 65:23). It is reasonable to think that mortals will continue procreating as they have always done. We cannot say that for the immortals during the millennium.

While debating with the Sadducees, Jesus said, "Are you not in error because you do not know the scriptures or the power of God? When the dead rise, they will neither marry nor be given in marriage; they will be like the angels in heaven" (Mark 12:25).

It may seem to be a great loss for immortals not to procreate. In keeping with this, however, Jesus said to the Sadducees that they did not understand the power of God. It therefore remains certain that an area of understanding and supernatural power will come to immortals, and I am sure that they will be surprised and grateful for the new arrangement.

The fact that mortals will still give birth to children, means that over the span of the thousand year period, millions of babies will be born, and each will have a free will to choose or reject the Lord.

Some mortals will die during that millennium, although it will be rare. As it was before and during the days of Noah, people will live for centuries.

Speaking of the new millennium, Isaiah said, " Never again will there be in it an infant who lives but a few days, or an old man who does not live out his years; he who dies at a hundred will be a mere youth; he who fails to reach a hundred will be considered accursed" (Isa. 65:20).

A few verses later, he said, "They will not toil in vain or bear children doomed to misfortune; for they will be a people blessed by the Lord, they and their descendants with them" (Isa. 65:23).

In the new millennium, even mortals will live long, wonderful lives. Many, especially the newborns, will no doubt live for the entire length of the thousand-year reign.

Chapter Fifty-six

Revelation is About the Nations in the Millennium

They came to life and reigned with Christ a thousand years. This is the first resurrection. Blessed and holy are those who have part in the first resurrection.
The second death has no power over them, but they will be priests of God and of Christ and will reign with him for a thousand years. (Rev. 20:4–6)

CHAPTER TOPICS

1. Judging the nations
2. The saints in hiding
3. Unsaved survivors in the millennium
4. Children in the millennium
5. The nations of the saved
6. The blessings of the nations
7. Mortals and immortals
8. A population explosion
9. Contempt among the mortals

THE NATIONS

THROUGHOUT HISTORY, GOD FORMED the nations and gave them their boundaries and their allotted time (Acts 17:26). On the whole, they have fallen prey to the lies of the devil, and by the time the great tribulation arrives, the nations will be excessively evil. Worse than that, the majority of people who are still alive at the end of the tribulation will be sold-out servants of Satan. They will be an abomination to the Lord.

The Lord will rescue and redeem most people during the tribulation, but many who are alive at the end will hate him. The Lord will judge them for how they have treated Israel and for the many sins they have committed against his Anointed One and against the innocent. The Lord will destroy them and cast them into Hades where they will wait for one thousand years. Then they will be brought forth to stand before the great white throne for final judgment.

SOME UNBELIEVERS ARE SPARED

While the vast majority of people belong either to the holy or the wicked, some seem to be caught in the middle. They will not serve the devil, but neither will they follow the Lord. God will not destroy them. When the Lord comes to judge the nations, some fence-sitters will be allowed to live. The Bible speaks of them in several places and refers to them as survivors. They will live beyond the second coming, and strangely enough, they will enter the new millennium along with the redeemed. They will be given another opportunity to be saved.

We read, "The earth is defiled by its people; they have destroyed the laws, violated the statutes and broken the everlasting covenant. Therefore a curse consumes the earth; its people must bear their guilt. Therefore earth's inhabitants are burned up and *very few are left*" (Isa. 24:5–6; italics added).

"Then *the survivors* from all the nations that have attacked Jerusalem will go up year after year to worship the King, the Lord Almighty, and to celebrate the Feast of Tabernacles" (Zech. 14:16; italics added).

"For with fire and with his sword the Lord will execute judgment upon all men, and *many* will be those slain by the Lord" (Isa. 66:16; italics added).

"In that day the Lord will reach out his hand a second time to reclaim the remnant of his people" (Isa. 11:11).

"The wedding banquet is ready, but those I invited did not deserve to come. Go to the street corners and invite to the banquet anyone you find. So the servant went out into the streets and gathered all the people they could find, *both good and bad*, and the wedding hall was filled with guests. But when the king came in to see the guests, he noticed a man there who was not wearing wedding clothes … Then the king told the attendants, 'Tie him hand and foot and throw him outside, into the darkness where there will be weeping and gnashing of teeth'" (Matt. 22:8–13).

Jesus will allow some survivors to enter the millennium, who do not have the proper wedding garments. They will be given another chance. Many undeserving will come to the great marriage supper of the Lamb. We read that both the "good and bad" will be brought in so that the hall will be filled. Some will refuse to wear the robes of righteousness, and they will eventually go to hell after the millennium is over and the great white throne judgment is complete.

CHILDREN ARE WELCOME

The ambiguous survivors are not the only ones who will enter the millennium as mortals. Unborn children and many young people will also enter without glorified bodies. They, as with adult survivors, will be mortal. They will not have know the Lord or have received the forgiveness of sins for eternal salvation. They will not be caught up into the clouds to meet the Lord when he appears, so they will not receive glorified bodies. This will happen because some will be in the womb of an unbeliever when Jesus comes. Some will be unsaved teens that the Lord will not send to hell. Many more children will be born to these survivors during the millennium and each of them will need to receive the Lord for themselves.

Jesus loves children. In all of the synoptic Gospels, Jesus says, "let the children come to me and don't refuse them." He says "the kingdom of God belongs to children."

"Let the little children come to me, and do not hinder them, for the kingdom of heaven belongs to such as these" (Matt. 19:14, Mark 10:14, Luke 18:16).

HIDDEN BELIEVERS

Many undercover believers will be alive when the Lord returns. They will be incognito in the nations, watching and waiting for the second coming. At the very end of the tribulation, Israel will be the only place on earth where believers will be open about their faith. Israel will have many enemies, and the world will be at war with Israel. The Holy Land will be inhabited with redeemed Jews, Old Covenant Jews, secular Jews, and Christian gentiles. When the Lord comes to Jerusalem, he will rescue all who live there. Many will be saved from wrath even though they did not previously accept Jesus as Messiah.

BELIEVERS RULE THE NATIONS

In the millennium, those who served the Lord will be given special blessings. They will become kings and priests and rule over the nations of the earth. The nations will look to Israel as the nation that hosts the government of God's kingdom. Jerusalem will be the capital city of the world. Jesus will live and rule from Jerusalem, and the nations, which will be rebuilt and will operate in righteousness and peace will worship him.

THE NATIONS REFORMED

All countries during the millennium will be called the nations of the saved. Each chosen nation will be rescued from extinction to be ruled by the sons and daughters of God.

Speaking of the temple in Jerusalem, scripture says, "The nations of those who are saved shall walk in its light, and the kings of the earth bring their glory and honor into it" (Rev. 21:24, NKJV).

The scripture also says, "And they shall bring the glory and the honor of the nations into it" (Rev. 21:26 NKJV).

Every nation will have a special and distinct destiny given by God. Some will be peacemakers; others will be inventors. Some nations will be rich in the arts and others will reflect amazing gifts of service, worship, leadership, athletics, hospitality, farming, or business administration. During the millennium, all countries will have experts in all realms of life, but each will excel with some distinction—a skill that is superior to that of other nations. Each nation will be known for its own excellence.

Like individual people, each will reflect a beautiful aspect of the glory and character of God. No person has the full measure of God shinning through them; they must partner with other saints to see a display of glory that even approaches God's. The nations likewise, will partner with other nations to demonstrate God's glory. The heavens declare the glory of God; so do individual people, and so do nations.

The glory of each nation will be brought to Jerusalem to be presented to the Lord. We are not told that every nation will be in the millennium, but I believe that most will be resurrected for the new world. We know that people from every nation and language are in heaven. Jesus purchased them with his blood and their nationality and ethnicity are recognizable as they stand around God's throne (Rev. 7:9).

"On this mountain the Lord Almighty will prepare a feast of rich food for all peoples, a banquet of aged wine—the best of meats and the finest of wines. *On this mountain he will destroy the shroud that enfolds all peoples, the sheet that covers all nations*; he will swallow up death forever. The Sovereign Lord will wipe away the tears from all faces; he will remove the disgrace of his people from all the earth. The Lord has spoken" (Isa. 25:6–8; italics added).

The Lord will take away the shroud that covers the nations. This shroud hides their inherent talents and gifts. Presently people and nations are robbed of their identity, their destiny, and their godly heritage. All of that will change in the millennium; during that time period, they will shine in God's glory. The nations will be reformed for the new millennium. The shroud will be removed from them. They will bring their special grace, honor, talents, distinctions, and glory to Jerusalem.

THE GLORY OF THE SAVED

The saved will be immortal, and their bodies will be incorruptible. They will be supernatural and spiritual. In many ways, they will be like Jesus; they are his family. They will take the mandate given to the first Adam to subdue the world, steward it, and manage it in righteousness. Adam failed, but they will not.

Billions of animals will be there, living in peace, and all of creation will flourish to its optimum potential. Humankind will fully enjoy the pleasures of creativity, invention, work, and prosperity.

People will be blessed with fun, recreation, and glorious fellowship and thrilled with a wealth of friends, and they will experience rich fellowship with the Lord. The kingdom of God will have come to earth in answer to the Lord's Prayer.

"Your kingdom come, your will be done on earth as it is in heaven" (Matt. 6:10).

It will happen, and God's people will fully enjoy their reward. Nonbelievers among the nations will live in the glory of God's people. They will be blessed because of the blessing that rest on the saints and on the land, but some will be unthankful.

MORTALS ARE BLESSED

In many ways, immortals and mortals will live differently during the millennium. One difference will be childbirth and population growth. As the years pass, more and more babies will be born to the mortals, but none to the immortals. The mortals are the unsaved survivors of Armageddon. They will have come into the millennium without making Christ their Lord.

In just twenty years, children become adults, marry, and begin to have children of their own. In the millennium, they will have grandchildren and great grandchildren and so on, for many generations. Because very few will die, untold millions of mortals will fill the world. Many of those will become followers of Christ, but a vast multitude will not bow the knee willingly.

MORTALS BREED CONTEMPT

As the millennium endures and moves toward its end, a growing disquiet will begin to surface. It will not come from the immortals. They will remember the old life when they had frail bodies. In the millennium, they will be sons and daughters of God and will not trade that glory for anything. They will know the fullness of God's fellowship and live like angels. They could not and will not turn away from the Lord. They will be totally one with him for all eternity.

Some mortals, on the other hand, will drift away from the Lord. Presently, we know the truth about waywardness. Isaiah said, "We all, like sheep, have gone astray, each of us has turned to his own way" (Isa. 53:6).

Some mortals in the millennium will take their blessings for granted, and their hearts will fall from gratitude and grace. Most will not have experienced the ravages of sin or the temptations of the devil. They will have only lived in the millennial kingdom. All they will have known is the rule of Jesus and his holy ones.

Many will earn positions of authority and responsibility and will begin to influence their community in a direction away from Jerusalem. Some will want to skip out on the feast celebrations.

The Lord says that all who refuse to come up to Zion for the Feast of Tabernacles will find that the rains will not fall on their nation, and their national productivity will begin to fall. Some will begin to show signs of rebellion (Zech. 14:17–19). It will soon be time for Satan to appear from the Abyss for his final campaign.

Chapter Fifty-seven

REVELATION IS ABOUT ISRAEL IN THE MILLENNIUM

They came to life and reigned with Christ a thousand years ... they will be priests of God and of Christ and will reign with him for a thousand years. (Rev. 20:4–6)

CHAPTER TOPICS

1. The chosen people
2. He who rules from Zion
3. Ruling with a rod of iron
4. Israel's blessings
5. Miraculous water
6. The feasts of Israel
7. The nations celebrating with Israel
8. Israel's second chance to find salvation

THE CHOSEN PEOPLE

THE JEWS ARE AND will be a distinct people before God. They will enjoy the blessings of a special inheritance. They will lead in global worship and in the international celebration of holy feasts. They will live in close proximity to Christ's throne room in the city of Jerusalem and the nation of Israel. That city will be the most honored on the planet. Redeemed Jews will be honored among the nations throughout the millennium.

JESUS RULES FROM ZION

Jesus will live in and rule from Jerusalem. From there, he will give the Jewish people and the nations of the world everything that was ever promised to them through the prophets.

"The Lord will rule over them in Mount Zion from that day and forever" (Mic. 4:7).

Although he is the most compassionate and gracious of kings, Jesus will rule with a rod of iron. The iron sceptre will be operational from the moment he returns to earth.

Revelation says, "Out of his mouth comes a sharp sword with which to strike down the nations. He will rule them with an iron sceptre" (Rev. 19:15).

He will rule, but he will not rule alone. He will delegate many to rule alongside him, and each will have the authority of the iron sceptre. Christian leaders will rule over the nations, and Jews will rule alongside Jesus in the land of Israel. Jesus is the king of the Jews.

"To him who overcomes and does my will to the end, I will give authority over the nations. He will rule them with an iron sceptre" (Rev. 2:26–27).

Jesus will rule with a rod of iron. His name will be the only name (Zech. 14:9). That means some matters are not negotiable:

1. Jesus will demand righteousness in his kingdom.
2. There will be no hurt or destruction in all his holy mountain.
3. He will not tolerate wickedness.
4. No other religions will be acceptable on the earth. All religion that originates outside of God's throne room is of the devil, and none of that will be permitted to linger on the earth.
5. No crime will be allowed.

6. No abuse, extortion, or killing will be tolerated. The entire world will be safe, joyful, and righteous.

The nations will experience the productivity of Eden and the glories of heaven. God's blessings will cover the entire planet, but Israel will be given a special place of honor.

ISRAEL WILL BE BLESSED FOREVER

The nation of Israel will be blessed in an unusual way. God will fix that which has been broken and will bless her with all that was promised.

"In that day I will restore David's fallen tent. I will repair its broken places, restore its ruins and build it as it used to be" (Amos 9:11).

Jesus will live in Jerusalem. The Jewish people will be around him, and he will give them their full inheritance. We read in Isaiah, "Rejoice with Jerusalem and be glad for her, all you who love her …" (Isa. 66:10).

"For this is what the Lord says: 'I will extend peace to her like a river and the wealth of nations like a flooding stream'," (Isa. 66:12).

Israel will be established in her mandated borders. The land from the Nile to the Euphrates will forever be the land of Israel (Gen. 15:18). It will overflow with temple worship, industry, agricultural productivity, and amazing beauty.

"Lord you established peace for us; all that we have accomplished you have done for us. O Lord, our God, other lords besides you have ruled over us, but your name alone do we honor. They are now dead, they live no more; those departed spirits do not rise. You punished them and brought them to ruin; you wiped out all memory of them. You enlarged the nation, O Lord; you have enlarged the nation. You have gained glory for yourself you have extended all the borders of the land" (Isa. 26:12–15).

Israel's population will also increase rapidly. It seems that the Lord wants more people as part of this special nation. Perhaps this is one of the reasons why many Jews will still be mortal during the millennium.

"They will not toil in vain or bear children doomed to misfortune; for they will be a people blessed by the Lord, they and their descendants with them" (Isa. 65:23).

"Then will all your people be righteous and will posses the land forever. They are the shoot I have planted, the work of my hands, for the display of my splendor. The least will become a thousand, the smallest a mighty nation. I am the Lord; in its time I will do this swiftly" (Isa. 60:21–22).

"As the new heavens and the new earth that I make will endure before me," declares the Lord, "so will your name and descendants endure" (Isa. 66:22).

MIRACULOUS WATER

Water, at present, must be carefully managed in Israel because, like in the surrounding nations, water supply is limited. In the millennium, it will flow freely from springs and gush forth in powerful rivers. This is God water, and it will have special healing qualities. Even the desert between Jerusalem and the Dead Sea will flow with living water. The new water will bring renewal and restoration to the entire nation.

"Then will the lame leap like a deer, and the mute tongue shout for joy. Water will gush forth in the wilderness and streams in the desert. The burning sand will become a pool, the thirsty ground bubbling springs. In the haunts where jackals once lay, grass and reeds and papyrus will grow. And a highway will be there; it will be called the way of holiness" (Isa. 35:6–8).

Even the Dead Sea will receive so much of this unique water that it will experience a new identity. People will no longer be able to call it the Dead Sea. Now, it is totally dead. No fish or creature of any kind lives in the Dead Sea. The oceans are 3 percent salt; the Dead Sea is 33 percent salt. Nothing can live there. In the millennium, the Dead Sea will abound with aquatic life.

"This water flows toward the eastern region and goes down into Arabah, where it enters the Sea. When it empties into the Sea, the water there becomes fresh. Swarms of living creatures will live wherever the river flows. There will be large numbers of fish, because this water flows there and makes the salt water fresh; so where the river flows everything will live. Fishermen will stand along the shore; from En Gedi to En Eglaim there will be places for spreading nets. The fish will be of many kinds—like the fish of the great sea" (Ezek. 47:8–10).

Wealth, joy, and peace will fill the land of Israel, and nations all around the world will see the glory of God that rests on her. The wealth of the nations will stream into the Holy Land, and people will desire to go up to Israel and serve the people and the land of the Jews, because Jerusalem will be the city of the Great King.

Many details are given in scripture to specifically describe Israel's glory and wealth during the millennium. There are too many verses to record them all. For those who want a more detailed picture of Israel's national prosperity during the thousand-year reign, I encourage you to read Isa. 60–66. There you will find more than one hundred verses that focus on the theme of Israel's coming glory. Israel will become the praise of the whole earth.

Concerning Israel, the scripture says, "Arise, shine, for your light has come, and the glory of the Lord rises upon you ... but the Lord rises upon you and his glory appears over you. Nations will come to your light, and kings to the brightness of your dawn ... The wealth of the seas will be brought to you, to you the riches of the nations will come ... Foreigners will rebuild your walls, and their kings will serve you" (Isa. 60:1, 2, 10).

"You who call on the Lord, give yourselves no rest, and give him no rest till he establishes Jerusalem and makes her the praise of the earth" (Isa. 62:6–7).

THE FEASTS OF ISRAEL

The feasts of Israel are God's appointed gatherings. They are not manmade but God-made. They highlight specific times when God's people gather for worship and celebration. They are special times of remembrance, thanksgiving, and honor. They are memorials, and the Lord will insist on these feasts during his thousand-year reign on the earth. He will command the nations to celebrate the feasts along with Jerusalem.

The Jews have been chosen by God to organize, administrate, and lead the world in the celebration of the feasts. In a list of eight things, this privilege—called the temple worship—belongs to the Jews. In Romans 9:3–5, Paul mentions the eight things that are parts of Israel's inheritance.

"My brothers, those of my own race, the people of Israel. Theirs is the adoption of sons; theirs the divine glory, the covenants, the receiving of the law, *the temple worship* and the promises. Theirs are the patriarchs, and from them is traced the human lineage of Christ" (Rom. 9:3–5; italics added).

This is not an Old Testament verse, but a New Testament verse. The leadership of the temple worship during the millennium has been allocated to the Jews. The most memorable feast will be the Feast of Tabernacles.

"Then the survivors from all the nations that have attacked Jerusalem will go up year after year to worship the King, the Lord Almighty, and to celebrate the Feast of Tabernacles. If any of the peoples of earth do not go up to Jerusalem to worship the King, the Lord Almighty, they will have no rain" Zech. 14:16–18).

The Feast of Tabernacles is called Sukkot. It has special significance.

In, *The Race to Save the World,* Sid Roth wrote, "Sukkot commemorates the forty-year period during which the children of Israel wandered in the desert, living in temporary shelters. Sukkot is the feast that we also celebrate the birth of Yeshua, who is the Son of the living God and who is our Salvation and our Provision, our Shelter, and our Provider."[ac]

During the millennium, the Lord will insist on the nations coming to Jerusalem to celebrate the Feast of Tabernacles. The world must recognize that God alone is their shelter. They must remember that man's time on earth has been a journey through the wilderness and God alone has brought mankind through it. Like the children of Israel in ancient days, the nations in the millennium will have come to their promised land. The feast is a joyous yet solemn reminder of man's frailty and his total dependency on God.

THE NATIONS GO UP TO ZION

Representatives from every nation will go up to Jerusalem to celebrate the Feast of Tabernacles. These will be glorious occasions, rich in fellowship and worship.

"In the last days the mountain of the Lord's temple will be established as chief among the mountains; it will be raised above the hills, and all nations will stream to it. Many peoples will come and say, "Come, let us go up to the mountain of the Lord, to the house of the God of Jacob. He will teach us his ways, so that we may walk in his paths. The law will go out from Zion, the word of the Lord form Jerusalem. He will judge between the nations and will settle disputes for many peoples. They will beat their swords into plowshares and their spears into pruning hooks. Nation will not take up sword against nation, nor will they train for war anymore. Come, O house of Jacob, let us walk in the light of the Lord."' (Isa. 2:2–5)

SALVATION EXTENDED AGAIN

Worshipping Jesus as Lord will become the obvious choice for Jews who once would not accept Jesus as Messiah. Orthodox zealots always believed in Messiah, they just did not want to believe that Jesus was the one. That delusion will instantly pass when he appears on the Mount of Olives. They will become believers, but they will have to wait for the great white throne judgment at the end of the millennium to receive glorified bodies. They will wait with enthusiasm for the next official resurrection.

"The calf and the lion will yearling together; and a little child will lead them … In that day the Lord will reach out his hand a second time to reclaim the remnant of his people" (Isa. 11:6; 11).

God will reach out to them a second time. These late blooming

Jews will be grafted into their own olive tree at the end of time, even when it seems that all hope is gone. Notice that it will happen when the calf and the lion yearling together in the new millennium. A second time, the Lord will reach out to his chosen people.

"How much more readily will these, the natural branches, be grafted into their own olive tree?" (Rom. 11:24).

This offer of eternal salvation will no doubt be extended to all mortals during the millennium. It seems strange to think that many will refuse even though they are living in the kingdom of God. Yet when Satan appears, many will rally to his evil call. Their hearts will be exposed, and their secret malaise of defiance will be uncovered for all to see.

Chapter Fifty-eight

Revelation Is About Satan's Last Campaign

When the thousand years are over, Satan will be released from his prison and will go out to deceive the nations in the four corners of the earth—Gog and Magog—to gather them for battle.
In number they are like the sand on the seashore. They marched across the breadth of the earth and surrounded the camp of God's people, the city he loves.
But fire came down from heaven and devoured them. And the devil, who deceived them, was thrown into the lake of burning sulfur, where the beast and the false prophet had been thrown. They will be tormented day and night for ever and ever." (Rev. 20:7–10)

CHAPTER TOPICS

1. The new Garden of Eden
2. The removal of temptation
3. An opportunity to sin in the millennium
4. The release of Satan
5. The lie of Satan
6. The army of Satan
7. Gog and Magog

9. A muster against Israel
10. Fire from heaven
11. Satan going to hell

A GARDEN OF EDEN

THE THOUSAND-YEAR REIGN OF Christ will be the most glorious era in earth's history to date. It will be a global Garden of Eden. Billions will inhabit the world in peace and productivity. The environment, although wild, will not be hostile, and all animals will be like wonderful outdoor pets. Children will be extra special because abuse and poverty will be gone. Multitudes of creative people will exercise their gifts and talents in an atmosphere of freedom. Righteousness will flow from the throne of God, producing a lifestyle of love and participation for all. The entire world will worship the Lord and glorify God Almighty. Jesus will rule the world. No one could design a better world to live in, but this era will not last forever.

NO EXCUSE FOR SIN

To whom much is given, much is required. That statement will never be truer than during the millennium. Whether Jew or Gentile, mortal or immortal, each person will live under the rule of Christ and enjoy the benefits of his kingdom. Satan will be far away in prison and will not be able to tempt or hurt anyone.

No person on earth will need to sin for there will be no lack of provisions or opportunities to enjoy life. Lust will not be promoted by Babylon's seductions because Babylon will be no more. Lust will not be flaunted in the media, and people will not dress or act flirtatiously.

It is amazing to visit a nation in the world today where technology and modern trends are not prevalent. Human sensuality in those countries is private, and lust battles are greatly reduced. In the millennium, all good and healthy desires will be readily met through godly means.

In the new Garden of Eden, one dynamic will stand out above all others. The life of Jesus will shine brilliantly. The loving example of the Lord will inspire and encourage people beyond their imaginations. Jesus will open the heavens, the doors, and he will open eyes, minds, and hearts so that each person will be able to discover and complete his or her destiny.

"No longer will violence be heard in your land, nor ruin or destruction within your borders, but you will call your walls salvation and your gates praise. The sun will no more be your light by day, nor will the brightness of the moon shine on you, for the Lord will be your everlasting light, and your God will be your glory" (Isa. 60:18–19)

Even when the Lord becomes the light of life, many will allow rebellion to fester in their hearts. Perhaps mortals will be jealous of the Jews or the immortals. Some may want to shake themselves from under God's authority simply because they want no authority over them. Perhaps some will want to be God themselves. Some may feel that their creativity is squelched because it cannot be mixed with sin, at least not out in the open. Whatever the reasons, sin will fill the minds and hearts of many people.

OPPORTUNITY FOR DISOBEDIENCE

We do not know what will inspire the rebellion against Christ, but it will come. Humans do not need the devil or enticements from other humans to be sinful. It comes down to a personal choice; will people bow to Jesus or refuse to give him allegiance?

A person may put on a good show for others, but still allow wickedness to grow in his or her heart. People may live a lie and fool others; they may even lie to themselves by allowing empty excuses to legitimize evil thoughts, but God is not fooled. The Lord does not want a kingdom of phony saints who follow him outwardly, but despise him in their hearts. That is why the millennium must end.

Sometimes sin is not evident because it has lacked opportunity. That will be true for multitudes in the millennium. Opportunity to express choice will come at the end of the thousand years when Satan is released from prison as the new choice.

SATAN GATHERS AN ARMY

After the thousand years are over, Satan will be released from the Abyss. He will muster a hoard of demons to help him with his task. We know that many demons will be present after Armageddon for they will eat the flesh of the fallen ones. Where they will be during the thousand-year reign of Christ, we are not told. They might be in the Abyss with the devil. Perhaps they will be somewhere on earth, under the earth, or in the planet's atmosphere. We know that they will not cause trouble for humanity during the millennium; for evil will be given no place under the reign of Christ.

Once Satan is released, he and his demons will deceive the nations, and God will allow it. They will fit in with his plan. Satan deceived Adam and Eve in the first Garden, and he will do it again in the millennium. During the first temptation, he told Eve that disobedience would allow her to become like God.

"You will surely not die," the serpent said to the woman. "For God knows that when you eat of it your eyes will be opened, and you will be like God, knowing good and evil" (Gen. 3:4).

I think this same lie will be the basis of the devil's deception in the millennium. Many blame Adam and Eve for the pain they brought to mankind. They had a perfect life in a perfect world, but they wanted more. Satan came and revealed the sin in their hearts, and they chose his counsel and rejected God's.

The serpent will be active in the garden once again. This time he will deceive the nations. Many mortals will choose deception because they are looking for an opportunity to rise above God. Pride and listening to the devil's lies will always control a sinful heart. Many mortals will be drawn away by their own desires, and Satan will entice them to fall. (See James 1:14.)

Positions of power will be given to leading men and women, and an army of rebels will rise among the nations. Jesus will instruct his people to let it happen.

MYSTERY OF GOG AND MAGOG

Those who gather to fight the Lord are called Gog and Magog.

"Satan will be released from his prison and will go out to deceive the nations in the four corners of the earth—Gog and Magog—to gather them for battle. In number they are like the sand on the seashore" (Rev. 20:7–8).

This representation of Gog and Magog does not refer to Russia, China, the European Union, or the Muslim Arab nations. Revelation 20:8 depicts Gog and Magog appearing at the end of the millennium, one thousand years after the present nations have been judged.

The nations will be different during the millennium. The complexion of the nations will not be as they are today. NATO, the European Common Market, the Alliance of Arab Nations, and the G8 will not exist. To be more clear, we are told in verse eight that Gog and Magog are not representatives of select nations, but they come from the four corners of the globe. They represent people of every nation except Israel.

WHO ARE GOG AND MAGOG?

There are three main groups referred to as Gog and Magog in the scriptures. References to these groups are found in Gen. 10:2, 1 Chron. 1:5, Ezek, 38 and 39, and Rev. 20:8. We will discuss Gog but first, here are the three different groups who are referred to as Magog are:

1. Japheth's children who become the Assyrians and rebel against God
2. The nations who gather against God for the battle of Armageddon at the end of the tribulation period
3. The nations who gather against God at the end of the new millennium

The first Magog mentioned in scripture was a son of Japheth, the oldest son of Noah (Gen. 10:2; 1 Chron. 1:5). Japheth was a survivor of the flood, which was God's first global judgment on Adam's race. Some of his grandchildren became the people of Magog, and they became the nation of Assyria. Assyria as a whole became an enemy of God and Israel.

The second group referred to as Magog is those nations who will survive the judgments of the seven years of great tribulation. They will rally together against Israel before the second coming of Jesus. They will come to the valley of Armageddon to attack Israel, and there they will be judged by God.

In Ezek. 38–39, Gog is a leader, and Magog are the people he leads. In Ezekiel 38:2, we read, "Set your face against Gog, of the land of Magog, the chief prince of Meshech … prophesy against him."

The NIV Study Bible notes assert, "Since the Hebrew prefix *ma-* can mean 'place of,' Magog may here simply mean "land of Gog."[ad]

The context of Ezek. 38–39, regarding Gog and Magog, points to a leader (Gog) and the rebels of the nations (Magog) who come to fight against Israel at the end of the great tribulation. Men and nations will attack Israel at the great battle of Armageddon, and the Lord rescues Israel and destroys the armies of Magog (the rebel army).

The third group referred to as Magog includes the mortals who will survive the second coming of Christ. Like the survivors of Noah's flood, *many grandchildren* of the Armageddon survivors will become the new Magog. The survivors will enter the millennium, populate the nations, and rebel against God. Satan will gather Gog and Magog for battle. They will come from across the breadth of the earth, and there will be so many of them that they will appear as the sand on the seashore.

ISRAEL SURROUNDED AGAIN

Fear will fill some of the hearts of the mortals who live in Israel. This will be true for some of those who remember the last age or those who have heard the story of Jerusalem's violent history. Gog and Magog will surround the city of Jerusalem.

God will allow Satan's military maneuvers to go that far, but no further. They will not have time to strike. Not one person will be killed before God intervenes. This muster will produce no godly casualties of war. The uprising will be permitted for one reason, to reveal the hearts of evil men—to let the world and the universe see who has chosen to be God's enemy.

God loves his people and will not allow them to suffer pain anymore. The fears of the mortals in Jerusalem and the rest of the world will soon be quelled.

FIRE FROM HEAVEN

When all of Magog has gathered for battle, God Almighty will make a preemptive strike. No enemy weapon will fire before the heavens open. Suddenly, and without warning, fire will fall on the enemies of God. Jesus will be on his throne in Jerusalem, but the Almighty will fight this battle from heaven. No angel will appear, and no human will lift a militant hand; it will be God himself who will destroy the enemy.

The unexpected fire will be powerful but focused. Like a laser, it will strike down its target without hurting the environment. All God's human enemies will be vaporized by the fire.

John wrote, "But fire came down from heaven and devoured them" (Rev. 20:9).

SATAN'S DESTINY

The devil, who deceived the nations, will be cast into the lake of fire where the beast and the false prophet were thrown one thousand years earlier. It is a lake of burning sulfur. There, fallen angels will suffer in torment day and night. They will have no relief for all eternity. That is Satan's destiny. He cannot avoid it or delay its coming. His eternal doom is sealed already, and his schemes for chaos and destruction will not affect the final outcome.

Satan cannot take a human soul with him to hell by wishing for it. Each person will stand or fall before God alone. The devil has hindered and hurt many during their lifetimes, but he has no eternal claims on the souls of men and women. He does not rule in hell. He is a prisoner there, as are all of God's enemies.

All humans who chose to hate God and side with the devil will suffer his fate, although I am convinced that many who were deceived by him or wounded because of him will escape his company by the end of the great tribulation. They will come through the narrow door of Jesus and no other way, but they will come. God will bring every soul possible into his kingdom, and those who do not make it will have no excuse.

Satan will never be released again. He will never again tempt the nations or hinder the flow of God's blessings on human beings. He will arrive at his final destination. He will find himself in hell.

Chapter Fifty-nine

REVELATION IS ABOUT THE GREAT WHITE THRONE

Then I saw a great white throne and him who was seated on it. Earth and sky fled from his presence, and there was no place for them.
And I saw the dead, great and small, standing before the throne, and books were opened. Another book was opened, which is the book of life. The dead were judged according to what they had done as recorded in the books.
The sea gave up the dead that were in it, and death and Hades gave up the dead that were in them, and each person was judged according to what he had done.
Then death and Hades were thrown into the lake of fire. The lake of fire is the second death. If anyone's name was not found written in the book of life, he was thrown into the lake of fire.
(Rev. 20:11–15)

CHAPTER TOPICS

1. The last resurrection
2. The great white throne
3. The dead will rise
4. The final judgment
5. No children in hell

6. Judging those from the millennium
7. Hell fires

THE LAST RESURRECTION

THE FINAL RESURRECTION WILL come at the end of the great millennium and will lead to the final day of reckoning. We know of no further judgments.

Since the days of Adam and Eve, men have lived and died. No human spirit, however, has been annihilated; the human spirit is eternal.

"He has also set eternity in the hearts of men" (Eccles. 3:11).

Every person will experience a resurrection. Resurrection is the reforming of the body and the reentry of the spirit into that body. All who died will live again, but each in their own order.

"For as in Adam all die, so in Christ all will be made alive. But each in his own turn: Christ, the firstfruits; then, when he comes, those who belong to him. Then the end will come" (1 Cor. 15:22–24).

Here are the three main resurrections:

1. Christ, the firstfruits
2. Those who belong to him when he comes
3. The end or final resurrection

The last resurrection will be the most sobering event in man's history. It will be the point of no return, the cliff that overlooks the grand canyon of eternity, and all who have refused salvation and godliness will dread it.

THE DEAD WILL COME

Every human (except the very young) has sinned, but Christ has removed the sins of all who have received him. All who will not receive him will be dead by the end of the new millennium. From the days of Adam to the end of the millennium, all rebellious souls will be waiting for the resurrection. When the last resurrection is finally called, no sinner will be left alive on the earth.

No person will escape the great white throne judgment, except those in Christ. All others will be escorted by angels to stand before God's throne. John wrote, "The sea gave up the dead that were in it, and death and Hades gave up the dead that were in them, and each person was judged according to what he had done" (Rev. 20:11–15).

Three domains will be summoned: the domain of the sea, the domain of death, and the domain of Hades. Each will surrender their dead. The domains of the sea and death refer to the domains of physical human bodies while Hades speaks of the domain of souls or spirits. Both bodies and spirits must appear before God.

The sea domain will release the bodies that have decomposed in oceans, lakes, or rivers. The death domain will release those bodies in tombs and those that have decomposed on land. All of these bodies will come together and be resurrected to life.

Hades will also yield her dead; she will release the human spirits. These are spirits of evil men who, before they died, demonstrated a life of wickedness and rebellion. Some will have waited in torment for thousands of years.

As the sea, the land and Hades give up their dead, spirits unite with bodies to appear before the great throne.

THE GREAT WHITE THRONE

God Almighty sits on the great white throne. He is called the Judge of All (Heb.12:23). None has been more patient, compassionate, or merciful, but God is also just, and those who chose evil will receive punishment. There is no higher court of appeal, and God will never delegate this responsibility to another. Hell is final, and he alone will send someone there.

MORE PEOPLE IN HEAVEN

I believe that more people will live in eternity with Christ than will go to hell. Vast multitudes will be saved during the great tribulation. Souls who lived throughout history in ages and cultures where many did not hear the truth of the Gospel will find that God will be more gracious in his judgments toward them. During this present age, statistics tell us that there are more people on the earth who claim to be Christian than there are those aligned with any other religion. I do not believe that all who claim the title of Christian are genuine, nor do I think that those who do not claim to be Christians are beyond God's reach.

Many think that the vast majority of humans will end up in hell, and only a very select group will go to heaven. That makes no sense to me. I find it hard to fathom that God, the master designer, would plan an end like that.

A popular scripture, which seems at face value to suggest that such a small group will go to heaven is found in Matthew's Gospel. It reads, "Enter by the narrow gate. For wide is the gate and broad is the road that leads to destruction, and many enter through it. But small is the gate and narrow is the road that leads to life, and only a few find it" (Matt. 7:13–14).

There can be no doubt that the way to life is narrow, and few are able to find it. The question remains, what life is Jesus talking about? Is it eternal life or a spiritual life with God that determines our experience on earth?

Many live lives of regret in this world, because they do not enter the narrow way and find a living relationship with the Lord. Most people live lives full of destruction rather than godliness. The word *life* in Matt. 14 is the Greek word zoe. *Zoë* speaks of quality of life and not necessarily eternal life. The context does not suggest the theme of eternal life. These verses are part of the Sermon on the Mount. The verses that immediately precede them talk about not judging others, asking the Lord for spiritual gifts, and loving our neighbor. The verses immediately following them give warning not to follow false prophets.

In other words, the focus of these verses is given in the context of quality of life on earth, not whether one makes it to heaven.

Another verse that seems to infer that only a few people will get to heaven is Matthew 22:14, which reads, "For many are invited but few are chosen."

Jesus is telling a story about the marriage supper of the Lamb, the great millennium. Many are invited, but of those few come as the chosen.

In verses leading up to verse fourteen, Jesus says, "Those I invited did not deserve to come. *Go to the street corners and invite to the banquet anyone you find. So the servants went out into the streets and gathered all the people they could find, both good and bad, and the wedding hall was filled with guests* (Matt. 22:8–10; italics added).

With closer inspection, we discover that the words "few are chosen" point to multitudes more being saved. Everyone who could be found was brought in, even the bad. In the end the wedding hall was filled.

A good friend of mine recently said, "Heaven is a big place." I believe that God will find a way for the majority of people to come to him through Christ.

We will find out how many go to hell when judgment day comes. Regardless of how many come to the Lord, the fact remains that multitudes will stand before the throne to be judged, and many will be sent to hell.

THE JUDGMENT

God will judge each person individually. He will take whatever length of time is necessary. The Almighty will judge with understanding, fairness, truth, and wisdom. He will not be rash, and he will not fail on his determinations. God cannot lie, nor can he change. In him there is no shadow of turning, no blinders; nor is their any unfounded indignation. His word is true, and the verdicts on judgment day will be final. Many books will be opened, and the details of every person's life will be exposed.

"And I saw the dead, great and small, standing before the throne, and books were opened. Another book was opened, which is the book of life. The dead were judged according to what they had done as recorded in the books. The sea gave up the dead that were in it, and death and Hades gave up the dead that were in them, *and each person was judged according to what he had done*" (Rev. 20:12–13; italics added).

God's judgment relates to activity—the things a person has done. It will also focus on people's acceptance or rejection of Jesus Christ, his Son. The judgments will be stricter for those who have received more understanding and more lenient for those without.

We read, "We who teach will be judged more strictly" (James 3:1).

Gentiles who do not have God's law will be judged according to their own conscience.

"(Gentiles, who do not have the law … show that the requirements of the law are written on their hearts, their consciences also bearing witness, and their thoughts now accusing, now even defending them.) This will take place on the day when God will judge men's secrets through Jesus Christ" (Rom. 2:14–16).

The standards for judgment will not be the same for every person. Less will be expected of the man who has never heard of Christ, the truths of the Bible, or the living God. He will be judged by his deeds and the attitudes of his heart.

The disciples asked Jesus, "Who then can be saved?" (Matt. 19:25, Mark 10:26, Luke 18:26).

Jesus' answer was simple: "With man this is impossible, but with God all things are possible" (Matt. 19:26).

Salvation is impossible for any man, but all things are possible with God. I could never say that someone cannot be saved; only God can make that determination. The thief on the cross next to Christ was a criminal, but in his final hour he believed in Jesus and asked to be remembered in his kingdom. Jesus told him he would make it to heaven.

WORKS WILL COUNT

While all have sinned, most people throughout history have done their best to deny wickedness and do good. Everyone has failed miserably, but contrary to some beliefs, generosity, kindness, and goodness will not be overlooked by God at the great white throne. John wrote, "Each person was judged according to what he had done" (Rev. 20:13).

Many non-churched people have spent their lives being kind and serving others. I have met many. I do not know how, but I believe that God will rescue them through the narrow door of faith in Jesus. Their expressions of kindness, goodness, and love will be a major factor on judgment day. Listen to the words of Jesus:

"All the nations will be gathered before him, and he will separate the people ... the King will say to those on his right, "Come ... Whatever you did for one of the least of these brothers of mine, you did for me." Then he will say to those on his left, "Depart from me, you who are cursed, into the hell fire prepared for the devil and his angels. For I was hungry and you gave me nothing to eat, I was thirsty and you gave me nothing to drink, I was a stranger and you did not invite me in, I needed clothes and you did not cloth me, I was sick and in prison, and you did not look after me." They also will answer ... "When?" He will reply, "Whatever you did not do for one of the least of these, you did not do for me." Then they will go away to eternal punishment, but the righteous to eternal life" (Matt. 25:32–46).

Acts of kindness will be in the equation on judgment day. God will look at the things people have done. He will look for deeds such as clothing the poor, visiting prisoners, helping the sick, and feeding the hungry. These acts are important to God, and they expose one's heart.

Man cannot be saved by works alone. Nothing can wash away one's sins, except faith in Jesus. God, nevertheless, takes notice of human kindness and a person's love for the truth. Those who demonstrate these qualities will be drawn to the narrow way of the cross. There, they will find opportunity to chose or reject the Lord. Those who receive him will become sons and daughters of God.

This is what happened with a kindhearted gentile named Cornelius. We read about Cornelius in the Acts of the Apostles: "At Caesarea there was a man named Cornelius, a centurion in what was known as the Italian Regiment. He and all his family were devout and God-fearing; he gave generously to those in need and prayed to God regularly" (Acts 10:1–2).

An angel appeared to Cornelius and said, "Your prayers and gifts to the poor have come up as a memorial offering before God" (Acts 10:4).

Following the angel's instructions, Cornelius called for Peter, who came and preached the message of Jesus to him and his family. The outcome was great; Cornelius and his family believed the words Peter spoke about Jesus. Before his sermon was over, the Spirit of God came upon the entire family. God found a way to bring these good people to the knowledge of Jesus so that they might be saved.

The good works that Cornelius did touched the heart of God. Cornelius had a faith in God although he did not know who he was. God made a way for him to find Christ.

Speaking of Jesus, the scripture says, "Salvation is found in no one else, for there is no other name under heaven given to men by which we must be saved" (Acts 4:12).

THE WICKED GO TO HELL

Those who choose a life of evil will be judged for their wickedness, and those who reject Jesus will go to hell. In order to understand God's definition of the wicked, scripture gives us an example.

Jude wrote, "Sodom and Gomorrah and the surrounding towns gave themselves up to sexual immorality and perversion. *They are an example* of those who suffer the punishment of eternal fire" (Jude 1:7; italics added).

The story of the Sodomites is in the Bible. Jude said that they are an example of those who will go to hell. They were full of violence and sexual perversion, and they abused the most vulnerable and the poor.

(See also Gen. 18–19, Isa. 1:10, Jer. 23:14, and Ezek. 16:46.)

Their sins were so vile that God destroyed their city. First, he sent two angels to Sodom to rescue Lot and his family. A homosexual mob surrounded Lot's house to attack and sodomize the angels, who they thought were men. Lot refused and offered them his daughters instead. The Sodomites refused the girls and continued to press in on the house. The angels blinded their eyes. Even though they were blind, they continued to break into the house in order to have their way with Lot's guests. God rescued Lot, even though he was an awful man to offer his daughters to the mob. The city and the Sodomites were burned with fire, and in the book of Jude, we are told that they will be cast into hell. That is an example of wickedness.

Most people are not so vile, but many will go to hell. God is the judge, and we cannot be.

Following are the words of Jesus that describe the verdict on judgment day. Note that the judgments will be based on the measure of light an individual has received. You may draw your own conclusions.

"God did not send his Son into the world to condemn the world, but to save the world through him. Whoever believes in him is not condemned, but whoever does not believe stands condemned already because he has not believed in the name of God's one and only Son. This is the verdict: Light has come into the world, but men loved darkness instead of light because their deeds were evil. Everyone who does evil hates the light, and will not come into the light for fear that his deeds will be exposed. But whoever lives by the truth comes into the light, so that it may be seen plainly that what he has done, has been done through God" (John. 3:17–21).

Five things stand out in this scripture:

1. God came to save, not condemn.
2. Believing in Jesus will save a person.
3. Rejecting Jesus will ultimately send a person to hell.
4. Evil deeds will send a person to hell.
5. Loving truth and doing good deeds will draw a person to God and salvation.

Daniel made reference to the severity and the joys of judgment day: "Multitudes who sleep in the earth will awake: some to everlasting life, others to everlasting contempt" (Dan. 12:2).

THINK OUTSIDE THE BOX, BUT IN SCRIPTURE

On judgment day, all the dead will be resurrected. Each person will be judged and will live in God's kingdom or be thrown into hell. The book of life will be opened. Recorded in it will be the names of those who belong to Christ. If anyone's name is not in the book, he or she will be thrown into the lake of fire.

The spirits of those who died before Christ died were kept in Hades. When Christ died he visited them and preached to them, and they believed that he was the Son of God. Their spirits ascended to heaven with him, and they are waiting in heaven to receive their bodies in the first resurrection (See Eph. 4:7–9).

Multitudes have died since then. Many have not had a chance to hear the Gospel. They have not had adequate opportunity to accept or reject Christ. They will be judged by their deeds and given opportunity to believe in Christ.

My question is whether the names of those who lived godly lives on the whole without knowing Jesus will be in the Lamb's book of life. God alone knows the answer. Only he knows how their names might be written in it.

They cannot make it without Jesus, but somehow, he has a way in Christ for them. Perhaps they will have a vision of Jesus or an angel will be sent to show them the way.

If Jesus preached to and revealed himself to dead souls in Hades because they never had opportunity to meet him or hear of him prior to their death, could it happen again? I do not know, but I know that with man salvation is impossible, but with God nothing is impossible. I am sure that I underestimate the extent of his reach!

The Bible says, "Man is destined to die once and after that to face judgment" (Heb. 9:27).

This scripture says nothing about what may happen between

death and judgment. If there is any uncertainty regarding a person's standing on judgment day, I am confident that God will have a way of completing a person's journey and filling in any gaps. Jesus is the author and finisher of our faith (Heb. 12:1–2). He will throw no one who does not deserve it into hell.

NO CHILDREN IN HELL

Some misinformed people think that God would send some children to hell. Nothing could be further from the truth. Some think this because they believe that God elects some people to hell and some to heaven. They also think that children of atheists and those born into religions other than Christianity will go to hell. I can only address this subject briefly in this book, but address it I must.

We should look at the big picture. What does the Bible tell us about the nature and character of God? Among many other things, scripture shows that he is gracious, compassionate, and the very definition of love. His grace and mercy will always triumph over justice. God is love; he will not send children to hell.

Furthermore, God is just and true; he cannot lie or be unfair. He will not extend to people an eternity of evil that they do not deserve. Concerning children, he is a defender of the innocent and helpless. While harsh judgments have fallen and will fall on families and communities in this life, they do not carry into eternity. Like all people, children suffer and die in this life because of the sins and curses of others, but that is a momentary pain. Judgment in eternity is not the same as judgment on earth. It is outside of God's character as the "Defender of the Innocent" (Ps. 68:5-6) and the "Judge of All" (Heb.12:24) to send children to hell.

Children are spiritually alive until they understand God's law and willfully disobey it as mature individuals. Paul recognized this. He taught that he was alive spiritually when he was a child, but when he was old enough to know and rebel against God, he sinned and that is when he died spiritually. He wrote, "Once I was alive apart from the law: but when the commandment came, sin sprang to life and I died" (Rom. 8:9).

Paul is speaking of his personal life as a child; he is not taking a theological position regarding the Law of Moses. Once we become young adults, we are held accountable for our actions and need salvation through the cross. Babies are not eternally accountable for their actions, nor are children. God, who is fair and just, will apply the benefits of the cross to them while they are young, and if they die in youth, he will bring them to himself.

Some think this to be true only if the parents believe in Christ. They unadvisedly quote 1 Corinthians which, they think, qualifies their reasoning.

It says, "For the unbelieving husband has been sanctified through his wife, and the unbelieving wife has been sanctified through her believing husband. Otherwise your children would be unclean, but as it is they are holy" (1 Cor. 7:14).

This thinking—that some children will go to hell—is due to a misunderstanding of the word *sanctified*. It is not the same as being eternally saved, or born again. No Christian that I know believes that a spouse will go to heaven simply because their partner is a believer, yet the scripture here says that a partner is sanctified by their believing spouse.

The word sanctified means to be set apart and made holy so that one might receive God's blessings, purpose, and destiny for their lives.

Vines Expository Dictionary of New Testament Words defines sanctification as "separation to God ... separation of the believer from evil things and ways ... the setting apart of the believer for God." [ae]

The verse is saying that an unbelieving partner may receive God's blessings and provision because they are married to a believer. Their children will likewise be set apart and be made holy, so they will be able to receive their rightful blessings and destiny. They will not be hindered from God's plan because one of their parents is an unbeliever.

This verse has nothing to do with eternal salvation, and it certainly does not infer that children without a believing parent will go to hell.

The truth is that all people are fearfully and wonderfully made in God's image, and he will not send the undeserving to hell. Children are at the top of the list of those God will bring to himself. They belong to God.

Concerning children, Jesus said, "I tell you that their angels in heaven always see the face of my Father in heaven" (Matt. 18:10).

He sealed the matter of salvation for children with these words: "Let the little children come to me, and do not hinder them, for the kingdom of heaven belongs to such as these" (Matt. 19:14).

God will not send children to hell. For those who thought differently, I trust that you will find this discovery refreshing.

MORTALS FROM THE MILLENNIUM

Mortals who die during the millennium will also stand before God's throne. They will have entered the millennium lacking a faith in Christ, but before dying, many will believe on him and on judgment day they will be resurrected with glorified bodies. Others will be judged worthy of hell.

Mortals who are still alive at the end of the new millennium will receive glorified bodies on judgment day. Like those who were alive on earth at the second coming of Christ, they will receive their reward.

HELL FIRE

Those who deserve it will be cast into hell with the devil and his angels. First, they will experience the second death. Their resurrected, but mortal, bodies will die a second time as they hit the fires of hell.

"Then death and Hades were thrown into the lake of fire. The lake of fire is the second death" (Rev. 20:14).

Lazarus and others who were raised to life in the time of Christ did not go directly to heaven. They lived on the earth, and in time they died again. It will be like that for sinners in the last resurrection. They will be raised to life, then die again. After the second death, they will spend the rest of eternity as they did in Hades. They will be spirits without bodies. They will have all of the sensations that people in bodies have. Although they are only spirits, they will feel pain and know sorrow.

"They will be punished with everlasting destruction and shut out from the presence of the Lord and from the majesty of his power" (2 Thess. 1: 9)

The sinner's foremost punishment will be the horror of being forever separated from the presence of the Lord.

"They will throw them into the fiery furnace, where there will be weeping and gnashing of teeth" (Matt. 13:42).

""and be thrown into hell, where their worm does not die, and the fire is not quenched" (Mark 9:47-48).

They will suffer great pain, for their thirst will never be quenched, and their worm will not die. Their carnal passions will be alive, eating away at their souls, but they will never be quenched. Their passions will become like tormenting maggots (their worm) that eat raw flesh. The cravings, however, will never be satisfied. Those in hell will live in darkness. They will weep and gnash their teeth in unbearable pain. (See 2 Thessalonians 1:9; Matthew 9:44, 46, and 48; and Matthew 25:30.)

Hell is a place designed for the devil and his angels. It is a sad and sober thought to realize that many humans will be there as well.

Chapter Sixty

Revelation is About a New Heaven and a New Earth

Then I saw a new heaven and a new earth, for the first heaven and the first earth were passed away, and there was no more sea. I saw the Holy City, the New Jerusalem, coming down out of heaven from God, prepared as a bride beautifully dressed for her husband. (Rev. 21:1–2)

SUGGESTED READING: REVELATION 21:1–10

CHAPTER TOPICS

1. The great beyond
2. The coming of the bride
3. The wedding feast
4. The voice of God
5. God's warning to hypocrites
6. A great new world

THE GREAT BEYOND

REVELATION 21–22 COVERS A massive time frame, including a review of the millennium and an introduction to eternity. The focus is on God's people in the hereafter. Sin and demons will be washed from the earth, and the people of God will enjoy intimate fellowship with him. The further into the future we look, the fewer details we see. What we do see, however, is amazing. The millennium will be great, but God has much more to give his people in eternity. In these chapters, he emphasizes the glory that will come.

COMING DOWN FROM HEAVEN

Revelation chapter 21 begins by reviewing a great paradigm shift. The righteous souls who went to heaven will come down upon the earth. Old things will pass away, and all things will become new. The chapter starts with the announcement that "there was no more sea" in heaven. The sea is a sea of people—the multitude of spirits gathered around the throne worshipping God. The people have been waiting for the resurrection, and they will leave heaven and receive bodies, so there will be no more sea.

We see the sea of saints at the end of the tribulation period, descending with Christ at his second coming, as warriors on white horses; now, in chapter 21, we see them from a different perspective—we see them as the bride. "I saw the Holy City, the New Jerusalem, coming down out of heaven from God, prepared as a bride beautifully dressed for her husband. (Rev. 21:1–2)

She comes as one dressed in righteous robes, prepared for the marriage banquet, the millennium.

A few verses later, John wrote, "And he carried me away in the Spirit to a mountain great and high, and showed me the Holy City, Jerusalem, coming down out of heaven from God. It shone with the glory of God, and its brilliance was like that of a very precious jewel" (Rev. 21:10).

The city, or bride, shines with the glory of God. It looks like a gorgeous gemstone, clear as crystal. It is covered with God's glory, it is absolutely transparent, and it is beautiful.

AN UNUSUAL ANGEL

When the drama of the tribulation is over, John saw a new heaven and a new earth. A fresh feeling of joy and relief washed over him as he realized that the light at the end of Revelation's tunnel is bright. Once its events have concluded, there will be no more death, pain, or crying. Everything will change for the people of God.

THE GLORIOUS BRIDE

"One of the seven angels who had the seven bowls full of the seven last plagues came and said to me, 'Come, I will show you the bride, the wife of the Lamb'" (Rev. 21:9).

At that moment, an angel approached John. This is not the same angel who guided him through the book of Revelation. John recognized the second angel as one of the seven who he'd seen pouring the plagues of wrath from the seven bowls—one of the seven spirits of God who goes out into the world. The demeanor of the angel, however, has completely changed. He was fierce before, now he was cordial and gentle. He came as a friend, like a loving brother, desirous to show John the sights around town at a family reunion. Previously, the angel was the ultimate warrior of war, now he is like a loving family member acting as a tour guide.

The bride of the Lamb is the New Jerusalem, which is the Jerusalem from above, the body of Christ, the one new man, and the completed olive tree. It is made up of all people who are part of God's family. All redeemed Jews and gentiles are part of the bride.

While the natural Jerusalem is the city of the Jews, the New Jerusalem is a spiritual city comprised of all of God's children. "The Jerusalem above is free, which is the mother of us all" (Gal. 4:26).

The New Jerusalem, is called the mother of us all: both redeemed Jews and gentiles are included in her. She is the bride of Christ, the reason for the drama of the tribulation, the reason why God created the world in the first place and the reason why Jesus died on the cross. The bride is the focus of God's attention. He loves his people; they are a bride for his Son.

THE WEDDING FEAST

The millennium is a thousand-year wedding feast. It is called the marriage supper of the Lamb. Jesus spoke of it often. He told us that many who should be there will not be there, but the unexpected will be included. He will invite many from the highways and byways and bring them into the wedding feast so that his house will be full. He will include those whom we may think are undeserving. Even some bad people will be there. Recall the scripture in Matthew.

"The wedding banquet is ready, but those I invited did not deserve to come. Go to the street corners and invite to the banquet anyone you find. So the servants went out into the streets and gathered all the people they could find, *both good and bad,* and the wedding hall was filled with guests. But when the king came in to see the guests, he noticed a man there who was not wearing wedding clothes … Then the king told the attendants, 'Tie him hand and foot and throw him outside, into the darkness where there will be weeping and gnashing of teeth'" (Matt. 22:8–13; italics added).

Jesus will allow many who are undeserving to enter the millennium, but some will refuse to wear the robes of righteousness and will go to hell after the great white throne judgment.

GOD SPEAKS

At the beginning of a royal marriage feasts, special guests and important dignitaries are introduced to the crowd as they enter the room. God Almighty will be introduced as he comes to speak to his family. The introduction will be passionate and compelling. A loud voice will come from heaven announcing the Almighty. Listen to the herald: "Now, the dwelling place of God is with men, and he will live with them. They will be his people and he will be their God. He will wipe every tear from their eyes. There will be no more death or mourning or crying or pain, for the old order of things has passed away" (Rev. 21:3–4).

Then Almighty God will enter the scene, and, for the first time, he will give a personal announcement, which John wrote down: "He who was seated on the throne said, 'I am making everything new! … Write this down for these words are trustworthy and true … It is done, I am Alpha and Omega, the Beginning and the End. To him who is thirsty I will give to drink without cost from the spring of the water of life. He who overcomes will inherit all this, and I will be his God and he will be my son" (Rev. 21:6–7).

God will announce that the great paradigm shift has arrived. He will tell us that he is making everything new, that evil is finished, and that the days of everlasting life are about to begin. All that was promised for those who have overcome sin and the devil will be given. The bride will inherit all things as joint heirs with Christ. God has given his word, and his words are true.

While these words have not yet been spoken, except in John's vision, they will be spoken at the end of the age. We are permitted to know them in advance, and they give us strength for the war that must come.

GOD SAYS MORE

The Almighty will not finish at this point; he will have more to say. He will not finish with a blessing, but with a warning for hypocrites. He will reach back to those who will live during the great tribulation. He speaks to all who will be tempted by the beast and the false prophet and tells them what he expects of them.

He will say, "But the cowardly, the unbelieving, the vile, the murderers, the sexually immoral, those who practice magic arts, the idolaters and all liars—their place will be in the fiery lake of burning sulfur. This is the second death" (Rev. 21:8–9).

These words were written by John so that we and those who face the great tribulation might hear them. People will read Revelation more during the tribulation than at any other time in history. These words are powerful now, but then, they will be even more potent.

It is easy to understand that all murderers, perverts, witches, and idol worshippers will go to hell, but what of the cowardly and all liars? The two phrases, "all liars" and "the cowardly" tell me that this list is for those who will live during the tribulation and not for people of every era.

"All liars," is an inclusive phrase. It does not refer exclusively to the worst of lies, but to all, including the least of lies. Think of children or those who have lied about a minor failure in life. If one says they did not steal a cookie or cheat on a test when they did, they are lying. Surely they will not go to hell for that. Multitudes in this present age are under God's grace even though they lack perfection.

In the great tribulation however, a special sanctifying grace is given to live spotless lives. Not even a little lie will be found in their mouths.

The same applies to the cowardly; it is also such an inclusive word. Many true Christians have suffered from fear and have turned away from a fight because of cowardice. It does not make sense to me that all of these people throughout history will go to hell. Think of a godly but frail grandmother who has been traumatized. She is fearful and will shrink back from battle. Surely she will not go to hell because she is cowardly. In the tribulation, she will have a special anointing. No matter what she faces, her heart will be full of faith.

This entire chapter 21 in Revelation is a review of the last days. It is reasonable to assume that God will be speaking to those in the tribulation as he gives this list of who will go to hell. The saints during that time will have a special anointing to displace fear and cowardice. Read what was said about the tribulation saints earlier in Revelation:

"They overcame him [the devil] by the blood of the Lamb and by the word of their testimony; *they did not love their lives so much as to shrink from death*" (Rev. 12:11; italics added).

There are no Christian cowards in the great tribulation. The saints during the tribulation will not run or shrink from death. At that time all will be courageous. The special anointing for saints in the tribulation is mentioned again in chapter 14. We read,

"They follow the Lamb wherever he goes. They were purchased from among men and offered as firstfruits to God and the Lamb. *No lie was found in their mouths: they are blameless*" (Rev. 14:4–5; italics added).

Only Christ is blameless in history, but in the tribulation, the saints will be blameless as well, and no lie will be found in their mouths. Surely, that is a special anointing.

NEW HEAVEN, NEW EARTH

"Then I saw a new heaven and a new earth, for the first heaven and the first earth were passed away" (Rev. 21:1).

A new heaven and a new earth means that everything will become new. Satan and his fallen angels will no longer fly through the heavens accusing the saints or fighting the angels of the Lord. War in the heavens will be over.

Changes on the earth will be even more dramatic than those in the heavens. The world will be washed of evil. Nature will be released to its created intention. Humankind and animals will be immortal and will live in harmony. There will be no pollution in the environment. Productivity on the planet will thrive at maximum potential. People will be higher in rank and authority than the angels and will fellowship with God and with the Lamb. Welcome to the new and improved world. Old things will pass away and all things will become new.

Chapter Sixty-one

Revelation is About the New Jerusalem

And he carried me away in the Spirit to a mountain great and high, and showed me the Holy City, Jerusalem, coming down out of heaven from God. It shone with the glory of God, and its brilliance was like that of a very precious jewel, like a jasper, clear as crystal. It had a great, high wall with twelve gates, and with twelve angels at the gates. (Rev. 21:10)

SUGGESTED READING: REVELATION 21:11–27

CHAPTER TOPICS

1. The bride of Christ
2. The city of God given in symbols
3. The dimensions of Jerusalem
4. The walls of the city
5. The gates of the city
6. The gold in the city
7. God's temple in the city
8. The light in the city

HERE COMES THE BRIDE

THE NEW JERUSALEM IS the bride of Christ. The people of God will come down from heaven with the Lord at his second coming. John saw them shinning with the glory of God. The Lord will be proud of the bride; she will be clothed in glory, dressed beautifully for her husband (Rev. 21:2).

Many details reveal the splendor of the saints as they descend from heaven. Revelation 21 is about that beauty. The picture of the city is symbolic. The New Jerusalem that is depicted coming down from heaven is not a physical city. Buildings, gates, and high walls will not be floating down through the atmosphere on an island of dirt with plumbing pipes and electrical wires hanging below.

The walls, foundations, streets, and gates represent strength, beauty, character, and all manner of godly qualities that portray the bride's glory. She is not a city of bricks and mortar, but of people. She is the community of the redeemed, the family of God. How could we envision a city like New York or London and call either of them a bride? God's family is the city, and this city is the bride of Christ.

SYMBOLISM

As we study the city, we discover many details. The city as described in Revelation 21 is a massive illustration, a great object lesson, that helps us picture the glory of the bride.

I will suggest a spiritual meaning for most of the details in the illustration. The Bible is its own best commentary, and the individual parts of the city are mentioned elsewhere in God's word. Looking through the Bible helps us discover what each part represents. I will give scripture references for those who wish to investigate the spiritual parallels in more detail.

I am glad that the prize of our inheritance is not stone walls, golden streets, or pearly gates. All those things will be present in the world to come, but our prize is much greater than material things. Revelation 21uses material riches to illustrate the spiritual beauty of the bride.

DIMENSIONS OF THE CITY

The city of God described in Revelation 21 has specific dimensions that include the number 12, or 12 times 12—144. The city is square, symbolizing balance and equal importance to each side. Its height, width, and depth have the same dimensions. No matter which way you look at it, you see the same value. Every piece and pattern regarding God's people is precious. We cannot pick and choose what we like and don't like about God's family. He says that every part of it is precious to him.

Each, dimension of the city is twelve thousand stadia. Twelve is God's number for family or nation. He has twelve tribes of Israel and twelve disciples of the Lamb. The width, depth, and height of this city tell us that we are family. God is not looking for a business organization or a plastic church; he wants a family.

This is further emphasized by the thickness of the walls. (See Isaiah 62:6, Psalms 51:17–18, and Psalms 122:7.) The walls are 144 cubits thick. That translates to a thickness of 216 feet. They are very thick and strong, but their significance is found in the number *144*. He sent his Son to earth to bring him back a family, and he will not be denied.

THE CITY WALLS

God's family is a city with walls, which represent his protection. The angels of the Lord camp around those who fear God. (See Ps. 34:7; Zech. 2:5.) Angels provide a wall of fire around the saints.

In ancient times, walls around a city protected the people from invasion. Our city walls speak of God's covering. They are high and wide. The New Jerusalem will be heavily fortified. God's protection over his family will be impregnable.

The walls around God's people have strong foundations with the names of the twelve apostles engraved on them. The early church met to study the apostle's doctrine. (See Acts 2:42.) These apostles wrote the New Testament, and they gave us understanding of the New Covenant and the word of God. When we allow these words to be the foundations of our lives, we discover the protection of the walls. The walls of God stand on the Apostle's doctrine.

The walls are made of precious gems called jasper, and their foundations are decorated with twelve jewels, which include jasper, sapphire, chalcedony, emerald, sardonyx, carnelian, chrysoprase, jacinth, and amethyst. Precious stones represent godly character. These are the same jewels that the Old Testament priests wore, and they represent the twelve tribes of Israel. They also represent the beauty of family. (See Exodus 28:15–21.) Scripture says that we can choose to build with wood, hay, and stubble or with gold, silver, and precious stones. (See 1 Corinthians 3:11–17).

In this life, we can live with substandard activity or build with godliness. Many lack integrity, honesty, courage, kindness, love, joy, gentleness, and peace, and they build instead with wood, hay, and stubble.

We may be saved by God's grace, but all our earthly accomplishments will burn up, and our rewards in God's future kingdom will be limited.

On the other hand, we may live by the fruit of the Spirit and build with love, joy, peace, faith, longsuffering, gentleness, kindness, goodness, and self-control. (See Galatians 5:22.) That is how we build with gold, silver, and precious stones, which will not be burned, but will last for eternity.

The symbolic gold, silver, and precious stones will be the building material of the new city. The foundations of God's people in the world to come will be decorated with quality gems. His family will exhibit the elements of godly character—the bride will shine with integrity.

THE CITY GATES

Revelation 21 says that there will be twelve gates around the city, three on each side. The details of the gates reveal a lot about God's family. City gates were important sites in ancient times, and they had many purposes.

They were entrance points to the city. One could not come into the city except by the gates. If a person was unwanted, he or she was not allowed in. An angel will stand at the entrance to each of the twelve gates around the celestial city, and only the family may come in.

City gates were the ports of commerce. The area outside and inside the gates formed a large plaza for commerce. Trading and marketing took place around the gates. Money was exchanged, and business deals were transacted there. It was a high-traffic area, and business people wanted to be the first to engage a traveling merchant who came to their city so they set up business at the gates.

Courts of justice were set up at the gates. The elders of the city met there to discuss civil and personal concerns. Judges heard arguments and handed down verdicts to administer justice. Rules, edicts, and wisdom were given to encourage good behavior between neighbors. The gates were a place where peace and protocol were established.

Protection was found inside the city gates. (See Exodus 20:10, Deuteronomy 5:14, 14:21, and 31:12.)

The gates were the first place of celebration when a city wanted to honor one of its citizens. As they entered the gates, crowds would rejoice with accolades of praise for those who had accomplished great things. This was the place to receive conquering heroes returning from a successful tour of duty.

The gates of God's city represent the industry and activity of her people. (See Psalms 24:7–9). They illustrate the comings and goings of God's family. The Lord did not create people to be in cages like zoo animals. His sons and daughters will be free to explore and be enterprising and creative. God loves to see his children stretching out to accomplish their creative best. The gates of the city represent the enterprising freedom of his family.

The gates represent the purposes of God. In eternity, no one will enter God's blessings without being a part of his family. All must come through the gates.

During the millennium, even the kings of the nations that rebel against the Lord will have to enter the purposes of God through these family gates. On no day will the gates ever be shut during the millennium. There will be access to the light of God and the people of God. His grace and availability will remain to the end.

Each gate is made of a single pearl (Rev. 21:21). This illustrates the enormous value of the gates. Each has a name of one of the twelve tribes of Israel written on it. God's family will always embrace the teachings of the Old Covenant patriarchs. We will always be reminded that Jacob's children, the patriarchs of old, have a special place of honor in our family. Our family will never lose its Jewish roots. Our Jewish beginning will never be forgotten or overlooked. They are eternally special to God and to his family.

CITY OF GOLD

Gold has special significance in the scriptures; it represents the trials of our faith. The troubles that true Christians and Jews have faced in this life have served to bring out the best in them. The trials are compared to the fires of a furnace where gold is refined. The refiner's fire brings impurity to the surface of the gold where it can be recognized and removed. Like with gold, the saints will be purified to shine like glass. That is the process of sanctification. Legally, we are made holy by the sacrifice of Jesus on the cross, but the working out of that sanctification is a process of time and endurance. In the world to come, our sanctification will be complete.

We learn in Revelation 21 that the city is made of pure gold. The buildings, the streets, and all of the chattels within its walls are gold. The gold symbolizes the glory of God shinning in and through his people.

THE TEMPLE

Symbolically, there is no temple in the city, because God Almighty and the Lamb are its temple. This is the spiritual city of Jerusalem. We know that the physical city of Jerusalem that parallels it will have a temple during the millennium.

The temple has always been a place for the focus of worship. It is a meeting place for man and God. The temple has served as a provision for fellowship with God during the time of the world that man was under Adam's curse.

There was no temple however, in the Garden of Eden. The Lord walked in the garden with Adam, and the need for props and buildings was unnecessary. The temple worship will become complete as man and God meet face to face at the end of the millennium.

The Almighty and the Lamb will be the new temple. Wherever they are will become the meeting place for men and women with God. Humankind will have an open door into their presence. God is omnipresent; he can be with everyone at the same time and have a personal conversation with each person. Our worship unto him will be constant. We will always be in the spiritual temple for we will always be with the Lord.

LIGHT, SUN AND MOON

Symbolically, there will be no need for a sun or a moon to give us light during the millennium or beyond. The glory of God and of the Lamb will be the light of our lives. They will light our way, light our minds, and illuminate the world around us. The nations will walk in the light of God as he shines through his family. The kings of the earth will walk in that light. Even rebellious mortals will enjoy the light of the Lord that shines from the people, the city of God.

And the kings will bring their wealth and splendor to the Lord's family. The light of the Lord will be so prominent during the millennium that there will be no night there. There will be no depression and no evil. No darkness will ever shadow the light of God, and his lamp will never dim. I believe that the physical sun and moon will still exist, but all our spiritual light will come from God. Spiritually speaking, we will need no other light.

In the millennium, the worldwide family of God will shine brightly, and no hypocrites or phonies will be part of God's family.

We read, "Nothing impure will enter it, nor will anyone who does what is shameful of deceitful, but only those whose names are written in the Lamb's book of life" (Rev. 21:27).

Chapter Sixty-two

Revelation is About Eternity

Then the angel showed me the river of the water of life, as clear as crystal, flowing from the throne of God and of the Lamb down the middle of the street of the city. On each side of the river stood the tree of life, bearing twelve crops of fruit, yielding its fruit every month. And the leaves of the tree are for the healing of the nations.
No longer will there be any curse. The throne of God and of the Lamb will be in the city, and his servants will serve him. They will see his face, and his name will be on their foreheads.
There will be no more night. They will not need the light of a lamp or the light of the sun, for the Lord God will give them light. And they will reign for ever and ever. (Rev. 22:1–5)

CHAPTER TOPICS

1. Heaven on earth
2. Serving God in eternity
3. The river of God
4. Special trees in eternity
5. The tree of life
6. Seeing God face to face
7. The final removal of the curse

8. The light of the world

HEAVEN ON EARTH

"UNTO HIM BE GLORY in the church by Christ Jesus throughout all ages, *world without end*. Amen" (Eph. 3:21 KJV; italics added).

Eternity will yield great resources. The first five verses of Rev. 22 point to life beyond the thousand-year reign of Christ. Whatever blessings were afforded the saints during the millennium will be extended into eternity, and many more besides. Man will remain on earth for eternity, although that will not limit travel to other planets and galaxies. We do not know these details, but we know we will have a world without end. It will be a world without end of time and probably a world with no end to discovery or expansion.

Jesus prayed, "Your kingdom come, your will be done on earth as it is in heaven" (Matt. 6:10).

That prayer will be fully answered. God's kingdom will come to earth just as it is in heaven. His kingdom stretches to the outer banks of the universe, but earth will become his new headquarters. Whatever the Bible has told us of heaven will then be on earth.

"No eye has seen, no ear has heard, no mind has conceived what God has prepared for those who love him—but God has revealed it to us by his Spirit" (1 Cor. 2:9–10).

SERVING GOD

"The throne of God and of the Lamb will be in the city, and his servants will serve him" (Rev. 22:3).

To serve God in eternity will be the greatest honor. Man is never fulfilled unless he serves. He must accomplish something useful to find satisfaction. Laziness is boring and uncreative, that is not our destination. We will be served as we serve one another, but we will receive ongoing assignments from the Lord.

As we serve, we will exercise our creative talents, and we will absolutely love it. It will be exciting to be a part of God's procurement team.

"And his name will be on their foreheads" (Rev. 22:4).

People will not have a tattoo or an implant that reflects the name of God. Like the mark of the beast, it has to do with our mindset. In eternity we will think as our heavenly father thinks. We will have the mind of Christ. No unclean or rebellious thought will wander through our minds. It is difficult to imagine a mind without distraction, but that is the way of the angels, and it will be our inheritance.

THE RIVER OF GOD

The river of God is mentioned throughout scripture. It proceeds from under the throne and brings life wherever it flows. Ezekiel recognized that the river flows from Jerusalem. (See Ezek. 47.) He gave a great description of the river, explaining its life-giving power and its eastern destination in the desert of Arabah and the Dead Sea. The river starts small, but it grows to a massive, uncrossable waterway. Ezekiel's prophecy encourages us to wade in its shallows and swim in its depths.

In eternity, the river is more than a vision. Although it will be an actual river, it will also have a symbolic quality. It represents all the goodness of God that flows from his throne. All life comes from the Almighty. The river is called, "the river of the water of life." The river releases health, revelation, gifts, talents, provisions, joy, peace, faith, and so much more. God has more to give than we can consume.

The river will run down the main street of Jerusalem. The road will be on both sides of it, and it will be part of a beautiful boulevard. The river will flow to the new sea far to the east. It is now called the Dead Sea; perhaps then, it will be called the Living Sea.

TREES, GLORIOUS TREES

"Fruit trees of all kinds will grow on both banks of the river. Their leaves will not wither, nor will their fruit fail. Every month they will bear, because the water from the sanctuary flows to them. Their fruit will serve for food and their leaves for healing" (Ezek. 47:12).

It is common for trees to line the banks of a river, and this river is no exception.

Along the entire length of the river will grow the most amazing trees. They will be fruit trees of every kind. The miracle water will produce miracle fruit on the trees. Every month a new crop will ripen, and the fruit will always grow to its potential best. To eat this fruit will be an amazing experience. I imagine that it will be shipped all over the world, and people will wait for its arrival with great anticipation. We are told that their leaves are for healing, like the leaves of the tree of life. They are for the healing of the nations (Rev. 22:2). The fruit from the trees will be nutritious as well as delicious.

Why will God's people need healing in eternity when no one will be sick? I believe the healing spoken of is the full release of God's blessings that will allow us to complete our eternal destiny. We will receive all that God has for us and be all he has destined us to be.

Even now, we know that humans only use ten percent of their brains. Our bodies do not function as they will then, and our spirits are dull compared to what they will be. We need healing, and we don't even know it. The healing will come as we receive all of the provisions that God makes available to us. The Lord will bring us into his fullness. The water and the trees are part of his provision for us.

Life will not be static in eternity. God's kingdom will be always increasing. Likewise, we will continue to experience more and more of God's blessings. That is the purpose of the trees. They symbolically represent the continual life-flow of God's amazing supply that will come to us. That is our on-going healing.

THE TREE OF LIFE

We also read about the tree of life: "And the leaves of the tree are for the healing of the nations" (Rev. 22:2)

The special tree of life is also in the city of God. It creates an archway over the river and has a trunk with roots that go down on either side of the river. It reminds me of the two branches of the olive tree, one representing Israel, the other the gentile nations of the saved.

Like the trees that we noted earlier, the tree of life will also bear fruit every month, and all will eat of it. This tree represents the life of Christ. The life of Christ will be our daily portion of sustenance, and we will live and reign with him forever.

The tree of life was in the Garden of Eden. In Adam's day, it represented the life of Christ, and whoever would eat of it would live forever. Because Adam ate of the forbidden tree instead of the tree of life, he was cursed and kept from eating the fruit from the tree of life. The curse was the fall of man. It brought pain and death for thousands of years. It has hindered and plagued man since Adam left the Garden.

The tree of life and the water of life have significance for us today. Even though all of humankind is presently under Adam's curse, those who draw near to God may partake of his life. They may fellowship with him and receive the indwelling of his Holy Spirit. They may receive direction, teaching, comfort, protection, and provisions, and they may taste of the Lord's miraculous power.

The last chapter of Revelation addresses those who want to walk with Christ today. They are given spiritual rights to the tree and to the river of life.

"Blessed are those who wash their robes, that they may have the right to the tree of life" (Rev. 22:14).

"Whoever is thirsty, let him take the free gift of the water of life" (Rev. 22:17).

FACE TO FACE

"The throne of God and of the Lamb will be in the city, and his servants will serve him. *They will see his face*" (Rev. 22:4; italics added).

Eternity has still more blessings. For the first time since the Garden of Eden, the Bible says that man will be able to see God - face to face. Throughout history, no man could see God's face and live. It is amazing; in eternity - finally, we will see his face This happens only after every bit of the curse is fully gone. Finally, all barriers between God and man will be removed. Both the Almighty and the Lamb will dwell in the newly formed Jerusalem on earth.

During the great millennium only Christ's throne will appear on earth, but at the end of the millennium, after the Father's final judgments, God Almighty will also live and rule on earth. The throne of God will move from heaven to earth and our fellowship with him will be made complete.

NO MORE CURSE

"No longer will there be any curse. The throne of God and of the Lamb will be in the city, and his servants will serve him. They will see his face" (Rev. 22:3–4).

Every part of Adam's curse will be removed. There will be no more besetting sin, no sorrow, no corruption, and no impediments to hinder our destiny.

Once the curse is gone, nothing will get in the way of man's glorification. The blessings of Christ's work on the cross will be available in every detail. The Lord Jesus will have successfully completed his assignment. He will have brought many multitudes of humans into glory.

The book of Hebrews says, "He suffered death, so that by the grace of God he might taste death for everyone ... In bringing many sons to glory," (Heb. 2:6–10).

This is not a partial glory with fragments of the past life still lingering; it is absolute glory, which was accomplished by Christ. The book of Revelation is the revelation of Jesus Christ. The final revelation we are given of him is one of total victory and immaculate perfection.

"Then the end will come, when he hands over the kingdom to God the Father after he has destroyed all dominion, authority and power. For he must reign until he has put all his enemies under his feet" (1 Cor. 15:24–25).

Now Christ will give the kingdom back to his Father. This is the climax of eternity as we know it. Ages before, God gave his Son the kingdoms of the earth. He accomplished his task. Everything will have now been brought under the feet of Christ. When everything has been made perfect, it will be time to give the kingdom back to God the Father.

LIGHT OF THE WORLD

Jesus has always been the light of the world and the light of men. (See John 1:4–5). That means that the right direction for humankind and the total provision for people's lives will only be found in him. All who try to make their own light or follow a different light have found a false light. They have only found darkness and no light at all.

In eternity, God will give us new light. He and the Lamb will be our light and our lamp. All knowledge, wisdom, instruction, and direction will come from him. There will be no other source for intelligence, and every shadow of doubt regarding that will be removed as we enter eternity. Forever, Jesus and the Almighty will be the light of man, the light of the world, and the light that extends to the far reaches of the universe.

All will live in that glorious light. That means that no one will be inferior or be in lack. Each person will fly to the height of his personal destiny. We will not just serve, but we will reign with Jesus. We will conquer new horizons and bring uncharted territory under the domain of Christ. We will receive authority from God and rule beyond the stars.

Chapter Sixty-three

Revelation is About Powerful Closing Words

Behold, I am coming soon! Blessed is he who keeps the words of the prophecy in this book. (Rev. 22:7)

SUGGESTED READING: REVELATION 22:6–21

CHAPTER TOPICS

1. The truth of Revelation
2. The words of the last angels
3. The angel's encouragement and warnings
4. The words of Jesus in the Bible
5. Jesus' encouragement and warnings
6. The words of John
7. John's encouragement and warnings

REVELATION IS TRUE

JOHN'S VISION OF REVELATION has come to an end. Revelation is so relevant, so up-to-date, and so detailed that John could not have fabricated it. The knowledge of present times and the conclusion to the scriptures tell us it is true. Even if we were not a people of faith, the facts of Revelation speak for themselves.

ENCOURAGEMENT AND WARNING FROM THE ANGEL

What remains are words of encouragement and warning. In the last chapter of Revelation, an angel speaks, the Lord Jesus speaks, and John speaks. Each says profound things that must be heard.

First we hear the angel. John wrote, "The angel said to me, "These words are trustworthy and true. The Lord, the God of the spirits of the prophets, sent his angel to show his servants the things that must soon take place" (Rev. 22:6).

"Do not seal up the words of the prophecy of this book, because the time is near. Let him who does wrong continue to do wrong; let him who is vile continue to be vile, let him who does right continue to do right; and let him who is holy continue to be holy" (Rev. 22:10–11).

On the heels of revelation come sober words. John's vision had vanished, but the angel remained. He knew that John had received a vision greater than any given in the history of man. He knew John would write the vision down, and it would be saved for generations to come. One day these words would even come to us. In fact, he told John not to seal or hide it, but to release and expose it.

We can feel the passion of the angel's heart. It was as if he was asking humanity: What more do you want? What more can heaven give you? It was as though the angel was telling the human race that we have all we need and the decision is now up to us—that we can choose, after receiving this message, to still be evil, and if that will be our choice, then so be it. The angel seemed to be telling us that, on the other hand, if we want to do right, then we should press in with all of our hearts, for the time is short.

He assured John that the words were "trustworthy and true." In other words, he was saying that the King would be coming, and the people of earth had better get ready and warning us not to mess up, for so much is at stake. Finally, the angel tells us to walk with God.

THE LORD JESUS SPEAKS

Then Jesus spoke:

"Behold I am coming soon! My reward is with me, and I will give to everyone according to what he has done. I am the Alpha and the Omega, the First and the Last, the Beginning and the End.

Blessed are those who wash their robes, that they may have the right to the tree of life and may go through the gates into the city.

Outside are the dogs, those who practice magic arts, the sexually immoral, the murderers, the idolaters and everyone who loves and practices falsehood.

I, Jesus, have sent my angel to give you this testimony for the churches. I am the Root and the Offspring of David, and the bright Morning Star" (Rev. 22:12–16).

Jesus spoke to John, but his words transcend time and space. They are for all people in every generation. His words are for us today, and no words are more profound. Jesus is the "bright" and "Morning Star"—the new dawn and the end of darkness and night. His coming will end the great tribulation and the pains of history.

Jesus was speaking to us today and he was speaking to those who will go through the great tribulation. He reminds us that he is "the Beginning and the End." There is no way to experience life or to find a future, except through him.

He also reminds us of the domestic and eternal scope of his own life. He is Jewish—the "Root" of David—and he is king of the universe—"the bright Morning Star." It is difficult for us to keep these two extremes connected, but Jesus is both man and God. It is a mystery, but he insists that his full identity remain intact.

Like the angel who told John not to seal up the words of the prophecy, Jesus reminds John to make sure that Revelation gets to the churches. He says that the book is for his people. It is for us.

Here, at the very end of the Bible, Jesus calls people of every nation and time period to enter his kingdom. He calls all of us to enter his city, to be part of his family, and have fellowship with him. He says we will be blessed if we wash our lives in his kindness and grace.

That involves repenting of our sins, believing in him for salvation, and living lives of obedience before him. Then, and only then, will we be blessed. He further encourages us to eat of the tree of life and enter the city.

Multitudes of people around the world, for thousands of years, have taken his advice. They have walked in the joys and blessings of the Lord and experienced wonderful fellowship with him.

JESUS REFUSES SOME

Jesus also describes those whom he will not have fellowship with. He will not welcome everyone into his family. Those he refuses, he calls dogs. He tells us that those people worship false gods, follow idols, and practice the occult. He includes in this list: the sexually immoral, murderers, and those whose lifestyle is full of lies and falsehood.

No person can live a perfect life, but everyone can refuse evil. They can refuse the occult, murder, sexual perversion, and a life of lies. Everyone has a choice. God expects us to flee from these things. They are sins that lead to spiritual and eternal death (1 John 5:16–17). People who do these things will remain outside of Christ's kingdom, unless they come to him, repent of their sins, and confess him as Lord.

Other sins such as besetting sins (Heb. 12:1–2) are not as wicked, but can still keep us from fellowship with Christ. They are the sins of the heart. They cover every detail where a man falls short of perfection. Only the grace of God can cover these sins. If we repent of them and ask the Lord to forgive us, we, in effect, wash our robes clean. The more we obey the voice of the Holy Spirit and live holy lives, the greater will be the blessings we will receive from the Lord in this life.

"Behold, I am coming soon! Blessed is he who keeps the words of the prophecy in this book" (Rev. 22:7).

AN INVITATION TO COME

"The Spirit and the bride say, 'Come!' And let him who hears say,

'Come!' Whoever is thirsty, let him come; and whoever wishes, let him take the free gift of the water of life" (Rev. 22:17).

The operative word is come. It is both a call from the earth for Jesus to come quickly and a call to the people of the world to come to Christ. The Holy Spirit releases the call and the church, Christ's bride, echoes it. The Lord Jesus calls to all who are thirsty. The grand invitation has been extended to the entire human race. Whoever wishes is welcome—Come!

JOHN'S CLOSING WORDS

"I John am the one who heard and saw these things" (Rev. 22: 8).

After his Revelation experience, John was never the same again. I trust that is also true for you as you read Revelation. John was so shaken by the awesome authority of the vision that he warns us not to change it in any way. The fear of God came over him as he received the testimony. It was layered on him, and he was in awe with the seriousness of what he received. John prophesied regarding these words.

He said, "If anyone adds anything to them, God will add to him the plagues described in this book. And if anyone takes words away from this book of prophecy, God will take away from him his share in the tree of life and in the holy city" (Rev. 22:18–19).

In closing, Jesus says, "Yes, I am coming soon" (Rev. 22:20).

John replies with the amen arrow of agreement that sends the word of God forth: "Amen. Come, Lord Jesus" (Rev. 22:20).

The closing words of John are gracious. He released a blessing from God on all people who read his report, from the first who see it to those at the very end of time.

He wrote, *"The grace of the Lord Jesus be with God's people. Amen"* (Rev. 22:21; italics added).

With those final words, the chapter closes, the outcome is inevitable, and the love of God is set in place to win the world.

Glossary of Terms

(Most of these terms are substantiated in the scriptures. Terms identified as probable suggestions are noted.)

Antichrist: the beast, a spirit, a fallen angel, Apollyon, ruling spirit of humanism

Babylon: city of darkness made up of all evil creatures and all evil people

Bema: judgment seat of Christ, for rewarding the saints

Bowls: censers for collecting prayers that come to heaven or containers that store the wrath of God

Dragon: Satan, the devil, the serpent, the ruler of the darkness of the world

False Prophet: the second beast, a spirit, a fallen angel, ruling spirit of the New Age Movement

Great Prostitute: queen of Babylon, mother of prostitutes, the rider of the beast, ruling spirit of lust

Great Tribulation: seven-year period of judgment to end this present age

Hades: temporary hell, waiting place of the wicked and the righteous before the cross having two parts—one of torment and one called paradise or Abraham's bosom

Harps: spiritual prophetic instruments that release God's word and will

Heads: spirits of power, angels, fallen angels, government leaders of the spirit world

Horns: spirits of power, angels, fallen angels, government leaders of the spirit world

Humanism: religion of man, anti-God, substitution for God, philosophy declaring that man is the sum of all things

Island: hidden place of security and power, financial stronghold (author's suggestion)

Israel: The Jewish people

Lamb of God: Jesus, Christ, Son of God, Messiah, sacrifice for man's sins

Lampstand: the church, churches

Lion of God: Jesus, Christ, Son of God, Messiah, Jesus the warrior

Messiah: the anointed one, Christ, Jesus, Son of God, King of the Jews

Midair: middle heaven, the second heaven, the place between God's throne (the third heaven) and earth's atmosphere (the first heaven), Satan's dwelling place

Millennium: the thousand-year reign of Christ on the earth, the marriage supper of the Lamb

Moon: The gentile Church (author's suggestion)

Mountain: high place of security and power, fortress, financial stronghold (author's suggestion)

New Age Movement: the full composite of all religions outside of God, the occult, the spirit of witchcraft, the supernatural element to humanism (author's suggestion)

New Jerusalem: all of God's people, the bride of Christ, Zion, the body of Christ, the two olive trees, the two olive branches, the one new man

Oil and Wine: compassion of the saints, mercy ministry of God's people

Rapture: when the bodies of a group of saints are caught up from the earth and taken to heaven

Revelation: apocalypse, an unveiling
Revival: when a multitude is converted to Christ
Saints: all of God's people
Saved: converted to Christ, born again, saved from eternal damnation and hell
Second Coming: the next appearance of Christ on the earth, the only coming of Christ in physical form between his death, burial, and resurrection - and the millennium
Seraphim: powerful six winged angels, leaders of God's angelic armies
Sky: God's covering, tent over humanity (author's suggestion)
Stars: angels
Sun: Jesus or God
Woman Dressed with the Sun: all God's people

Approximate Timeline of Events

YEAR ONE OF THE GREAT TRIBULATION

- Sin and evil abound in the nations
- Seven seals begin to open
- Four spirit horses are released from heaven
- The first campaign is launched from heaven
- War, famine, and plague kill more than a billion people on the earth
- The saints minister kindness and care to a dying world
- The first tribulation revival takes place
- Earthquakes come
- Vast numbers of angels descend to earth for the purposes of God
- Earth experiences a moment of hell
- Israel defends herself in war and gains her promised boundaries, from the Nile to the Euphrates
- The Muslim nations are decimated
- All nations become democracies
- The Jews experience revival

- Redeemed Israel and the church begin to partner as one new man
- Ancient prayers are answered

YEAR TWO OF THE GREAT TRIBULATION

- Israel experiences her renaissance
- Israel is inhabited with a mixture of orthodox, secular, and Messianic Jews
- The temple is rebuilt in Jerusalem
- The church suffers great persecution but grows in favor with the multitudes
- Wicked people become more wicked
- Vast multitudes die and go to heaven
- Christian leaders become so popular that they are elected to govern the nations
- The second campaign is launched from heaven
- The seven trumpets begin to sound
- More intense judgments come
- Meteors destroy much of the planet
- Great persecution falls on the church
- A seraph warns the earth that demons are coming—the three woes

YEAR THREE OF THE GREAT TRIBULATION

- The Abyss is opened
- Demons torment the multitudes
- The saints receive divine protection
- Apollyon the beast appears at the three and a half year mark
- Four demon generals incite the world to war
- Redeemed Israel and the church rule the world in righteousness
- Their leaders become spiritual prophets who have amazing supernatural power

- A major paradigm shift occurs at the three and a half year mark of the tribulation
- An evil military coupe led by Apollyon erupts in every nation except Israel
- The leaders of the nations who are saints are murdered and left on the streets to rot
- Those leaders are resurrected and raptured
- Another revival happens

YEAR FOUR OF THE GREAT TRIBULATION

- The days of the seventh trumpet begin
- Michael overpowers the devil and expunges him from the heavens
- Satan comes to earth, full of anger—that is the third woe
- Satan makes war against the rest of God's people who are still on earth
- God protects his people and gives them added favor
- The beast and the false prophet set up their kingdom
- Multitudes of saints are killed
- The world is forced to worship the beast who receives assistance from the false prophet
- The beast's philosophy of humanism dominates the world, even the temple in Jerusalem, and it is the abomination that causes desolation

YEAR FIVE OF THE GREAT TRIBULATION

- The beast rules the world, but must secure the services of the mother of prostitutes, which is the ruling spirit of lust; and she controls, manipulates, and rides him
- The beast hates the spirit of lust but needs her to control humanity
- The beast, the false prophet, and the prostitute continue to slaughter the saints as much as they can

- When so many saints are killed, multitudes of people see the beast for who he is and turn to Christ
- An elite group of intercessors, symbolically called the 144,000, evangelize the world in the face of grave danger
- The saints are anointed with miraculous power and sanctifying grace
- Angels assist the saints with the eternal gospel
- The saints inspire the greatest revival in history, called the harvest of the earth

YEAR SIX OF THE GREAT TRIBULATION

- The third campaign is launched from heaven
- The bowls of God's wrath are poured out and the judgments on the earth intensify
- The heavens enter a new level of rejoicing
- Desolation falls on the planet
- All vegetation is burned, everything in the sea dies, all surface water becomes poisonous, the sun's rays burn skin, 100 lb hailstones fall on the earth, and the worst earthquakes in history demolish the nations
- Man reverts to a survival-only mentality, causing the power of lust and humanistic philosophies to become irrelevant
- The beast turns on the great prostitute and destroys her
- The beast initiates marshal law around the world and kills anyone who will not conform to his tyranny

YEAR SEVEN OF THE GREAT TRIBULATION

- The saints go undercover
- Most people are dying because the planet is almost uninhabitable
- The infrastructure of society is completely destroyed
- The people who remain on the planet are greatly disillusioned

- The beast rules the world through his ten spirit kings
- The beast musters the armies of the world and marches them toward Jerusalem
- The battle of Armageddon begins
- The second coming of Christ happens
- The dead in Christ are raised
- Jesus lands on the Mount of Olives
- Jerusalem is rescued
- Jesus judges the nations
- Most sinners are killed and their bodies are eaten by vultures
- The beast and false prophet are cast into hell
- Satan is cast into the Abyss

TRANSITION PERIOD BEFORE THE MILLENNIUM

- The cleanup of the earth begins
- The environment is supernaturally restored
- The judgment seat of Christ is in session
- Rewards are given to the saints
- Many more Jews receive Jesus as their Messiah

MILLENNIUM

- The reign of Christ comes from Jerusalem
- The saints rule with Christ
- The animals receive the blessings of God
- The kingdom of God comes to earth
- At the end of the millennium, Satan is released to tempt the nations
- Satan musters Gog and Magog against Jerusalem and is defeated
- Satan is cast into hell
- All the dead are raised to life
- The great white throne judgment begins

ETERNITY

- God moves his throne to earth
- The Lamb and the Almighty are the only light needed
- God removes the curse
- The people of God see his face
- The people of God rise to their full potential
- The people of God enjoy the tree and the river
- The people of God serve him in the world-without-end

NOTES

a Derek Prince, *Atonement* (Grand Rapids, MI: Baker 2000), 37.

b William Byron Forbush, ed., *Fox's Book of Martyrs: A History of the Lives, Sufferings, and Deaths of the Early Christian and Protestant Martyrs,* New Kensington, Whitaker House 1985).

c The NIV Study Bible, 10th Anniversary Edition (Grand Rapids MI: Zondervan 1995), 1,933.

d Iain H. Murray, *The Puritan Hope; Revival and Interpretation of Prophecy,* (publishers, 3 Murrayfield Rd. Edinburgh, UK), 61.

e Iain H. Murray, *The Puritan Hope; Revival and Interpretation of Prophecy,* (publishers, 3 Murrayfield Rd. Edinburgh, UK), 72

f Iain H. Murray, *The Puritan Hope; Revival and Interpretation of Prophecy,* (publishers, 3 Murrayfield Rd. Edinburgh, UK), 113.

g Iain H. Murray, *The Puritan Hope; Revival and Interpretation of Prophecy,* (publishers, 3 Murrayfield Rd. Edinburgh, UK), 256.

h www.everydaycounsellor.com - A short Introduction to the History, Customs and Practices of the Moravian Church, by Herberty Spaugh – Prayer life

i *Encyclopedia Britannica,* Volume 18, Pompeii, (Chicago 1960), 201.

j Derek Prince, *They Shall Expel Demons* (Grand Rapids, MI: Baker 1998), 91 k The NIV Study Bible, 10th Anniversary Edition (Grand Rapids MI: Zondervan 1995), 1,934.

l *Encyclopedia Britannica*, Volume 20, Scorpions, (Chicago 1960), 136.

m The NIV Study Bible, 10th Anniversary Edition (Grand Rapids MI: Zondervan 1995),, 117.

n *Columbia Encyclopedia*, (Internet Reference).

o The NIV Study Bible, 10th Anniversary Edition (Grand Rapids MI: Zondervan 1995), 1,303.

p Francis Schaeffer, *The Christian Manifesto*, (Westchester, IL: Crossway Books 1982), 54.

q The NIV Study Bible, 10th Anniversary Edition (Grand Rapids MI: Zondervan 1995), 1941

r Frank Turek, I Don't Have Enough Faith to Be an Atheist, (Wheaton: Crossway Books, 2004), 163

s Fyodor Dostoevsky, *The Brothers Karamazov* (New York: Norton, 1976), 72.

t Quoted in D. James Kennedy, *Skeptics Answered* (Sisters, Ore: Multnomah, 1997), 154.

u Strobel, *Case for Faith*, (Grand rapids, Zondervan Publishing 2001), 91.

v From the audiotape "Reaching Evolutionists,' at Southern Evangelical Seminary's 2001 Apologetics Conference. Tape AC0108. Posted online athttp://www.impactapologetics.com.

w Bob Dylan, *Gonna Serve Somebody*, http://www.bobdylan.com.

x Edward H. Flannery, *The Anguish of the Jews: Twenty-three Centuries of Antisemitism*, (New York, Paulmist Press, 1985) 109, 111.

y Michael L. Brown, *Our Hands Are Stained With Blood: The tragic Story of the "Church" and the Jewish People, (Shippensburg PA, Destiny Image Publishers, 1992) 78*

z Sister Pista, *The Guilt of Christianity Towards the Jewish People, (Darmstadt, Evangelical Sisterhood of Mary, 1997)*

aa The NIV Study Bible, 10th Anniversary Edition (Grand Rapids MI: Zondervan 1995),, 1,945.

ab C. S. Lewis, *The Complete Chronicles of Narnia,* (Hong Kong, Harper Collins, Jacket 2000), 132.

ac Sid Roth, *The Race to Save the World,* (Lake Mary, Charisma House Publishers 2004) 129, 130.

ad The NIV Study Bible, 10th Anniversary Edition (Grand Rapids MI: Zondervan 1995), 1,272.

ae W. E. Vine, Merrill F. Unger, William White, Jr., *Vines Complete Expository Dictionary of Old and New Testament Words* (Nashville, TN: Thomas Nelson) 545,546.

Another must read book by - Dr. Peter Wyns

FIGHTING DEATH AND OTHER DESPERATE BATTLES

"If you are facing a dark battle for life or staring at hopeless impossibilities, this story is for you. From a certain death tragedy comes unbelievable recovery. From hopeless diagnosis comes a report so incredible that everyone fighting for life should read it. Too many give up without fighting, often because they lack the knowledge of how to win. Against all odds Clarice Holden, armed with faith, fought a battle and saved the life of her husband. She would not go into the night quietly. Neither should you."

"I met the main character in this story several years ago and was captivated by his story. Peter has done a great job capturing this truly remarkable testimony."
—Rick Joyner

A must read for all serious Christians
To order a copy direct from the source: Contact
Great Reward Publishing
ISBN 10: 0-9771633-0-X
Second Printing, January 2007
ISBN 13: 978-0-9771633-0-4
PO Box 36324
Rock Hill, SC. 29732 U.S.A.
Or e-mail the author at: wynsusa@comporium.net
Check out our website: www.peterwyns.org